Candy Floss Collection

Social Fictions Series

Series Editor

Patricia Leavy (*USA*)

International Editorial Advisory Board

VOLUME 32

The titles published in this series are listed at *brill.com/soci*

Candy Floss Collection

3 novels

By

Patricia Leavy

BRILL

SENSE

LEIDEN | BOSTON

All chapters in this book have undergone peer review.

Library of Congress Cataloging-in-Publication Data

Names: Leavy, Patricia, 1975- author. | Leavy, Patricia, 1975- Low-fat
  love. | Leavy, Patricia, 1975- Blue. | Leavy, Patricia, 1975- Film.
Title: Candy floss collection : 3 novels / by Patricia Leavy.
Description: Leiden ; Boston : Brill Sense, [2020] | Series: Social
  fictions series, 2542-8799 ; volume 32
Identifiers: LCCN 2020006130 (print) | LCCN 2020006131 (ebook) | ISBN
  9789004428256 (paperback ; acid-free paper) | ISBN 9789004428263
  (hardback ; acid-free paper) | ISBN 9789004428270 (ebook)
Classification: LCC PS3612.E2198 A6 2020 (print) | LCC PS3612.E2198
  (ebook) | DDC 813/.6--dc23
LC record available at https://lccn.loc.gov/2020006130
LC ebook record available at https://lccn.loc.gov/2020006131

ISSN 2542-8799
ISBN 978-90-04-42825-6 (paperback)
ISBN 978-90-04-42826-3 (hardback)
ISBN 978-90-04-42827-0 (e-book)

PRAISE FOR
CANDY FLOSS COLLECTION

"Epic! Brilliant! Absolutely delicious! *Candy Floss Collection* is Patricia Leavy's definitive statement. Her books – the people, scenes, dialogue – always feel natural; whatever or whomever she is describing feels authentic. Leavy manages to normalize persons and relationships that have been ignored or stigmatized, and she does so in a genuine way. People are people. I really like that she doesn't make identity politics the center of the story, but focuses on our similarities as we search for meaningful lives. Her talent for weaving pop culture into her narratives is on full display in this collection. Pop culture matters; in these books, it's a part of who the characters become in their hearts and souls. Leavy both critiques and celebrates pop culture, while showing how we can all make and remake the culture we consume. This unconventional trilogy is luminous, generous, heart-rending, and fulfilling. I have read and loved all three of these novels individually, seeing myself and loved ones in the pages, and I'm in awe of the impact of placing them in a collection. I have followed Tash's life across three books, and I rejoice at how she has grown up and chosen a healthy love relationship and a creatively fulfilling career. I want her to "have it all." It's clear that Patricia Leavy wants readers to imagine they too can have it all, whatever that means to the reader. The message is an important one: we can all live "big" lives by focusing on what matters most. *Candy Floss Collection* offers a template of *possibility*. It will inspire you to believe in possibility in your own life, and in those around you. I don't think you'll ever be able to settle again."
Laurel Richardson, Ph.D., The Ohio State University, and author of *Lone Twin*

SELECTED PRAISE FOR *LOW-FAT LOVE*

"I couldn't put it down! *Low-Fat Love* is a remarkable novel that every women's studies class and interpersonal class would do well to read.

The title is indicative of the search for meaningful, deep, enriching relationships beyond the artificial, low-fat love that is all too pervasive in society today. I wholeheartedly recommend this book."
Robin Patric Clair, Ph.D., Purdue University

"Based on my students' responses and my own enjoyment of the novel, I highly recommend it!" **Barbara Gurr, Ph.D., University of Connecticut**

"My students LOVE the book. One keeps saying, 'I feel as if I am inside this story... so colorful, so contemporary!'"
Jeasik Cho, Ph.D., University of Wyoming

"More than anything, *Low-Fat Love* proves the astonishing talent that Leavy possesses as both a writer and social commentator... It manages to be a short, 'can't put it down' book to read on the beach or on a plane, while still inspiring the sort of reflection usually reserved for self-help novels and sociology tomes. A wonderful and inspiring read that I will be using for years to come. Every student should read this book."
U. Melissa Anyiwo, Ph.D., Curry College, and editor of *Gender Warriors: Teaching Contemporary Urban Fantasy*

"This book is a great read. Leavy writes characters that you care about. I read this book over a weekend, barely able to put it down. The story is well-developed, fun, and has great pacing... I am using this book in my Introductory Sociology course, not only to springboard discussions about gender identity and women's roles, but also to demonstrate the power of sociology beyond the classroom."
Jessica Smartt Gullion, Ph.D., Texas Woman's University, and author of *Writing Ethnography*

"The characters are deep and complex, the storyline intertwined, and I couldn't put it down."
Linnea Rademaker, Ph.D., Northcentral University

"A joyful, inspiring and painfully beautiful novel written by gifted scholar and writer, Patricia Leavy. *Blue* shows all of us how to move forward through times of pain, crisis or complacency with hope and love."
Norman Denzin, Ph.D., University of Illinois at Urbana-Champaign

"What a treasure this novel is… Here's the thing: while this is a short book, it's an eminently readable, thoughtful, satisfying one – the kind of book where you start and then just read until you're done, no interruptions and much joy. It can – and should – be used in university classrooms for a variety of subjects, but it is also meant to be read outside of the university – for yourself, or with your book club. There's much to ponder, and discuss, but also much to ingest, reflect upon, and relate to your own life. I couldn't put it down, absolutely loved it, and can't stop thinking about it. Highly recommended."
Jessie Voigts, Wandering Educators

"An engaging piece of public scholarship, *Blue* provides rich food for thought about the pop culture landscape and how its shapes our own stories. With a subtext about privilege, opportunity, sexual assault and gender, this would be a useful and fun teaching tool."
Sut Jhally, Ph.D., University of Massachusetts at Amherst; Founder & Executive Director, Media Education Foundation

"*Blue*… reminds me of what it meant to live through the blue of young adulthood, a time spent working through the complexities of a life that's constantly changing like the sky while struggling toward self-love, spiritual balance and happiness. I was immediately pulled in as a reader by Leavy's refreshing use of language, her descriptions helping me see the world she's creating, a world that feels as familiar as one I remember as if it were yesterday."
Mary E. Weems, Ph.D., author of *Blackeyed: Plays and Monologues* and Cleveland Arts Prize winner

"Leavy's strength lies not just in writing relatable yet complex women, but also in the level of cultural and social research she puts into each page. *Blue* is more than a great read, it is the embodiment of sociological art, grounded in theory and method and mixed with all the fun pop culture has to offer. The result is stunning! I can't wait to use it in the classroom!"
Adrienne Trier-Bieniek, Ph.D., Valencia College, editor of *Gender & Pop Culture*

"In her new novel *Blue*, Patricia Leavy maps the contemporary landscape of love by narrating a vibrant tale where complex and compelling characters dance with the possibilities of longing and romance like light and shadow dance a tango, full of wisdom, wit, and wonder, swirling with vibrant voices that conjure the hope and loss we all know is the heart and truth of love, always more confounding than found, always calling us forth with indefatigable desire. *Blue* is a novel we all need to read now!"
Carl Leggo, Ph.D., University of British Columbia; Poet

SELECTED PRAISE FOR *FILM*

"With a subtext of sexual harassment and inequality especially relevant in the #MeToo era, this timely novel illustrates the cultural context in which girls and women live their lives. An engaging read, *Film* is sure to stimulate reflection, both personally and more broadly in book clubs and courses on media and gender."
Jean Kilbourne, Ed.D., author, feminist activist, and creator of the *Killing Us Softly: Advertising's Image of Women* film series

"*Film* is a tour de force!… *Film* is a page-turner, but also dives deep beneath the surface. This is Leavy's greatest skill, along with her ability to write characters with whom we empathize. The people in this novel bring with them their familial histories, their #MeToo experiences, and their desire to make it in La La Land. They have 'big' dreams, and we root for them as they overcome their obstacles and discover what

really matters... I couldn't put this book down. *Film* takes you inside yourself, and outside, too... absolutely gorgeous."
Laurel Richardson, Ph.D., The Ohio State University, and author of *Lone Twin*

"An engaging reminder of the struggles that come and go in the course of a life, *Film* captures the experiences of multiple women at transformational times in their lives and demonstrates the importance of persistence, creativity, and support for the achievement of one's dreams."
J. E. Sumerau, Ph.D., The University of Tampa, and author of *Palmetto Rose*

"Her characters help us all realize that we only really see shades of people, tips of icebergs that often hide deep wells of pain... use this novel in your Contemporary History, Social Work, Communication, Film, Women's and Gender Studies, Sociology, and Capstone courses. In the end, you should just read it and judge for yourself."
U. Melissa Anyiwo, Ph.D., Curry College, and editor of *Gender Warriors: Teaching Contemporary Urban Fantasy*

"This novel is written for anyone who has ever confronted the shadow side of their life to find the courage to light their own fire. *Film* provides inspirational fuel for forging the life, work, and art we need... *Film* is a feminist fist bump and a gorgeous visual of what women helping women and being your own muse looks like on the big screen of our lives."
Sandra L. Faulkner, Ph.D., Bowling Green State University, and author of *Poetic Inquiry: Craft, Method, and Practice*

"*Film*... is a love letter to popular culture, and in particular, illustrates how art may sustain us through life's challenges when those around us may not. Leavy has delivered another title in her original and unique voice, yet again demonstrating her mettle as a masterful writer of fiction."
Alexandra Lasczik, Ph.D., Southern Cross University

Also from Patricia Leavy

Film

Privilege Through the Looking-Glass

Low-Fat Love Stories
By Patricia Leavy and Victoria Scotti

Blue

American Circumstance: Anniversary Edition

Low-Fat Love: Expanded Anniversary Edition

Gender & Pop Culture: A Text-Reader
Edited by Adrienne Trier-Bieniek and Patricia Leavy

For more information, visit the author's website
www.patricialeavy.com

To every Prilly,
every Tash,
every you,
and every me

CONTENTS

Preface   xix

LOW-FAT LOVE

Part One

Chapter 1   5

Chapter 2   21

Chapter 3   29

Chapter 4   39

Chapter 5   53

Part Two

Chapter 6   77

Chapter 7   89

Chapter 8   93

Chapter 9   97

Chapter 10   103

Chapter 11   107

Chapter 12   125

Chapter 13   135

Part Three

Chapter 14   143

Chapter 15   147

Chapter 16   151

Chapter 17   165

Chapter 18   179

BLUE

Part One

Chapter 1   189

chapter 2   199

Chapter 3   213

Chapter 4   219

Chapter 5   227

Part Two

Chapter 6   243

Chapter 7   257

Chapter 8   277

Part Three

Chapter 9   287

Chapter 10   297

Chapter 11   301

FILM

Part One

Chapter 1   317

Chapter 2   325

Chapter 3   329

Chapter 4   335

Chapter 5   343

Chapter 6   351

Part Two

Chapter 7   359

Chapter 8   367

Chapter 9   375

Chapter 10   381

Chapter 11   391

Chapter 12   401

Chapter 13   409

Chapter 14   413

Part Three

Chapter 15   421

Chapter 16   429

Chapter 17   435

Chapter 18   441

Chapter 19   449

Suggested Classroom or Book Club Use 453

Afterword   455

Acknowledgements   457

About the Author   459

PREFACE

Candy Floss Collection is a set of three previously released novels: *Low-Fat Love, Blue,* and *Film.* Each novel can be read on its own, but together, these novels convey an overarching message. This is not a trilogy. Rather, this collection can be understood as installation art. When all three novels are read together, a full picture emerges. I'm delighted to have this opportunity to present my full artistic vision for these works. For those who are coming to these novels for the first time, I offer a synopsis for each one, before explaining the interconnections between them.

    Low-Fat Love unfolds over three seasons as Prilly Greene and Janice Goldwyn, adversarial editors at a New York press, experience personal change relating to the men (and absence of women) in their lives. Ultimately, each woman is pushed to confront her own image of herself, exploring her insecurities, the stagnation in her life, her attraction to men who withhold their support, and her reasons for having settled for low-fat love. Prilly lives between who she is and who she longs to be. She falls for Pete Rice, an unemployed, ever-sexy, curiously charming aspiring graphic novelist. Prilly thinks she is finally experiencing the "big" life she always sought but feared was beyond her grasp because she was "in the middle" (not beautiful or ugly, not greatly talented or totally hopeless – someone who could work for it). Pete's unconventional, free-spirited views on relationships unsettle Prilly, ultimately causing her to unravel over the course of their on-again-off-again love affair. Meanwhile, Janice, a workaholic, feminist-in-name-only editor, overburdens Prilly, her underling, with busywork, and undercuts Prilly's professional identity. Janice's regimented life is set on a new course when her alcoholic father becomes injured in a car accident and she is forced to face her own demons. Along with Prilly and Janice, the cast of characters' stories are interwoven throughout and eventually connected in the third and final section of the book. The offbeat characters include: Melville Wicket, Pete's awkward friend who lives one beat outside the moment; Jacob, Melville's younger, pothead brother; Kyle Goldwyn, Janice's seventeen-year-old son, who appears ordinary in every way but is actually quite extraordinary; and Tash, Kyle's wild-child, flighty, sexpot cousin who attends NYU and ends up dating Jacob. In the end, momentum builds as the characters struggle to escape the consequences of their decisions. Unexpected events cause changes in the characters that appear minor but carry significant implications for their futures. With a subtext about commercial pop culture, *Low-Fat Love* questions the cultural landscape against which we live our stories, day by day.

Blue follows three roommates as they navigate life and love in their post-college years. Tash Daniels, the former party girl, falls for deejay Aidan. Always attracted to the wrong guy, what will Tash do when the right one comes along? Jason Woo, a lighthearted model on the rise, uses the club scene as his personal playground. While he's adept at helping Tash with her personal life, how does he deal with his own when he meets a man who defies his expectations? Penelope Brown, a reserved and earnest graduate student, slips under the radar but has a secret no one suspects. As the characters' stories unfold, each is forced to confront their life choices or complacency and choose which version of themselves they want to be. *Blue* is a novel about identity, friendship, and figuring out who we are during the "in-between" phases of life. The book shines a spotlight on the friends and lovers who become our families in the fullest sense of the word, and the search for people who "get us." The characters in *Blue* show how our interactions with people often bump up against backstage struggles of which we are unaware. Visual art, television, and film appear as signposts throughout the narrative, providing a context for how we each come to build our sense of self in the world. With a tribute to 1980s pop culture but set in contemporary New York, *Blue* both celebrates and questions the ever-changing cultural landscape against which we live our stories, frame by frame.

Film follows three women who moved to Los Angeles to pursue their dreams. Tash Daniels aspires to be a filmmaker. Her short film was rejected from festivals, she has a stack of rejected grant proposals, and she lost her internship at a studio when her boss sexually harassed her, forcing her to take a job as a personal shopper.

Lu K is a hot deejay, slowly working her way up the club scene, but no one is doing her any favors. Fiercely independent, she's at a loss when she meets Paisley, a woman who captures her heart. Monroe Preston is the glamorous wife of a Hollywood studio head. As a teenager, she moved to LA in search of a "big" life, but now she wonders if reality measures up to fantasy. When a man in their circle finds sudden fame, each of these women is catapulted on a journey of self-discovery. Tash struggles with staying invested in art-making when she has nothing but rejections to show for her efforts. She begins to spiral into old habits and question her path and identity. Lu and Paisley may be the perfect couple, but the idea of a perfect connection bewilders Lu. She has always pushed uncomfortable thoughts out of her mind, but when she enters Paisley's world of close friends and family, Lu finally allows herself to remember her past. Monroe develops crippling insomnia as she begins to obsess over turning points in her youth and a painful revelation about her mother. As the characters' stories unfold, each is forced to confront how her past has shaped her fears and to choose how she wants to live in the present. *Film* is a novel about the underside of dreams, the struggle to find internal strength, the power of art, and what it truly means to live a "big" life. Frequently bathed in the glow of the silver screen, the characters in *Film* show us how the arts can reignite the light within. With a tribute to popular culture, set against the backdrop of Tinseltown, *Film* celebrates how the art we make and experience can shape our stories, scene by scene.

    Low-Fat Love was my debut novel. It was a secret project. My partner, Mark, who I later married, was the only person who knew about it. I was writing it for myself as a way to purge the cumulative insights I'd developed over a decade spent collecting interviews with women about their lives, teaching intimate sociology courses about love, gender, and popular culture, and amassing my own life experiences, including a few toxic romances. As the title suggests, *Low-Fat Love* is about settling in life and love because we devalue ourselves. I never imagined how deeply the book would resonate with others. It struck a chord. After the release, I was bombarded with messages from readers. At conferences and book events, people lined hallways for a chance to whisper their own stories of low-fat love to me. I will always be enormously moved by the experience. I never intended to write a sequel and went on to write another, unrelated novel.

Several years later, my daughter's biological father died of lung cancer. I found myself in a state of what I came to think of as "messy grief." He had been a dark force in my life, but also a source of inspiration. It was complicated. I turned to creativity and began writing *Blue*. At the outset, I took Tash Daniels, a supporting and deeply flawed character from *Low-Fat Love*, and made her the protagonist. Tash was surrounded by a new cast of characters. While it was not a sequel, *Blue* was the next piece in an installation. It had to work both on its own and as a piece of a larger whole. At its core, *Blue* celebrates possibilities.

When I finished *Blue*, I knew there was another story to tell. However, art needs room to breathe and artists need room to grow, so I first wrote another, unrelated novel in a different genre and completed a few nonfiction projects. When the time was right, I wrote *Film*, which chronicles the next part of Tash's journey and introduces new characters. It was a daunting task. *Film* had to work as a stand-alone novel, as a sequel to *Blue*, and as the final piece in a three-part installation. I loved writing all three of these novels, but *Film* just flowed out of me. It completed a decade of creative work and was a gloriously immersive process for which I'll always be thankful.

Each of these books is about the relationships we have with popular culture, with others, and with ourselves. *Low-Fat Love* explores the effect of toxic popular culture on women's lives, *Blue* explores how we may positively use the stories in popular culture to illuminate our own stories, and *Film* explores how the popular culture and art we create sustains us. Further, the characters in *Low-Fat Love* show how people may suffer in isolation, the characters in *Blue* show the importance of having people in our lives who understand us, and the characters in *Film* show the importance of developing a strong sense of self as individuals if we are to participate in healthy and affirming relationships with others.

To honor the interconnections between these works, each book has nods to the others, including specific pop culture references, images, and themes. For example, A-ha's "Take on Me" comes up in *Low-Fat Love*, denoting a character's self-esteem struggles, and then resurfaces in *Film*, as another character fully comes into her own. There are numerous examples of references reappearing and taking on entirely new meanings, as the three novels illustrate a journey to self-actualization. Other items, such as food the characters eat, repeats in this way. For instance, characters in all three novels are shown eating Chinese food, each scene denoting something quite different. In *Low-Fat Love*, one such scene shows the protagonist, Prilly, eating Chinese takeout and struggling with chopsticks, symbolic of her self-esteem struggles. By the time we reach *Film*, Tash eats Chinese takeout with chopsticks in a scene that illustrates joy and coming into one's own. Even words, such as edge, recur across the novels, the contexts creating different meanings and an overarching message. Great care was taken to create each novel as an independent read *and* to weave connections through the collection, making the sum larger than the parts. In terms of tone or mood, the books form an arc from darkness to light. It's no coincidence that film, as an art form, is light-driven.

I've never shared this before, but when I was writing *Low-Fat Love*, I used a placeholder title: *Candy Floss*. To this day, all my electronic files from the first draft are labeled *Candy Floss*. When I decided to publish it, I felt I needed a catchy title to break through the clutter, especially because it was a debut novel. I also wanted a title that encapsulated the concept of the book. I'm very glad I landed on *Low-Fat Love*, which has developed a life of its own as a term people use to describe settling in life and love. Yet in my own heart, the title has always secretly remained *Candy Floss*. I'm glad to honor what this decade-long journey has meant to me by titling the complete work *Candy Floss Collection*. It's intentional that cotton candy pops up in both the first and last books, signifying different moments in the journey to selfhood. I'm profoundly grateful to my publisher and readers for allowing me the opportunity to present my full artistic vision.

I hope this collection inspires you to love yourself just a little bit more and to chase your dreams just a little bit harder. We are possibilities.

LOW-FAT LOVE

PART ONE

CHAPTER 1

"'Casey bombed into town with her daily organizer.' It's the worst first line I've ever heard! I mean, you're left with this organizer, just sitting there, for no reason. You never mention something so irrelevant right in the beginning. It's awful. Nowadays everyone thinks they can write. There are no real writers anymore," he said, flinging the manuscript on Prilly's desk.

"Just real editors, right Stuart?"

"Ah, you're just soft Prilly. You can't coddle them. There's no point."

With a friendly roll of her eyes, she agreed to the inevitable. "I know, I know," she said shaking her head. "I'll tell him we can't go forward with publication."

"Good. We have to start streamlining our list. Bad writing that sells millions of copies is one thing, but unsuccessful bad writing is an embarrassment. I don't have to remind you that we can't afford the drain."

Prilly smiled, thinking his remark about unsuccessful bad writing was dead-on. "Got it. I'll take care of it."

Stuart left her small, drab office, inadvertently knocking a teetering stack of mail off the corner of her desk. The piles on her desk taunted her. She desperately desired to have everything organized and in its place, but she just couldn't manage it for more than a couple of days at a time. She had seen an episode of Oprah where an expert said that clutter in one's office or home represented clutter in one's emotional and spiritual life. As she wondered whether that was true, she reread the beginning of the manuscript. *Is it really such a bad opening line?*

***

That night when Prilly entered her apartment she immediately kicked off her comfort heels and slipped on her at-home uniform: Old Navy black pajama pants and worn out Ugg boots. She poured a glass

5

of Beaujolais and lay on the couch. Remote in hand, she flipped between her usual stations and landed on *Access Hollywood*. They were featuring a story about Brad Pitt and Angelina Jolie. She always bought tabloids when they were on the cover. Although she despised the idea that they were mostly adored for their good looks, she was fascinated. Sometimes she fantasized about what Angelina's life was like. More than any other celebrity, Angelina seemed to have it all. She was ridiculously gorgeous, the kind of beauty that doesn't seem to go out of style or age. She had lived a wild life, and now she had a massive, multicultural family (that she probably never had to take care of with all her nannies, assistants, and so forth), a fabulous partner who undoubtedly worshipped her, and an amazing career. Somehow she had managed to be both an artist and a commercial success, or at least she could reasonably claim to be both. People admired her. People like Prilly. As Prilly watched the story she felt a familiar storm cloud of envy, longing, and self-loathing.

Access Hollywood was just the prelude to whatever "movie of the week" she could find. Tonight she was watching a Lifetime movie about a woman who worked as a newspaper reporter and, while reporting on a local crime, became the next target of a psychopath. As Prilly picked up each forkful of the vegetable stir-fry she made during the commercials, she couldn't help but think, *In some ways the reporter is lucky. At least her life is exciting.*

Prilly lived in between who she was and who she wanted to be. She had moved to Manhattan from Boston in search of a *big life*. She had always felt she was meant to have a big life. To date, she had barely lived a small life. Although she was an atheist, she blamed God for all her problems (when she wasn't blaming her parents). She thought it all came down to looks, to genetics. She was convinced that beautiful people have a much greater shot at a big life. Ugly people have no shot. People somewhere in the middle, which is where she was firmly located, had to work hard for it, but it *was* possible. So ever since Prilly was about seven years old and she realized that she was regular looking at best, she blamed God and her parents for her lot in life. As a teenager, she admired the beautiful, popular girls. To her, they had been graced with the best gift of all: the gift of possibility. When you are beautiful, all you have to do is add on to that to get what you want, to be who you want to be. When you aren't beautiful, you spend your life making up for it, filling in what is lacking. Compensating. At times Prilly even envied the ugly girls. If you are ugly and know it, you have no hope for a big life. Ultimately, that could be very freeing. You could focus on being content with your life as it is. Ugly girls don't have to waste time or money on makeup, hair care, exercise, beauty treatments, and fashion. What's the point? No one fabulous would ever get close enough to reject them, so they must be free from disappointment too, she thought – once they accepted their situation, at least. The ones who had it the worst were those in the middle, the girls who, with enough work, could be considered pretty but never beautiful. Those girls could taste the big life, they could see it close enough to want it, to reach for it. Prilly was in the middle.

***

Pete Rice picked up the latest Neil Gaiman book, planning to spend the next several hours reading while drinking dark roast coffee. He loved the smell of coffee brewing. It was his favorite smell.

Waiting for the coffee to brew, he replayed the scene of Rachel storming out of his apartment the night before. He decided not to call her; he didn't care. He had a theory about women. If they loved you, you could control them. If they loved you too much, it was a disaster. He had many disasters. (There was Alice, who showed up to a party at his friend's house, plastered, shouting that he had an STD. He didn't. Then there was the catalogue model, Georgia, who slashed his vintage T-shirt collection and trashed his apartment. This, of course, brings to mind Sophie, who upon catching him in bed with Georgia, used his dirty clothes to make a bonfire on the fire escape outside of his apartment. Worst of all was Sadie, who would stake out his usual haunts – a local teahouse, a sandwich shop, a pub – waiting to see him arm-in-arm with another woman. This would cause her to scream publicly as if the world was burning and only she could see it. Interestingly, this would cause the woman currently with Pete, in her guiltiest of thoughts, to want him even more.)

Pete's days depended primarily on three factors: whether or not he was screwing someone steadily (steadily for him being a long series of intense relationships that lasted about two months each), whether or not he had been out all night (he had a penchant for dance clubs, though at thirty-eight he was nearly two decades older than everyone else there), and whether or not he was working (although he resisted any kind of long-term commitment or "career" that would interfere with his art, he did take very occasional part-time jobs doing things like telemarketing or working in a one-hour photo shop, which also never lasted for more than two months). He vacillated between feeling invincible (he had an unknown genius complex, one that was imprinted with the arrogance of a guy who was better looking than behaved) and feeling utterly depressed. That day, Pete had expected to be alone.

His studio apartment consisted of one small room that served as his bedroom and workspace, a kitchenette with a cutout wall that looked into the bedroom, and a small hallway that led to the bathroom and front door. The main room had two large windows, one of which led out to a small fire escape that he used as a teeny tiny porch. Sometimes he grew pot out there, but his neighbors usually stole it.

He used an old queen-size mattress and box spring, but no bed frame, so his bed was low to the floor. Gaiman book in hand, he propped two pillows against the white stucco wall and sat down in his black and white checkered boxers and old David Bowie T-shirt. He placed his oversized "I Love NY" mug on the cinderblock to the right of his bed and opened the book. He always read the dedication first. He felt you could learn everything about the soul of an author by reading the dedication page and thus, the soul of the book. Books without dedications always disappointed him. As he flipped to the first page, there was a knock on his front door.

He walked to the door and shouted, "Who is it?"

"Melville."

Pete opened the door. Neither said a word, and Pete walked back down his narrow hallway to his bedroom while pulling at a wedgie. Melville locked the door and followed. Pete plopped down on his mattress and picked up his coffee. Melville pulled out the rolling computer chair tucked under the desk opposite the bed. He turned it to face Pete and sat down. Then he stood up, took off his jacket, and sat down again, placing the orange garment across his lap.

"So what's up?"

"Oh, nothing, I was downtown visiting my cousin so I thought I'd stop in. I thought that maybe we could get some coffee or something. What are you doing?"

"Nothing. I got the new Gaiman book and I was just going to start it."

"I could have gotten you a deal on that. I hope you didn't pay full price, not for the hardcover. I know a store where you can get hard covers half-off, even new ones. If you get 'em used you can get them for a few bucks. Hard covers are a rip-off anyway."

As Melville spoke, slowly as ever, Pete wished that he would shut up. He was the cheapest person he had ever met. He had holes in his sweaters and had sported the same worn-out, ugly, orange windbreaker for the whole time Pete had known him – more than a decade. Pete hated going out to eat with him because Melville refused to tip appropriately. He left spare change, usually about a four percent tip at most. Pete was cheap too, but only privately. In public, he intentionally gave the impression of being generous, but in private, he often screwed friends who loaned him money, haggled with the landlord over the rent if any minor repair was needed (real or imagined), and while he always had money for expensive restaurants, liquor, books, art supplies, and all things entertainment, he never seemed to have money for anything else. For example, he had no health, dental, or life insurance. Nor did he have any property beyond the books and odds and ends in his tiny rented apartment. He routinely bought an overpriced cappuccino from the café down the street, only to drink a sip and forget about it, but he couldn't manage to pay his utilities on time and consistently ended up paying late fees and even reinstallation charges. As the flaws in others are always much more apparent than those in ourselves, Pete was oblivious. He wished that Melville wasn't so cheap or at least that he'd have the good sense to shut up about it. The truth was that he was embarrassed to be friends with Melville. Pete prided himself on chasing the muse, being in tune with the zeitgeist, and living in the moment. To Pete, Melville was the embodiment of all that he disdained. Pete decided that Melville lived one beat outside the moment. That was why he was slow to relay the simplest of information and why, at the age of thirty-six, Pete suspected he might still be a virgin. Yet despite his harsh evaluation of Melville, he remained the only reliable presence in Pete's life.

Totally ignoring Melville's inane hardcover commentary, Pete shot back with, "Yeah, okay, let's go grab a bite. I need to shower. You can make yourself some coffee if you want. I'm out of filters but there's paper toweling there. Flip through that book, or look in that folder over there," he said, pointing to a pile of papers on the desk behind Melville. "I've expanded the carnival part of the story and I'd like to know what you think. No one's read it yet. You're in for a treat. I'll be out in a jiff," Pete hollered as he walked to the bathroom, coffee mug in hand.

Forty-five minutes later, they were sitting down in a diner three blocks away. Pete was an inconsistent regular. He went through spurts of eating there nearly every day, sometimes more than once a day, but then he didn't go for months at a time. Just as the waitresses were getting to know him, he took a hiatus and they had forgotten him by the time he returned. When the waitress came to take their order, Pete couldn't help but notice how unusual looking she was. He had a knack for noticing atypical faces, and this face intrigued him. It was fairly old but probably appeared older than its biological age. It had very long features and a strong nose. After further examination he determined that the nose was in fact so ugly that he actually found it quite wonderful. He expected an interesting accent to match the face, but when she said, "What'll it be?" it was with the same New York accent he had come to tire of during the last five of the fifteen years he had been in the States.

"I'll have two eggs over easy with wheat toast. I'd like marmalade on the side, not jam. And coffee, with cream."

"And you?" she asked looking at Melville, who was still staring directly into the oversized plastic laminated menu.

"Um, what does the special egg sandwich come with?"

"Home fries."

"Does it come with a drink?"

"No, just home fries."

"Um, okay, I'll have that."

"Something to drink?"

"Just water."

Pete, growing tired of these uncomfortable exchanges, occupied himself by doodling in the small notepad he always carried. By the time Melville looked up from his menu, Pete was in another world.

"So I read the new pages."

"Yeah, and?" Pete asked, both eager to hear the response and annoyed that he had to coax it out of him.

"They're good but you're missing some commas in a couple of places. I can show you where." (Melville had been an English major in college, until he dropped out sophomore year.)

"Commas? Fucking commas? This is your insight? I don't give a fuck about commas! I hate fucking commas. Do you have anything useful to contribute or are you just taking up space?"

Although visibly hurt by Pete's patronizing rant, Melville ignored it, as he was accustomed to doing. Wanting to show Pete he had more to offer, that he wasn't just "taking up space," he quickly retorted, "Well I don't get where you are going with the main character. The writing is good but there's nowhere to take it."

"Ha! You should stick to commas," Pete said through hearty laughter.

Melville shrugged, looking down. Although Pete didn't notice, Melville never looked him in the eyes. Never. He normally looked down and sometimes to the side.

"You'll get it when it's all there. That's your problem, you need it all spelled out. Can't feeeeel where it's headin'. But don't worry, it'll all be there and you'll get it."

With that, the waitress brought their breakfast. Melville ate swiftly, looking down at his food the entire time. Pete spent a few minutes dunking the corner of his toast into his egg yolks before eating.

At the end of the meal, there was some typical squabbling about the bill. Melville left his usual four percent tip. Anyone else would have just thrown some extra money down, but Pete, being secretly cheap himself, guilt-tripped Melville into putting down a couple of dollars. Pete either didn't realize or didn't care that when Melville gave in it was just to get him to shut up. Melville couldn't stand the sound of Pete's voice. Although he envied him, particularly with women, he also found Pete laborious. Walking out, Pete noticed a flyer in the entrance of the diner. It announced a book reading by Jeanette Winterson that Saturday afternoon at a local bookstore. He ripped down the flyer and said, "We should go to this. It would be good for you to hear the work of a real writer. No one uses metaphor quite like Winterson. She's good."

Not acknowledging the condemnation, Melville simply replied, "Yeah, okay."

***

On the train, Melville Wicket sat still and silent. Weeks earlier he moved into his younger brother Jacob's apartment in Brooklyn, which he shared with a manic-depressive named Jeremy.

Melville was a telemarketer for a medical insurance company. He only worked twenty-eight hours a week so his employer could avoid paying him benefits, like medical insurance. With hardly enough income to live, Melville had been staying in a small basement room in a rooming house for the past three years. He paid month-to-month. Some residents had week-to-week deals. The room was half above ground and half below. There were two small rectangular windows high on the right wall, nearly touching the ceiling, with rusty iron bars. Underneath the windows was a small refrigerator, the kind you would expect to find in a college dorm room, a microwave, and an electric Crock-Pot that violated building codes. Across from the windows was a twin bed with old, off-white sheets, one flattened pillow, and a worn out, queen sized down comforter with a few holes. Sometimes when Melville woke up in the morning, there were feathers in his hair. In his mind, he called them *chicken feathers*. To the left of the bed was a small, unfinished wooden desk and brown leather chair. On the desk, he kept a stack of library books, a few pieces of old mail, notebooks and pens, an old word processor from 1995, and a small alarm clock with a CD player. On the floor beneath, stacks of CDs. To the right, a tall halogen lamp. There was a shared bathroom in the hallway. Melville was allotted one shelf in the medicine cabinet for his personal items, which he used, although he didn't feel good about it.

Melville would have stayed there forever, but was asked to leave at the end of the previous month. One of the female residents complained to the super that Melville had been peeping on her while she was in the bathroom. She reported that she saw him through the slit of the barely-opened door, a door she claimed to have closed. He must have pushed it ever so slightly open, she had argued. Two years earlier, another woman had made a similar complaint. Melville denied it, in his usual quiet manner. The super took pity on him and let him stay, but now with a second complaint, he was out. When he told Pete what happened, Pete said, "Spying? You were spying on the girls? Ha!" Melville insisted he hadn't done it, but Pete rolled his eyes and didn't say anything else. He always assumed that Melville was guilty, not because he was a pervert, but because he was shy, and awkward, and terribly lonely.

Jacob hadn't wanted Melville to move in with him, but what could he do? The guy was basically homeless, and he *was* his brother. Besides, he could get money for rent and utilities, leaving more money for pot and the occasional celebratory mushroom. Jacob was twenty-four and worked in what he called a "vintage music store" in the Village, near Washington Square Park. The store sold rare vinyl and used CDs, dealing largely in trade. Melville wondered how a store like that could stay in business in the age of eBay and iTunes. He once asked Jacob about it and was told to "shut the fuck up." Melville never mentioned it again. Melville didn't know what Jeremy did for a living. Most days he stayed in his room all day, sleeping, Melville assumed. But every Tuesday, he was up and out of the house by eight o'clock and didn't return until after six in the evening. Melville didn't ask questions.

After spending the morning with Pete, Melville returned to his apartment at three o'clock. He went straight into his small bedroom. It was actually a two-bedroom apartment with a small living and kitchenette combo room and one tiny bathroom with a stall shower. The apartment also had a very small sunroom that Jacob turned into a makeshift bedroom for his brother. With no room for a bed, Melville slept on a small couch. The room was drafty, and Melville was worried about winter. He thought about it all the time. On that day, as most, he entered his room, took off his sneakers, and put on a Puccini CD. He lay on his couch with his jacket still on, listening.

***

Prilly's search for a big life hadn't amounted to much. She was in her office from eight until six-thirty every weekday. By the time she got back to her apartment, it was time for *Access Hollywood* and a healthy dinner, followed by a bad junk food binge with a side of guilt and a movie about women who steal other women's babies or who murder their young repairmen lovers. Although she had been in New York for several years, she hadn't managed to make more than a couple of friends, and she didn't really like them. Much like the fat girl in high school whom she befriended, this, for now, was the best she could do. The single women at work routinely went to local bars together, and, although they always invited her, she never once went. She felt uncomfortable and feared it would be awful. After a while, she noticed that they didn't actually invite her, but rather said, "We're heading to Maxwell's." She assumed she was welcome to join them, or else why would they bother to announce where they were going. But she wasn't sure.

She took one stab at Internet dating. The Internet appealed to her for two main reasons. First, no one had to know about it, so if it didn't work out, she wouldn't have to explain her failure to anyone. Second, she could screen the men based on income, education, looks, and interests. She wanted a man who earned more money than she did, not because she had any intention of becoming dependent, but because it would be hard to have a big life in Manhattan without more money, and a lot of it. She also wanted to get out from under her mounting credit card debt, which weighed on her, particularly on the nights she drank excessively. She hoped to meet someone interested in the arts, who could take her to the best shows. Although she wanted to be with a good-looking man, which she believed made a so-so looking woman seem much more attractive, she didn't want to be with a man that was too good looking. Men like that always left average women eventually. It was hard to fool them into thinking you were prettier than you actually were. If she managed to get a decent man and turn it into a steady thing, she didn't want to have to do it all over again someday. She also feared being part of a couple that made other women wonder: *What is he doing with her?*

The Internet dating ended up costing her $199, a weekend's worth of screening time, one terrible evening, and an untold sum of shame. She had made a date with Henry. He seemed promising. He was an accountant who owned his own apartment and claimed to see every foreign film that came out. They planned to meet at a Spanish tapas restaurant a few blocks from her office for a drink and quick bite. She thought about the date incessantly for five days. She got a manicure, bikini wax, and bought two new outfits (neither of which she wore; she decided one was weird and the other looked too "datey"). On the night they were supposed to meet, she got to the restaurant, stood outside for a minute panicking, walked around the block, and then decided that if he had seen her walk around the block he would already think she was a freak. She went home, drank nearly a bottle of wine, and watched four hours of a nine-hour *Murder, She Wrote* marathon on the Hallmark channel. Henry sent her an email the next morning asking what happened and if she was okay. She never responded and removed her profile from match.com. She felt guilty for months, thinking of Henry often.

Without many friends to go out with and no real effort made at dating, her life was fairly lonely. She decided to invest energy into her weekend routine. Convinced that if you lead an interesting life you will meet interesting people, Prilly made being interesting her full-time weekend occupation. For her, there was nothing more interesting than the arts. Had she been braver, she might have been some sort of artist, or at least a journalist. She took to surrounding herself with the products of others' bliss. The monotony of the workweek was soon juxtaposed to weekends of ballet, theatre, concerts, gallery openings, craft markets, spoken word performances, independent films, museums, and poetry readings. It was exhausting.

***

"Well I wanted to tell you in person. I know it's difficult, but please don't take it personally. We're a mid-sized press and we need to be very careful about which books we publish, particularly for our trade market. Usually we don't even consider unsolicited works."

"But you've sold fifteen thousand copies of my last book. That should count for something. That's why I came to you first. I just don't understand this. Isn't there anything I can do?"

"Yes, I understand how you must feel," Prilly responded in a hushed tone, "but that was an introductory geography textbook. It was an academic printing with a built-in audience we could market to. If you talk with Marcy, I'm sure she can explain it to you. The trade market is very different and we publish very few new fiction authors each year. I'm sorry but we can't go with this and I don't want to waste your time. I encourage you to submit it elsewhere."

After a moment of silence, during which Prilly could hear her own breath, Charles matter-of-factly said, "Well, I'm very disappointed. Very disappointed." With that, the large, pear-shaped man got up, outstretched his arm over Prilly's desk for a sweaty handshake, and left.

Prilly felt awful. Normally she just sent rejection emails or letters. She never saw the person she was rejecting, but because Charles was already published with the house, Stuart suggested she do it in person the next time Charles stopped by to see Marcy, the geography editor.

Before Prilly could regroup, Janice popped her head in the door, left ajar by Charles. The sight of Janice made Prilly crave Advil. Janice was a long-time acquisitions editor with the press and Prilly had been her assistant for nine months before being promoted to editor. It was the longest nine months of her life. At first she thought she was incredibly lucky. She was told that there were very few women in publishing who had made it to Janice's level, with her list of accomplishments. After ten years of working in their geography division, Janice was given a new list to build, history, a market the press had never ventured into before. With a degree in history, Janice had purportedly been thrilled. She introduced herself to Prilly as a feminist. She boldly said, "Prilly, this is a male-dominated industry. It's not easy, but it *can* be done and we have to support each other." She also prided herself on including women's history and Black history in her line, books she swore other editors would forego.

Prilly soon discovered that feminism was more of an abstract concept with Janice. She really enjoyed talking about supporting "women's issues," but she didn't support *actual women*. In fact, over time Prilly learned that Janice was particularly harsh on the women she worked with out of some irrational fear that they would become more successful than her, and what's worse, that they wouldn't have to work as hard to do it. Janice had to work for everything she had, and unlike the "spoiled bitches" she went to college with, she scraped for everything she got, including her education. As a result, Janice only liked women in positions beneath her, those that she could easily manipulate and therefore control.

Janice liked Prilly well enough at first, but when she realized that Prilly wouldn't be content being an assistant forever, she grew weary. This weariness led to a quiet resentment. Prilly often found herself working outrageously long hours that mostly consisted of doing secretarial work for Janice, which was not in her job description. Assigning these kinds of tasks helped Janice on two levels. First, it made it clear to Prilly and anyone else paying attention that she was in charge, that she was Prilly's boss. Second, and even more importantly, it prevented Prilly from doing the kind of work that the publishers would notice, the kind of work that would get Prilly promoted. What Janice failed to recognize was that the publishers had always intended Prilly for an editorial position. They only made her an assistant first so the others wouldn't complain about rank jumping. When Prilly was promoted, she immediately went to Janice, hoping to avoid future unpleasantness.

"Thank you so much, Janice. Without your mentorship, this never would have happened."

"Well, actually I did put in a good word for you, too. I had to push for this. I had to make this happen. But you deserve it," Janice replied in her usual quiet, monotone voice.

Prilly thanked her although she knew it wasn't true. In fact, she suspected that Janice secretly gave her mediocre performance reviews so she would remain her assistant indefinitely. Ever since, Janice went out of her way to be nice to Prilly, so much so that it alarmed her. Once in a while, Janice found a way to say something cutting under the guise of being helpful, like the knock about having to convince the bosses to promote her. It was no wonder that the mere sight of Janice at her door caused a sharp pain in her spine.

"Hi Prilly. What was that about? Charles looked pretty upset when he left. He used to be one of my authors you know."

Prilly relaxed a bit, hoping Janice was just nosing around for gossip, as she was prone to do, and didn't want anything beyond chitchat.

"Oh, that's right. He's one of Marcy's now. Same old, same old. He's an academic who thinks he can also be a novelist. I had to tell him that his manuscript isn't for us. He took it pretty hard, but what can you do, you know."

Janice shimmied her way into the doorway, allowing her back to gently tap the door closed as if unintentionally. *Oh great*, Prilly thought. *There's more.*

"Do you want to come in and sit down?" Prilly asked entirely out of obligation.

"Oh sure, just for a minute."

Janice always had a way of making things seem like they were someone else's idea, as if *she* was doing *you* a favor.

"Prilly, I wanted to run something by you."

"Sure, what's up?"

"I want to build a list of memoirs, focusing mostly on unknown female authors."

"That sounds great, Janice. You should give Stuart a proposal."

"Well I did actually, and that's where you come in. Stuart said that memoirs would fall under your list, that they're sold as trade books and since we don't publish non-fiction trade, they'd have to be a part of our current trade list. He thought it would make sense for someone in your division to partner up with me."

"Hmm."

"So I suggested that you and I work on it together. We could do it as a book series instead of a line, at least as a sort of pilot test. If we solicit authors who have already drafted manuscripts, we could premier at Trade Launch this spring. You and I could serve as co-editors-in-chief for the series, with my name listed first. If it does well, we could eventually build a full line. I think this would be an excellent opportunity for you."

Yeah, I bet you do, Prilly thought. She learned long ago that Janice only cared about opportunities for herself. Anytime she framed something as an opportunity for someone else, Prilly thought that the poor soul should run like the wind. A part of Prilly actually liked Janice, despite all the obvious reasons not to. At times, she even thought that her fondness for Janice grew in direct proportion to her manipulative behavior. Although she was very different from Janice, deep down she knew that a part of them was the same. A part of each of them had been shafted and was clawing their way out the best way they knew how. Janice's claws were simply sharper. She also wanted to believe in Janice's tale of great feminist heroism in publishing, even though she knew it was all a lie. If Janice would just be more forthright, Prilly could even be friends with her. She kept this thought to herself.

"Well it does sound interesting. Why don't you give me your proposal? I'll look it over and we can talk more. I'm really swamped as it is, but I'll definitely look at what you have."

"I'm telling you, this is a great opportunity for you. In fact, Stuart didn't think you were up for it yet, but with my convincing, he's willing to give you a shot."

"Well I appreciate that," Prilly said, the way a child thanks their parents when they're given socks for Christmas. "It sounds like a great opportunity but I'd like to look over the specifics and think about it."

Janice couldn't conceal her irritation as she fiddled with her pin-straight, light brown hair, but she played along. "Okay, I'll email you the proposal and Stu's notes. We can talk about it early next week."

"Okay, great. Thanks, Janice."

Janice left her office, shutting the door behind her. Prilly took four Advil.

* * *

The weekend couldn't come fast enough for Prilly. She spent Friday night at home with half a bottle of red wine and Chinese takeout. (She always ate right out of the container with the disposable chopsticks. She thought it was more sophisticated, even though no one was there to see it, and she had no idea how to use chopsticks properly, so food invariably landed on her couch. This also prevented her from ordering the veggie fried rice she liked, since she couldn't possibly eat rice with chopsticks). On Saturday, she woke up late with a wine and MSG headache and took two Advil.

With no plans until Sunday (when she was meeting an old friend for a several-times-rescheduled lunch), she sipped her French roast while perusing one of her favorite New York websites, which listed events of interest. Jeanette Winterson was doing a book reading and signing at four o'clock. The bookstore was near the shoe repair store where she had left her silver shoes for heel reinforcement. Prilly liked to multitask. Plus, *there are sure to be interesting people at the book reading*, she thought.

CHAPTER 2

"Hang on a minute. Fuck, Melville's banging on the damn door. No, we're going to a book reading. I'm not even dressed so I'd better get movin'. I'll call you later. Hang in there. Bye."

When Pete hung up the phone, he stammered down his hallway and opened the door. He turned around and walked back to the kitchenette without saying a word. Melville shut the door and followed.

"Christ, I was on the phone. Can't you wait a minute?" Pete asked with a tone that made it clear he was not looking for an answer. "I'm making coffee, do you want some?"

"No, thanks," Melville said as he grabbed a comic book off Pete's desk and sat in the chair, flipping through its pages. Melville didn't care for comic books; he thought they were juvenile and beneath him, but like so many other thoughts, he kept this to himself.

"I just need to throw my clothes on. I'll bring the coffee to go."

"Okay," Melville said as he read a random page from the middle of the comic book.

***

The bookstore was crowded, and by the time Pete and Melville arrived, fifteen minutes late (though Winterson hadn't yet begun her reading), there weren't any seats left. Melville was secretly annoyed that Pete, per usual, wasn't ready on time. They stood in the back, leaning against a wall. Pete, burnt out from a sleepless night, sipped his coffee steadily.

When Winterson appeared, everyone stood up and began clapping ferociously. She began by talking about her new work, from which she read several passages. She then took questions from the audience about her first novel, *Oranges Are Not the Only Fruit*, and fan favorites like *Sexing the Cherry*. Prilly, who sat in the corner of the back row, hadn't read any of Winterson's books, although she owned several. They were amidst the collection of "important artistic works" she thought everyone should own, and someday even read.

At the end of the question period, there was a book signing. The mob scurried to the front, forming a swerving line through the store. Prilly detested standing in lines. She also hadn't brought any books with her and wasn't committed to buying the new book. She picked up her unmarked brown paper bag that contained her newly repaired shoes and turned to head out. The bag didn't have a handle and was cumbersome. She stuck it under one of her arms and threw her handbag on her opposite shoulder. She fumbled a bit as she made her way past the rows of arranged chairs toward the door. Melville, still leaning against the wall with Pete, noticed her immediately. *She is lovely*, he thought. It was his irrepressible staring that made Pete aware of her. As Prilly walked by, Pete said, "You're not getting a book?"

"I'm sorry. Did you say something to me?" Prilly asked, catching a glimpse of Pete for the first time. He had striking teal eyes framed with a few soft lines that made her think, *he's really lived.*

"I just asked if you were getting a book, like everyone else seems to be doing."

"Oh," noticing how sexy his voice was. "The line is too long."

"My friend and I are going to get a coffee and talk about the reading. Would you like to join us?"

Stunned by the invitation from a tall, dark-haired man whose name she didn't yet know, Prilly stammered. Pete quickly responded, "It's okay, no worries, but if you're not busy, come along."

Pete walked ahead of Prilly, opened the door, and let her pass through. He then stepped outside with Melville following. He turned to Prilly, who was shocked by both the unexpected invitation and the willingness with which this man would let her just leave. "Well, have a good evening," he said as he turned and started walking down the street.

Prilly watched as he and Melville went into a café halfway down the block. She turned to walk in the other direction, but as if in slow motion, she stopped mid-movement and turned back toward the café. *I'll hate myself if I don't check this out.* When she walked into the café, Pete was sitting on a long, red velvet couch. He smiled and said, "Well, you changed your mind."

"I thought I'd just come for a quick coffee."

"Great." He jumped up and got in line next to Melville, cutting in front of several people who didn't seem to mind.

Prilly put down her brown bag and sat on a wooden chair opposite Pete's vacated spot on the couch. "What'll ya have?" he hollered.

"Oh, a cappuccino. A non-fat cappuccino, please."

He took only a minute to place the order and soon returned with drinks in hand. "Thank you," she said as Pete handed her the foamy beverage.

"My name is Pete, and this is Melville, my editor," Pete said with a smirk as he plopped down on the couch.

"I'm Prilly. Prilly Greene." Turning to Melville, who was sitting in the chair to her right, she said, "You're an editor? Me too, that's so funny. I'm at WISE. Which house are you with?"

Pete laughed and said, "The house of Jacob."

Melville stuttered a bit and Prilly, not knowing what was so funny, turned to Pete. "Are you a writer?" she asked.

"Yes. Graphic novels mostly, but I do a little of everything."

He's very sexy, too sexy for me really, but he seems interested. Prilly was disproportionately impressed by him, considering they had just met. She loved his British accent though she was embarrassed by her own trite thoughts. He immediately reminded her of the lead singer from the '80s band A-ha. She had always loved the video for their song, "Take On Me," in which the singer is transformed into a cartoon illustration who falls in love with a plain-looking diner waitress. Every time she saw that video she wondered why they didn't get a more glamorous woman to play the love interest, but she cherished the video because it gave her hope. That was exactly how she felt with Pete.

After talking about the book reading for quite a while, they decided to go out for dinner. Although clearly a bit full of himself, Pete was well read and Prilly was enamored. Prilly said that she wanted to stop at her apartment first to drop off the bag with her shoes. She actually wanted to freshen up and throw a toothbrush and some makeup in her pocketbook just in case she didn't make it home that night. Although she had no intention of sleeping with him, this was the most exciting thing that had happened to her in a long time and she wanted to be prepared for spontaneity.

Suddenly worried that she just invited two strangers into her apartment, she felt a mix of trepidation and exhilaration as she clumsily turned the key in the lock. "I'll just be a couple of minutes. Feel free to look at those books," she said, pointing to her bookshelf before she darted into her bedroom. She returned ten minutes later with a larger handbag and without the brown paper bag that had become a source of gags on the way to her apartment. "Are you ready to go?" she asked.

"I'm going to head home. I forgot that I promised my brother I'd watch a movie with him tonight," Melville said. "He already rented it."

"Oh, okay," Prilly responded, not knowing if it was true or if Pete had asked Melville to make himself scarce so they could be alone. Though she was hoping that the latter was true, the thought also made her stomach knot. She had never been with someone so good looking before.

The three walked out together, and Melville headed left while Pete and Prilly turned right.

***

When he entered his apartment, Jacob was sitting on the couch with three guys that Melville had seen there before but had never been introduced to. They were passing around a joint and listening to country music. Melville walked over to the refrigerator and took out a small bottle of Orangina and a Tupperware with leftover macaroni with meat sauce that he made a few days earlier. He popped the macaroni into the microwave. The ninety-second cooking time felt like eternity as Melville awkwardly waited for the beep. "Hey, I thought you were hanging with Pete tonight. Did he ditch you?" Jacob hollered from the couch. Suddenly, there were four sets of bloodshot eyes peering at him.

"He met a girl. Wanted to be alone with her. She's beautiful," Melville quietly said, embarrassed that, in fact, he had again been ditched. Jacob and his friends returned their focus to their joint, and Melville took his dinner into his room where he ate while listening to Stravinsky and thinking of Prilly.

***

"'Casey bombed into town with her daily organizer.' Ha! That's terrible," Pete said as his voice became higher and his laughter morphed into a cackle.

"Really? You think so? It's not Pulitzer material but I don't think it's that bad. You should have seen the guy. He looked … he looked like he was trying to pretend he wasn't shattered. He's one of our established authors. I felt really badly for him."

"You've got to be kidding. It's dreadful. That could be an example in a book about how *not* to write. Maybe you could use it for that," Pete said, again punctuating his suggestion with laughter.

Pete was bordering on hurting her feelings, and he was definitely arrogant, but she let it slide and just said, "Yeah, I guess it's pretty bad," even though she still didn't understand why.

After a two-hour dinner at the bar of a pub that Pete recommended, where they split the bill, Prilly was in Pete's apartment sharing a bottle of red wine they picked up along the way (which Prilly had paid for because Pete suddenly became fascinated by plastic lighters when it was their turn at the register). Normally Prilly would have been put off by such a scruffy little apartment, but on that night she saw the simplicity differently. *He's living like a real artist*, she thought.

With only one chair in the apartment, Pete invited her to sit on the bed. When she hesitated he said, "Don't worry, you don't have to sleep with me or anything," followed by a short burst of laughter which she was beginning to realize was a regular part of his communication.

"Oh, I know," she said uncomfortably as she went to sit on the bed, careful not to spill her wine. Wanting to change the subject, Prilly asked, "What have you written? You said something about graphic novels. I don't know much about that genre but would I know your work?"

"Oh, no. No, you wouldn't know my work. I haven't been ready to publish. Haven't sent it out anywhere. But soon."

As an editor, Prilly didn't know what to make of this. She dealt with writers every day who were desperate to publish, who wanted it more than anything else. "When you say you're not ready to publish, do you mean that you haven't completed a work or are you one of those perfectionists who wants to get it all just so before you hand it over? Because you'd be amazed by how useful copyeditors can be."

"Well, I'll put it to you this way: if I were a gardener I would have the most beautiful, unusual flowers in the most unexpected and glorious colors. Everywhere the eye darted would be unimaginable wonder. However, I would forget to water them and they would all die." He laughed. "Besides, Melville does my copyediting."

"Ah," Prilly said, choosing to ignore the warning she knew the universe might be sending her. She also chose not to ask how he earned a living. (Days later, he would tell her that he lived mainly off an inheritance from his parents who had both died young of lung cancer although neither were smokers. Instead of wondering about his work ethic, she just felt sorry for him.)

They moved on to childhood tales (he had stories about eating candy floss on autumn days; she had no idea what candy floss was but it sounded wonderful), his days in college (he was a philosophy major who dropped out during his third year because there was nothing more to learn from the professors), his subsequent adventures in London (where he befriended many drug-addicted counter-culture artists), and eventually his move to New York (for "the energy"). She briefly told him about how much she loved her career, but mostly she just listened. After a few hours of talking, listening to new wave music that Prilly couldn't believe she had never heard before, and flipping through folders of Pete's work that appeared to be fragmented bits of rambling sprinkled with something magical, she realized it was past midnight.

"I should probably go."

"Don't be silly, spend the night. We can go out for breakfast in the morning. There's a wonderful little diner nearby with a fabulous waitress. She has the most unusual face, you have to see it. Do you have plans tomorrow?"

Prilly did have tentative plans with her friend Yvonne, and she wasn't sure if she wanted to sleep with Pete yet, but she said, "No, no plans."

"Settled. I have only the one bed so you'll have to sleep with me but don't worry, we can just sleep. I'll get you a T-shirt to wear."

Prilly went into the bathroom and put on the oversized Smiths T-shirt he had given her. She looked in the small, toothpaste-splattered mirror above the sink and wondered, *What am I doing? Thank God I brought my toothbrush.*

She timidly returned to the bed and carefully crawled in. Pete smiled and said, "Good night," as he flipped off the light switch. She lay awake for hours pretending to sleep.

The next morning, she heard Pete wrestling around in bed. She slowly turned to him, conscious of her morning breath. He looked her in the eyes and softly said, "Good morning."

Not wanting to breathe on him, she looked down and whispered, "Good morning." She turned around, lying with her back to him. He put his hand on her shoulder and she moved closer to him. He slid his hand under her T-shirt and rubbed her breasts. Then he moved his hands down and gently pulled her panties off. He put his hand on her and started slowly motioning. He slid into her and they made love, never turning to each other, never kissing.

CHAPTER 3

After blowing off her friend with a text message in order to spend the rest of the weekend with Pete, Prilly floated into her office Monday feeling exhilarated. Even though she knew Pete probably wasn't terribly successful, all she could think about was how sexy he was and how lucky she was to have met him. Filled with excitement over plans to see him that evening, and wearing her lucky bronze colored slingback heels, Prilly barely noticed Janice pop into her doorway, before she even had a chance to turn on her computer.

"It's nine fifteen. You're always here right at eight o'clock. I was concerned. A little bit longer and I would have called you just to make sure you were okay."

Considering they had almost no relationship whatsoever, she wondered why Janice was feigning concern for her. That thought temporarily distracted her from wondering why Janice was keeping tabs on what time she got into the office.

"Oh, I had a late night, so I decided to come in a little later today," Prilly said, suddenly realizing it was none of Janice's business.

Too focused on her own agenda to recognize an opportunity to prod for more information, Janice simply asked, "Well, what do you think?"

"About what?"

This caused Janice to roll her eyes, flip her hair, and sigh all at once. Prilly was worried she might hurt herself. She hijacked the chair facing Prilly and responded sharply, "About the memoir series."

"Oh, right. I'm so sorry, but I was really busy this weekend and I didn't have a chance to look over the materials. Can I get back to you later in the week?"

"Prilly, this is really an excellent opportunity and it's time sensitive. We need to get moving on this."

Time sensitive? Prilly wondered to herself. *It's not that time sensitive.* But she realized that Janice was fixated and would be relentless. If Prilly ultimately turned her down, Janice would be out to get her, and may not be subtle about it any longer. If she agreed to work with Janice, she would probably end up suicidal. It was a toss-up. Feeling invincible from the two orgasms she had the night before, Prilly decided that with her personal life taking this wonderfully unexpected turn, it wouldn't be such a bad time to take on a new work challenge. Maybe the series would be a hit. Memoirs were interesting. Best yet, Pete would be impressed.

"Well, I still want to review the materials in order to under-stand the scope of the commitment and what the compensation will be, but I think it's a good idea. I'd like to do it with you."

"Great! This is a terrific opportunity for you. I mean, I don't really have time for it either, but I think it will really strengthen our line and help your career." As Prilly was contemplating this last remark, Janice stood up and smiled. "I'll let Stu know. Let's set up a meeting later this week to go over the details and draft our work plan." Janice turned on her heel and left Prilly's office, closing the door behind her. Prilly worried about what she had just gotten herself into.

***

That night, feeling good about cajoling Prilly into the memoir series, Janice arrived home at a quarter to eight with a canvas bag of groceries hanging on one shoulder and her maroon leather laptop case in her hand. She hurriedly entered her house as the grocery bag started slipping. From the kitchen she shouted, "Richard, are you home?" as she unpacked green grapes, sliced turkey, wheat rolls, and three bottles of Pellegrino sparkling water. To break the silence she hollered, "Kyle, Kyle please come here." Nothing. *He's probably out with his friends again,* she thought. After making a turkey sandwich with a slather of Miracle Whip, the one taste of her childhood in which she found comfort, she flung her canvas bag on the coat rack near the front door, grabbed the computer case she had abandoned there, and headed into the dining room, which over time had become her office. Sitting alone at the end of a long, rectangular, dark mahogany table covered with stacks of manila folders and books, she took out her folder labeled

"Ideas for the Memoir Series" and started to work. The sandwich sat untouched beside her.

***

Janice Goldwyn prided herself on three things: her career, her family, and her house. More accurately, she prided herself on the appearance of her career, the idea of her family, and while she truly loved her house, she always feared that she best not get too comfortable there. So she didn't.

Growing up, Janice didn't have much. She lived on the outskirts of Detroit. Her father was a nasty drunk. Janice desperately wanted his approval, so she worked her absolute hardest in school. Each afternoon, she came bounding into the house where she found him half reclined in his old sky blue Lazy Boy, drinking a beer and watching *Family Feud*. She gently tapped him on the shoulder (after learning not to jump right in front of him, thus obstructing his view). He always ignored her. Unable to contain her enthusiasm she happily said, "Pop, Pop, guess what? I got an A on my geography test," or, "Pop, Pop, guess what? Miss Murphy hung my painting up in art class," or, "Pop, Pop, I beat my obstacle course record in gym class. Maybe I can be a Marine like you someday."

To her excitement and accomplishments, her father always had the same response: "Biiiig nothing. Scatter. Scatter you pissant." Unlike Janice's younger sister, Marge, who despised their father and didn't care what he thought, Janice never stopped trying. Day after day, year after year, this scene repeated. Over time, Janice came to resent her mother, Myra. Janice saw their situation as her mother's fault. She thought her mother must be inadequate, weak, a loser. When she hung all of Janice's crayon drawings on their refrigerator, Janice concluded that she was too easily impressed. After long days at a factory clear across town, four bus rides, two there and two back, cooking, cleaning, sewing, and countless other acts of sheer survival, Myra inevitably had to face the lifeless eyes of a drunk and the scorn-filled eyes of her daughter, who looked at Myra as if *she* were the pathetic one. A quiet, devout Catholic who believed her duty to her family disavowed her of the perils of wants of her own, she took it. She took it all, without request or complaint.

Janice grew both ambitious and resentful. Her efforts to impress her father resulted in acceptances to seven high-ranking colleges, all of which were conveniently located far away from Detroit. She found it impossible to make friends in college. She had two part-time jobs (a scholarship and student loans paid for the rest). One job was as a research assistant, which actually meant errand girl, but she told her sister in weekly phone calls that it was "important work that would be published." She also worked at the check-in station at the school fitness center, where she watched the "spoiled bitches and dumbass jocks" hang out while she read Proust or Dostoyevsky, always for a class, never for pleasure.

When she wasn't working, she was studying, regularly pulling all-nighters. One night, as she fought sleep at her desk while trying to get through Adam Smith's economic theory, she pulled a yellow post-it note off her pad and wrote, "I'll sleep when I'm dead." She stuck it to her desk and used it for motivation. Anything less than an A devastated her. This often prompted her to rewrite papers and do extra credit assignments. If professors told her "grades weren't everything," she instantly detested them. Her initial sweet tone darkened and she accused them of "low balling" her.

Her schedule wasn't the reason she didn't have friends. She resented the other students so intensely that she mistook the smallest politeness for veiled criticism, often causing her to say something cutting and totally unwarranted. For example, when her roommate offered to loan her "anything in her closet," Janice wrongly assumed the roommate was insulting her wardrobe (which she felt self-conscious about since she couldn't afford expensive clothing). Thus she responded, "Thanks, but I think I'm smaller than you," which she wasn't. Although she did have three lackluster lovers, she hadn't had a single true relationship or one true friendship.

Building her career was at the top of her life's to-do list. Like everything else, Janice had to work for it. Nothing came easily. She constantly felt that the glass ceiling was preventing her from excelling. She believed she was overlooked for promotions in favor of lesser men. When women were promoted ahead of her, it was because they had slept with the right person or were being controlled by someone – "handled," she would say. What Janice failed to realize was that although she was legitimately quite skilled at her job, she rubbed people the wrong way. The only thing standing in Janice's way was Janice.

As a result of her prickly personality, Janice never became the great success she felt she deserved to be. She had been stuck as an acquisitions editor without hope of becoming publisher. Although she was eventually given the history line to build, she had to fight for each author, each contract, each new idea. And while she found the work more interesting, it was a lateral move. She was merely re-positioned. Despite what she told Prilly, she had been trying to start a memoir line for nearly four years. When Stuart finally agreed, he didn't want her involved with the project at all; he wanted to give it to someone else in-house. Janice had a fit, threatening to sue him for sexual harassment, so he agreed to let her co-edit the line, committing only to a test series. He suggested Prilly because he knew she was able to work well with others, which would balance out the Janice-factor. Janice agreed because after being Prilly's supervisor she had a firm handle on Prilly's weak spots. She also knew that Prilly would never mistakenly see them as partners, as equals.

Janice incessantly boasted to her husband, Richard, that she was much more successful than she truly was. He knew it wasn't true; he saw her paycheck and attended the annual WISE holiday party, where it was very clear that Janice was neither important nor liked. Richard was a highly successful investment banker. He and Janice had met at a bagel store when they were both waiting for a fresh batch of poppy seeds to come out. He was short, only 5'5" (she was two inches taller), and the little hair he had was dark and curly.

Although not terribly attracted to her, he slept with her that night to scratch the itch. *Why not*, he figured. Janice called him twice that week. He was still itchy, so he took her out to Docks Seafood Grill for dinner and then back to his house for a quickie. On their third date, which he thought would probably be their last, they went to a movie and then back to his house where they slept together again. He didn't even get undressed. He just pulled her underwear off from under her dress, pulled his pants down to his ankles, and got on top. He kept his eyes shut so that he could fantasize about his dental hygienist, a fair-skinned redhead who rubbed his arm while the dentist drilled. Janice was fantasizing about one of the college football players she often checked into the fitness center years earlier. He had always smiled at her, revealing his dimples, and he smelled like cedar.

Richard didn't return any of her calls after that night. Three weeks later, he received a message from her saying that she was a week late getting her period. Once a doctor confirmed that she was pregnant, he asked her to have an abortion. She refused, claiming Catholicism as her reason, though she had long ago deserted the idea of a God, all-loving or otherwise. Richard wasn't the kind of man who wanted to have a child with a woman to whom he wasn't married. This wasn't because he believed in "doing the right thing" as his aging mother urged, but rather because he was embarrassed by it and perceived it as a hassle. After a period of dating, during which they developed a mild friendship, they married at City Hall, with Marge as their only guest, when Janice was seven months pregnant with their only child, a son they named Kyle. He made her sign a prenuptial agreement in exchange for a 2.5-carat, emerald-cut Tiffany diamond. She told everyone that they had eloped in Saint Martin. Janice and Richard hadn't had sex in over four years.

Kyle, now a high school senior, had been Janice's project for years. Desperate to turn him into "something" (he was fairly homely with unwieldy dark hair, a large nose, and oily skin), she schlepped him to museums, sporting events, and ethnic food restaurants. She made him take piano classes (though he had no interest or talent) and karate (though he was terribly uncoordinated). Although Richard was very wealthy with serious family money in addition to a lucrative career, they sent Kyle to public school. This angered Janice but allowed her to tell anyone who would listen all about how important it was that people support the public school system. Always a quiet boy, Kyle had become much more withdrawn in recent years, spending a lot of time alone in his room or out with friends. Janice was initially concerned, but in time, she came to accept it as a normal part of being a teenage boy. She was just glad he had friends. She was too busy to pay much attention. Richard worked twelve-hour days at the office, and then generally spent the remainder of his time, including weekends, locked in his home office, secretly watching televised golf.

Their home was magnificent. Richard bought their multi-level brownstone apartment during the big real estate boom in the '90s when the widow of an old cultural attaché finally agreed to sell. It featured high ceilings and mahogany floors and was filled with stunning pieces of antique furniture (many of which were Richard's family heirlooms). Anyone would be jealous of a home like this. Janice truly loved it. She speculated that most of her equally fortunate neighbors barely noticed their own homes. Each day, as she walked through the large, sculpted double doors, she appreciated what she had, often catching herself wandering through the house and looking up, her eyes following the Victorian moldings.

Janice loved being able to say she was married to an investment banker. She loved wearing her diamond ring, which she religiously Windexed once a week for maximum sparkle. She loved showing up at the Christmas party every year with Richard who, at her request, always dressed in an Armani suit. And she loved showing off pictures of Kyle (she always made sure to have blurry pictures, because even she knew what he looked like) who, she bragged, was both musical and athletic. In short, Janice loved the appearance of the life she had pasted together, and tried to suppress the relentless fear that it was all a house of cards.

***

The next few weeks were the most intense of Prilly's life. Every day after work, she hurried to her apartment to freshen up and grab an overnight bag. Then she'd head out to meet Pete at his place or at a teahouse where he often hung out. Some nights they picked up takeout Indian food and ate on Pete's bed, listening to music and talking about art and politics. Other nights they went to underground dance clubs where everyone seemed to know Pete, especially the women. He held her hand as they walked around. It was extraordinary.

She found herself doing things she never thought she would do. The Saturday after they met, they were browsing in a vintage clothing store in the Village when Pete insisted she try on a pair of faux black leather pants. After resisting to no avail, she tried them on. "Well look at you. You're hot, girrrl!" Prilly happily bought them. She wore them four nights later to a club where they danced until three in the morning to wonderful trip-hop music she had never before heard. At his suggestion, Prilly wore silver body glitter on her neck and arms. The next day at work when Janice was in her office babbling on about the potential author list for their series, Prilly had to muster up all of her strength not to blurt out, "I wore body glitter last night. Body glitter! Can you believe it?"

Every night ended the same, with the most intimate lovemaking of Prilly's life. Pete always unflinchingly locked his eyes to hers, except when he entered from behind. She had never felt anything like it. Some nights she took a cab home at four in the morning, others she slept at Pete's. It was always an inner struggle. Although there was nothing that made her happier than falling asleep and waking up with him (sometimes he spooned her and she thought her heart might break from the beauty), she was invariably late to work when she stayed there. Some days she was very late, too late. One day she didn't arrive until almost ten fifteen, which Janice immediately pointed out to her, out of concern of course. Prilly thought tardiness was a small price to pay for the fullness she suddenly felt. She imagined that after another week or so, things would settle down and she would be better able to manage everything.

She knew she was in love with him by the Thursday morning after they met. He slept soundly as she waited for the alarm clock to beep. He had one of those alarm clocks that begins with four quiet beeps and increases in volume at seven-minute intervals. She was always worried that she wouldn't hear it and often woke herself up shortly before it went off. This, of course, contributed to her increasing exhaustion resulting from her new schedule, a schedule she knew full well couldn't be maintained. He slept for hours after she left, but she had to race to work and then race to meet Pete, who seemed to blossom after ten o'clock. The dark moons under her eyes were becoming more difficult to mask with concealer. On that morning, as she lay awake waiting for the alarm to beep, she kept thinking, *Just a few more minutes, just a few more minutes. Let me lie here with him for just a few more minutes. Don't make it end.* Lying on that old mattress was the most alive she had ever felt. *This is a big life.*

Late one night a week later, lying back to back, Pete whispered, "I love you." It was so quiet she wondered if she had imagined it. She lay awake tightly holding onto the possibility. Two days later, when he said it again, once again as they were falling asleep after making love, she whispered, "I love you, too."

***

Soon Prilly realized that she was working hard to keep Pete's interest. Naturally there was the nearly endless effort to look good: leg shaving, bikini waxes, makeup application, makeup touch-ups, high heels, and assembling "artsy" outfits that looked effortless. All this dwarfed in comparison to trying to be interesting, which was getting considerably harder. He was always saying clever and insightful things. For example, when they went to the Modigliani exhibit at the MoMA, he explained why the eyes in Modigliani's paintings were so special. She would have missed that. She tried to contribute her own insights about the peculiar shapes of the bodies. Apparently, this was a "pedestrian" remark. Sometimes he was very impressed by her, particularly her quick observations about the use of language (most of which were ideas she had borrowed from her authors). She reveled in the affirmation. Other times he looked at her the way one looks at a dirty puppy that will have to be cleaned. She felt as though there was elixir running through her veins, and she would do anything that she could to keep it flowing. It was a lot of work.

CHAPTER 4

"Hey, Melville, over here," Pete shouted as Melville twice scanned the teahouse. When Melville walked over, he was greeted with, "Fuck man, are you blind?"

Melville sat down at the small table, took off his jacket, and hung it on the back of his chair. "What have you been up to?" Melville asked. "Haven't seen you much lately."

"Aren't you going to order something?"

"No, I don't want anything. If I'm thirsty later I'll just use the water fountain."

"You can't just sit here if you're not going to order anything. You think these people want you coming in here just to sit?" Pete said, gesturing to the staff behind the espresso bar.

Melville didn't say anything. He stood up and got in line. He returned a couple of minutes later with a single shot of espresso. He didn't drink espresso but it was the cheapest thing on the menu and he couldn't afford anything else. When he returned to the table, Pete was reading. He sat there for a few minutes and then repeated, "What have you been up to? Haven't seen you much lately."

"Been writing. I've nearly got the carnival part just right. And I've been hanging out with that girl, Prilly. Remember the one we met at the Winterson reading?"

Remember? he quipped in his head. He had hardly thought of anything else. "Yeah, she seemed nice."

"Yeah, I like her. She's in publishing, you know. She's been spending most nights at my place. She's meeting me here in about an hour. You can hang and have a coffee with us if you want."

"Sure."

"Clyde's been calling me lately, too. She broke up with that loser and is coming out of her latest bender, so you know. Whatever."

Pete started reading again. Intrigued by this last remark, Melville took a small paperback novel out of his inside jacket pocket and pretended to read.

***

Prilly stared at her watch as she waited in Stuart's office. At first, all she could think about was that she was supposed to meet Pete in twenty minutes. She was going to be late. She tapped her pen against the legal pad on her lap. Soon, she wondered why Stuart had asked to see her before she left. Prilly knew she had been trimming her hours lately and she felt nervous. *I wonder if I look tired. Am I in trouble?* Just as her palms started to sweat, Stuart walked in.

"Sorry to keep you waiting. Marcy cornered me in the mailroom, and you know how hard it is to get away from her."

"No problem. What's up?" Prilly said as a feeling of indigestion bubbled up.

"I wanted to know how it's going with Janice."

"Oh," Prilly said feeling relieved. "It's fine. Everything's going well. She's put a lot of thought into this idea, so I'm really just along for the ride." This wasn't entirely true. While Janice was relentless with emails, voicemails, and unscheduled meetings at her discretion, she also demanded that Prilly implement many of her ideas. In short, she left Prilly to do most of the grunt work. Nevertheless, Prilly didn't want to create any bad blood. Her newfound bliss also made her feel badly for Janice, whom she now saw as obviously miserable.

"That's good to hear. I bumped into Janice earlier, and she led me to believe that there might have been some friction, division of labor and so forth. I told her I was confident that it could be resolved."

"Oh," Prilly said, stunned. "I'm surprised to hear that."

"I wouldn't give it too much thought. Janice is a bit of a workaholic. I think she holds everyone to her standards. I'm sure it'll be fine."

"I have been working hard Stu. I've just been swamped with everything and this series is taking up a lot of time."

"I know, I know. Don't worry. I just needed to check in. Just wanted to let you know I'm here if needed."

As Prilly stood up and thanked Stu, she remembered that she was late to meet Pete. She had to hurry.

***

Standing at the opposite end of the dining room table from where his mother sat working, Kyle quietly said, "I'm going out now."

"Okay, see you later," Janice softly replied without glancing up from her laptop.

Kyle grabbed his olive green backpack and left, walking two blocks before heading down into the subway. While waiting on the platform, he took his red iPod out of his bag and listened to the Cocteau Twins' *Live BBC Sessions*. A minute later, he was sitting on the train between two elderly women. He got off at the fifth stop and walked with his earphones on up to street level where one of his friends was waiting for him.

"Hey."

"Hey."

***

Prilly, who usually arrived to everything fifteen minutes early, was so late that she skipped her routine stop at home before rushing to the teahouse. She left a toothbrush and some clothes at Pete's place, and had taken to shoving her cosmetic case in her workbag in case of such an emergency. Worried that she might look worn down, she stopped in a Starbucks a block away from the teahouse. After waiting in a long, slow line, she went into the foul-smelling, one-person bathroom and quickly retouched her makeup. She then raced to meet Pete.

"Hey girl," Pete shouted from a corner table.

Oh great, Melville's here, Prilly thought as she made her way over, trying to slide between cramped tables without knocking her large bag into anything or anyone. She thought that Melville's sunken, drooping eyes made him look like a weirdo, and she also found him oddly quiet. Besides, she was in a bad mood and wanted to be alone with Pete.

"Hey," she said, flopping down on an empty chair and dropping her bag on the floor. "Were you waiting long? I'm really sorry, I got held up at work. You wouldn't believe the crap I'm dealing with."

"All good. No worries. I've been reading a wonderful book," Pete replied.

"I'm beat. Would it be okay if we picked up some takeout and just ate at your place?"

"Yeah, sure," he said as he put his jacket on. He and Prilly left with a quick "See ya later" to Melville.

***

"She's just so two-faced," Prilly said as she maneuvered some lo mein into her mouth.

"Here, let me show you. You're not holding them right," Pete said as he illustrated how to properly place one's fingers on chopsticks.

Embarrassed, Prilly tried to copy him, but moments later resorted back to her own way of holding them.

"Well, is there any truth to it? Have you been pulling your weight?" Pete matter-of-factly asked as he knocked a container of spicy pea pods over onto the old towel that lay across the bed as a makeshift tablecloth.

Unable to control her frustration at what felt like the second betrayal of the day, Prilly snapped back, "She's just a bitch. Don't you get it? I'm doing *most* of the work, not just a little, but most of it. And I never wanted to do this in the first place – she bullied me into it. What the hell is that to say something to my boss when she hasn't said a word to me? She's obviously up to something."

"Well then, you've got to confront her. Take the venom out of it." Before Pete could continue his phone rang. He leaned over and grabbed it off the floor. "Hello?" He turned his back and lowered his voice. "Hey, this isn't a great time. I'm eating with a friend. Where? What's the address? I'll try to make an appearance, but no promises. Yeah. Okay, bye."

Friend??? Prilly thought. *Am I just a friend?* she wondered, as the speed of her animosity built like a runaway car on a rollercoaster straight out of a childhood nightmare.

"Who was that?" she asked.

"A friend of mine, Clyde. She's having some issues, just broke up with some guy, blah blah blah. She wants to see me. She's going to a small gothic club downtown in a bit. She was hoping I'd make an appearance."

"Oh. Well, I thought we were gonna stay in tonight. I'm tired and upset. I don't really feel like going to a club."

"How about this: why don't you stay here and relax, maybe read or go to sleep, and I'll slip out for a couple of hours?" Pete asked.

Prilly didn't know what to say. *I can't believe that he would leave me here alone. And who is this woman that he wants to see more than he wants to be with me? A woman to whom I am just "a friend?"* She felt like bursting into tears but refused to show him how upset she was, so she coldly said, "Well, I guess, if that's what you want to do, I can just go home."

"No, no, stay here. Stay, relax, listen to music, eat this food, and I'll be back in a couple of hours."

Pete jumped up and walked to the bathroom, bringing the container of lo mein with him. Prilly sat there. She heard the shower turn on. She heard it turn off. She heard the sink faucet turn on, then off. She heard him open the bathroom door. She mostly heard the angry voice in her head, a high-pitched voice that wouldn't shut up. She just sat there, silently fuming. All she wanted all day was to be with Pete, and now he was ditching her for some other woman. He came into the room and casually said, "Hey girl," and smiled, as if totally unaware of the angst he was causing her. He put the nearly empty Chinese food container down on the bed and said, "That's delicious. I couldn't stop myself," and laughed. As he bent over, she could smell his newly spritzed cologne. She wanted desperately to remain silent, to stay cool. She had been telling herself over and over again during his twenty-five minutes in the bathroom that she needed to play it cool. But after that whiff of his cologne, she blurted out, "Who is this friend? Is she an old girlfriend?"

He chuckled. "If you're asking if I've slept with her, yeah, sure, but we're just friends. She's going through a bad time and she wants to talk. I kind of feel like getting out tonight, and you don't. Even if you did, I don't think it would be the best time to introduce you. I broke up with her, and now she just broke up with someone, and you know."

No, I don't know. I don't know why the man I am crazy about, the man I am running all over town to see while utterly exhausted is leaving me to see another woman whom he's slept with, a woman who may still have feelings for him! She could feel rage brewing and feared it would slip from her lips. She held onto it as tightly as she could; worrying that she might induce a stroke.

He leaned down and kissed her on the forehead. As he bent over she heard his black leather pants squeak. They were tight, and with a black and silver long-sleeved T-shirt over them, he looked sexy. He smelled good, and he looked sexy. She was livid.

***

When Pete left with a "See ya, girl," Prilly experienced physical paralysis and mental Tourette's. She couldn't stop wondering what had just happened. In her mind, over and over again, *What just happened?* Then she started to obsess about Clyde, this woman Pete was so eager to see. She knew he had slept with other women of course, and by his unmatched sexual talents she figured there had been many of them, but she didn't want to think about it; she didn't want to know about them. She mostly didn't want him to care about them. *Clyde, Clyde. She's probably really beautiful. She sounds beautiful. She's probably really cool. She probably wouldn't mind if he ran out to see an old girlfriend. She's probably beautiful.* As she sat in his little apartment that now stunk of Chinese food, a smell she couldn't get rid of long after putting away the leftovers and washing the dishes, she felt sick. The longer she waited, the angrier she got. *Who the fuck is he to leave me like this? What kind of fucking man does this? He doesn't care. He doesn't care about how I feel!*

She decided to get ready for bed and then pretend to sleep until he got home. She wanted to look good, assuming they would make love after he apologized and told her how wonderful she was, so she brushed her teeth but slept with her makeup on. She didn't want to really fall asleep, afraid she would have bad breath and messy hair by the time he returned, so she just lay in bed, thinking, spinning, seething. Four and half hours passed, with each minute experienced like the labored breaths of an old woman on her deathbed. She twice got up to rinse her mouth with Listerine and to powder her nose. She felt pathetic, really pathetic, and she knew she should just get up and leave without a note or phone call, but instead, she lay there counting the seconds. Her thoughts vacillated from Pete to Clyde to Janice and Stuart. Her big life was shrinking.

Shortly after two-thirty, she heard a key in the door. Pete went straight into the bathroom, and ten minutes later, made his way to the bed where Prilly was still pretending to sleep, afraid he could hear her overpowering heartbeats. When he got into bed, she rustled around a bit so he would think he woke her up. He didn't say anything and she could feel his back to her, so eventually she went to sleep. She woke up at five in a cold sweat, and then fell back asleep.

The next morning Prilly got up, showered and dressed, and made two mugs of coffee with Pete's one-cup coffee maker. There was only a little cream left, and she used most of it in her coffee. *Screw him.* She stood in the kitchen, looking through the cutout wall, trying to read his mind as he slept. *Am I overreacting? Am I being too sensitive? Did it mean anything? Why didn't we make love when he got home?* She couldn't wait for him to wake up and somehow make it better.

After an hour and forty-five minutes of waiting, trying to subtly make just enough noise to wake him without being obvious, he finally woke up, rubbing his eyes and clearing his throat. "Hey. I smell coffee," he said in a low voice.

"Yeah, I made you a cup. You might have to nuke it, it's been sitting for a while."

"K. Thanks," he said as he stood up, wearing the same long-sleeved T-shirt he had left in, now paired with his black boxers. He lifted his arms high into the air and made a loud yawning noise as he stretched upward. "I have to go to the bathroom. I'll be right there."

The next two minutes seemed somehow to be a hundred times longer than all that preceded them. Prilly stood in the kitchen, sipping her cold coffee, not knowing what to do. Pete came in and kissed her on the forehead, grabbed his coffee, and went to the refrigerator for cream. He spilled the last drops into his mug and said, "We're out of cream."

"I know."

He took his mug and walked past her into the bedroom. He propped his pillow against the wall and sat on the bed, legs outstretched, drinking his coffee. Furious, Prilly made a loud sigh and walked into the bedroom with her mug in hand. She sat in the computer chair, and just as Pete started to smile at her, she said, "So, you got home late last night."

"Yeah, sorry. After midnight I figured you were asleep and that it didn't matter, so I stayed a bit longer. Didn't want to call and wake you."

In a sharp tone she responded, "Well, did you have a good time? Is your friend okay?"

"Oh, you know, she's always going through something. She has a tinsel heart, you know. She's like a bird that you want to take care of."

What the fuck is this? Prilly screamed to herself. *Doesn't he know how upset I am? Can't he see that I'm upset?* The silent anger quickly turned to hurt. *Tinsel heart? Bird? Is everything about her beautiful? It sounds like he loved her. Maybe he still loves her.* Despite all of the thoughts swimming in her mind, she managed to stay silent. It took a lot of effort, but the more special Clyde sounded, the less she wanted to reveal how very not-okay she was with all of this.

"The club was cool. You would like it; we should go sometime. It was very small and dark, and the walls were covered with dark purple fabric, like a flowing translucent kind of fabric. The music was wonderful, a terrific deejay. He played lots of trippy stuff like Portishead. I danced all night."

Fighting every inclination she had, she remained quiet, just looking at him and silently screaming, *What the hell is wrong with you?*

"I'm gonna hop in the shower. Starving. You want to go to that diner again, the one with the fabulous waitress?"

"Sure," she said, feeling relieved that they were spending the day together, but also angry and utterly confused.

Pete got up and went to the bathroom to shower.

***

An hour later, they were sitting in the diner, waiting for someone to take their order. "I'm ravenous; feel like I could eat a horse," Pete said. *He seems particularly jolly this morning,* Prilly thought.

"Hmm. So you said."

The waitress walked over, and Pete smirked at Prilly; it was not the waitress with the wonderful face. This much younger waitress had a very long, thin face with long, thin features and elfin ears.

She's a bit birdlike, Prilly thought. *Not a pretty bird, but a bird.* She looked at the nametag on her canary-colored uniform: Ruth. *Clyde is probably a beautiful bird,* Prilly imagined.

"I think I'll try an omelet today," Pete said, as if the waitress knew his regular order, or cared. "With mushrooms and cheese, cheddar cheese."

"What kind of toast?"

"Wheat. With marmalade, not jam."

"And for you?"

"Oh, um, I'll have the blueberry pancakes please."

Shit, Prilly thought to herself. *What am I doing? First the lo mein and now pancakes. I'll have to suck in my stomach all day.*

"So what do you want to do today? There's a Shepard Fairey exhibit at the Guggenheim I'm dying to see. Do you know his work?"

"No."

"Oooh, he's wonderful. He's famous for that Obama poster you know, but his other work, his real work, is marvelous. It's all very subversive, like the guerrilla art I told you my friends in London were into. There's a marriage between word and image in the work. Very carefully done. Sharp and sardonic. And the Guggenheim, well fuck, that building is an orgasm itself."

"Uh, huh," Prilly said, totally unable to focus on anything he was saying. She then blurted out, "What happened last night? I mean, you totally ditched me and went out with some woman you've slept with before, and then you don't come home until the middle of the night. Do you know how that makes me feel?" As soon as the words came out, she regretted saying them but was desperate to hear his response.

He laughed. He laughed, and then with a close-mouthed smile, he managed to make her feel even more pathetic than she already felt. "It was nothing. A friend called me and she needed me. You could have come but you weren't up for it. You know how I feel about you. What we have is what we have; it has nothing to do with Clyde or with anyone. It shouldn't matter whether I've slept with her or not."

"Well you might not feel that way if it was you."

"If it were the other way around, I wouldn't care. I know what we have, and I wouldn't worry. I wouldn't want to stop you from doing something you wanted to do."

Unsatisfied, Prilly asked, "Were you … were you in love with her?"

"Love? I don't even know what love is. Love is just a word people say to each other. I care about her, sure."

Love is just a word people say to each other? He doesn't even know what love is? What the fuck is he saying? How can he say this when he told me that he loved me? He said it first, and he said it twice. How can he be saying this? "I felt like you abandoned me. I was really upset; you knew I had a bad day at work, and we made plans. Then you just left. What's worse, you left to see some woman you had a relationship with. How did you think that would make me feel?"

Ruth brought the food over. Pete thanked her and started eating immediately, sprinkling salt on his omelet with one hand as he ate a forkful of home fries with the other. Prilly just sat there, staring at him.

A few moments later, he put his fork down and said, "Look, I'm sorry if you were upset. Honestly, I didn't think it was a big deal. I thought you were cool with it."

"Okay, I guess we can just drop it," Prilly responded, not quite sure if she had blown it all into something bigger than it was, but certain she didn't want things to escalate further. She cut up her pancakes, drizzled on some syrup, and ate, trying to convince herself she wasn't really as upset as she was.

After a few bites Pete said, "You know, I don't believe in the traditional monogamy thing. I mean, I thought we were cool, that we had an unspoken understanding, but maybe it's best to lay our cards on the table." Unable to take in the oxygen necessary to comprehend this information or formulate a response, Prilly sat silently. Pete continued, "I mean, we're having a wonderful time and it's very special, so there's no reason to label it. What a person has with one person doesn't diminish what they have with someone else. Like with Clyde. What I had with her doesn't take away from how I feel about you. It's totally different."

Too many thoughts, too many thoughts to process, Prilly frantically thought to herself. She took another bite of blueberry pancake in order to buy enough time to steady her voice. "I don't understand. We've spent every day together since we met." Leaning in and lowering her voice, she said, "You told me you loved me."

He again smiled, close-mouthed. "I said what was in my heart in the moment. I always do and it is always true. This you can count on. So who needs false promises when you have that?"

She thought to herself that maybe this Clyde woman, whoever she was (and she did sound wonderful), could see the beauty in what Pete was saying; she probably could, "tinsel heart" and all, but to Prilly, it just felt hurtful, deeply hurtful. She wondered if they had been in the same relationship at all. She felt foolish.

"I still don't understand. Are you saying that you're seeing other people or that you want to? Did something happen with Clyde last night? Is that why you came back so late?"

He offered up another close-mouthed smile. "No, no, nothing happened with Clyde if that's what this is really about, but even if it had, it wouldn't need to change anything we have. Clyde was once a special person in my life, and she is still sort of in my life, but I haven't slept with her since we broke up before I met you. I think she wanted to last night. She was very vulnerable. But truthfully, all I could think about was you at my place, in my bed, waiting for me. I thought it was sweet how you let me go, how you knew it was fine."

Again, too many thoughts; too many thoughts to process at once, Prilly thought, feeling overloaded. He had thrown so much information at her, and she feared none of it was good. She wanted to be cool. She wanted to be the sweet, cool, tinsel-hearted girl who waited in his bed. But she wasn't. So, she responded sharply, "It would matter to me."

"Look, two people can be together forever and be only with each other, but not because of some artificial promise. I don't believe in that. Sure, you can find a thousand men with who will give you hollow promises, but that's not me. That's not what I'm giving you. You have to live moment to moment, and the moments string together. And eventually you can string together a lifetime, but not because of promises, just because it is true to your heart, to your soul. You cannot cage a bird, as they say."

Great, more birds, Prilly thought. "It wouldn't be all right with me if you were with someone else. That's not what I want."

He smiled again, letting out the quietest of laughs as if she were too provincial to understand what he was saying or too insecure to deal with it, the latter of which may well have been true.

"Okay, I understand. If anything were to ever happen with someone else, or if I wanted it to, I would tell you. You have my word. I would be honest with you and you could do as you needed to."

"Okay," Prilly softly said, not knowing how to make this dreadful conversation end in a way that would leave them both sitting there, and ideally in a way that would restore the feeling to her numb feet.

"But I don't want to be with anyone else right now. I like being with you," he said, as if he were giving her a gift. Just as she had so many times in earlier years, she felt like Charlie Brown dumping out a Christmas stocking full of coal.

***

On the way to the Guggenheim, Pete wanted to "dash into Starbucks for a doppio espresso." He said he was still feeling "wiped and the diner coffee sucked." When he and Prilly hurried in, she noticed

Melville sitting by the window. This time, she was glad to see him. "I'll just have a bottle of water please," she said to Pete as she plopped down next to Melville. Pete put his hand out. Embarrassed on every level, Prilly reached into her bag scrambling for her wallet. She pulled out a five and handed it to him. "Do you want anything?" she asked Melville. Not accustomed to being offered anything, he just shook his head. "So, what's up?" she asked.

"Um, nothing really. Just reading a book," Melville shyly replied.

Prilly grabbed the book from him. "Wow, this looks good. I love novels set in Victorian times." She glanced over to spot Pete whooping it up with the pretty, young barista behind the counter. Suddenly, she was replaying their relationship in her head. She thought these had been the best weeks of her life, but now, as she rewound, all she could picture were the times he flirted with waitresses, made small talk with female bartenders, or spoke to strange women in cafés after she had hurried from work to meet him. Feeling terribly insecure and in need of affirmation she looked at Melville, who she had an inkling might like her, and said, "You know, Melville, I met you when I met Pete. Remember? Did you ever think it might be different? That it could have been different that day, and you and I might have ended up together?"

With a stone face concealing his astonishment, he stuttered a bit and said, "Well, you and Pete seem to make a good couple." Secretly, he thought, *Yes, yes, I think about it all the time, and I hate myself for not having been able to talk to you first, knowing it never would have been me.*

Totally distracted by his last "couple" comment, she was markedly unaware of the effect she was having on Melville, who felt increasingly tortured. She slumped down, balancing her elbows on the table and putting her head in her hands, and muttered, "Yeah, well, couple. What's a couple, right?"

Melville was too caught up in his own thoughts to realize how incoherent she was. Like most people, Prilly was speaking to an audio in her head that no one else could hear. "Hey Melville, do you know Clyde?"

"Yeah, sure."

Prilly leaned in closer, "She and Pete were a thing, right?"

"Yeah, I thought they were the real thing."

As Melville's heart raced at the smell of Prilly's apple-blossom shampoo, Prilly's heart sank at the confirmation of her worst fear: Pete had been in love with Clyde.

Suddenly, Prilly heard Pete say, "Thanks, hon" to the barista in his ever-sexy voice. She leaned back, feeling defeated. When Pete returned, he handed Prilly the bottled water – without change, she noticed – and remarked, "You know the plastic in these things is probably worse than the tap water. Ha. All these supposedly environmentally conscious people drink these, but what do they think all of these plastic bottles do to the environment? That's an inconvenient truth," Pete said through intermittent laughter.

Prilly was in no mood to be criticized. She was heartbroken and he was lecturing her about her beverage choice.

"Ready to go?" he asked.

Oblivious as ever, Prilly thought. "Sure. Why doesn't Melville come along?" Prilly suggested, surprising them both.

After a brief pause Melville said, "Oh, no it's okay."

"No, come on. We're going to the Guggenheim to see some art exhibit Pete's all excited about. Come with us. It'll be fun."

"Come with us, don't just sit here all day," Pete said. Somehow even his invitation made Melville appear feeble.

"Okay."

And with that, the three made their way on foot to the Guggenheim.

CHAPTER 5

Janice had a very particular weekend routine. Every Saturday she woke up bright and early and hurried out of bed with great urgency only to discover her family was nowhere to be found. Her husband was already out. She invariably assumed that he must be at the squash club, which was his weekend morning ritual. Kyle was either sleeping or out; she assumed he left early in the morning, but never quite knew for sure if he had ever returned the night before. It never occurred to her that surely they would be gone, so she always went through the ritual of searching for them before concluding they were out.

Then she raced to the kitchen in her long, tangerine kimono purchased when "Asian styles" were in, and made a pot of decaffeinated coffee. She always bought whatever brand was on sale, normally some sort of dry-roasted Colombian blend in a large canister covered with dust. She emptied the dishwasher as the coffee dripped. Then she filled her Cornell College mug, adding only one Splenda, and trotted off to her bedroom to make the bed, complete with military corners. She then scurried to her makeshift office in the dining room, checked her email, and read her favorite blog, a humorous pop-feminist blog by a Canadian writer from whom she stole many ideas. Next, she decided to "do a little work." She typically worked for several hours, getting up occasionally to refill her coffee or grab a bunch of grapes. She rarely had work that required her to work these extended hours, so she simply obsessed about the work that she did have, often coming up with piles of "new ideas" that Stu later rejected. She also enjoyed creating lists of "things to do" for her various projects, followed by lists of what could be outsourced (mostly to Prilly).

By late morning, she needed to "clear her head," which she accomplished by riding her stationary bicycle in the windowless guest room across from her second-floor bedroom. Sometimes she watched public television on the small, old TV in the room. After exercising she showered and got ready for the day. Next, lunch. Typically this consisted of a sandwich of some kind, which she ate at the dining room table and usually decided to "do a little more work while she's sitting there." By late afternoon, Kyle made an appearance. Although he often stopped by the dining room to chat with her, by then she was deeply engrossed in her unnecessary work. She wouldn't look up, so Kyle would leave. By five thirty, with the day gone and no longer able to stare at her computer screen, she wandered around her house until it was time to go out with her husband. They usually had a work-related dinner with his colleagues. She did her best to make conversation but found it tiresome. She often complained to Richard's colleagues that she was overloaded with work. She'd say, "I had to work all day, yet again. Can you believe it? I can't remember the last time I had a day off." Sensing his colleagues felt badly for her, she felt free to talk more about the demands of publishing "at her level." She always thought these dinners went very well considering how stressed she was. On nights when there was no business obligation, they sometimes went out to dinner alone, making small talk about getting the car checked or taking Kyle to the dentist. Other nights Janice spent the evening by herself, eating takeout in bed and watching television. Sundays were almost exactly the same except she called her sister and they never went out to dinner.

By the time she got to work on Monday, she was angry that she had been so swamped with work that she hadn't been able to enjoy her weekend. She was especially difficult to deal with, particularly to those who made the mistake of telling her about how they had spent their weekend.

There were only two exceptions to her weekend routine. First, Janice and Richard took a vacation twice a year. Every spring they spent one week in Phoenix visiting Richard's sister, Vicki, and brother-in-law, James. Janice and Vicki usually spent afternoons together going to local craft markets. Janice always bought silver and turquoise jewelry crafted by Native Americans. She haggled over the price well past the point of acceptability by anyone else's standards. Vicki was mortified but never said anything, since it was the only time all year she "had" to see Janice. Over lunch, Janice would go on and on about how she liked to "buy the local crafts to support the Native Americans." Desperate for an anesthetic, Vicki usually ordered a glass of white wine with her lunch and said that it was a "special occasion, a girl's day."

Richard and James spent mornings at a local health club. James hated playing squash with Richard; Richard took it far too seriously and had James running around the court the whole time. When they returned to the house, Richard excused himself to work. Not only did he bring his laptop, Blackberry, and Bluetooth headset, but he scheduled lengthy conference calls. Late in the afternoon Vicki would say she was a bit tired from the wine at lunch and would excuse herself for a nap. She usually lay on her bed watching the Travel Channel on mute. Janice sat outside on their wrap-around porch admiring the exquisite scenery. The dramatic landscape composed of shades of burnt umber impressed her. Before marrying Richard, she had never seen anything like it. After half an hour on the porch she invariably wound up at their dining room table with her laptop, working.

In the evenings, they all went out to dinner. When Kyle and his cousin Natashya were younger, they were there too – requiring parental attention so that there was little need for the adults to come up with conversation. Since Natashya went to college to study film at NYU two years earlier, Kyle refused to go on the trips. This allowed them to talk about their kids when they had exhausted their supply of small talk about "how wonderful dinner is" and "how great it is to take some time off for family." Vicki secretly harbored anger toward Janice and Richard for not extending themselves more to Natashya while she was living in New York. They had invited her over for dinner only once (Chinese takeout) and taken her to one Broadway show (*Wicked*) in the two years she had lived in the city. James didn't know why Vicki found that so offensive.

On their other annual trip, Janice and Richard visited a Caribbean island for a week. They stayed at a five-star resort. Janice loved being waited on by the staff. When they stayed at the Four Seasons in Nevis, the cabana boys walked around on the beach spraying guests with Evian water. Janice couldn't get enough of it, although she also felt that she had snuck into a member's only club and might be caught at any moment. To compensate for her insecurity, she was overly demanding of the staff, to make sure they knew she belonged there.

This was the only time all year when Janice and Richard really spent time together. Mostly they lounged on the beach, each reading their own book. Richard often worked on his laptop in the evenings after dinner, and Janice went to sleep alone. When she returned from these trips she boasted about her fabulous vacation for weeks to anyone in the office she could corner long enough to listen.

The other exception to her weekend routine was when she met one of her girlfriends for lunch, sometimes followed by shopping or a museum visit. She only had three friends with whom she spent time by herself, and although she enjoyed an occasional lunch, during which they caught up on work, kids, and so forth, she never created any real intimacy. The conversation, at least on her end, was always superficial. She liked having friends who would share their problems with her, and to whom she could complain about how hard she was forced to work and how undervalued she was. These conversations made her feel good about herself.

On this particular Saturday, she had lunch plans with her friend, Sarah Cohen, a feminist historian she met at a WISE event years ago. As usual, she woke up with the sun that morning to discover Richard was already out. *He's probably playing squash at the club*, she thought. After making her decaf coffee and checking her email, she decided to jump on the exercise bike for an hour and then get ready to meet Sarah. She chose her favorite charcoal gray pencil skirt paired with a thin, black V-neck sweater. While she dressed, she started to regret making plans with Sarah. She wasn't in the mood to hear about her boyfriend, a public school teacher whom Janice had met once at a book party. Sarah had a way of being particularly draining. As she unrolled her black tights up one leg at a time, she thought about how Sarah would go on and on, and Janice wished she could stay at home to get some work done.

Janice arrived everywhere early. When she went out on weekends, she carried the streamlined black Prada pocketbook Richard had given her for Christmas two years earlier (he always gave her a "statement piece" on Christmas, her birthday, and their anniversary, and she adored them). She was able to slide one manila folder of work into the thin rectangular bag. She felt less self-conscious waiting for someone if she had a project to occupy her. It also sent a powerful message to the person who, in Janice's mind, was late and wasting her time. (To Janice, "late" was anything after she arrived, though she routinely arrived fifteen minutes early, making it nearly impossible for any normal person not to be "late.")

Despite trying to feign interest in the folder of memoir series notes, Janice noticed Sarah immediately when she arrived at the restaurant at noon (Janice naturally clocked her in at fifteen minutes late). It was hard not to notice Sarah. An ex-hippy, she wore long, flowing, Indian-inspired, multi-colored skirts with tank tops adorned with many long layers of ornate chains or large beads. On this day, Sarah was wearing a long, merlot-colored skirt with a black pattern of some indiscernible kind, a white tank top, and four multi-length necklaces of silver coins that sounded like wind chimes every time she moved. Sarah was petite and very pretty, with waist length, nearly black hair in natural spiral curls. Janice thought Sarah would be beautiful if she dressed in more sophisticated clothing and tamed her hair. Paradoxically, she admired her for having her own unique style. Janice always experienced some dread before seeing Sarah, but when they were together, she remembered the many things she liked about her. On this day, the always-effervescent Sarah couldn't stop talking.

"Oh, there's my friend," Sarah hollered as she floated past the hostess, who pointed to the far corner where Janice had taken the booth seat. "Hi, hi, hi. Oh, don't get up," she said as she slid into the chair across from Janice, throwing her large canvas tote on the chair beside her. "Hope I didn't keep you waiting. I'm starving."

"Oh, no, it's fine. I was just catching up on some work."

"Busy?" Sarah asked as she read the menu.

Janice sighed and gently moved a strand of hair that was aggravating her eye. "I'm swamped. I'm telling you, you can't even imagine."

"I hope they appreciate you over there."

"Ha. You can't imagine. It's a real mess there. I work more than anyone and they don't like it. They're threatened by me. I'm a big producer, and it makes others look bad, so they try to marginalize me as much as they can. No one's doing me any favors, that's for sure. If I wasn't committed to my authors, I'll tell you, I wouldn't bother."

"That's awful. There's so much of a bias against women, too. I bet if you were a man they'd be in awe of you, but because you're a woman they're threatened."

"Absolutely," Janice said as she nodded while thinking to herself that sometimes Sarah was really spot-on.

"Well, have I got a story for you. It'll take your mind off of work," Sarah said as the waiter came over and asked if they wanted to order a drink.

"Actually, I think we're ready to order lunch," Janice responded. Sarah nodded as she scoured the menu. "I'll have a club soda with lime and the chicken tortilla salad," Janice said.

"And for you, Miss?" the waiter asked, unable to stop staring at Sarah.

"An iced tea, unsweetened, and the beet salad without cheese. Thanks."

"Very good."

"I stopped eating dairy a month ago, and I feel terrific," Sarah told Janice, as if to explain her order.

"What do they call that? Vegan?" Janice asked.

"Yeah, now I'm a full-fledged vegan. I read an op-ed in *The New York Times* that reported reducing meat intake by twenty percent is the equivalent of going from driving a Toyota Camry to driving a Prius. Can you believe it? I figured since I didn't miss meat when I gave that up I would try the non-dairy thing too. It's been terrific. I'm full of energy."

"Uh huh," Janice said, suddenly thinking Sarah sounded stupid.

"So, you're not going to believe this. Remember that Israeli-Palestinian peace group I'm in?"

"Uh huh," Janice said, even though she didn't. Sarah was always hung up on some new cause or joining some new group, none of which interested Janice so she didn't keep track.

"Well, we lined up a panel of speakers to coincide with the New York City Human Rights Festival. Remember I forwarded you that email?"

Janice nodded.

"Anyway, I somehow volunteered for the party planning committee for the opening reception. Just a low-key social event, wine and appetizers kind of thing. We had, like, no budget, so there's only so much you can do. Someone suggested doing the food potluck style, which I thought was a great idea. Save money, get the people on the committee involved, easy for me."

"Uh huh," Janice said, looking intently at Sarah despite being bored with the story.

"Well, days before the reception I get a call from Joanne, who is also on the planning committee and is kind of the main de facto organizer of our group. Apparently, a couple of kosher people who aren't members of our group wanted to come to the event, but requested that only kosher food be served. Joanne told them that wasn't going to be possible since arrangements had already been made, but that they were welcome to contribute kosher dishes to the buffet."

"Uh huh. Did that satisfy them?" Janice asked, trying to show that she was paying attention.

"Nope. Not at all. They said that it would not be acceptable to serve non-kosher food at this kind of event. I'll spare you every detail, but suffice it to say, Joanne wanted to get this person off the phone so she told him to call me. I talked to the guy and got a long education about what it means to prepare and serve a kosher buffet and that simply adding a kosher-made dish would not suffice. I told him we did not intend to serve shrimp wrapped in bacon, but that we had some Palestinian committee members who were planning on serving hummus and salads. I thought that maybe dishes that didn't contain meat might be okay."

"And?" Janice asked, totally missing Sarah's humor regarding the bacon-wrapped shrimp.

"He said that he understood but wouldn't be able to attend. So after a year and a half of volunteering with this peace process group, I couldn't even get people to agree on a politically and culturally acceptable buffet! How do you like that?"

Janice smiled. "Religion is a tough thing to battle. People are very sensitive about it," she said in a serious tone that was incongruous with Sarah's zealous storytelling.

"Doesn't give me much hope for world peace," Sarah said, now unable to control her laughter. The waiter returned with their salads and they ate lunch.

Sarah was meeting her boyfriend that afternoon to see a series of documentary shorts at a nearby independent movie theater. She invited Janice, who insisted she needed to get some more work done. They hugged at the door of the restaurant and parted ways. It was such a beautiful, crisp day that Janice decided to walk home. On the way, she stopped at a corner grocer. She looked at the flowers extensively but hated spending money on something fleeting. She ended up picking up some pink lady apples and a bottle of cranberry juice and headed home.

***

That night, Melville approached his apartment with dread. He could hear hip-hop music blaring from the downstairs corridor and knew Jacob was probably having another party. When he opened the apartment door, a wave of smoke assaulted him. He coughed as he made his way through the small, darkened living room lined wall-to-wall with people he had never seen. No one seemed to notice him as he went straight to his room. He flung his jacket on his chair, staring longingly at the Mozart CD case on his desk. He lay on his couch with his hands behind his head. He thought he could see his room vibrating with each blast of reverberated noise. Eventually, he shut his eyes. He wanted to masturbate but was scared someone would walk in so he pulled his blanket up to his chest, unzipped his pants, and did it quickly.

***

As they arrived back at Pete's apartment, Prilly felt increasingly anxious. All she could think about was Pete leaving the night before, Clyde (a stranger whom she suddenly couldn't stop wondering about), and worst of all, those awful words at the diner: *love is just a word ... I don't even know what love is ... I don't believe in promises ... I will tell you if I want to be with someone else.* Over and over she replayed his words and Melville's remark that Pete and Clyde were "the real thing." Her brain was a muddled mess interspersed with images of Pete intently looking at her while they made love and how she felt so alive she could see sounds and hear colors.

She mindlessly followed Pete into the apartment. He was still talking about the Fairey exhibit.

"The consumerism stuff is a bit pedestrian but good anyway. I mean, I've seen more inventive stuff. The whole church-state thing has been done. But you gotta hand it to him, the collection as a whole makes a statement."

"Uh huh."

"There was some filler, though. The portraits of the musicians are fun but disconnected from the larger work. I mean, yeah, they're all resistive counter-culture artists, but they're not political in the ways he's suggesting. I mean, I get the subversive artist thing, but it didn't all hang together like the other work. I would have done it differently."

"Uh huh. Yeah, I liked those pieces though. Music gets at people in its own way," Prilly said as she plopped down on the edge of the bed, tossing her bag on the ground.

"Hey you," Pete said in his sexiest voice as he glanced over through the cutout wall from the kitchen where he was guzzling a canned energy drink.

She smiled at him.

As he made his way over to her, she couldn't quiet her mind. *What's going on? What is this? What am I doing here? How does he feel about me? Why does he look at me that way if he doesn't love me? Why? How could he want to be with someone else when I can only think of him?*

With one touch of his hand to her shoulder, her thoughts scampered and she looked up at him, hoping for a sign. As they made love, her eyes locked onto him. She kept thinking, *He will see what I am trying to show him. He will see what I feel and he will tell me he feels the same. I know he does.*

Afterward, she lay in his arms waiting, making a conscious effort not to fall asleep. If he held her long enough, after that beautiful, intimate lovemaking, he would give his whole self to her, as she thought he once did.

"You're beautiful."

She smiled softly as she looked up into his eyes.

"Are you hungry? I'm starving. I think I have some pasta. I could make a little spicy tomato sauce. I think I have some olives and capers. Want to help?" he asked as he sat up and grabbed his boxers from the floor.

"Sure, that sounds good," she said as she sat up.

They fell asleep two hours later after a pasta and red wine dinner eaten in bed followed by Pete reading more pages from his latest work. Prilly thought she was happy, but that night she woke up three times in a cold sweat. The last time she awoke, Pete was holding her as he slept.

When she woke up in the morning, she was surprised to find Pete already out of bed. "Hey girrrl. You're a sleepyhead. I made you some coffee."

"What time is it?" she asked, rubbing the corners of her eyes. "It's only ten thirty. I woke up feeling inspired this morning and had to get some stuff down. Funny how the brain works. That stuff we saw yesterday gave me some new ideas."

"That's great," Prilly said as she sat up and reached over the side of the bed in search of her underwear.

"I've been onto the word-image thing for years. I mean, that's the whole graphic novel game when it's done right, but the way Fairey has whittled it down to literally marry the singular word and image, it's clever."

"Uh huh," Prilly said as she realized she was putting her tank top on backwards. Pete was still talking as she went to the bathroom to brush her teeth. She usually got up first expressly to freshen up before he awoke. When she came out, he said, "Come see this," and motioned over to her from in front of his computer.

"Sure, let me grab my coffee," she said sleepily.

With her coffee in hand, she walked over and stood next to Pete, who put his right arm around her and pointed to the screen with his left. She scanned the words in front of her while sipping her coffee. "I like it. It's ironic, right?"

"Yeah. It's supposed to be humorous. But notice how I do that without diminishing the message."

"Yeah, it's good. I ..." but before Prilly could continue, the phone rang.

Pete jumped up and pushed past her. "Hang on, babe. Hold that thought." Prilly sat down in front of the computer and started scrolling down. "Hey, it's not a good time. Yeah, sure. Will do. Bye." He hung up the phone and returned to the computer. "So girl, tell me what you think."

"Who was that?"

"Clyde," he nonchalantly replied.

"Oh."

"I told her I'd call her back," he said as he kissed the top of Prilly's head. "I know how it bothers you, so I can wait and talk to her later after you've left."

"So basically you're saying that you'll just talk to her behind my back?" Prilly shouted as she leapt up, knocking Pete back.

"What the hell?"

As Prilly hurried across the room and knelt to the floor where her clothes lay strewn, she continued her tirade, "You just don't get it. You don't understand how I feel. You don't care." She frantically picked up her things and jammed them into her overnight bag.

"What are you talking about?" Pete said, now sounding annoyed. "Of course I care about your feelings. That's why I didn't talk to her now. I wanted to avoid this melodrama. It's not behind your back. I haven't lied to you," his voice rapidly elevating.

Putting her shoes on as quickly as possible, she shouted, "You don't get it. You don't fucking get it," and she jumped up with her bag in hand.

"Fuck you. I don't need this shit. I haven't done anything wrong. You're crazy," Pete hollered.

Prilly stormed out, slamming the door so loudly Pete was afraid it would come unhinged like she had.

***

Prilly opened the door to her apartment with her shoulders slumped, feeling physically unable to take another step. On the way home, her rage had given way to a heaviness that she had never felt before. She dropped her bag by the door and went straight into her bedroom. She took off her shoes, got into bed, and pulled the covers over her head. She shut her eyes and begged God to let her fall asleep. When she woke up a couple of hours later, she started crying and couldn't stop. After several hours of uninterrupted sobbing, she got up, put her robe on over her clothes, and went to the kitchen. She opened a bottle of wine while an emergency frozen fish sticks dinner cooked in the microwave. Feet dragging, she brought her meal into the living room where she nibbled and watched two Lifetime movies starring Valerie Bertinelli. The second movie was based on the true story of a mentally ill woman who stormed an elementary school with a gun and randomly shot a child in a brutal conclusion. In an earlier scene that Prilly would never forget, the increasingly fragile woman compulsively bought raw meat at the grocery store and filled her otherwise empty refrigerator with it – the meat eventually started to spill out into her apartment. It was insane. Prilly wondered why the woman did that. Did it make her feel better? Then she imagined the feeling of her hand penetrating a lump of ground meat.

***

Janice's phone rang at two thirty in the afternoon. The ringing was a jarring interruption to the usual stillness. She got up from her dining room table where she was checking her email and walked into the kitchen to answer the phone. "Hello?"

"Hey sis, it's me."

Surprised because they had already had their weekly call several hours earlier, Janice stumbled a bit before saying, "Oh, hi. What's up? Did you forget something?"

"Something happened. Something bad."

Janice leaned against the wall and lowered her voice. "What is it, Marge? What happened?"

"Dad was hit by a car. It's bad."

Janice stood against the wall, breathing slowly and trying to process what Marge had said. "How bad? Where is he?" she asked.

"He's at Mercy. He's in critical condition, Jan. We don't know if he'll make it. They don't know the extent of his injuries yet. His legs were mangled. If he survives, he may not ever be able to walk again. Mom is hysterical. Scott is watching the boys while I wait with her. Depending on how things go, he and I will take turns staying here with Mom."

"Well that's good. That's good," Janice mumbled. Calmly, she asked, "How did this happen?"

"The guy who hit him said he was just walking across the freeway. It was a college kid, Jan. We're told he's devastated. I feel so sorry for him. I mean, who would expect an elderly man to be walking across the freeway? I mean, not a street but the middle of the damn freeway!"

"What freeway? Why was Pop walking across the freeway?"

"Mom said he was going to sit by the lake. It's a beautiful day, which we don't get many of this time of year. She said he likes to watch the birds. There's a pedestrian overpass for people to cross the freeway safely, but Mom said he always complained that it was too long. I guess he decided to take a shortcut and cross the freeway instead. Crazy. I mean, who would cross a damn freeway on foot? Scott and I feel really sorry for the kid who hit him."

"That's awful."

Without hesitation Marge continued, "It's probably his drinking spot, Jan. I mean, watch the birds? Give me a break. I never thought of Dad as a nature lover." Marge took a long pause before saying, "I don't have the heart to say anything to Mom. She believes his bullshit. Jan, he was probably drunk and didn't know what he was doing. That's the only explanation I can think of."

"If he was drunk, the doctors would have said something. They test people for that stuff, Marge. We don't know what happened yet. Let's wait and see."

Marge sighed, knowing she and Janice would never see their father the same way – or their mother, whom Marge became fairly close to once she was old enough to take pity on her. They had long ago agreed not to talk about their parents. "I think you should come home. I think you should get on the first flight you can. Ask Richard to come with you."

Flustered, Janice swiftly responded, "I can't. I'm inundated at work. I can't just pick up and leave right now. I have too many responsibilities, too many commitments. What good would my presence do? There's nothing I can do. Richard can't do anything, and he couldn't leave work even if he wanted to. Richard doesn't even know Dad. And you don't even know what's what at this point."

After a long pause, during which Marge seemed to be trying to collect her thoughts, she said, "Mom could use the support, Jan."

"I'll call her. I will. I'll call her as soon as you let me know she's back in the house. If things get worse, I'll come but I can't drop everything now. I have no choice. Try to understand."

Not surprised, Marge replied, "I'll call you later and let you know what's going on. Please think about coming. I could use you here too, Jan."

"Okay. Keep me posted. Take care of yourself," Janice whispered.

"Will do. Bye."

"Bye."

As Janice hung up the phone, she felt a bit dizzy so she stood for a few moments, balancing, trying to reclaim her equilibrium. Then she walked back into the dining room, sat down in front of her computer, opened her memoir notes, and began working.

At five thirty, Kyle came home. "Hey Mom," he shouted as he walked upstairs to his room.

"Hi," she said, still mesmerized by her computer screen.

Half an hour later Richard came home. He had something big going on at work and spent most of the day in his office. He walked past her on his way to the kitchen.

"Should we order Chinese?" he asked as he twisted the cap off a small bottle of Vitaminwater.

"Sure, that's fine. I'll have my usual."

"Is Kyle here?"

"Yes, he's in his room," she said without diverting her eyes from her computer.

"Kyle? Kyyyle," Richard shouted.

"Yeah, Dad?" he replied from the top of the stairs.

"We're ordering Chinese. What do you want?"

"Beef and broccoli, and some of those ravioli – the fried ones. Thanks."

"Okay."

Richard picked up the phone, hit 3 on their speed dial, and placed their order.

An hour later, they quietly ate dinner together, all seated at one end of the table as Janice's folders occupied the other. They used paper plates. After dinner, Kyle went to his room for the rest of the evening while Richard watched a football game in the living room and Janice watched a PBS special on Irish stepdancing in bed. At eleven thirty, Richard came up to their room. Without speaking, they carried out their nightly routine of taking turns at the bathroom sink to brush their teeth. When Richard switched out the lights and got into bed, Janice said, "My father was in an accident today. He was hit by a car."

"That's terrible," Richard said loudly, turning to her.

Lying on her back and staring at the ceiling, Janice replied, "Yeah, Marge is really upset. It's bad."

"Is he going to be okay?"

"Don't know."

"How did it happen?"

"I don't know. He was just crossing the street," she softly said. She turned onto her side, away from Richard, and said, "Goodnight."

He lay looking at her back for a moment and then said, "Goodnight." He rolled over and they fell asleep back-to-back.

The next morning Janice was in her office at eight fifteen.

***

Prilly called in sick for only the second time since starting at WISE (the first time she had eaten some bad sushi for dinner, which caused her to wake up at three in the morning and left her unable to get off the toilet until the next afternoon). She spent the day lying on her couch, curled up under a pink chenille blanket, watching talk shows and court TV. She kept thinking Pete would call to apologize, but he didn't. As the hours rolled on, she thought about the things he said to her. *Maybe I was being irrational. He's allowed to have friends.* By that evening, Prilly was sure that she had blown it. She overreacted. She wanted to call to tell him but felt frozen. She didn't know what to say, and she was embarrassed. By late evening, her thoughts drifted from Pete to work. She wondered how she would be able to go to the office the next day. She felt like crap. She wasn't ready to face the world. She decided to set her alarm for the usual time and take it from there. When the alarm went off the next morning at six, she felt too depressed to get out of bed. She called in sick again and watched a *Judge Judy* marathon on TV while napping intermittently on her couch.

When she arrived at work at nine fifteen on Wednesday morning, Janice immediately cornered her in her office, walking right into the open door without knocking or saying a word.

"Oh, hi Janice. How are you?"

"Is everything all right, Prilly?" Janice asked in a demanding voice as she made herself at home.

"Yeah, everything's fine …"

Before she could continue, Janice sternly asked, "Well where have you been? I've been swamped here, neck deep in our series and you've been nowhere to be found."

"I was home sick. I had the flu. I called in."

"Well, you should have called or emailed me too, Prilly. I mean, we're working together now and I need to be able to count on you. Authors are emailing me queries, agents are sending me proposals, and you're nowhere to be found. I've been on my own dealing with all of this and with all of my other responsibilities. I've emailed you several times."

Prilly had no idea why Janice seemed so angry; it wasn't as if she had missed any deadlines or scheduled meetings. "I haven't checked my email yet. Sorry if you've been stuck because I was out. I was really sick and there's no way I could have come in. I never miss work; you know that. Anyway, I'm sorry."

"Uh huh," Janice replied in a sharp tone while nodding. She then stood up and said, "Please deal with the emails I forwarded to you."

"Okay," Prilly said as Janice walked to the door.

Right before Janice left, she turned to face Prilly and said, "I'm just looking out for you, Prilly. People were talking, wondering where you were. I don't want to see you under the gun." She walked out in a huff, leaving Prilly to wonder why she had ever agreed to work with Janice and whether people had really been talking.

Prilly spent the rest of the week trying to concentrate on work. She stayed in the office until after eight thirty each night. Janice thought Prilly was trying to show that she was on top of things. Really, Prilly was wasting so much time during the day because she was unable to focus – time spent daydreaming about Pete and berating herself – that she needed the extra time in order to get a bare minimum of work done. She also couldn't stand to be alone in her apartment, waiting for the phone to ring. Even though just a month earlier, spending time alone in her apartment would have been fine, everything was different now. She wished she were with Pete every moment she was alone there. In those long solitary moments, she grew to blame herself even more. She had tasted happiness and spit it out, too afraid to swallow.

Saturday morning she slept until eleven. With nowhere to go, she didn't bother to shower. Wearing the robe that had recently become her at-home uniform, she drank her coffee and decided to do something drastic. She would show up at the teahouse Pete frequented, and maybe she could accidentally bump into him. She knew it was pathetic and she hated herself a little for wanting to do it, but after two hours spent getting ready (making sure her hair was shiny and her outfit was artsy-sexy-casual), she found herself approaching the teahouse.

Her heart was racing and her palms were sweaty. She feared passing out. *This might be a mistake. This might be a really big mistake.* These fears echoed in her head as her hand reached for the door, now so sweaty that she left a perspiration handprint on the gold knob as she walked in. She tried to appear casual, but she hurried to the counter so fast that she wasn't able to scan the whole room to see if he was there.

When it was her turn in line, she stuttered. "Uh, uh, I'll have a … a latte, non-fat. Uh, small please."

As she waited for her beverage, she noticed Melville sitting in the corner by the front window. He was writing in a spiral notebook and didn't seem to notice her. As she went to the condiment counter to get a napkin, she discretely scoured the place only to discover that Pete wasn't there. She felt stupid. She decided to talk to Melville, though she didn't know what he did or didn't know about her and Pete, which made her even more anxious.

"Hi," she said, standing beside him.

He shuddered, so engrossed in his notebook that he hadn't noticed her. "Oh, oh hi. Hi Prilly," he stammered, as he closed his notebook and slipped it into an old backpack beside him.

Suddenly with no idea what to say or do Prilly said, "Oh, well I noticed you were here so I just wanted to say hi. I have some work to do, so I'm going to go sit down over there," while pointing to the overcrowded back of the teahouse; there wasn't a free seat in sight. Melville didn't notice her mistake. As she started to turn around he said, "You can sit here if you want."

"Oh, sure, thanks," she said as she pulled out a chair, which made several squeaking noises. She placed her latte on the wobbly table. Nervous to begin with, her slippery hands knocked the mug a bit, and some of her drink spilled on the table.

"Oh, that's okay," Melville said as he placed his napkin over the spill.

"Thanks," she said, sitting down. She stared straight into Melville's eyes, causing him to look down at his hands. "What are you up to?"

"I'm waiting for Pete. Aren't you?" he queried.

Melville doesn't know we broke up. Prilly's heart raced with excitement. She would see Pete; he would walk in at any minute. If Melville hadn't heard about their fight, maybe it wasn't as bad as she thought. Maybe it would be okay. Noticing the growing silence, she quickly said, "No, no I don't have plans to meet him. I was just in the neighborhood. I'm going to an art show later, so I thought I'd grab a coffee and do a little work while I have time to kill." (She instantly regretted the art show lie as it would be hard to keep up if he pressed for details.)

Before Melville could respond, Prilly heard Pete's unmistakable voice shout, "Hey." As she turned her head, she realized he wasn't alone. Next to him stood a tall woman with long red hair, dressed all in black with a dog collar necklace tightly wrapped around her pale neck. She looked like she was twenty. "Oh, hey you," Pete said, now noticing Prilly.

"Hi," Prilly said, not knowing what to do.

"Hey, I'm glad to see you," he replied. "Melville, Prilly, this is my friend Veronica."

"Hi, nice to meet you," Prilly said as she extended her hand out in horror.

"Hey, yeah, you too," Veronica said, keeping her hands in her pockets. "Pete, I gotta go, I'm gonna be late. I'll call you later," she continued.

"Okay hon," Pete said as he hugged her goodbye. "I'm gonna get an espresso. You two all set?"

Prilly and Melville nodded awkwardly and Pete was off. The next four minutes felt like an eternity as Prilly tried to acclimate herself to what was happening. She had a splitting pain in her stomach and was afraid she would be sick. She imagined herself unable to leave the toilet in the one-person bathroom with mobs of tea drinkers pounding on the door.

When Pete returned, he stood between Prilly and Melville because there weren't any free chairs around. Terrified of what he might say, Prilly blurted out, "I was just stopping in for a coffee on my way to some plans I have and I saw Melville so ..."

With his characteristic close-mouthed smile that this time made him look sexier than she had remembered, he said, "Well I'm glad to see you. I've been meaning to call you, but ... but you know."

"Yeah, yeah I know. Well I have to go," she said jumping up.

"Don't leave. Why don't you join us? We're going to a poetry reading."

"Oh, thanks, but I really can't. I have plans. Some other time," she replied as she frantically tried to grab her bag off the floor without knocking the table and spilling more coffee. "Thanks anyway. Good seeing you. Bye. Bye Melville," she hurriedly stammered as she walked toward the door.

"Prill, you sure?" Pete shouted after her.

"Yeah, yeah, I have plans, sorry. Good to see you."

"Okay, bye," he said, now smiling ear to ear.

Prilly hopped in a cab outside the teahouse and went back to her apartment. She spent the rest of the day thinking about how pathetic she was, how sexy Pete was, whether or not she should have gone with them, and whether or not he was sleeping with Veronica. When all her other thoughts started to quiet down, the last one overtook her. She fell asleep on her couch watching a Hallmark movie about a woman who battled her health insurance company to get an experimental breast cancer treatment. The woman died.

The next morning at seven, she was awoken by her telephone. She stumbled into the kitchen and picked up the receiver.

"Hello?" she answered sleepily.

"Hey you. Did I wake you?" Pete asked.

"Yeah, it's okay though," she whispered. She wondered if he tried to make his voice so impossibly sexy or if it just came naturally.

"Sorry. I thought your machine would get it if you were sleeping. I've been up all night. I couldn't stop thinking about you. Come over, okay?"

Prilly stood frozen. Like a child climbing a tree who wanted to go just one branch higher but was too scared to look down, she knew it was dangerous. Still, she kept clinging, afraid to let go. After a moment passed she said, "I have to shower and stuff. I'll come over later."

"Okay. Hurry."

***

Three hours later Prilly arrived at Pete's apartment. He greeted her in his boxer shorts, bathrobe, and signature smile. "Hey. Come on in. I have something for you. I wrote you a short story," he said as she followed him into the bedroom. "It's right there," he said pointing to the bed. "I'll get you some coffee while you read it. I worked on it all week."

Prilly dropped her oversized handbag on the floor (which contained a makeup bag, toothbrush, and change of underwear, just in case) and picked up the papers. There were two single-spaced pages. *All week?* she thought.

By the time Pete came back with a mug of coffee, she had finished reading. It was a beautifully written piece about a man who wandered into a graveyard at night to protect the "sleeping dead." She didn't understand at all how this could be for her. She tried to think of it as a metaphor or allegory, but any connection to her or to them completely eluded her.

"What do you think?" he asked, sitting down on the edge of the bed.

"It's beautiful. Your writing is like a painting. I can see it all so clearly."

He blushed, looking down. "I paint with words."

"Thank you for giving it to me."

Sitting there next to him, she felt just as alive as she had when they first met, but now her head was spinning with questions, fears, and doubt. She still didn't know what had happened, why he hadn't called all week, and who Veronica was.

"I've been really upset since … since what happened last weekend."

"Let's just forget about it. People overreact. I'm sorry I shouted at you. I was hurt. I thought you knew how I felt about you so I felt insulted."

Wishing he would elaborate she said, "I'm sorry if I overreacted too."

He leaned toward her, rubbed the tip of his nose to hers, and then leaned back and smiled. Prilly looked down and asked, "Who was that woman yesterday?" and then looked up, waiting for an answer.

Pete smiled again and said, "Just a friend. She's just a friend.

PART TWO

CHAPTER 6

Kyle Goldwyn was not an average seventeen-year-old. Despite his mother's not-so-secret anxiety that he may be below average in almost every conceivable way, Kyle was, surreptitiously, quite exceptional. He was enormously perceptive. He not only saw things that other people seemed to miss, but he saw them in remarkable ways.

At the age of three, an older and larger boy bullied him at preschool. When Kyle built a block fortress, the other boy came and kicked it down while mocking him. One day the boy pushed Kyle off a swing, causing him to badly scrape his knees. After Janice repeatedly yelled at the director of the preschool, threatening to sue if her son was hurt again (she made such a scene that the woman forever cringed at the sight of her), Janice told Kyle, "Ignore the boy. He's a loser."

Kyle replied, "I think he must be very unhappy."

Janice rolled her eyes and feared that Kyle was a wimp. When he was eight years old, a discussion about Christmas in his third grade class prompted him to ask his mother why Jesus Christ was killed. Only partly hearing the question she answered, "That's what the Bible teaches, that's all. You don't have to agree if you don't."

Kyle responded, "I think Jesus Christ must have been very special. Maybe his ideas were so special that they frightened people." Janice was preoccupied with opening junk mail and just said, "Uh huh."

Kyle ran upstairs to his room, where he spent the rest of the afternoon lying on his bed, wondering what made good people afraid. During the next several years as Janice schlepped him from museum to museum hoping to "make him interesting," Kyle began to see the world through different lenses. When Janice got the free audio headset tour so that Kyle could "properly learn about the great art," he always muted it. He looked at the paintings, sculptures, and photographs and tried to imagine where the artist was from, how they grew up, how they came to see the world, and how much of that vision lay before him, lopped off in a frame. This process made him wonder about different cultures and how they produce different kinds of people. He wondered where innovation came from, why some people's work seemed derivative and others stood on its own, unable to be defined or judged. He came to see beauty in her many guises, which so too made him clearly see her falsehoods.

Kyle was keenly aware of people's emotional centers, as if he could almost feel them immediately. A kind soul, he used this skill only to the advantage of others, never his own. This gift of perception helped him in innumerable ways, not the least of which was related to his mother. Of all the things that Kyle could perceive in his environment, what he saw most clearly was when there was a need for silence. Therefore, Kyle Goldwyn knew that the greatest kindness he could show his mother was not to show her all the things he saw, and so he didn't.

Although quiet and not terribly good looking in the traditional sense, Kyle was not considered unattractive by his peers. Contrary to his parents' assumption, he had dated several girls (including fooling around with a few and sleeping with two). He had many friends at school, and more importantly, no enemies. Outside of school, he spent most of his time with his best friend, Sam.

Kyle and Sam hung out in Central Park playing cards; they went to music stores and browsed old vinyl; they walked around the Village, talking about the evils of organized religion or politics (they were both fiercely on the left, though unimpressed by most politicians and surprisingly missing the idealism often characterized by leftie youth); they went to parties at friends' houses or met girls at the movies; and most often, they went to Sam's place and watched movies. Kyle frequently crashed on a small futon in Sam's room. Sam lived in a tiny, two-bedroom apartment with his mother, Melanie, a paralegal at a Wall Street law firm. She had long blonde hair, and Kyle thought she was incredibly beautiful and looked far too young to be a mother, though he knew not to mention this to Sam.

Sometimes they stopped by the NYU dorms to see Kyle's cousin, Natashya. Neither Kyle nor Natashya ever told their parents, but they had become close friends during those brutal family vacation weeks. They texted every week (sometimes daily) and hung out at least once a month since Natashya (Tash as Kyle and Kyle alone called her) moved to New York. When one of them had a problem they needed to talk about, they met at their favorite boisterous deli, where they always waited until a booth opened up. They shared a platter of blueberry cheese blintzes and a pot of weak coffee, which they complained about. Although she looked naïve with a freckled face and preppy clothes that stood out in the artsy punk crowds in her neighborhood, Natashya was a rebel. She used to tell Kyle that she was "sexually free" when he questioned why she always seemed to be "hooking up with some random guy." In response, she teased him that he was just uptight because they were cousins. He thought that she was a little too free. He feared that she didn't know how foolish she could look. Natashya also had a fake ID that she used to buy beer for Kyle and Sam. Kyle and Sam never drank more than one or two cans. From time to time, she also smoked a joint. Sam always took a hit or two but Kyle never did. This wasn't because he was a "straight edge," as Natashya would say while giggling, but rather because he knew that if there were ever an emergency, one of them needed to be sober. He only trusted himself with that responsibility.

Kyle was acutely aware of Tash's propensity to morph free-spiritedness into a lack of consideration for others. He didn't let it bother him until Halloween. Tash invited Kyle and Sam to a party at an underground club. She insisted that they dress in costume. When they arrived at her dorm, both made up to look like mimes, Kyle immediately noticed that Tash seemed a little out of it. Her eyes didn't focus when she offered them a beer while she finished styling her hair. He figured she had smoked a bit. She was wearing a Playboy bunny costume, complete with a white fluffy tail, white fishnet stockings, and stripper-style white patent leather stilettos. With her innocent face covered in makeup and her fine light brown hair long and stick straight, Sam thought she looked hot. She had a Lindsay Lohan look. Kyle thought that a long dress revealing one bare shoulder was far sexier than her hookeresque ensemble, but he kept this thought to himself to avoid being teased and called uptight, which he wasn't. Tash was too special to distract the eye in such cliché ways.

"What do you think?" she asked, throwing her arms up in one of her over-the-top model poses.

"You look awesome," Sam said enthusiastically.

"Weeell?" she asked, looking at Kyle.

"I think you're more beautiful than you know," he answered.

She smiled brightly and said, "Let's roll; cabs will be tough tonight."

Three hours later Kyle and Sam were getting bored. The large red club decked out in an excess of black streamers and hanging paper skeletons was massively crowded, and over time, the heavy synthesizer sounds of the techno music grated on their nerves.

"Come on, let's get out of here, man," Sam said.

"Yeah, okay. I have to find Tash to tell her we're going and to make sure she's okay getting a cab on her own."

"I'll wait here."

"Okay," Kyle shouted as he made his way through the crowded dance floor to the last place he had seen her, which was over an hour ago. He wandered around, squinting when the strobe lights flashed in his face. He stood outside of the women's bathroom for fifteen minutes, thinking that if she were in there she'd have to pass him when she left. He sent her three text messages without reply. Tash was nowhere to be found. Eventually, he made his way back to Sam.

"Hey dude, what happened to you? I didn't think you were coming back."

"Can't find Tash. I don't like just leaving her here. She's probably wasted."

"She brought us here man. I'm sure she can handle herself. Let's go to my place. My mom's out with that jackass again. We can do whatever we want."

Kyle scanned the room one more time before acquiescing, "Yeah, okay, let's get out of here."

From the subway, Kyle sent Tash two more text messages. Never drifting off for more than an hour at a time he checked his phone religiously all night in hopes of a reply.

The next day at five in the afternoon, Tash finally texted:

```
Hey. Sorry 2 worry. Met a friend. Hope
you had fun. Hugs. T.
```

Kyle wasn't the type to get angry and certainly not one to hold a grudge, but something in him shifted ever so slightly that night. He never mentioned it to her or to anyone.

***

Halloween proved to be a turning point for Pete and Prilly too. They had been inseparable since the day Prilly returned to Pete's apartment. She stayed in his apartment from Friday night until Monday morning every week, as well as most weeknights. They made romantics dinners, read poetry, and went to movies. They listened to music, drank cheap wine, and made love without ever saying the word love. There were only two problems, both of which Pete seemed oblivious to.

First, Prilly's commitment to her work was dwindling because of her preoccupation with Pete (combined with utter exhaustion, also caused by her preoccupation with Pete). She had yet to adjust to her routine of racing to and from Pete's and was often late to work. In an effort to spend as much time with him as possible, she tried to rush out of work at the end of the day, and she no longer checked her email over the weekend. In short, she was working far fewer hours. Tired and distracted, when she was at work she wasn't terribly productive. She knew that she wasn't getting as much done as she used to, but felt it was a small price to pay for finally living a *big life*. At the heart of it, though she would never say it aloud, she feared no one else could make her feel the way Pete did.

Second, she existed on the edge of worry all the time. She didn't trust Pete. She spent many nights lying awake in bed replaying everything he had said (and not said) that particular day. Every comment became suspect. She was consumed by questions like: *What is the message he is sending me? Is our relationship fizzling? Is he happy? Is there someone else?* That last question never quieted down and slipped into her mind at the most inconvenient times, like when she was in meetings with Janice, talking on the phone with her family, or looking in the mirror searching for flaws to cover up. The louder the voice in her head, the more flaws she found. Pete didn't help matters by continuing to flirt with every young, attractive woman he saw, often right in front of Prilly. Nights dancing at clubs that had once felt magical were now a game of "I spy" gone awry. *I spy a slut. I spy Pete looking at the slut. I spy Pete talking to the slut.* All of the spying was exhausting. If trying to be interesting was tiring, trying to be *more* interesting than every other woman he encountered was utterly depleting. Fearing that many of them were prettier than she was, she felt she had no choice. Sometimes she suspected that Pete knew how worried she was; at times, she actually thought he tried to make her jealous. During happy moments, he said things like, "I'm happy with you...well, right now at least," followed by his signature close-mouthed smile and a laugh. He made comments like, "That woman is beautiful, don't you think? Her bone structure is phenomenal," leaving Prilly to stare at him in astonishment, not sure of how to play it. She once asked him if he was trying to make her feel insecure. He laughed at her and said, "Only you can make yourself feel insecure. That's not on me, girl." She didn't bring it up again until Halloween.

Halloween fell on a Friday. Pete wanted to go to a costume party his friend was hosting. When trying to convince Prilly to go with him, Pete said, "My friend Luke is a wonderful cartoonist, very cutting-edge. He does wonderful things with strong female characters that you'd love. He's a bit of an opiate boy, but hey, everyone's got a monkey on their back, right?"

"What? Opiates as in opium? As in heroin? Uh, no," Prilly said, horrified at both the information and the casual way that Pete revealed tidbits like this. "Not everyone has a drug addiction or anything like it. I don't know about going to this guy's place. It doesn't sound good."

Pete rolled his eyes, and in his most annoyed voice said, "He's not an addict; he uses occasionally but he's got it managed. Not everyone who dabbles is an addict. Don't believe everything they tell you on the ten o'clock news. He's an artist and he's very successful. He's fabulous. I shouldn't have mentioned anything, and then you would have gone and had a wonderful time. Step outside the box, girl."

Prilly wondered if she was being provincial. She loved art, and now she had a chance to hang out with a cool artist crowd. Why was she looking for problems? At moments like this, she questioned what Pete saw in her at all. He seemed to think she was limited, and sometimes he actively made her feel that way. She never quite knew if it was she who couldn't get outside of traditional thinking or if in fact he just had a very convenient way of justifying bad behavior, including his own. Every time she started to believe it was him, he said something cutting that hit her insecurity-center, and she refocused on herself. Even though she noticed the pattern, she still didn't know who was to blame. Ultimately, she wanted to believe it was her problem so that she could fix it.

Per Pete's suggestion, they dressed up as Sid and Nancy. This required Pete to simply spike his hair a bit and wear pretty much the same black vinyl pants and white T-shirt he normally wore on weekends, kicked up a notch with an old black leather jacket. Prilly wore a blonde wig that Pete had in one of his drawers. She didn't ask why he had it, afraid to know the answer. She wore tight black jeans, a long-sleeved black shirt, a sequined black leather choker around her neck, and an armful of silver bangles she bought in the children's section of a drugstore. She did her makeup severely with dark black liquid eyeliner and hot pink lipstick.

"Wow girl, you look very punk meets pop art!"

"What does that mean? I don't look stupid, do I?"

"You look terrific."

In the cab on the way to the party, Prilly thought, *Playing dress up is actually fun. I should forget the nonsense about the opiate boy and just have a good time.* She leaned against Pete and held his hand, bumping her head on his chin as they plowed over potholes.

They walked into the party hand-in-hand, which made Prilly feel like the luckiest woman there. The industrial style loft with exposed brick and silver pipes hanging from the ceiling was surprisingly big. *Pete was right – this guy is successful*, Prilly thought. There were large windows, but unfortunately, they overlooked the building next door. Dimmed red light bulbs in lamps around the apartment complemented the seductive background music. As they made their way through the crowd of thirty or forty people, a guy wearing a long-sleeved, electric blue shirt unbuttoned a third of the way down his hairy chest and skintight black jeans grabbed Pete's arm. He shouted, "Hey man, hey! You came! Phenomenal!"

"Hey, Luke. Your new place is wooonderful. Those pieces, are they yours?" Pete asked pointing to the left.

"Yeah, yeah, I did those ages ago. I'm too lazy to frame anything new."

Feeling self-conscious just standing there, Prilly casually rubbed her hand against Pete's arm. "Oh, Luke this is my girlfriend, Prilly."

Prilly smiled and put her hand out, "It's nice to meet you. Your apartment is great."

Luke grabbed Prilly by the shoulders and kissed her on both cheeks. Before Prilly could say anything else, Pete said with a laugh, "So what's your costume, man?"

"Fuck that," Luke replied. "I'm me, man. I'm just me," and he walked off. Prilly watched him grab someone else exuberantly.

"See, he's all right," Pete said.

"Sure. This place is really cool," she said looking around the room.

"Let me find the bar. What'll you have? Some wine?"

"Sure, that'd be great. But I'll come with you," she said, not wanting to be alone in a crowd of strangers.

"Hey, see that spot on the leather couch?" he said pointing to the other end of the room. "Go grab us a seat and I'll be right back."

"Okay," she said as they parted ways.

Twenty minutes later, after two awkward exchanges, one with a guy who wanted to debate whether or not Mighty Mouse was on cocaine and the other with a gay couple who asked her if she could move over (leaving her squished in the corner of the couch), she started to have a mental meltdown wondering where Pete was. Just as she decided to get up to go look for him, she noticed him walking toward her. He was with a beautiful woman dressed in a long, white, flowing, see-through dress with green petals on it (that matched her exquisite eyes), white face makeup, and very long brown hair with side-swept bangs that nearly covered one eye. Pete was smiling and Prilly already knew what he was going to say.

"Prilly, this is my friend, Clyde."

Prilly felt her insides twitching. She was hot and a bit dizzy. Clyde was even more beautiful than she had imagined. *And for Christ's sake she's dressed as Ophelia. Ophelia!* she silently screamed. It couldn't get worse.

"Here," Pete said as he handed Prilly a small plastic cup of red wine, keeping one for himself. As she took the cup she said, "Hi, it's nice to meet you."

"You too," Clyde said in a voice that was every bit as lovely as her face.

"Clyde's dressed up like Ophelia. It's wonderful, don't you think?" Pete asked smiling.

"Yeah, yeah. I thought it was Ophelia. It's great," she stammered, desperate to conceal how rattled she was.

"Clyde's here with a friend. He's in the kitchen trying to make a martini without vermouth," Pete said as he laughed. Clyde looked at him and smiled.

"Wouldn't that just be vodka?" Prilly asked before nervously taking a gulp of her wine.

Pete and Clyde burst into laughter. Prilly didn't know what was so funny but she felt stupid, excluded, and increasingly nauseated.

"Well, it was nice to meet you," Clyde said as her laughter subsided. Then she turned to Pete and said, "I'll talk to you later," before giving him a peck on the cheek.

"Sure," he said.

"Nice meeting you too," Prilly said as Clyde walked away.

"Hey, move over, girl," Pete said, indicating he wanted to sit down.

"There's no room. I tried to save you a seat but it's too crowded. I couldn't hold it."

"No worries," he said as he sat down on the wide arm of the couch just to her left. "Sorry I got held up. I bumped into Clyde in the kitchen when I was getting our drinks. She told me about some wonderful new band she discovered, blah, blah, blah. I didn't want to be rude."

"It's okay," Prilly softly replied.

Pete leaned in, and with his free hand, touched her chin and kissed her.

They stayed at the party for nearly four hours and chatted with Luke, talked to cartoonists and musicians, flipped through photography books, nibbled on hummus, pita chips, and olives, and occasionally held hands. Through all this, although they didn't see her again, Prilly had a singular thought: Clyde.

***

In the cab ride to Pete's, which Prilly thought of as home, she agonized over whether to say something to him. She couldn't get Clyde out of her mind and she was terrified of blurting something out that she wouldn't be able to take back. Biting her tongue, she sat quietly all the way back, holding Pete's hand as he leaned his head on hers.

When they got back to his place, Pete put some soft music on. Smiling, he said, "Come here." She went over to his extended arms. He took her hands in his and started to sway back and forth. She leaned into his chest and they danced.

Overcome by a wave of emotion, "Did you know she'd be there?" quietly slipped out.

"What?" he asked, leaning back, still holding onto her hands.

"Clyde. Did you know she was going to be there? Because if you …"

He cut her off. "This is what you're thinking about?" he said as he let go of her hands. "This is what you're thinking about while we're having this marvellous night?" he asked in a disgusted tone as he walked into the kitchen.

Mad at herself for ruining the moment and mad at him, she stood there and said in a louder voice, "Well, if you knew she was going to be there, I just think you should have warned me."

"Oh fuck, Prilly," he said as he opened the refrigerator and looked at the nearly empty shelves. "What's the difference? No, I didn't know she was gonna be there. I mean, I guess I knew it was pooossible. She knows Luke, she knows lots of people I know, but she didn't teeell me she was going to be there or anything." He shut the refrigerator door forcefully.

"Well, I just felt caught off guard. I think you should have told me she might be there."

Now filling a glass with tap water he said, "I was there with you. She was there with some guy. What's the difference? I wanted to avoid this. I didn't see any reason to get you all freaked out when, for all I knew, she wouldn't even be there. I know how insecure you are about this," he said in a hostile tone as he shut off the tap and started drinking.

"Fuck you. I would never bring you to a party where my ex might be without warning you. You disappear for ages and then bang, I'm faced with you and your ex."

"Fuck me? Fuck *me*?" he yelled, staring at her through the cutout wall. "Fuck you!"

Prilly frantically grabbed her overnight bag from the floor and stormed into the bathroom where she shoved her makeup and toothbrush into the bag and left the apartment in a frenzy, slamming the door behind her.

***

Prilly was falling over herself as she tried to rush down the stairs and quickly exit Pete's building. Her insides were racing and she felt as if she were on fire. As she flung the building door open and felt a wave of cold air smack her face, she heard, "Wait … Prill, wait."

She turned to see Pete standing there. "Don't go like this. Let's not end things like this."

She stood motionless trying to resist both the urge to tell him to go to hell and the urge to run into his arms. She wanted to leave as a sign of pride, but was afraid that if she did, it might be for good. So she just stood.

"Hey, come on. It's cold out there. Come back inside. I'm sorry I shouted. Come inside."

Prilly stepped back into the building and followed Pete to his apartment. But there was no going back.

CHAPTER 7

Over the next six weeks, Prilly started to unravel. She was consumed by jealous impulses. When Pete was in the shower, she glanced at his Blackberry. When glances didn't suffice, she scrolled through his emails, texts, and phone logs. Sometimes when his apartment phone rang, she answered it. Knowing that would probably bother him, she never mentioned those calls. To compensate for her fears, she tried to spend as much time as possible with Pete. She tried to be interesting, she tried to be sexy, and mostly she just tried to be there. No longer wanting to run home after work to get an overnight bag and freshen up, she brought a makeup case to work and left two drawers full of clothes at Pete's. She rushed out of the office as quickly as possible and raced to meet him. Every time she caught him chatting up another woman, she found a way to punish him without telling him why.

One Friday night when she arrived at the teahouse, he was sitting and reading something he had written to some woman. Prilly went out of her way to be rude to the woman, who took the hint and left abruptly. Pete smirked and said, "Hey girl, she noticed my drawing and asked what it was, so we ended up having a nice little chat and I read her something. That's all."

Prilly responded, "I don't care." She put on a happy face that night and then went out of her way to be disagreeable for the rest of the weekend. She refused to go to a house party he wanted to pop in on, she told him the art at a gallery they went to was ugly after he said he loved it, and she made enough noise in the mornings to disrupt his sleep without appearing like she was trying to wake him. Worse than anything she was doing to Pete was the mental anguish she was putting herself through. Every time the phone in his apartment rang, she imagined it was Clyde, but on this and this alone, she bit her tongue.

Then one Friday afternoon she got a call at work. "Hello?"

"Hey babe."

"Pete?"

"Yeah, of course."

"Oh, it's just that you've never called me at work before. Is everything okay?"

"Yeah, everything is fine. Listen, I need to ask you to spend the night at your place. I have a situation I need to deal with."

"What's wrong?" Prilly asked solemnly.

"Nothing girl, just got to take care of something. Come over tomorrow night and we'll spend the rest of the weekend together, all right?"

"Okay, sure. I hope nothing is wrong. If you need something, call me."

"Thanks. Bye."

"Bye."

Prilly hung up the phone wondering what was going on. She was filled with questions that all asked the same things: *Is this about me? Is this about us?*

That evening, Prilly returned to her apartment for the first night in ages. The first thing she noticed was a foul stench coming from her kitchen. She hadn't taken the garbage out in over a week, and something reeked. As she pulled the drawstring bag out of the plastic can, she nearly hurled. She looked at the bottles under her kitchen sink desperate for an odor-eating product of some kind. Absent anything like that, she grabbed a bottle of perfume and sprayed some in each room of her small apartment. It didn't help. She sat on her couch trying to decide whether to order Chinese food, but she was too consumed with thoughts of Pete. *What is going on with him? Why didn't he say why he canceled?* She became increasingly agitated. The putrid smell in her apartment was taunting her. *I shouldn't be here. I should be at Pete's.* She thought about going down to the teahouse in his neighborhood to accidentally run into him, if he was there. Knowing it was too transparent, she decided to order some food and curl up on the couch. An hour later she was eating chicken in a spicy brown sauce with chopsticks, right out of the container, while watching a Lifetime movie about a woman who had an affair with her best friend's husband. She drank half a bottle of red wine and passed out in her work clothes.

The next morning she went through the motions of her former morning routine: French roast coffee and her favorite New York website. She wasn't really looking for something to do; she was just passing time until her plans with Pete, whenever that would be. She wasn't particularly eager to spend time with him but she was desperate to find out how he had spent the evening. After a night of panic, she tried to convince herself that it must be something benign and that she was freaking out for nothing. *If he was spending the night with another woman he would have made up some excuse, but he hadn't. It must be nothing.*

After showering and getting ready, she sat on her couch and tried to figure out what to do. She was having a really good hair day, and her outfit was spot-on. She was wearing a long-sleeved, black, sheath-style dress with black tights and new mauve Mary Jane high heels. *I look good and I don't want to sit at home wasting it. I want Pete to see me before the end of the day when I'll undoubtedly be more haggard looking. I'll throw some work in a bag and go to the teahouse near Pete's. Janice has been on my case to mark up the drafts of the first three memoirs, and with any luck, I'll bump into Pete while I still look good.*

An hour later and a block away from the teahouse, her hands began to tingle. This feeling had become familiar so she knew it would soon pass. As she approached the teahouse, Pete was coming out. Just as her adrenaline was pumping hard with wonder about his reaction to seeing her, Clyde emerged. Tremors coursed through her body as Pete turned and saw her. She wanted to turn around and run away, but concerned with saving face, she kept moving forward.

"Prilly, hey, what are you doing in this neck of the woods? You remember my friend Clyde," he said as he touched Clyde's arm.

"I had some work to do and … and there's a problem in my apartment, so … so I just thought I'd come and get some work done. My apartment reeks. It's unbearable and I need to work. I didn't think I'd see you."

"I was just going to walk Clyde to the subway, but if you wait I'll come back after," Pete said as if nothing was wrong.

"Pete was nice enough to help me out with something last night. I thought the least I could do was take him for a coffee," Clyde interjected, gently brushing her long bangs from her eye.

Unable to stop thinking about Clyde's beauty, Prilly's tremors morphed into full-on waves of rage. Clearly sensing she was upset, Pete said, "Yeah, I'll tell you about it in a bit, okay? Wait for me."

Unable to control herself she blurted out, "No, no I don't think so. I'm not going to wait," and she turned around and walked away so quickly that she twice tripped on her own feet.

Pete hollered after her. "Hang on there," but Prilly just threw one of her arms up in disgust and kept walking.

When she got home, she went straight into her bedroom where she lay on the bed, too worked up to fall asleep. A few hours later Pete called. "Hello," he said tersely.

She screamed, "*Fuck you*" at the top of her lungs and hung up. She waited for him to call back but he didn't. Prilly knew it was over.

CHAPTER 8

During the weeks after her father was hospitalized, Janice received regular updates from her sister. Marge also insisted that Janice call their mother every Sunday. The Sunday following Halloween was particularly stressful for Janice. Her father had been released a few days earlier, wheelchair bound and forced to use a catheter, which, like many other things, her mother had been trained to assist with. Again, Marge urged Janice to visit, and again, Janice claimed that she was too swamped at work. She leaned against her kitchen wall and paused before making the dreaded weekly call to her mother. After hearing things like, "Dad's in diapers, Jan. Diapers," from her sister, she knew it would be a brutal call.

"Hello?" Myra answered.

"Hi Mom."

"Oh, hi Jan."

"How's Dad?"

"Oh, not so good."

"Why? What's wrong Ma?"

"It's much harder for him now, being at home. I thought he would be happy to have his foods again and watch his TV. You know he couldn't watch his programs at the hospital. The other man in his room – he didn't have his own room, you know, and we couldn't do anything about it – the other man in his room would sleep all the time and your father couldn't watch his programs. Scott brought him some headset contraption to use to watch his programs, but he wouldn't have any of it. So …"

"Mom, Mom," Janice interrupted, frustrated that she had to hear yet again that her father was forced to share a room in the hospital, which she was convinced was just a tactic her mother used for pointing out the fact that she hadn't visited. "Mom, you were telling me how Pop is."

"Oh, right. Well, I thought he'd be happy to have his programs and his food. I made him the noodle casserole he likes so much but he hardly ate any of it. He usually takes two or three portions. This time he only had a few bites. I even put those fried onions on top that he likes so much. I made him creamed potatoes, which you know he can't resist, and Jell-O, the red Jell-O, but nothing. Just a few bites. I made him eat some chicken soup that Ellie from next door brought over, but he just sits in his chair in the living room or sleeps."

"Uh huh."

"I don't think he likes me taking care of him, you know. It was easier in the hospital. There's a nurse coming to the house once a day to check on him, but that's only for another week or so. Her name is Betsey. He can't be alone, you know. So I can't leave the house unless Betsey is here, or your sister and Scott. And he's so stubborn, you know your father."

"Do you need money Mom? I might be able to get a little something together to send you. You could hire someone to help you."

"No, no Jan. We're okay. We're just fine."

"You can't do it forever Mom. Not like this. People don't need to live like this nowadays. You can hire help."

"I know, I know. We'll see. We'll see what happens. Each day as it comes, like I always say."

"Uh huh. Right, Mom. It sounds like Pop is just a little depressed. It's a big change. Or maybe he's in pain. Is he in a lot of pain? Does he have the right medication?"

"He doesn't say much, you know. He's on all these pills, and I have to keep track of them. I think he's just tired mostly."

"I'm sure he'll be better soon Ma. I have to go. I have work I have to do, but I'll call you next Sunday. You can call me if you need something."

"You have to work? It's Sunday. You work too hard. You need to take care of yourself Jannie. I worry about you. And …"

Janice cut her off. "I know, I know, Mom. I'm fine, I'm just busy. I really have to go. I'll call you next Sunday. Tell Pop I said hi."

"Sure. Bye. I love you."

"Bye."

Janice hung up. She took a deep breath and walked over to a bowl of fruit on her kitchen counter. She shuffled the fruit around, selected an apple, and polished it on her shirt as she walked over to the dining room table. She stared at her computer for a moment and then made a beeline across the hall and into the living room. She manually turned on the television, sat down in the middle of the couch, and watched the last half of a jazz retrospective.

After six weeks, Janice decided this torturous weekly call to her mother was the most unpleasant development in her life in recent memory. She didn't adjust to change well in general, nor did she deal well with family issues. Growing up in a home in which things could quickly shift at any moment, she had learned the value of routine and distance. While it was easy to put geographic space between herself and her family, she became skilled at creating other distances too. Others did not see her discomfort with any disruption to her normal schedule because, true to type, Janice never discussed her problems. However, although they may not know the cause, everyone who encountered Janice could see the manifestations of her angst. Richard sensed he should work even later than usual. He also knew it wasn't the best time to make dinner arrangements with colleagues. He knew this just by observing the energy with which Janice shut kitchen cabinet doors. Unfortunately, unable to see her heart, he couldn't see when it was broken. Kyle knew it was time for invisibility. Only he knew his mother was sad, not angry, even though he didn't know why. So, he spent as much time outside the house as possible, doing his duty of being neither seen nor heard. Her colleagues knew she was "in a way" because she sighed loudly as she walked from her office to the copy machine; she threw the leftover part of her tuna sandwich in the receptionist area garbage without bothering to seal the Ziploc bag, thus stinking up the office; and worst of all, she popped her head into people's offices to say things like, "Watch out, I hear the guys are making cuts, trimming the fat." When it came to these kinds of jabs, Prilly bore the brunt of Janice's wrath.

CHAPTER 9

Kyle hadn't seen Tash since Halloween. They sent each other text messages sporadically. She was busy with finals and didn't have time to hang out, and Kyle was happy to have a break, though he thought of her from time to time and wondered what she was up to. The Saturday before Christmas, Kyle received a text.

> Hey stranger. Gotta go home 4 the big
> xmas family thing, free tom am? Wanna
> meet @ the usual for blintzes? Much 2
> catch up on.

Kyle responded: Yeah. C U @ 11.

The next morning on his way to meet Tash, Kyle stopped at the base of the staircase when he heard his mother on the telephone. She sounded strange. He stood quietly and listened to what he gathered was the tail end of a conversation. His mother was speaking in a hushed tone reserved for the most private or troubling exchanges.

"I can't do that. I can't do that Marge. … I'm sorry. I told you weeks ago that we've been invited to a Christmas dinner with Richard's colleagues. He said we have to go. It's important; it's business. … Uh, huh. … I know, I know. I just can't do it. I'll explain to Mom again when I talk to her tomorrow. And I've sent her some money. … Yeah, okay. Bye."

Janice hung up the phone and stood perfectly still. Kyle waited for the sound of movement, for a sound that indicated she was all right, but he heard nothing. He thought about going to her. His father had told him that his grandfather had been in an accident. Kyle went to his mother that day and said, "I heard about your dad. I'm really sorry."

She said, "Oh, thank you. I'm fine." Nothing more was said about it after that and he didn't ask. His mother was very weird about her family. They never saw his grandparents, although his grandmother faithfully sent him birthday, Christmas, and Easter cards, each containing fifteen dollars. The fifteen dollars, his mother's silence, and quips Marge had made over the years all told him that his grandparents weren't well off. He knew there was more to it but he didn't probe. He liked Marge a lot the few times she visited. She was fun and down-to-earth, and told him funny stories about his mom that he'd never know otherwise. She also swore quite a bit, which he found refreshing. He wished she visited more. He wanted to know his mother's family.

After standing and waiting for a noise to indicate that Janice was okay, he decided to leave. Instead of just taking off as he usually did, he shouted, "Bye Mom, going out with Tash. See you later."

Startled, Janice leapt from the kitchen wall that she was propped against and hollered, "Bye," as he was locking the door. She hadn't caught the name of whom he was going to see.

Twenty minutes later, Kyle walked into the deli and was surprised to see Tash was already sitting in a booth. She smiled and waved as soon as she saw him, reminding him how much fun they had together. As he approached the table, she jumped up and hugged him.

"Dude, it's been so long. Crazy."

"No, no way, don't *dude* me," Kyle said as he gave her a disapproving look followed by a small burst of laughter. "What have you been up to? How'd finals go?"

"My finals were a joke. They were all really easy. I had one twenty-page paper to write, which sucked, but whatever. I think it's all fine," she said, rolling her eyes. "I have sooo much more to tell you."

Before Tash could continue, the waitress came over. "Do you know what you'd like, or do you need another minute?" she asked as she put down a complimentary plate of bagel chips and spread.

Tash glanced at Kyle and asked, "The usual?" He nodded. "We'll have a large order of blueberry cheese blintzes and two coffees. Thanks," Tash said as she handed the large plastic menus back to the waitress.

"What's up? What trouble have you gotten yourself into?" Kyle asked as he dipped a marble rye bagel chip into the cream cheese olive spread.

Tash picked up a bagel chip and broke off a corner, which she promptly threw at Kyle while laughing. "Trouble? *Trouble*? I don't get into trouble. I'm a good girl. You know that," she said, giggling.

"Yeah, right. So, what trouble have you been up to?" Kyle asked with a laugh.

Tash tossed another piece of a bagel chip at him but it flew past his shoulder. "Aww … sucker," he said, now hysterical.

The man in the booth behind Kyle turned and looked at Natashya. She mouthed, "I'm sorry," and then Kyle proceeded to make funny faces at her, trying to provoke her to throw another chip. "You're so bad," she said. The waitress returned to drop off two mugs of coffee. "So," Tash said as they poured mini creamers into their mugs, "I met someone really cool. You have to meet him."

"Does he go to NYU?" Kyle asked.

"No, my friend Lyric and I were …"

Kyle cut her off. "Lyric? Lyric? You actually have a friend named Lyric?"

"Yeah, her name is Lyric," Tash said as she broke off another bagel chip piece and tossed it at him, hitting him right in the face because he was laughing so hard he forgot to move his head. "Anyway, Lyyyyric and I were hanging out in the Village and we stopped in this used music store. She wanted to look into selling a bunch of her old, shitty CDs. She wants to buy this totally overpriced pair of Gucci boots on eBay, so she's trying to sell her old junk. Anyway, she started talking to the guy behind the counter, and the next thing you know, we were all talking. He ended up asking for my email and we hung out, and he's so cute and it's been like three weeks of constant hanging out. He's awesome and you've got to meet him."

The waitress delivered their platter of blintzes with two small plates, and asked, "You all set here? Anything else I can get you?"

"We're good, thanks," Kyle said.

"These look awesome," Tash said as she smeared a dollop of sour cream onto the tops of the blintzes.

"Yeah, I haven't had these in a while," Kyle said. He cut into a blintz and watched the blueberry cheese mixture ooze out. "Does he go to school? Is he older?"

"He's a musician. He plays the guitar, and he's only like a few years older than me, so it's fine," Tash said, cramming a big forkful of blintz into her mouth.

"Your parents aren't gonna be happy that you're dating some random guy who works at a CD store. Good luck telling them that one," Kyle said with a smirk.

"Oh it's fine. Don't take it so seriously. Besides, why do they need to know, right?" she said with a laugh. "He's having a New Year's Eve party at his place. You should come with me so you can meet him. He lives in Brooklyn."

"I thought you were going home."

"Yeah, I am, but I told my parents that I need to come back at the end of December for a winter session seminar. What do you say? Will you come with me? You can bring Sam if you want."

"Sam is going on a cruise with his mother and her boyfriend."

"Ugh, poor Sam. That sounds heinous," Tash said with a wince. "So, will you come?"

"Yeah, sure, I'll go."

"Thanks, it'll be great. So what's going on with you?" Tash asked. She loaded her fork with another bite of blintz.

"Same old, same old." For the next few minutes, they ate and caught up on the minutia of their lives. Then, seemingly out of the blue and without looking up from his plate, Kyle said, "My grandfather was in an accident. Did you hear?"

"No, I haven't heard anything. Gee, I'm really sorry. Is he okay?"

"I don't really know. My mom doesn't like to talk about it," Kyle said, still looking down.

"You don't really know your grandfather, do you?" Tash asked.

"No. Never met him."

"Crazy."

"Yeah. My mom is pretty upset. I heard her on the phone this morning talking to my aunt. She hasn't gone to visit or anything, though."

"It's probably too depressing for her," Tash said. She balanced her fork on the edge of her plate, looked straight at Kyle who looked up at her, and in a lowered voice said, "Look, a long time ago my parents told me that your mom's family is, like, trailer park or something. I don't know if it's true, but …"

Trying to spare Tash from coming up with a way to finish the sentence, Kyle interjected. "Yeah, I know. I think she's embarrassed by them or something. Let's talk about something else; I didn't mean to be a total downer." Kyle looked back down at his plate and took a large bite.

"Sure," Tash said, picking up her fork. "I need some more of this shitty coffee. Where's the waitress?"

CHAPTER 10

After spending the rest of the weekend on her couch watching TV, napping, and drinking in her Old Navy pants and a ratty gray sweatshirt, Prilly pulled herself together to go to work on Monday. She spent the next couple of days focused entirely on work, blocking everything else from her mind by making herself emotionally numb, a skill she learned while being bullied on the playground in third grade. She shut down so she could show up. This also helped in her dealings with Janice, who now appeared downright angry.

She edited the first batch of memoir manuscripts that Janice had been nagging her about. The more work she did, the more Janice seemed to relax. The memoirs came in handy too; she lost herself in the stories of others. One of the books was absolutely riveting. It was about a middle-aged woman, Joyce, who was married with two grown children. She was a university professor who, along with some colleagues, volunteered for a 9/11-related charity. The group was composed of 9/11 widows and other volunteers who worked to help improve the conditions of Afghani women. Joyce ended up going on a trip to Afghanistan where she met a poor man with one leg, with whom she had a three-year, bi-continental affair. She fell madly in love and experienced "the emotional, cultural, and intellectual journey of a lifetime." Her husband never found out. Prilly was captivated.

Prilly's newfound use of work as Prozac was short-lived. She had put in for extended vacation time from Christmas Eve through New Year's Day. The press virtually shut down during that week anyway. She had intended to spend the time with Pete. Much to her parent's disappointment, she had told them she wouldn't make it home for the holidays. After she and Pete broke up, she knew she would be alone; she was resigned to the solitude and never told anyone that she no longer had holiday plans. She considered working to avoid blowing through her vacation days, but when she broached the subject with Stu, he brushed her off and told her to enjoy her vacation. He was concerned about how tired she seemed lately.

Christmas Eve morning, Prilly was in her office organizing some folders to take home with her, just in case she ended up working. Suddenly Janice was standing in her doorway.

"Prilly, do you have a minute?"

"Oh, hi Janice," Prilly said, startled. "Sure, what's up?" Janice walked in and stood behind the chair in front of Prilly's desk. "Do you want to sit down?" Prilly asked.

"Oh, no, I'm fine," Janice responded. Prilly thought Janice seemed odd, even for her.

"I think we should start planning the spring launch," Janice said in a faraway voice. "This launch is important. It will set the tone for the series and I really want to be on top of things."

"Yeah, sure," Prilly said. "What do you want to plan?"

Janice rolled her eyes. "We need to plan the organization of the booth, the signage, author book signings, support staff, everything. We can't just show up with a few books. We need to make a splash."

"Absolutely," Prilly responded. "What if the books don't make it through production by then? What if they're not ready? It's an incredibly tight schedule."

"They'll make it. It'll be close, but a small run of the first batch will be there and we'll have covers and flyers for the second group. We can promote them even without the books. We need this to go well."

As Janice turned to leave, Prilly realized that other than Stu, they were the only people who had come in to work that day. "What are you doing for Christmas?" Prilly asked. Janice didn't respond, so Prilly added, "I hope you have a good vacation."

"Thanks," Janice softly said, before walking out.

***

An hour later, Janice came home to an empty house. Richard decided to take an impromptu ski trip to their family house in Stowe, Vermont. Janice said she was too busy to go. Richard wasn't surprised since she didn't ski.

Richard and Kyle left early that morning. They would be gone for four days. Janice was used to being alone, but on that day, she felt uncharacteristically lonely. She stopped at a local grocer near her house and picked up some ready-made food from the salad bar and a chilled bottle of white Zinfandel. When she entered her house, she dropped her work bag at the front door and headed to the kitchen to unpack the food. She poured a glass of wine and walked back through the dining room, returning to the front door to retrieve her work bag. She sat down, sipped her wine, and got to work.

The next day, after making a pot of decaf, Janice called her sister's cell phone to wish her a Merry Christmas. Marge was at their mother's house so Janice was forced to speak to her as well. She spent the rest of the day working, exercising on her stationary bike, and watching a Christmas double feature on TV: *Miracle on 34th Street* followed by *It's a Wonderful Life*. During the second movie, Richard and Kyle called to say Merry Christmas. They both asked her to join them the next day, but she said she had too much to do and that they should have fun. She planned to go back to the office the next day and was already feeling resentful of her many colleagues who had taken a proper week of vacation.

***

By Christmas, Prilly had fallen into the depression she knew was coming. She mustered up all of her energy to call her parents. She managed to have a three-minute conversation without falling apart, which she counted as an accomplishment. She spent the next several days lying on her couch, watching women's television, eating takeout, drinking, and fantasizing about Pete. She wondered what he was doing, if he was with someone, and if he was thinking about her. She didn't shower or check her email. She didn't even brush her hair.

As the days dragged on, she felt worse and worse. There was living, and then there was living a life worth living. Right now, she was barely living. Over this week, Pete came to represent a life that was worth living, the life she dreamt of possessing. While the tricks of memory are usually played out over time, in this case, it happened more quickly. All she could remember were the wonderful moments of music, dancing, and lovemaking. Nobody like him would ever make her feel that way again. Pete was a big life.

She woke up on the morning of New Year's Eve with a new resolve to reconnect with Pete. She needed to know if it was possible. Her life couldn't be any worse than it already was, she couldn't be any more hopeless, and so she had nothing to lose.

CHAPTER 11

Although it seemed like ages ago, Prilly and Pete spoke about New Year's Eve when they were still together. Prilly made sure to bring it up as a part of her many tests of Pete's long-term commitment. He mentioned a club he liked that hosts a big New Year's Eve bash, and so she reserved tickets online for them, for which he praised her. As far as she was concerned, his affirmation more than paid for the price of admission. In the wake of the breakup she looked into canceling, only to learn that the tickets were non-refundable. Prilly often got stuck on small stuff, almost obsessively. In this instance, while initially irked about losing the money for the New Year's tickets, she soon became enraged over it, with thoughts of those unused tickets cycling through her mind when she couldn't fall asleep at night. But with her new determination to try to reunite with Pete, she suddenly felt the universe had actually thrown her a bone by preventing her from hastily canceling the reservation. It was serendipity.

Prilly transformed from a woman on the verge of total collapse into a laser-sharp vixen with a plan. She planned to get herself looking as good as possible and go to the club in the hope that Pete would be there.

By the time Prilly left her apartment, she felt invincible wearing a long, full, black skirt with tulle peeking out from underneath, paired with a white, sparkly tank top, black tights, and high-heeled, patent leather boots. Pete had pointed out the skirt in a SoHo store window display. She went back on her own a few days later and charged it even though it was way out of her price range. Her hair was long and sleek and her makeup flawless with dark, smoky eyeliner and pale lilac shimmering lip gloss. On her way to the front door, she gave herself a final once-over in the mirror and thought, *I couldn't look better. Perfect.*

After having a hard time hailing a cab, Prilly was finally on her way. While sitting in traffic, doubts started to creep in. *What if he isn't there? What if I look stupid?* Worst of all, *What if he's with someone else?* Determined to see her plan through, she pushed these thoughts out of her mind, afraid he would be able to read them on her face.

Upon arrival at the club, Prilly got in the back of a long line of people waiting to show their IDs. It was freezing. She was wearing only a light, black trench coat and black leather gloves. She didn't wear her winter coat, scarf, or hat in case she saw him outside. She didn't want to look frumpy. When it was her turn, the bouncer couldn't find her name on the reservation list. She started to panic, but with a second look, he found her. She was in.

As soon as Prilly walked through the door, she feared she had made a horrible mistake. She had never been to a club, party, or anything like it alone. She didn't know what to do with herself. As she stood for a moment trying to get her bearings, the people behind her started to push past her, making her feel all the more awkward. She glanced upward and saw a blue neon sign that noted the coat-check was down the stairs directly in front of her. She headed straight down, where she then stood in a hallway with gray walls that reminded her of the cheap stucco that lined her elementary school. It was dark with blue lights hanging from the ceiling. She leaned against the right-hand wall, waiting in a long line for the coat-check. Opposite her were women in line for the restroom, which was followed by a men's room, which men entered and exited freely. The hallway was narrow and with people lined up on both sides, she felt claustrophobic. She was getting warm and started to worry that her perfectly done makeup might melt. She felt conspicuous, just as she had as a kid in school.

After finally hanging her coat, she decided to go to the ladies room since it was right there; she wanted to check her face and waste some more time. After standing in line on the left-hand side of the hallway, Prilly entered the overcrowded women's room to discover only two of the three stalls had doors. Naturally, the one that opened up was the one without a door. She squeezed to the side to wait for another one. When she finally got into a stall, the toilet hadn't been flushed and the floor was sticky. It was hard to balance while holding her large skirt up, and she was scared the tulle would drag across the stained floor. By the time she maneuvered her way to one of the two tiny sinks to wash her hands, she glanced in the foggy mirror and assessed that she didn't look as good as she did an hour ago, but she still looked okay. Deflated, she made her way upstairs.

At the top of the stairs, she surveyed the lobby as if for the first time. It was a large, garnet-colored room with black velvet couches and chairs. It seemed to be a mood room of sorts. People were sitting and standing everywhere. To her left was a large room with a dance floor. She peeked inside. It was incredibly loud. Techno music was blaring and the dark room, lit only with strobe lights and blue glow-in-the-dark necklaces around the necks of the club-goers, was absolutely packed with moving bodies. She went back through the mood room to the final room. This large, open space had a slightly less crowded dance floor, with gothic-style music playing. On the left side of the room was a long, packed bar. Prilly started to make her way over when, through all the other noise, she heard the unmistakable sound of Pete's laughter. When he was really laughing hard, it turned into a cackle that you couldn't miss. Her eyes zoomed to the end of the bar where Pete was sitting on a stool talking to a few people standing around him. Her blood coursed faster and faster. She tried to decide whether she should walk right over to him or if she should head to the middle of the bar, pretending not to see him, and wait until he noticed her. Just as she had chosen the latter plan, Pete spotted her. "Hey girrrl," he shouted loudly. *He looks happy to see me.*

She coyly tilted her head slightly downward and smiled. She hoped he would get up and come to her, but instead he waved her over to him. She felt like throwing up. As she approached the small group, Pete, sexier than she had remembered, jumped off his stool and hugged her. "You look beautiful," he whispered, his warm breath imprinted on her ear.

As he pulled away he said, "Prilly, this is Jay, Lacey, Kim, and you remember Veronica."

She smiled and nodded. "I was on my way to get a drink," Prilly nervously said.

"Allow me, my dear," he said in his sexiest voice.

She had never met anyone more charming. He turned to the bartender a few feet away and asked for a red wine. A few moments later, he handed Prilly the wine.

His friend Jay said, "Pete, we're going to dance; are you coming?"

Prilly held her breath in anticipation.

"No, you go ahead. I'll catch up with you."

As the group walked away, Pete turned to Prilly, leaned in, and said, "It's too loud here. Let's go find a nice spot to sit and talk."

"Okay."

He grabbed his cranberry-colored drink off the bar with one hand and took Prilly's hand with the other. She tried not to spill her wine as they pushed their way through the crowd to the mood room up front. There wasn't anywhere to sit. Just before he was going to say something, he saw a spot open up on a couch in the far corner of the room. "Let's go girl," he said as he hurriedly walked over, still grasping her hand.

They sat down on the small couch and he looked directly in her eyes. "I'm glad you came. I was hoping to see you here. You look wonderful."

Prilly smiled and looked down. "You look great too."

He caressed her cheek and she raised her head. He kissed her softly, and then made a beautiful close-mouthed smile.

"So, how have you been girl?" he asked before taking a swig of his drink.

"Okay. What about you?" she asked, sipping her wine.

"Ah, you know. Chasing the muse." Then he paused, looked down for a moment, and then right back into her eyes. "I've thought about you a lot. I've missed you."

"Me too."

She didn't think she could be any happier. Her fears subsided. She was right to have come, and for once in her life, her courage was being rewarded. Flooded with things she wanted to say but determined to hold onto them tightly, she felt a crack in her armor. Just as she was about to let something slip, she realized they were not alone.

"Oh, hey," Pete said. Veronica, dressed head to toe in black, was standing over them.

"Didn't mean to interrupt. Pete, just wanted to tell you that we're heading into the other room for a bit if you come looking for us."

"Thanks. We have some catching up to do but we'll find you all later."

At first Prilly was thrilled – this time, Pete wanted to be with *her*. But then she saw the look on Veronica's face. Veronica was pissed off.

As Veronica left, Prilly took a big gulp of her wine. Pete gently said, "Put that down." When she did, he took her hands in his and whispered, "Hey you, I really did miss you."

"Me too," she said. "I'm sorry if I've crashed in on your New Year's plans."

He shrugged his shoulders and smiled. "That's okay. I'm glad you're here."

"I hope your friends don't mind," Prilly said quizzically. He shrugged again. "Veronica seemed annoyed."

"No, she's cool." Pete said. "So my girl, what have you been up to?"

They talked about work, music, art, and how much they had thought about each other. Nearly an hour later, their drinks were empty.

"Hey, let's get a refill," Pete said.

"Sure."

They made their way back to the bar in the large gothic room. Pete's friends were hanging out. "Let's join them," he said as he started to head in that direction.

"Okay," she said, feeling exhilarated.

They spent the next twenty minutes drinking and hearing about the group's misadventures on the techno dance floor. Prilly would have been having a great time but she kept sensing bad vibes coming from Veronica. It began to gnaw at her. She did her best to ignore it.

Then Veronica leaned over to Pete and said, "Hey buddy, I need to talk to you," loud enough for Prilly to hear.

"Sure." He turned to Prilly and said, "Don't go anywhere. I'll be back in a jiffy. Go have a dance."

Prilly watched as he and Veronica walked away. Jay asked if she wanted to dance. "No thanks, I'm good," she replied with a smile. Jay and Lacey went to dance and Kim wandered off. Prilly was left standing there, but only for a few minutes. When Pete returned, he was alone.

"Hey girl, sorry about that."

"It's okay. Is everything all right? Where's Veronica?" Prilly asked.

"She needed some air, went for a smoke outside I think. She'll be back," Pete said while looking over at his friends on the dance floor.

"Pete, is there something going on with you two? Are you on a date or something?"

Pete looked at Prilly and smiled. "No, no, it's not a date at all. We all came together as friends."

"Oh, because she seemed kinda upset. She was glaring at me."

"What?" Pete hollered over the loud music.

Prilly leaned in close enough to smell his cologne. "Can we go back into the other room?"

"Sure. Let's go."

They walked back into the front room to discover there weren't any free seats. They leaned against a wall and Pete asked, "What were you saying before? I couldn't hear you."

"I was just saying that Veronica was giving me weird looks, and I was just wondering what was up."

"She's just protective of me, that's all."

Prilly was puzzled. "Protective of you, from me? Why? I don't understand."

"I was kinda messed up when we stopped seeing each other. She doesn't want me to get hurt, that's all."

Prilly was ecstatic to learn that Pete was so seriously impacted by the breakup. It wasn't just her. What she thought they shared was in fact real. Then Pete made a funny face and said, "There may be a bit of jealousy there too."

Suddenly Prilly's runaway happiness hit a wall. "Jealous? Why?" She paused. "Does she have a thing for you?"

"Oh, I don't know," he said in a blasé tone. "We slept together a couple of times, just like a friend thing with no strings, but I think she might want more."

"I thought you were just friends," Prilly quickly said, trying to hide her shock.

"We are. It was just a friends-with-benefits kind of thing. Scratch the itch. You know how it is."

"When? When was it?" Prilly demanded.

"What does it matter?"

"I just want to know."

"A couple of times after we broke up. Didn't mean anything, was just trying to get past you. It was more about missing you than anything else."

Prilly's heart imploded. While she had been devastated, he had been sleeping with someone who looked like a teenager. It was too much to handle.

"I can't believe it. I've made such an awful mistake," she frantically muttered as she started to leave.

Pete grabbed her shoulder. "Not this shit again. I told you it's nothing. It's you I've been thinking about." And then his tone sharpened. "Don't be stupid, girl."

With those cutting words, she turned around and walked straight out of the club. She knew she had left her coat and gloves, but she was too embarrassed to go back for them.

The streets were crowded and she couldn't spot any empty cabs. There were bright lights and she felt turned upside down. The ground was slick. In her hysteria, she stumbled several times and twisted both ankles. Freezing, she noticed a small convenience store and hurried in for warmth. Desperate, she bought a thirty-five dollar, white "I Love NY" sweatshirt, two sizes too big, which she immediately pulled over her head. She headed back outside in search of a taxi. After about ten minutes, she got lucky. She felt like puking and had to open the cab window even though it was freezing. She made it home just before midnight. After cranking up the heat in her apartment in an attempt to thaw out, she took off her boots, tights, and skirt, and got into bed. She tried to cry but couldn't.

Lying in bed, she wished she had never met him. Then she would still be able to hope, still be able to believe that something or someone big was ahead of her, and in the meantime, she wouldn't really know what she was missing. But it was too late.

***

Kyle met up with Tash outside her dorm at eight o'clock on New Year's Eve. To his surprise, she was outside waiting when he arrived. Her parents had given her some money for the holidays. Feeling it burning a hole in her pocket, she decided they would splurge on a taxi to Brooklyn, which she had wisely booked in advance.

Tash was wearing skintight black jeans (so tight that Kyle wondered how she was able to get them on). He thought about making a comment as she got into the cab, pushing him to the other side, but decided against it. He also noticed what looked like four- or five-inch black patent leather high heels. He sarcastically mused to himself how much fun it would be to help her walk later when she would undoubtedly be drunk and stumbling around. Her sweet face was caked with makeup. Her blue eyes were smoky and dark, and her lips glistened hot pink. She was wearing a long, low-cut, sequined, silver top and a black motorcycle jacket that struck him as odd. He had never seen her wear it, or anything like it, before. Right after telling the driver where to go, Tash started fiddling around in her hobo-style silver studded black bag.

"What are you looking for?" Kyle asked.

"Gum, but I have so much crap in here I can't find anything." She giggled and said, "I need one of those lights that you, like, tape into the inside of your bag. Have you ever seen those lights? You know, from the infomercials. They're hysterical." Before Kyle could respond, Tash continued while searching through her bag. "God, I love those infomercials. Don't you love them?" she asked exuberantly. "Sometimes when I can't sleep at night I watch them for hours. The stuff always starts out looking crappy, but by the fourth or fifth testimonial, I'm hooked! I swear! And the acting, that's the best part. It's like watching a soap opera or porn or something. At first it seems totally fake but then somehow it starts to seem believable. Did you ever notice that?"

"Yeah, it's kind of like watching wrestling. Sometimes Sam and I joke about …"

Before Kyle could finish his thought, Tash cut in. "A ha!" she said as she pulled a jumbo pack of Juicy Fruit out of her bag. "Want a piece?" she asked as she unwrapped two pieces and shoved them in her mouth.

"No thanks," Kyle replied. "Listen, Tash, what's the deal with the party we're going to?"

"What do you mean?" she asked as she zipped her bag. "I told you that the guy I'm seeing is having a party with his roommate. I've met a few of their friends too. They're cool. They're like indie musician types. You'll like them."

"It's a little weird for me going when I don't know any of these guys, and … and …" he paused briefly. "I want to hang together," he said, turning his gaze from the cab window to Tash.

As she spit out her huge wad of gum into the wrapper and dropped it on the floor of the cab, she quickly said, "Just don't worry about it. Just be yourself. It'll be fun. It's a small place; you couldn't lose me if you tried. We can totally crash there too if we want to."

Kyle turned away. He leaned his head against the door and stared out the window, hoping that the night wouldn't be too miserable and hoping he wouldn't end up sleeping on some guy's floor listening to him screw his cousin.

Finally, they arrived. Kyle got out of the cab while Tash paid the driver. Standing on the sidewalk, he could hear hip-hop music blasting from above. It was freezing and he wished Tash would hurry. When Tash hopped out of the cab, she grabbed Kyle tightly by the hand and said, "Let's go." The front door to the building had been propped open with a few bricks. As they made their way upstairs, Kyle could feel the stairs themselves vibrating from the overly loud music. He wondered if all the other tenants were unconscious or out for New Year's. It seemed like the kind of place where people without New Year's plans would live. The building was musty and foul smelling. Before he knew it, he was being led into an overcrowded, dark apartment that positively reeked of cigarette and pot smoke. The smell permeated the furniture and walls, and he suspected it would linger for years after the party ended. There were bodies everywhere and they all appeared to be in motion. The small apartment itself seemed to be throbbing from the wall-to-wall people and booming music. Tash pulled Kyle through the crowd in the living room. She approached a closed door and flung it open. As the bright lights and smell of pot hit them, Tash dropped Kyle's hand, flung her arms into the air, and announced, "Hey baby. I made it."

There were four or five guys crowded onto a twin bed and a couple of girls sitting on the floor on the far side of the room. One of the guys put his hands out and said, "I was waiting for you, but we had to start the party without you." He got up and crossed the room.

"Hey man, how are you doin'?" he asked as he put out his hand.

"Hey," Kyle said quietly.

"This is my cousin, Kyle," Tash interjected.

"Well, I'm Jacob, this is my room," he said as he casually waved one arm around. "These are my friends and that's my stash. Ha. That's funny, dude, I just realized Tash and stash rhyme. So now I got my stash and I got my Tash," he proclaimed as he took Tash's hand and broke out into hysterics. The guys sitting on the bed started laughing too. Turning back to Kyle, Jacob said, "Hey, seriously dude. Welcome to my humble abode. Mi casa es su casa. There's beer and shit in the living room, there's party supplies in here, go crazy."

"Thanks man," Kyle said, struck by how utterly unappealing this guy seemed. He was on the short side and had greasy-looking, straw-colored hair. He was clearly behind on a haircut too. He was wearing light blue jeans and a totally outdated flannel shirt. In the middle of talking to Kyle, he grabbed a plastic cowboy hat that had been perched on the corner of a chair and put it on his head. He tipped his hat to Tash and said, "You look mighty hot, little girl." All in all, Kyle thought he seemed like a loser. He was glad he put the hat on though, if only to reduce the chances of any lice jumping off his head and onto someone else's.

"Let's hang in here for a while," Tash said to Kyle. Kyle nodded as she and Jacob plopped onto the bed. The other people on the bed moved over to make room for them. "Have a seat here, Kyle," Tash said while giving him an encouraging look.

"I'm cool," he said as he grabbed the chair where Jacob's hat had been, turned it around to face the group, and sat down.

"Dude, give Natashya some of that," Jacob said to the guy holding a joint. The guy passed it to Jacob and Natashya put her hand out, but Jacob said "uh uh" with a shake of his head and a smile. He took a big drag, sucking it in deeply, and with his free hand, grabbed the back of Tash's head, pulled her lips to his, and blew the smoke into her mouth. The other guys on the couch exchanged juvenile looks and grins. Tash inhaled deeply, holding the smoke down while offering a closed grin. When she couldn't hold it any longer, the smoke escaped with a giggle. Jacob turned toward Kyle and offered him the joint. "Here you go man."

"No thanks, I'm good," Kyle said.

"Suit yourself, dude," Jacob replied as he passed the joint on to the next guy.

"Kyle's a straight edge," Tash said in between giggles.

"Hey, that's cool. To each his own you know," Jacob said.

Over the next hour or so, they talked a little about music (including how they were all too lazy to go and tell the people in the other room to turn it down), movies (mostly movies aimed at adolescent boys), and even politics (but this conversation was painfully limited). The major attraction of the room was the endless pot supply. After an hour of weed and conversation, Jacob pulled a sandwich-size Ziploc bag out of his front jean pocket. It was filled with little pills. "Come on baby, let's feel good," he said to Tash. He passed the bag around the room and everybody took one, everyone except for Kyle.

Tash leaned in close to Kyle and said, "It's just X, Ky. They make you feel reeeeeally good. It's awesome. You should try one. It's New Year's!"

"Nah, I don't think so. I'm good," Kyle said with one shake of his head.

"Suit yourself," Tash said as Jacob popped one into her open mouth.

"Didn't know you were doin' that kind of stuff," Kyle remarked with a serious look.

"Well, I'm a woman of mystery," Tash said seductively before laughing like a child.

The night dragged on for Kyle. He was infinitely bored, and soon, Tash was leaning onto Jacob who was not-so-discreetly rubbing her ass. Between their increasingly vulgar display and the incredible swirl of smoke in the almost entirely unventilated room, Kyle reached his limit. He stood up and said, "I'm gonna grab a drink in the other room, check out the music."

Tash barely noticed him leave, but as he walked out the door, Jacob hollered, "Have fun man, I'll take good care of Natashya."

Kyle left the room mortified for Tash, whom he heard giggling as someone kicked the door shut. Finding himself standing in a dark and overcrowded room full of strangers and blaring music he abhorred, Kyle knew he had made a horrible mistake. He made his way to the disgusting kitchen. It was overloaded with bottles of hard liquor and mostly empty bags of corn chips and Doritos. The kitchen sink was overflowing with beer cans floating in melting ice. There were dirty red plastic cups everywhere. Kyle looked for a clean cup and settled for what looked like the cleanest of the bunch. In search of something non-alcoholic, he opened the refrigerator and instinctively threw his head back in horror at the revolting smell. He quickly grabbed one of several half-empty bottles of Mountain Dew and slammed the refrigerator door shut. The smoke was killing his throat and he needed to drink. He filled his cup, chugged it down, and refilled it once more before returning the bottle to the refrigerator.

He surveyed the room but couldn't see anywhere to sit or anyone worth talking to. Instead, he stood by the kitchen counter and slowly drank his second cup of flat soda. In search of a bathroom, he saw a closed door that he assumed was it. With the music so loud that people on the street could hear it, he didn't see any point knocking so he just twisted the knob and gently opened the door. It was a very small bedroom of sorts with a guy lying on a small couch, wearing large, '80s-style headphones. His eyes were shut. As Kyle went to close the door, the guy looked over at him. "Hey, sorry man, just looking for the bathroom." Kyle stood there for a minute waiting for a response, but was met only with a stare. "Sorry man," Kyle said again as he pulled the door shut.

After using the bathroom, Kyle was able to grab a seat on the couch when somebody got up to go get a beer. He sat there alone for most of the night, occasionally chatting with whoever would sit down next to him. When people started to leave around two, someone mercifully turned off the music. He hoped Tash would emerge from Jacob's room. He hated the thought of having to go get her; he dreaded seeing the pathetic state she was in. Just as he was about to go check on her, Tash stumbled out of the room and made a beeline for the bathroom. Five minutes later, she came out and was heading back toward Jacob's room. Kyle jumped up and intercepted her.

"Hey. What's up? Are you almost ready to go?"

"Oh, Kyle. I'm so glad you're still here. I didn't know if you had left," she said with her eyes swirling. Her eye makeup was smudged and her cheeks were bright red. She hugged him.

"I wouldn't leave you, you know that. You're a mess. Let's get you out of here," Kyle said.

"No, I'm good. I'm reeeally good. I wanna crash here. I told you I wanted to crash here, remember? You can stay too, okay?"

"Come on, I'll take you to my place and you can have the spare room. We can go out for blintzes in the morning," Kyle rebutted.

"Naw, that's okay. I'm gonna crash here, but you can totally go home if you want to. I'm fine."

He knew she had probably stayed there many times before, and that it probably didn't matter whether he was there or not. He detested the thought of spending the night in that rat hole, but there was no way he was leaving her there, not in that condition and with those people.

He sighed and said, "I'll stay too."

"Oh, you're the best," Tash said as she grabbed him for a tighter hug, half-falling onto him. We can still do blintzes in the morning, okay?" she slurred.

"Uh huh," Kyle said with a nod. "Where should I sleep?"

"Stay here, I'll find out."

Tash went back into Jacob's room. Kyle waited for about ten minutes before Jacob came out holding a pillow. "Dude, when everyone gets outta here you can crash on the couch. There's a blanket thingie on the back of the couch you can use. Okay, dude? You all set?"

"Yeah, I'm all set," Kyle said, wondering how wasted Jacob was. He spent the next hour and a half sitting on the couch with a stained pillow on his lap waiting for everyone to leave. Eventually, although there were still a handful of people milling around the apartment, the couch was empty. Exhausted, Kyle took the pillow with cigarette burns in it and lay down. He never saw the "blanket thingie" that Jacob had been talking about, so he took off his coat and draped it over his chest.

***

The next morning, Kyle slowly awoke to the sound of someone stirring nearby. He opened his eyes just a little and was overcome by the sunlight pouring into the room. He closed his eyes and rubbed the crusty sleep out of the corners. When he slowly opened them again, just a crack, he saw a guy standing in the kitchen pouring cereal into a bowl. It was the same guy that had been lying alone in that room the night before. Kyle watched him through barely opened eyes. The guy took a carton of milk out of the refrigerator, sniffed it, and then poured some into his cereal bowl. As he fished around in a drawer, presumably for a spoon, Kyle became distracted by another noise. His half-opened eyes veered to the right where he saw Jacob's bedroom door open and a guy, wearing only boxer shorts, walk out of the room and go into another bedroom, shutting the door behind him. The mysterious cereal man was now on his way back into his room with his breakfast in hand. Kyle lay on the couch, awake but with his eyes shut, for about an hour and a half until Tash emerged from Jacob's bedroom. He pretended to be asleep as she stumbled out of the room wearing an oversized Rolling Stones T-shirt that he assumed was Jacob's. She went straight to the bathroom. Ten minutes later, she was tiptoeing back to Jacob's room when Kyle stretched his arms and made a noise as if he were just waking up.

"Oh, hey. Sorry. Didn't mean to wake you up," Tash said.

"No worries," he moaned. "I'm sure it's time to get up anyway." Kyle sat up and asked, "Where's Jacob?"

"Oh, he's still sleepin'. Knowing him, he could sleep for half the day. He really partied hard last night."

Tash walked over to the couch and sat down next to Kyle. Her shoulders were hunched over as if she were cold. Kyle put his coat on her bare legs. "Thanks," she said. She looked awful. Her thick black eyeliner was smeared all around her eyes, making her look like a raccoon staring at rapidly approaching car headlights.

"You hungry?" Kyle asked.

"Nah, not really. I'm just super tired. I only got up because I was bursting and had to pee. You wanna get out of here?"

"Sure."

"I just have to get dressed. I'll be right back."

Tash got up and went into Jacob's room. Kyle used the bathroom and when he came out, Tash was dressed and waiting, slipping on black sunglasses. Kyle grabbed his coat and they headed outside. Tash leaned against the building smoking cigarettes while Kyle tried to get a cab (which took nearly twenty minutes).

They sat in silence for the first few minutes of the cab ride. Feeling uncomfortable, Kyle finally said, "Last night I was looking for the bathroom and accidentally walked in on this guy lying alone in a room. I saw him again getting cereal this morning. Do you know who that guy is and why he stayed alone in his room all night?"

"Oh, that's Jacob's loser brother. Melvyn, or Melville, or Mel-something. He's a freak. Jacob just lets him crash there because he'd be, like, homeless otherwise. He's a total dweeb," Tash said. She was leaning against the car door and looking in Kyle's direction, but her dark sunglasses made it difficult to see if her eyes were open.

"Oh. I kind of felt badly for him. It was really loud there last night."

"Don't feel bad for him. He's a loser. He's lucky to be able to stay there at all," Tash quipped back.

Kyle was quiet for a minute, thinking about what to say next. After a moment passed, he asked, "So who else lives there? How many roommates does Jacob have?"

"You're full of questions today," Tash groaned. "He has one roommate, Jeremy, plus his loser brother who stays there, but he's not really a roommate exactly."

Knowing that Jeremy must have been the guy that came out from Jacob's bedroom nearly naked this morning, Kyle probed, "Oh, did I meet Jeremy last night?"

"Yeah, he was one of the guys in Jacob's room, on the bed. He's kind of a prick." She paused and then said, "I'm super fried. Can we just chill the rest of the way?"

"Yeah, sure," Kyle responded. It seemed like a perfect time to stop talking anyway.

Soon they arrived at Tash's dorm. When they pulled up to the curb, she started going through her bag. She was fumbling around, unable to find her money. She dumped the contents of the bag onto the backseat of the cab. Her money wasn't there. As she scooped everything back into her bag she said, "Hey, Kyle, I ..."

He cut her off. "Don't worry, I got it."

"I don't know what happened to my cash. Maybe it fell out of my bag or something. Sorry," she said unconvincingly as she leaned in and gave him a half-hearted hug.

As she stepped out of the cab, Kyle leaned toward her door and said, "Blintzes another time."

"Yeah, sure. See ya."

When the taxi arrived at Kyle's house, he asked the driver to please wait while he ran in to grab some money. He walked into the house, leaving the front door ajar while he hurried to his room for the cash. Janice was sitting at the dining room table wearing a long silk robe and working on her laptop. She hollered, "You left the door open."

Before she could get up to close the door or ask Kyle to do it, he was darting back down the stairs and racing out the door. When he came back into the house, he said, "Hey, Mom. Sorry about that. I didn't have enough money for the cab driver."

"Cabs are a rip-off. That's the great thing about the city: the subway," Janice said quietly, without looking up from her computer. "Yeah, I know," he said as he headed back up to his room. From halfway up the stairs he said, "Hey Mom, Happy New Year."

"You too, honey."

Kyle flung his shoes off, plopped down on his bed and checked his cell phone. There was a text from Sam wishing him a Happy New Year and complaining about his cruise.

Kyle responded:

```
Back @ u bro. That's nothing. I got stuck
in Brooklyn w T. She's into a bad scene.
Will tell u later.
```

Although he eventually told Sam all about the atrocious party and how Tash was smoking and popping pills, he would never mention the second guy that came out of Jacob's room to anyone.

Lying on his bed, he kept thinking about how Tash seemed to be spiraling downward and about how much it irked him when Jacob called her Tash instead of Natashya. He had never heard anyone else call her that, not even her roommate. He was afraid to even wonder what had happened to her behind closed doors.

CHAPTER 12

Prilly pulled herself out of bed at noon on New Year's Day, sweating in the oversized sweatshirt she bought the night before. She had to pee badly. She thought briefly about just going in the bed, but knew she would regret it almost immediately. While sitting on the toilet, she pulled the sweatshirt over her head, tossed it on the floor, and left the bathroom without washing her hands or flushing the toilet. Shoulders slumped, she shuffled back into her room where she opened her dresser drawer and pulled out an old pair of gray yoga pants and a matching long-sleeved cotton shirt. She changed, got back into bed, and forced herself to go back to sleep.

Two hours later, she woke up with a killer headache. She took four Advil and made a pot of coffee. She stood in the kitchen as the coffee brewed and stared at her answering machine. *No messages.* She took a cup of coffee and a box of crackers into the living room. She sat on her couch, flipping through stations looking for something to watch. Nothing. All of the things that usually comforted her, like movies of the week, seemed to be mocking her. She settled on a channel that showed infomercials all day long. Vacant and numb, she watched for hours, only occasionally getting up to get something to snack on or to use the bathroom. New Year's Day fell on a Thursday, so she had until Monday to pull herself together before leaving her apartment and returning to work. She couldn't imagine ever going anywhere again. She felt dead. She had never felt so empty, worthless, and lifeless. She spent the next few days in her apartment watching TV, sleeping, eating frozen dinners, and forcing herself not to call Pete. *I can never call him again* became her mantra.

***

Janice's alarm rang at five in the morning the Monday after New Year's. She sprung from bed and got ready for work, selecting her favorite gray pencil skirt, a white button-down shirt, and a long, black cashmere cardigan. She was in her office before seven.

Prilly arrived at ten after nine. She had psyched herself up the night before, telling herself that things would somehow get better if she could manage to get up in the morning, take a shower, and drag herself to work. She made it her mission to be on time, but a subway delay made her late. As she hurried into her office, throwing her work bag on the floor and flopping down in her chair, Janice appeared at her doorway.

"Did you hear?" Janice asked.

"Oh, hi Janice," Prilly nervously said as she pressed the power button on her computer. She was convinced that everyone could suddenly see what a worthless mess she was.

"Did you hear?" Janice repeated, this time agitated.

"Oh, I'm sorry. Uh, did I hear what?" Prilly asked as she typed her password into her email login screen.

"Charles Pruit committed suicide on New Year's Eve," Janice said matter-of-factly.

Prilly froze, looked up from her computer screen, and with trembling fingers softly asked, "What? What did you say?"

"Charles Pruit committed suicide. Jumped out of his apartment window or something on New Year's Eve. Hell Prilly, it's been all over the news and Stuart sent out an email days ago." She snidely finished with, "Where have you been?"

In shock, Prilly couldn't think of anything to say.

"He was one of your authors, right? Didn't you reject his latest book or something?" Janice asked, already knowing the answers to these questions.

"Oh my God. Yeah, yeah, Stuart didn't want to go with it," Prilly muttered, struggling to sound coherent.

"Well, it's not your fault. He must have been a nut," Janice said right before she turned and walked away.

Prilly just sat there. Not a minute later, her computer beeped indicating the delivery of a new email. It was from Janice and read: "Prilly: We need to get moving with our series. I have been working for several days and I have been here since early this morning. You need to pull your weight. I want to see your notes by the end of the day. I will be sending my notes attached to several forthcoming emails. J."

Prilly opened her desk drawer, pulled out her bottle of Advil, and then sat with it in her hands, unable to muster up the energy to open it. She put her head down on her desk.

A few minutes later, she heard Stuart's voice. "Hey, are you okay there?"

Prilly popped up, "Oh Stuart, I'm sorry, I ..."

"It's all right. I know," he said as he walked into her office, shutting the door behind him and sitting down across from her. "I know how hard this must be for you, but honestly Prilly, the guy must have been pretty messed up. It's got nothing to do with you or with us. He was depressed, chronically depressed. He needed help."

"Yeah. I'm sure you're right," Prilly responded, not knowing what to say but hoping Stuart, though always nice to her, would leave so she could be alone.

They sat for a long moment in uncomfortable silence. Then Stuart said, "Listen, Prilly, I realize this might be tough for you. If you're really troubled by it, you might want to talk to someone. I can get a name for you."

She was startled by his suggestion and wanted to take the spotlight off her emotional state. "I appreciate your concern, thank you. But I'm really fine. I barely knew him," she said in a way that she hoped made her sound together even though she was quite rattled.

With decades on her, Stuart thought of Prilly as a kid in some ways. He also liked her and felt protective of her. "Well you know where to find me if I can be of any help," he said as he stood up and pushed his chair back. When he reached the door he turned back and said, "By the way, Happy New Year. Hope you had a good break. Janice said you two are working on some exciting stuff. Look forward to catching up on it all."

"Thanks Stu. Uh, Happy New Year to you too," Prilly mumbled as he was walking away.

She sat for a moment until she realized that she was still clutching the bottle of Advil. She opened her desk drawer and dropped the bottle, never having opened it. She thought about Charles. She felt guilty. In her heart of hearts, she knew that the rejection had at least been a part of it. She even understood. Then she started to think about

Pete, about the last few days, and about how broken she was. A part of her envied Charles.

Her thoughts were interrupted by another beep from her computer. It was another new email from Janice that read, "P: My notes are attached. More forthcoming. J." Prilly's inbox had seventy-nine new messages, not including those from Janice. She needed to get to work and so she did.

She managed to work all day, catching up on emails and making final editorial notes on the memoir manuscripts. At six fifteen, Janice came to her office and suggested they have a working lunch together the next day to review their progress and to determine what they need to accomplish before Trade Launch. Prilly agreed and Janice told her to make a noon reservation at Nico's, an Italian restaurant two blocks from their office. Janice would meet her there. Prilly didn't have the energy to question how Janice was always able to turn her into a secretary, she just said, "Sure, no problem."

"I'm glad to see you're still here," Janice remarked before turning her back and saying, "See you tomorrow."

Prilly was about to pack up and leave, but feeling self-conscious she spent another half hour in her office, although she didn't get anything done.

When she got home, she changed into her comfy clothes, made a grilled cheese sandwich, poured a glass of red wine, and headed straight to her computer. She had waited all day to read the news reports about Charles. Worried her Internet usage might be monitored at work, she waited until she was home. While her computer was booting up, she took a few bites of her sandwich and set it aside. As soon as she typed "Charles Pruit" into Google, a slew of newspaper articles and YouTube news clips popped up. She sat reading, watching, and drinking for two hours, watching some clips repeatedly.

She was able to picture what happened that night. He was alone in his tiny studio apartment. There were stacks of books and a desk with a computer on it. He was wearing a white undershirt, pajama pants, and a robe. He was watching the New Year's Eve festivities around the world on his old television perched atop a small plastic TV stand. He was drinking Jack Daniel's. He kept refilling his glass.

He had been planning this for a while. Maybe in those final hours he hoped for a miracle, some great change to come and sweep over the defeat. But he was alone. At eleven thirty, he took a final swig from his glass and dropped it on the floor beside his chair. He walked over to the only window in his apartment, opened it, and climbed out onto the fire escape. Without hesitation, he jumped. Prilly wondered if he had intended to wait for midnight but just couldn't make it.

From the various reports, she was able to put together the facts of his life in a way that made perfect sense to her. Charles was forty-eight years old, never married, and didn't have children. From what she could tell, he hadn't had anyone special in his life. He was an only child and was survived by his seventy-four-year-old mother who lived in New Haven, Connecticut. Many of his colleagues and students were interviewed. They all said it was surprising, but that he was a quiet man who kept to himself. Several reporters asked his department chairperson if it was true that he had been denied a promotion recently. The chairperson had no comment. The president of the university made a statement "expressing deep sympathy for his mother" and "confidence that our community will rebound from this terrible tragedy." Prilly thought it was unspeakably sad that a forty-eight-year-old man had only left behind his mother. There may be no one else grieving for him. He was a kindred spirit. She felt increasingly guilty.

She lay in bed for more than an hour that night before falling asleep. At first, she thought about how isolated and disappointed by life Charles must have felt. He couldn't escape the smallness of it all. Then she started believing that's how she would end up. "Hell, that's how I've already ended up," she muttered to herself. She thought about how lonely she had been for so long and how connected she felt with Pete. She couldn't understand how she could love someone so much who cared so little for her. She wondered if maybe he *did* love her and that she had caused all of this. She had shown him that she didn't deserve him. He might not have figured it out until he was so in love that it wouldn't have mattered, but she revealed herself. And now she was utterly alone again, more alone then she could have imagined. If not for her newfound posthumous bond with Charles, she wouldn't have anyone.

***

The next day, Prilly arrived at the restaurant at five minutes to noon. Consumed with thoughts of Pete and Charles, she had barely slept the night before and was frazzled from a long morning spent trying to organize her notes for the memoir series before the dreaded lunch meeting. As she was giving her name to the host, she spotted Janice already waiting at a table across the restaurant. She told the host she was "all set" and started walking toward Janice, who was looking down and writing. Janice looked up and said, "Oh, there you are," as if Prilly was late.

"Oh, I'm sorry if I kept you waiting," Prilly said, wondering if she was somehow late. Janice's first move was always the same, throwing her opponent off balance. Janice was sitting on the booth side of a table for four. She had a yellow legal pad and pen in front of her and a stack of manila folders to her right. Prilly sat in a chair opposite her and placed her work on the chair beside her. There was a long rectangular mirror running the length of the wall behind Janice. Prilly immediately found herself distracted by it, vacillating from looking directly at Janice to looking just beyond her at her own reflection. *I look terrible*, Prilly thought. "So how are you doing?" Prilly asked, as she placed her napkin on her lap.

"Oh you know, busy busy. I'm always madly busy. I always take so much on. I think we should get to work because there's a lot to get through. Do you know what you're having for lunch? When the waiter comes I think we should order right away."

"Oh, um I haven't looked yet. What are you having?" Prilly asked as she opened her menu.

"The ravioli special," Janice said.

"Oh, that sounds good. I'll have that too," Prilly said, closing her menu just as soon as she had opened it. She then pulled a notebook and pen out of her bag as the waiter walked over and asked if they wanted to order a drink. Janice replied, "We're ready to order lunch. I will have a club soda with a piece of lime and the ravioli."

"I'll have the ravioli as well and a Diet Coke please," Prilly said, looking up at the waiter.

"Very good. I'll bring some bread over," he said as he reached to take their menus.

"Well, let's get started," Janice suggested.

They spent the next hour and a half reviewing their notes on the memoirs they had received to date. They talked about final editing, marketing, soliciting endorsements for the books, and many other issues. Janice did most of the talking, and Prilly did most of the note taking, although Prilly felt a strange synergy working with her. They bounced ideas off each other and seemed to have an impressive batch of books lined up along with an innovative marketing strategy. They continued talking through their wonderful meal of spinach and ricotta ravioli in a chunky tomato sauce. Prilly hadn't eaten a decent meal in weeks and realized she was starving for nourishment. It was so good that she used a piece of Italian bread to soak up the remaining sauce in her bowl, but felt awkward when Janice shot her a disapproving look.

As they were wrapping up their work, the waiter came over and asked if he could bring them anything else. Janice ordered a decaf cappuccino.

Prilly said, "That sounds good, I'll have one too. Regular, please."

"So, I think we're in pretty good shape here. We'll just need to hustle and lean on the production team to get these books out," Janice said as she put her manila folders back into her Louis Vuitton briefcase.

"Yeah, I think so too. This is going to be a great line. I will get on that list of reviewers for commentary as soon as we get back to the office," Prilly said as she also put her pad and pen into her bag.

The waiter walked over and handed them their cappuccinos accompanied by two pieces of amaretto biscotti. Janice picked up one of the pieces of biscotti and dunked it into her cappuccino. "I hope this is decaf. You never know," she said before breaking out into a high-pitched laugh.

Prilly smiled and feigned a quick laugh, thinking how she would hate to see Janice over-caffeinated. She dropped two lumps of sugar into her cappuccino and gave it a stir.

"So," Janice said, "What's been going on with you?" she asked before taking the last bite of her biscotti.

"Oh, not much. You know, nothing really new," Prilly said while playing with the biscotti. Janice stared at Prilly without expression or waver. Prilly dunked her biscotti into her cappuccino and, looking down at it said, "It's been kind of a tough time. I broke up with someone." She took a bite of the soggy biscotti. It felt surprisingly good to say it aloud. If naming something makes it real, Prilly needed to take something that was the most real thing in her life and make it known in a way she could control. It somehow made her feel less crazy. Although she hadn't had any intention of talking about anything personal with Janice, certainly not about Pete, it felt completely natural coming out of her mouth. "The holidays were kind of tough. You know how New Year's is, and … and I had thought we would be together."

As she swallowed the mushy cookie, Janice replied. "Oh, I'm sorry to hear that. What happened?"

"Well," she said, pausing to take a sip of her cappuccino, "I don't really know. I think he had commitment issues."

"Oh, I see," Janice said.

"He's very free-spirited. He's an artist. He's amazingly talented. He has that free-spirited artist mentality, you know? I just didn't know if I could handle it." Prilly consciously stopped to sip her drink, wanting to know what Janice would say.

"Those artist types are tough," Janice said with a laugh. Prilly laughed too. Then Janice returned to her stern face, looking right at Prilly. "Was it a serious relationship?" she asked.

"Yes. It was. I thought it was it. I thought he was the one."

Janice offered a sympathetic look and Prilly couldn't believe how easy it was to tell her all of this.

"If they're not ready, they're not ready. If the most they can offer is less than the minimum you're willing to accept, then there's no point. Sometimes it's better to cut your losses and move on. Women who try to change them only end up miserable. They waste a lot of time, and tell me, what do they have to show for it? What?" she repeated, again breaking out into cackling laughter. "Sometimes these things are for the best. You should focus on your career. Then you'll have something to show for yourself," Janice said firmly.

Prilly was a life-long romantic. She believed in soul mates, great loves, and above all, big lives. But she wasn't foolish enough to believe that everyone got to have those things. Being in the middle, her chances were slim. She tried to envision a life worth living without them, without him. She realized that there was no way Janice shared her romantic disposition and couldn't really understand her pain, so Prilly wasn't about to tell her. Still, she wondered if there was something to learn from a woman who had made career her priority but still wasn't alone, still had a family, or so it seemed.

"Thanks. I'm sure you're right. I'm going to try to focus on work and on myself. It's just hard. It's a letdown."

"Sometimes the best thing we can do is to pick ourselves up and keep going. That's what you've got to do. Trust me Prilly, at the end of the day, what do you want to have to show for yourself? This memoir series is a big opportunity for you. You don't want to blow it. You can't afford to be distracted," Janice said sternly. "We both need to do our part."

"Oh, of course," Prilly said, realizing the tenor of the conversation had slipped out from under her. "Absolutely, I won't be distracted. I'm actually very glad to have the work to focus on." Although Prilly was just saying it because she felt she had to, she genuinely felt grateful to have a project that demanded her attention.

"Stuart is expecting a lot from us. I promised him the sun and the moon," Janice said, again starting to laugh. "So now we have to deliver."

"Absolutely. I think we're in really good shape. I feel good about it," Prilly replied with newfound confidence.

"There's a lot of work ahead, but I think we'll get there. We'll pull it off," Janice said with an uncharacteristic smile.

"So what about you? How were your holidays?" Prilly asked.

"Oh well, they were fine. My husband and son are doing really well. We just decided to stay around here this year because my husband and I are both busy with work. He has a very demanding career too, and it never lets up," Janice said before sipping her cappuccino.

"Sometimes it's nice to stay at home and catch up on things," Prilly replied.

With nothing more to add, Janice said, "Are you ready? I think we need to get back to the office. We have an action plan now."

CHAPTER 13

Over the next five weeks, Prilly followed a strict routine as if her life depended on it. She was at the office every day by eight thirty. Janice usually arrived by eight, if not earlier, and often started Prilly's day by popping unannounced into her office to review her latest ideas. Prilly worked hard, both on her considerable normal responsibilities and, even more so, on the memoir series. She was determined to stay focused while at work. There were long-circulating rumors that the press was in trouble and cuts may be coming, rumors Janice was all too eager to spread. With the economy in the crapper and several years of declining book sales across the country in a world gone digital, Prilly took Janice's warnings more seriously than usual. She had been living off credit cards for years as it was, rotating debt from one low-interest card to another, accruing fees that she chose to "think about later." She was barely managing to keep all of those balls in the air. She needed her job. Prilly also began to appreciate her newfound working relationship with Janice. Most days they met several times in addition to the countless emails that Janice sent. On several occasions, they returned to Nico's for lunch meetings. Janice always ordered the ravioli, and Prilly usually did too. Other days, they had sandwiches delivered and ate in Prilly's office. Despite the difficulties Prilly still encountered working with Janice (incessant emailing, last-minute changes, and being "assigned" a disproportionate amount of busy work), Prilly also found herself, in spite of herself, enjoying Janice's company. More than that, she enjoyed having a collaborator. It was in stark contrast to the rest of her life.

Weeknights were different – less focused, more numb. When Prilly got home, she ritualistically changed into her at-home clothing, poured a glass of wine, and ordered takeout to be delivered (or warmed up takeout leftovers). She didn't do any real grocery shopping, but she did stop at the corner grocer when she ran out of wine, coffee, or cream. Sometimes she also picked up a salt bagel and cream cheese for the morning, although she inevitably felt guilty about eating it. She spent her nights curled up on her couch eating, drinking, and watching TV. The entertainment tabloid shows and movies of the week that she usually relied on immediately brought Pete to mind, and she knew she wasn't equipped to think about him without tumbling down a dark hole. So instead, she turned to the home shopping networks for comfort. Eventually, she started to feel as if the "home shopping ladies" were all members of a community that she belonged to. She knew the hosts; she knew their styles and senses of humor; she knew when they were exaggerating or even lying (although she didn't care); and she knew that they were always there, smiling and complimenting their viewers. She could count on them. Although routinely tempted, she only bought a couple of items: a new set of sheets for her bed that promised to be as soft as a favorite old T-shirt, and a beige patent leather work bag that gave her a rush in her heart as she opened the box and tore away the bubble wrap. The sheets turned out to be thin and cheap feeling, but she kept them and tried to convince herself that they were better than they were. She loved the bag, which she felt paid for itself when Janice called it "very cool" during one of their lunches at Nico's. Mostly, she just liked watching the programming. It gave her somewhere to go at the end of the day, somewhere she wasn't alone.

The weekends were much harder. She never left her apartment and found it hard to pass the time. She thought about organizing her closet, cleaning her apartment, and even working, but she wasn't able to do any of this. She didn't even bother to shower or dress. All the energy she was able to muster during the week left her completely drained by the weekend. She slept as late as possible, sometimes just lying in bed for hours to pass time. She frequently napped during the day and continued to watch home shopping. The worst part of the weekends was how much time she spent thinking about and missing Pete. He consumed her thoughts. She thought about how much better her weekends were when they were spent with him, back when she felt truly alive.

On the sixth Saturday, Prilly decided to make a change. Unfortunately, it was a change for the worse. Falling back into dangerous territory, she decided to make herself look as fabulous as possible and casually walk by the teahouse. She wasn't going to talk to him, she wasn't even going to go in; she just wanted a glimpse. She knew it was pathetic and a backward step, but once she got the idea, it took over and she couldn't stop herself. Her heart was racing during the entire cab ride, which she interpreted as being *alive* again. Before she knew it, she was pulling up to the teahouse. Her nervous rush of energy immediately transformed into something else. She couldn't believe her eyes. She couldn't believe the timing. Pete was standing outside with Clyde. Just as the cab stopped, Pete, looking hotter than ever, touched Clyde's face and leaned in to kiss her. Prilly was trembling. She heard a buzzing in her ear and she thought she might pass out.

"Drive! Drive!" she yelled at the cab driver.

The driver had already stopped the car, so he turned around and asked, "What? This isn't where you want to go?"

"Please just go. Take me back to my apartment. I'm sorry but I forgot something. I need to go back," she said in a panic.

"You got it."

As they pulled away, Prilly couldn't help but turn around and look through the rear windshield. Pete and Clyde were just standing there, and she wasn't sure whether they had seen her. They drove over a pothole and she gagged, choking back vomit.

All she could think about on the ride back was what a loser she was. She desperately hoped that he hadn't seen her. Even though she figured he must have known how pathetic she was, she didn't want to publicly confirm it, not again. Not in front of Clyde. After paying the outrageous taxi fare as well as a huge tip because she was too embarrassed to ask for change, she entered her apartment and walked straight to the bathroom. She stared at her reflection in the bathroom mirror. She wanted to remember how ugly this particular shade of desperation was. She wanted to hate herself. She spent the rest of the weekend following her usual routine of watching home shopping and sleeping. She didn't cry. She just tried to completely tune out.

Prilly picked herself up Monday for work. She and Janice were making a lot of progress on the memoir series. That Thursday night as Prilly was sitting on the couch and eating the last egg roll from her takeout, her phone rang. It was startling because her phone never rang. She muted the TV and sat, listening. It was Pete. She listened to him leave a message in his sexiest, hushed voice. "Hey there, you ... I've been thinking about you. I miss you. Give me a call. Bye."

Although there was an initial jolt of excitement that he called, it immediately morphed into mortification as she assumed he must have seen her that day in the cab. *Why else would he be calling now, after all this time?* She promised herself that she wouldn't call him, and despite every urge to the contrary, she didn't. It was torture.

As the days and eventually weeks passed, Prilly, still fighting the craving to call him, started to feel like she could expand the bounds of what was possible beyond Chinese takeout and home shopping. She began to incorporate some grocery shopping, cooking, and movie rentals into her routine. One Friday night, standing in her local video store, she found herself perusing the foreign films. She looked at some of the movies Pete had told her she "positively must see" that he couldn't believe she had never seen. She rented a couple of them and bought a tub of butter-flavored microwave popcorn. That night, she made spaghetti with jarred marinara, opened a bottle of Cabernet, and popped one of the movies in. It was a French film about an aspiring novelist and his tempestuous lover. It was beautiful, inspiring, romantic, and utterly devastating. It was just the kind of film she would have watched with Pete. Halfway through both the film and the wine, she thought that the story was reminiscent of the life she had imagined living with him. And then, all of a sudden, the narrator interrupted her thoughts. He was describing how the male lead viewed his lover and he said, among other familiar things, that she possessed a "tinsel heart." In her wine-induced haze, Prilly nearly slid off the couch. She paused the movie and sat upright. She replayed the scene several times. "Tinsel heart. Tinsel heart. Tinsel heart." It suddenly occurred to her that it wasn't just that Clyde was beautiful and had been with Pete that hurt Prilly so deeply, it was the way he spoke of her. He had a knack for making beauty where there was none, just as he made doubt. And he made what was already beautiful sound even more so, like Clyde. She had never been able to escape the "tinsel heart" remark until now. Until she realized, *It wasn't his original thought. It was a line he lifted from a movie.* Suddenly she couldn't stop wondering which other ideas he had espoused that weren't his own. That weekend, she watched the other films and Googled the many authors, artists, and books he had urgently recommended. Soon she realized that most of his ideas were derivative of someone else's, including his supposed insights about the artists they had seen, like Fairey and Modigliani. There was very little he'd ever said about art or philosophy that developed in his own mind. Even his ideas about love and relationships and being "in the moment" were rip-offs from one of his favorite authors, whom Prilly had never bothered to read before. Sunday night she watched the "tinsel heart" scene one more time and vowed never again. It was freeing. She felt stronger than she ever had before.

***

February was a very snowy month. The city was covered in white, then gray, then white again. The snow made Janice think of her childhood. By late February, she sat at her laptop at the end of her dining room table and would sometimes see a childhood memory in between her and the screen. They were usually happy memories at these moments, like sledding with her sister or making a pot of soup with her mother. But the memories always ended with either an awful image of her drunken father quieting their laughter or, more often, the memory of how badly she had always missed him in those happy moments. She wished he would have taken her sledding, even once. She shuddered at those thoughts and tried to avoid the distraction of nostalgia. This year the never-ending snow somehow made it difficult.

One brutally cold, dark night in early March, Kyle was making a cup of hot chocolate in the kitchen. Janice walked in to get some grapes to snack on, and he offered to make her a cup too. Usually, she would say "no thanks," but on that blistery night she paused. "Sure, that'd be nice. Thanks."

She returned to the dining room, and a few minutes later Kyle walked in holding two white mugs filled with piping hot cocoa. "We didn't have any whipped cream or marshmallows or anything," he said as he handed her a mug.

"Oh that's all right, honey. This smells good. I haven't had hot cocoa in as long as I can remember."

As he was walking out of the room, Kyle asked, "Why don't you come into the living room with me and we can watch a movie or something?"

"Oh, well …" Janice started, but then the smell of hot cocoa wafted into her nostrils. "Well okay. I guess I could wrap up early tonight." They walked into the living room, each holding their mug, and sat on the couch together. Kyle found a showing of the old film noir *Double Indemnity* that had just started a few minutes earlier. They sat silently and watched the movie while sipping their cocoa.

When the movie was over, Janice ordered a large spinach and mushroom pizza with wheat crust. Kyle took a couple of slices up to his room when it arrived. He wanted to try to get in touch with Tash, whom he had not seen since New Year's. They had texted a few times, but he was growing worried. Most of his texts went unanswered, including all of the ones asking her to get together with him. Janice stayed in the living room, watched *The Postman Always Rings Twice*, and ate another slice of pizza. When the movie was over, she went back to her laptop. She saved and closed her work documents, went to Expedia, and booked an open-ended round trip ticket to Detroit.

PART THREE

CHAPTER 14

Kyle was cool and calm in almost any circumstance, but as he sat in the deli waiting for Tash, he felt something unfamiliar: nerves. He'd barely spoken to her in two months, and he practically stalked her via text messaging before pinning her down for brunch. After New Year's he knew she was in bad shape, but he didn't know how bad. He was afraid to find out. He was on his third cup of coffee by the time Tash finally arrived.

"Hey, sorry I'm late. Did you order?" she asked robotically as she slid into the booth opposite him. "There's jelly on this seat, gross," she continued, making a face as she attempted to wipe it off with napkins she quickly pulled from the dirty dispenser on their table.

Kyle scanned her quickly. She was wearing a long, thin, white sweater with black leggings, silver-studded black boots, and a black leather motorcycle jacket. She had several long silver strands around her neck and large silver hoop earrings. Her stick-straight hair looked messier than usual and she was wearing her signature bright pink lipstick. She looked thin, too thin, and when she removed her large black sunglasses, he noticed dark circles under her eyes.

"So … what's been going on with you?" Kyle asked.

"I need coffee. Where's the waitress?" Tash asked while looking over her shoulder. "I need some fucking coffee, like, pronto."

Kyle put his hand up to signal to their waitress. The white-haired woman turned to them and asked, "What'll ya have?" while looking at her pad, pen in hand, ready to scribble down the order.

"She'll have a coffee, and we'll share a large platter of blueberry cheese blintzes please," Kyle said while handing her both menus. "Thank you," he said as he looked back over to Tash, who was still obsessed with the jelly on her seat.

"So, what's been going on with you?" Kyle asked again. "I guess you've been really busy lately."

"What's that?" Tash asked, finally looking up. "Oh, yeah, I have been really busy. Sorry to be out of touch lately. I lost my phone for a week, so I was out of touch with like everyone. It eventually turned up at Jacob's behind a couch cushion and with a totally dead battery. I didn't have a charger there either. What's going on with you?"

"Not much, same old same old," Kyle said as the waitress came over with Tash's coffee and a plate of bagel chips and spread. "Thank you," he said looking up.

Tash immediately poured sugar and creamer into her coffee. "It's about time, you old fossil," she muttered as the waitress walked away.

Kyle grabbed a poppy seed bagel chip and dipped it in the cream cheese spread. "I missed these, they're so good," he said as he took a bite. Tash was already halfway done with her coffee and trying to signal the waitress for more. "Hey, have a bagel chip. I see some of those nasty cinnamon raisin ones you like," he said pointing at the plate.

"No, not in the mood," she replied. "I just desperately need some more coffee. It's so freaking cold too."

"Yeah, it's been one big blizzard since we saw each other last," Kyle said. "So, what have you been up to?"

"Oh, you know, same old. School, hanging with Jacob, doin' my thing. Lyric and I have been shopping in the Village a lot lately, you know, the vintage clothes stores. It's super fun. We go on the hunt for, like, a Marilynesque stole or something, and we look around until we can dig one up. I'm going shabby-chic!" she said with laughter. "She's dating Jacob's roommate now, did I tell you that? So we hang out there at the apartment all the time. Jeremy's kind of a jerk but whatever. He hates women. He only likes to do her up the butt! Can you believe that? She puts up with him because he buys her anything she wants and she thinks he's super hot. She's basically like his whore, but whatever. Anyway, what about you? Anything new? How's Sam?"

Kyle could barely put his thoughts together after Tash's barrage. He couldn't understand why Lyric would be into a guy like that, and why Tash would think these guys were cool. He tried not to dwell on the last part of what she said and refocused the conversation.

"Sam is going nuts. Remember that guy I told you his mom is seeing, the cruise guy?" Tash nodded and Kyle continued, "Well he's worried they're gonna get married."

"Does he hate the guy or something? Is he an asshole?" Tash asked before gulping down the last of her coffee.

"No, it's not like that. He's just some nice, nerdy guy. He's been really nice to Sam's mom and he's pretty cool to Sam too. I don't know what Sam's deal is. I think it's more bullshit than anything."

"Uh huh," Tash said, though clearly distracted. She was motioning to her empty coffee cup as the waitress walked by. "Well, it doesn't sound so bad. Maybe he just doesn't want to be crowded, you know? To have another person to deal with," she continued as her eyes widened at the sight of the waitress approaching with a pot of coffee.

"Yeah, maybe," Kyle said. "I'm sure he'll get over it. He's close to his mom; he wants her to be happy." Kyle paused, watching Tash fix her second cup of coffee. "Listen, Tash, I've been kinda worried about you."

Tash didn't look as if she had registered the comment. Kyle took a breath in preparation to continue when the waitress plopped the platter of blintzes and two small plates down in front of them.

"Those smell good," Kyle said, thankful for the respite. He grabbed a plate and spooned three blintzes onto it.

"Yeah, I'm not that hungry," Tash said.

"Oh no. You have to have the blintzes," Kyle replied, holding his fork up as if throwing down a battle call.

Tash giggled. "Well, if you put it that way, I'll nibble a little."

"That's better," Kyle said, smiling. He stabbed a blintz with his fork, put it on Tash's plate, and they both started eating. After a few bites, Kyle tried again. "I've been a little worried about you. You've been impossible to get a hold of and …"

Tash interrupted him. "Yeah, yeah I know. I've been busy and I told you about my phone."

"Yeah, it's not just that you've been tough to get in touch with. It's more than that. You've seemed different lately. Maybe it's since Jacob, I don't know. I'm just worried about you. Do you really think this guy is good for you? He seems a little sketchy."

Kyle knew if he said too much Tash might completely withdraw. In an effort to keep it light, he kept eating while talking, even putting a second blintz on Tash's plate even though she hadn't finished the first one yet.

"Well, I mean, he's not the forever guy, that's for sure, but he's really into me and I'm just gonna ride the wave. I like having his place to veg in for a few days at a time. It's cool. Don't worry so much. I'm fine."

Knowing that when a woman said she was "fine," the conversation ends or enters dangerous territory, he let it go. "Okay, I don't mean to pester you. Just checking in."

"It's okay," she said, smiling coyly to show she was the same old Tash he always knew. "I'm good, just partying a little, havin' a thiiing, you know. It's all good."

Kyle nodded.

"You're so sweet though. Little cousin always looking out for me. I promise I'll try to be better about checking in." She fetched a cinnamon raisin bagel chip and said, "I just can't resist."

Kyle smiled but the smile was a lie. Tash had all but confirmed what he was thinking: she wasn't doing well but she still had enough spunk to pretend that she was.

When Kyle got home, he headed straight upstairs to his room and took his phone out of his pocket before throwing his coat on the floor. He was about to sit on his bed when he noticed a folded piece of paper on his pillow. He opened it. Three twenty dollar bills fell out, and there was a note: "Kyle, have to go out of town for a couple days. Order yourself some takeout, Dad will be home late. Fresh fruit in the fridge. Don't let it go bad. I have my phone. Mom."

Kyle put the sixty dollars on his dresser, kicked off his sneakers, and collapsed in bed, leaning his pillows against the wall for support. He sent Sam a text.

```
Yo. Wanna come over 2night + get pizza,
my treat? Folks gone. Finally saw T.
```

A few seconds later Sam replied.

```
Sure. C u in 2 hrs.
```

CHAPTER 15

Prilly played Pete's message over and over again. She wanted to delete it but couldn't quite bring herself to. She figured as long as no one else knew, there was no harm in deriving the little pleasure she got from playing it, the pleasure she got from allowing herself to wonder, if only the littlest bit, if he really did miss her. She promised herself that, no matter what, she wouldn't humiliate herself by daring to call him back. So now, she had a new routine. She did her best to work efficiently while in the office, trying to keep up with Janice, whom she continued to grow fond of despite the fact that every nicety or bit of normalcy that Janice threw her way was tempered with cutting comments and stacks of busy work. Prilly spent long hours at work. When she got home at night, she changed into her at-home clothes, opened a bottle of wine, ordered takeout, listened to Pete's message, and then made her way into the living room for a night of home shopping.

One particularly *blah* evening as she cut into her steaming egg roll, the telephone rang. The noise was so startling that she flinched, immediately hoping it was him. She wouldn't call him, but if he called her again, she wasn't sure what she would do. She stood over the answering machine as her away message ended and the incoming message began. "Hey you," Pete said in his unmistakable voice before taking a deep, throaty breath. He slowly continued, "Just wanted to see what you were up to, girl. Came across something that made me think of you … I miss you. Well …"

Prilly couldn't help herself and picked up the phone. "Hey."

"Oh," he said with his characteristic little laugh. "You're there."

"Yeah, I didn't hear the phone but then I heard you talking into the machine," Prilly nervously replied.

"Oh, I see," he said, again with that characteristic chuckle. "Well, I was just thinking about you and so I thought I'd be spontaneous and give you a call. I'm glad you picked up. It's good to hear your voice," he said in his sexiest.

Prilly's heart raced. *What am I doing? Why did I pick up the phone and how will I ever hang up?* "Good to hear yours too," she said sheepishly.

"You want to hop in a cab and come over?" he asked.

"Um, I don't think that's such a good idea."

"But do you want to?" he pressed.

"I want to do what's good for me and ..."

Pete cut her off. "Hey, we *were* good. We were really good, and I think you know it."

"Why are you calling now? So much time has passed, and ... and I never heard from you after New Year's. You must have known how upset I was."

"That's not true, I did call you. I left you a message recently. Didn't you get it?"

"I'm not talking about that. I'm talking about New Year's. You didn't come after me, you didn't call ... nothing. So why now?" Prilly felt stupid letting him know how she had expected him to chase after her, but she couldn't hold it in.

"Well, I miss you I guess. Just thought of you. Do I need a reason?"

"Are you seeing anyone?" Prilly asked with trepidation.

"Oh, not this again. There you go, girl; I call to tell you I miss you, and you ask if I'm seeing anyone else." Prilly didn't say a word, waiting for Pete to fill the void. "Right now, I just want to see you," he finally said.

After a long silence, Prilly said, "I assume you're seeing someone else by now. Are you?"

"Well hell, I'm just trying to follow my heart. I miss you. We had the beginning of something special. Didn't you know that? I know you did. No, I haven't been sitting around all this time waiting for you, but, fuck, so what?"

"Look," Prilly said quietly, before taking a deep breath, "I can't do this again. I know you're seeing Clyde. I saw you with her and ..."

Pete jumped in. "Oh, jeez girl, here we go again. You've got to be kidding. Are you following me or something?"

"No, not at all," Prilly quickly chimed in, mortified and wishing she hadn't answered the phone. "I was just driving by and saw you two a while ago and ..."

"Look, sure I've slept with Clyde a few times. She's beautiful, and it is what it is, but I've slept with lots of people. So what? We don't own each other. You're the one I miss. Keep your eyes on the big picture."

"I am, and that's why I can't do this. I just can't. Please don't call me again," Prilly said, trembling as she hung up the phone.

She balanced against the wall for a minute, waiting to see if he would call back. He didn't. She returned to the living room couch and refilled her wine glass. About fifteen minutes later, she ate her lukewarm Chinese food. More than anything, she wished she could have jumped in a cab to be with Pete just for a night, but she couldn't bear the humiliation anymore. It was enough that she was privately humiliated; she couldn't let him or anyone else see it. And she could never look at him without picturing him making love with Clyde and looking into her eyes, beautiful Clyde, not before he knew Prilly, but after. That image was a shameful reminder of everything Prilly feared she never was and would never be, which she felt he had just confirmed. She wanted to keep it secret. Two days later, she deleted the only saved message. She continued with her daily routine of work, takeout, and television.

149

CHAPTER 16

Janice only had a few minutes at the gate before boarding her flight. While waiting in the pre-boarding line, she called her mother from her cell phone.

"Hello?" Myra answered.

"Hi, Mom, it's me."

"Jannie?" Myra asked quizzically.

"Yes, Mom."

"Oh, hi dear! I'm surprised to hear from you in the middle of the week," Myra said, sounding both happy and genuinely surprised.

"Well, I'm actually calling from the airport, Mom. I'm on my way to see you. I wanted to visit Dad."

"The airport? You're at the airport, oh my. Let me call Margie and see if she can pick you up. I know Scott must be working with his big job and all, but maybe Margie can come and get you. Or maybe …"

As Myra started to trail off, Janice interrupted. "No, Mom. I'm at La Guardia in New York. I have to go in a minute; they just started boarding my flight."

"Oh, well when do you get in? I'm sure I can have Margie or …"

Janice cut her off, "Mom, Mom, it's okay. I've already reserved a rental car."

"Oh, okay, honey. Well how long are you staying for? Are Richard and Kyle coming with you? I so would love to meet that grandson of mine. The pictures you sent are all on the fridge." Janice tried to interrupt but it was impossible when Myra was all worked up like this. "Shall I set up your room for you? I have some of your father's things stored in there but …"

"No, no, it's all right, Mom. I've booked a room at the Westin down the road from you. It's only me and I can only stay for a day or two."

"All right. Well come over for dinner tonight after you freshen up at your hotel. I'll make something special. Your dad will be so happy to see you. He's been feeling …"

"Mom, I have to go. I have to board my flight."

"Okay, honey, have a good trip. I'll call Marge and see if she and the kids can come …"

Myra was going to continue, but Janice forcefully said, "I have to go Mom. I'll see you in a few hours."

"Bye Jannie."

"Bye Mom."

***

Janice brought her work bag, overflowing with manuscripts, book proposals, and notes about the memoir series launch. She intended to keep as busy as possible. She worked through the entire flight, sipping on club soda and snacking on whole wheat pretzels. Twenty minutes before landing, a flight attendant announced that tray tables must be placed back in their upright and locked position and personal items must be stored. Janice quickly put her work away and stared out of the window for the remainder of the flight. It was the first time she stopped to think about what she was doing. Suddenly she felt afraid – afraid of the state her father would be in and afraid to face her mother since she hadn't been back to visit in all this time, especially since the accident. She was also afraid to see Marge. Even though they were close, Marge had been stuck with the lion's share of dealing with their parents, and Janice knew it. Since the accident, Marge mentioned this in ways she never had before. Janice thought about all of these things, and she remembered how she had vowed never to go back. Despite these thoughts, as the plane taxied down the runway, she leaned her head against the window, looking out and feeling glad to be there.

After a long wait at the car rental kiosk and a longer drive in rush-hour traffic, she arrived at her hotel. She checked in, unpacked her small suitcase, and transferred her wallet and keys from her work bag into her Prada handbag. Then she washed her hands, brushed her teeth and hair, and put on some fresh deodorant before heading out. Minutes later she was pulling into the driveway of her family home.

When she turned off the ignition, she paused for a moment. She sat quietly inside the warm car and surveyed the tiny yellow house. The paint was badly chipped. The walkway was cracking. Unable to delay any longer, she threw her keys into her bag, walked to the front door, held the screen door open, and pressed the rusty, old doorbell.

The front door swung open. "Oh, Jannie, I'm so happy to see you! Let me look at you. Let me look at you!" her mother exclaimed. Myra was standing in a white housedress with blue polka dots shouting, "Let me look at you" over and over again while grinning ear to ear.

"Hi Mom," Janice said softly, noticing how impossibly old her mother looked.

"Well come in honey, come in."

As Janice stepped into the doorway, she felt as if she were entering a lost world in slow motion. It was as if the house had shrunk; it was a miniature version precisely preserved from her memory, a memory she didn't even know she had. As her mother closed the door behind them, she just stood, looking around, and felt as if she had walked into a haunted dollhouse. It was so much smaller than she remembered. She looked to the left into the cramped living room. Nothing had changed – the couch and her father's old recliner looked ancient, the buttercup walls were as dirty as ever, as were the sheer white drapes. The only difference was that their tiny old TV and stand had been replaced with slightly larger versions. In this sad little world, time seemed to have stopped.

"Well, let me look at you," Myra said again, staring at Janice who was staring into the living room.

"Oh, sorry Mom, it's been so long since I've been here, it just …" and then Janice couldn't find the words.

Myra helped. "It must have taken you back."

"Yes, well, I'm fine," Janice said, trying to regroup.

Myra flung her arms open, "Well, give me a hug, honey."

Janice leaned in and hugged her. As she began to pull away, Myra held on and hugged her tighter. It was a long, strong, complete hug. Janice couldn't remember the last time anyone had hugged her like that, so she gave into it, for a moment.

"Well, give me your coat and then come into the kitchen, honey. Come see your father."

Janice took off her coat and followed Myra into the kitchen. It too was exactly as she remembered, only much smaller. The rectangular Formica table sat in the middle of the light blue kitchen, with a small bouquet of multi-colored flowers in the center. Janice's father sat at the far end of the table. "Hi there Jan," he said, looking up at her.

"Hi Pop," she said, while giving him the once over. "How are you?" She walked over and bent down to hug him, noticing the bodily waste bag connected to him, peeking out from under his dark blue robe. As he started to put his arms around her, she pulled back and instead turned to her mother who was standing over the sink, looking out of the tiny window and drying her hands with a dishrag. "Something smells good; what is that, Mom?" Janice asked.

"Oh, would you look at that Mrs. Jensen? She's so nosey. Any unfamiliar car in the driveway and she finds an excuse to walk out onto her porch and look over. Even when it's freezing!"

"Mom, something smells good," Janice repeated.

"Oh, it's just meatloaf, dear. I wanted to make something more special but with Margie and the kids not coming until tomorrow, I thought …"

Janice interjected. "Marge isn't coming?"

"Oh, she wanted to. She felt awful. It's just that Greg has some band practice he can't get out of. He has a recital coming up, you know. I invited her over tomorrow night. I'm making pot roast, your favorite," she said gleefully.

"Oh, well I'm not sure if I am heading home tomorrow or the next day," Janice said as she noticed all of Kyle's wallet-size school photos on their old olive-green refrigerator, along with some crayon drawings Marge's kids must have made.

"Well I hoped you would stay for at least two nights. We haven't seen you in so long, Jannie. You can stay, can't you?" Myra asked, now turning directly to her.

"Sure," Janice said, taking a seat at the table and hanging her handbag on the corner of her chair as if she were a guest in a stranger's house.

Myra noticed and said, "Let me take that for you and put it in the living room."

"That's all right Mom, I'm fine," Janice replied. Next to a little vase was a large bowl of green grapes, just as there had always been. Janice picked a few, popped one into her mouth, and said, "You know Mom, grapes keep much better if you store them in the fridge."

"I put them in the fridge every night and take them out during the day. If I left them in there, I'm worried we'd forget to eat them," Myra said as she removed a large meatloaf surrounded by roasted carrots from the oven. The room suddenly felt warm and was filled with aromas that Janice hadn't smelled in years. Myra put a slice of meatloaf on each of the three plates stacked beside her, along with one carrot and a scoop of mashed potatoes from the stained pot on the stove. She served Janice first.

"Oh thank you, Mom. This looks delicious."

After serving everyone, Myra retrieved a pitcher of iced tea from the refrigerator and a basket of crescent rolls from the counter and finally sat down opposite her husband.

"Well, we're so glad you're here, Jannie, aren't we?" Myra said, looking over to her husband.

"We sure are," Janice's father said, as he mustered up a half smile.

"It's a blessing, a real blessing. Thank you Lord for this bounty and bringing our Jannie home. Well, let's start eating," Myra said. "Jannie, can I pour you some iced tea?" Myra asked, lifting the pitcher.

"Yes, thank you," Janice said, raising her glass. "This really smells good. I haven't had meatloaf in as long as I can remember," she continued. "You still do the tomato sauce strip on top the same way," she said as she took her first bite.

"Why mess with a classic, I always say," her mother replied.

"It's very good Ma," Janice said with a full mouth.

After a few minutes of eating in silence, Myra said, "So, tell us about the big city. How are Richard and Kyle?"

"They're fine. Kyle is doing very well in school. He's a hard worker and he's very gifted. Richard is doing extremely well at work. He's very busy, we both are. Everything is fine," she said, taking another bite of buttery potatoes.

"Tell us about your work, Jannie. It sounds so exciting, making books," Myra said, smiling at her daughter.

"Well I don't exactly make the books, but ..."

"Oh," Myra said, embarrassed. "I meant ..."

"No, it's okay Ma, I know what you mean. It is exciting. It's very exciting actually. I've been given a lot of new responsibilities. It's very demanding but it's worth it. I'm publishing a new line of memoirs. The press has never done anything like this and the whole project was my idea, my work, everything. It's going to be a big hit. The series is scheduled to premiere soon, so I've really been under a lot of pressure."

"Oh, well, that sounds very impressive. My, isn't that impressive?" Myra said, beaming and looking from Janice to her husband.

"Yes, it sure is," Janice's father said.

Silence fell over the table again, and the three focused on their dinner. Finally, Myra asked, "So, I was surprised to get your phone call. We were so happy you were coming to visit. What made you decide to come so last minute?"

"Oh, I hope I didn't put you out," Janice began.

"No, no dear, not at all. We are very happy you came, very happy. I was just taken aback."

"Well, I've been working so hard on my memoir series and ... and there is a potential author in Detroit whom I've been having trouble signing, so I thought I would come and meet with him in person."

"Oh, I see," Myra said, a bit deflated.

"So it was a chance to see you and Dad, which I've been meaning to do." Janice regretted the lie that made it sound as if visiting them was just another item on her to-do list, but she couldn't backtrack.

"We're just glad you had time to come and see us. So you'll take care of your business tomorrow and then come over for a big family dinner. We can celebrate all of your wonderful accomplishments," Myra said.

"That sounds great Ma," Janice said, feeling uncomfortable.

When they finished eating, Myra cleared the dishes and put on a pot of decaffeinated coffee. "I made a pound cake."

"Thanks Mom, but I'm stuffed and I'm really tired. I think I should get back to my hotel," Janice said.

"Oh, won't you have just a little slice, honey? I made that lemon icing you like," Myra said, turning to Janice and holding a plate with a small iced loaf on it.

Janice felt terribly bloated already, but said, "Sure, I'll stay for a sliver. It looks great, Mom."

"Some decaf?" Myra asked, holding out the pot.

"Sure. Thank you."

Fifteen minutes later Janice got up and walked over to her father. She leaned in and gave him a little hug. "Night Pop. See you tomorrow."

She grabbed her bag and headed for the door, followed by her mother.

"Are you sure you don't want to bring a snack back to your hotel? I can fix you something real quick," Myra insisted.

"Thanks, but I'm okay Mom. Thank you for dinner. Everything was delicious."

"Oh, we're just so happy to see you, honey. We're so happy you came. Your father has been saying so ever since you called. It's the first time he's eaten at the kitchen table since, since you know. I usually have to bring his meals into the bedroom."

Janice smiled. "I'll see you tomorrow night. Around six, okay?" Janice asked as she leaned in for a hug.

"We'll see you at six. Come earlier if your work is finished. We'll be here, come any time," Myra hollered as Janice walked to her car.

***

After an early morning workout in the hotel gym followed by a day of work in her room, Janice arrived at her parents' house at exactly six o'clock. She rang the doorbell and her sister immediately opened the door. "Hey, Jan! Great to see you! Come on in."

Marge hugged Janice as she entered the house, but before they could say a word, Greg, Marge's ten-year-old ran into the room whizzing a little airplane through the air, quickly followed by his younger brother, Tim, who was chasing him. Distracted, Marge turned and yelled, "I told you two to stop running, this instant."

"Come in, take your coat off," Marge said, returning her attention to Janice, who was still standing in the doorway. "It's so good to see you. I can't believe you're here."

Janice walked in, shut the door, and hung her coat and handbag on the coat rack. "Something smells good," Janice said.

"Mom's going crazy in there – roast beef, gravy, peas, stuffing, and all the fixings. She probably hasn't stopped cooking all day," Marge said as she plopped down onto the couch.

"She didn't have to go to all that trouble," Janice said.

"Don't be silly, you know Mom lives for this sort of thing," Marge replied.

Myra came into the living room carrying two glasses of iced tea. She placed them on the coffee table and gave Janice a big hug. "Hi honey, I'm just finishing up in the kitchen, so why don't you and your sister catch up. I bought that fancy port wine cheddar cheese spread you used to like. It's right there with some Ritz crackers," Myra said, pointing to a small plate on the coffee table.

"Thanks Mom, that looks great," Janice said. "Can I help you with dinner?"

"Oh no dear, just sit and catch up with Marge and dinner will be ready soon," Myra said as she walked back into the kitchen.

Janice sat beside her sister on the small couch. "The kids have grown so much. They look great. You look great," she nervously said, picking up her iced tea.

"You look great too. So skinny. You must be on one of those New York celebrity diets, right? What is it – the zone, the ozone, the …" Marge burst into laughter before she could finish her sentence.

"Well, I just try to eat healthy," Janice said, slightly defensively.

"Relax, I'm jealous," Marge quipped back.

"Where's Scott?"

"He felt terrible but he couldn't make it. He put in a bid for a big job downtown and got the contract. They broke ground a few days ago and he's been working late ever since. Honestly," Marge said, leaning in and lowering her voice, "as much as he wanted to see you, I think he's had enough of Mom and Dad. He's been here a lot helping out over the past few months, and I think he needs a break. This new job was the perfect excuse."

Janice understood.

Marge turned her attention to the cheese plate in front of them. "You know you're the only one that has ever gotten Mom to buy this cheese. And I love this stuff!" she proclaimed as she made a little cheese sandwich in between two crackers.

Janice smiled awkwardly and took a cracker with some cheese spread, which she thought looked vile. "Well it sounds like Scott is doing really well. That's great. I hope he gets paid for working late." Janice bit into her cracker, the taste of neighborhood Christmas parties coming back as the cheese oozed between her teeth.

"So, Jan," Marge said, leaning in and lowering her voice again. "What the hell brings you here?"

"Oh, well …" but as Janice tried to conjure an answer, Marge's kids barged in, complaining that they were hungry.

"Well take a couple of crackers," Marge said, "but don't get crumbs everywhere. Grandma won't like that." The kids walked into the kitchen with their crackers, so Marge turned intently back to Janice. "Sorry, what were you saying?"

"Oh, well …"

"Mom said something about an author you had to meet with?" Marge inquired. "She even told me I couldn't call you today and bother you while you were working."

"Yes, that's right. I'm editing a new line of books, a big line actually. I needed to meet with a potential author in Detroit, so I thought I could stop by and see everyone," Janice said. She popped the rest of her cracker into her mouth.

"Jan, come on, it's me," Marge whispered. "Give it up. What's going on? You haven't come in all this time and now …"

They were again interrupted, this time by Myra who came in and proclaimed, "Dinner is ready. The boys are hungry. I think you two should come in."

Marge shot Janice a look that said, "I'll get you later," as they both stood up and walked into the kitchen with their iced tea glasses. The table was overcrowded with platters of food. It looked like Thanksgiving or Christmas. The boys were already sitting on one side of the table. Myra told Marge to sit across from her boys and that Janice should take the end seat.

But where's Dad going to sit?" Janice asked.

"Oh, honey, your father isn't feeling well. Today's a bad day. He just can't make it to the table so I fixed him a tray. He feels terrible with you being here and all, but you can go and say hi after dinner," Myra explained as she sat down, setting down a bowl of peas to complete the feast.

"Well, everyone – let's eat!"

***

After dinner, Myra cleared the dishes. The boys asked if they could go and play, to which Marge said, "Just be good; don't make a mess." She then asked, "Mom, can I help you with the dishes?"

Janice chimed in. "Oh, can I help you Mom?"

"No, no, girls. I'm just going to get a pot of coffee going over here. You girls can bring dessert to your father. I know he really wanted to visit with you, Jannie."

"Oh, you don't need to go to the trouble, Mom. I'm stuffed," Janice said.

"It's no trouble. I made one of your favorites, apple cobbler. I would have made peach but you know they aren't in season yet. You can just have a little, dear. Besides, I know your father really wants to see you. He can't resist my cobbler, even at his crankiest." Myra removed the Saran wrap from the big casserole dish on the counter. As she peeled away the plastic, swirls of cinnamon filled the room. Janice suddenly remembered long days spent playing outside with Marge in their secret fortress. They returned to the house, dripping with dirt, to the smell of freshly baked cobbler just out of the oven. Before she knew it, Myra was handing Janice a dessert bowl with cobbler and a scoop of vanilla ice cream melting on top. "That's for your father. You and Margie can bring it to him and have a little visit. When you're done, the decaf will be ready and you can come in for dessert. I made gingersnap cookies for the boys, and I thought you might want to bring a few home for Kyle, Jannie. Oh Margie, there's plenty for Scott too. I'll make him a care package so he can have a nice hot dinner when he gets home."

"Thanks Mom," Marge said.

Janice didn't move from her seat at the table, holding her father's dessert. "Here you go, dear," Myra said, handing her a napkin and spoon. "Everything will be ready in about ten minutes."

Janice and Marge walked to their parents' bedroom. Marge knocked on the door. They heard grumbling on the other side that sounded like "come in." As Janice followed Marge into the small room that had seemed so much bigger as a child, she stared at the old, embattled man lying in his bed who also seemed so much bigger when she was a child. Two small, dim lamps on each nightstand provided the only light in the bleak room. Their father was sitting up in bed, propped against several pillows. Marge took the only chair in the room, in a corner near a small window. Janice handed her father his dessert, looked over at Marge, and then sat on the edge of the bed.

"Thank you, but I'm not hungry," he mumbled.

Janice reached out to the take bowl back, but Marge chimed in. "Just eat the cobbler, Dad. Mom made it special. Just try it."

He nodded.

"So Dad, how are you feeling?" Marge asked, sounding annoyed. Janice thought about how Marge always sounded annoyed on the phone when talking about her father, and apparently, even when talking to him. Things hadn't improved between them despite his ailments. She couldn't hide her resentment over the fact that he was still taking up space in her life.

"I'm okay," he said, fidgeting and trying to get comfortable enough to eat. "How are the boys? How is Scott's new job going?" he asked before taking a bite of his cobbler.

"Everyone's fine, Dad," Marge replied. "So, what about Janice? She came all this way."

"Yes. I'm just so glad you came Jan," he said, looking at Janice and trying to smile.

"I'm sorry you aren't feeling well Pop," Janice said.

He took another bite of the cobbler and said, "This is really good. Aren't you two having any?"

"We'll join Mom in a bit. We wanted to see you first," Janice replied. "It smells good. I haven't had cobbler since I lived here," she said, smiling at her father.

"Yeah, well I can see why you wouldn't want the tastes of home," Marge said sarcastically.

"I remember how much you and I liked Mom's peach cobbler in the summer; do you remember that, Dad?" Janice asked, trying to focus only on her father.

"He doesn't remember anything," Marge said.

Janice's father smiled half-heartedly at Janice and looked over at Marge, as if to plead for sympathy.

"You know what I remember?" he said.

"What, Pop? What do you remember?" Janice asked softly.

"That summer we went to the big fair in Ann Arbor. Do you remember that? This cobbler smells a lot like something they had there. Do you remember?"

"I think it was those apple donuts," Janice said. "Do you remember those donuts, Marge?" she asked. "We bought a bag and ate them the whole drive home."

Marge shook her head.

"Yes, that's what it was, the donuts," their father said with another small smile.

"That was such a fun day, one of the best I remember," Janice said with a sigh.

"You must not remember it then. Don't you remember all the beer Dad drank and him fighting with Mom about driving home? On the walk to the car, he jumped and slammed his hand into that big sign, that big, green, metal freeway sign. Don't you remember? There was blood everywhere, and he was screaming," Marge said angrily.

Silence hung like a shroud. After a couple of moments passed, Janice said, "I remember having fun that day. It was the prettiest place I had ever seen. We had all of those tickets, those tickets for the rides, and there was that rollercoaster. I had never been on anything like that before. And I remember you got us lots of treats that day," Janice said.

"Yes, that's right. I think you had cotton candy, and Marge, Marge you had an ice cream cone, right?" their father asked.

"I had a waffle ice cream sandwich," Marge said.

"That's right. Chocolate," he said.

"No Dad, it was strawberry," Marge said. She stormed out of the room, forcefully shutting the door behind her.

Janice looked lovingly at her father. "Your cotton candy, it was pink right, bright pink?" he asked.

"Yes, Pop."

"Jannie, I don't blame you for not visiting. I know that …"

Janice spared him from finishing his sentence. "I've been so busy, really, you can't imagine what it's like in New York. I just couldn't get away …"

"Jannie, it's okay. I understand."

"Pop, when you had your accident I wanted to …"

This time, he took her hand and looked her squarely in the eye. "Jannie, it wasn't an accident. It wasn't an accident."

Janice sat perfectly still, her hand resting limply in his. "What do you mean, Pop? Were you …" but she couldn't find the words.

"No. I wasn't drinking, Jannie. I know you have no reason to believe this but I've been sober for a few years now. Your mother finally threatened to leave me, and she meant it. She packed a bag and went to stay with one of those ladies from the church. And, well, I couldn't do it without her. It was a battle but I've been sober." He paused again. "I wasn't drinking that day."

He looked down and Janice moved her hand to really embrace his. "What do you mean Pop, that it wasn't an accident?"

"It's been real hard Jannie, real hard. I don't remember much, but I know what I am and I know what I've done to all of you. Your mother's been telling me for years how awful I was. When I think about …" He shuddered and seemed to be trying to gather his strength.

"She was a young, beautiful woman when I met her, and now she's almost done, she's almost done, and she's been stuck with me and my problem."

Janice could hardly believe what she was hearing. "What do you mean it wasn't an accident, Pop?" she asked again.

"I know what I am, and I couldn't take it no more. I thought I would release your mother, release all of you. That maybe you'd visit her, and your sister wouldn't be so angry anymore. Wastin' her life with that damn anger, like a cancer. I just didn't see what was left at this end. That's why, Jannie. That's why I did it. That's why I walked across that way like that. That's why. And now look at me. Look at your mother. I couldn't even do this right." He paused. "I never told your mother. She never asked."

Janice sat still and quiet with tears streaming down her face. They didn't say anything else. A few minutes later, she gave him a long hug and left him alone. She solemnly joined Marge and her mother in the kitchen. She sat in silence eating cobbler and drinking decaf while they spoke about some shopping trip they were planning for the weekend.

When Janice left the house, she hugged her mother as completely as her mother had hugged her. Although she didn't say a word, Myra felt grateful.

When Janice arrived home the next afternoon, Kyle was sitting in the living room watching TV. She pulled a Ziploc bag of gingersnap cookies from her bag and handed them to him. "I'm tired. I'm going to shower and maybe take a rest," she said.

"Okay, Mom. Thanks for the cookies," Kyle said, confused. He was preoccupied. He had a terrible feeling that something bad was going to happen, and he wished that Tash would respond to his many text messages.

CHAPTER 17

Jeremy Bransfield spent most days sleeping late, playing video games, smoking pot with his roommate, Jacob, and sleeping with his girlfriend, Lyric (or whatever girl he could get up to his apartment). Although ragged and unkempt, he was naturally good looking and tall, with great bone structure and intense, dark eyes. He looked even better when compared to his roommate. Women perceived Jacob as the grimy little pot guy and Jeremy as his hot roommate. But for all his foolishness, Jacob was, at his core, a decent person who meant no harm. Jeremy, on the other hand, was smart, slick, and far more dangerous than Jacob was capable of realizing.

Jacob met Jeremy when he came into the used record store looking for an obscure reggae artist. It wasn't long before Jeremy offered Jacob a "business opportunity" to deal dope out of the backroom of the store. With declining sales, Jacob had been worried about losing his job. He also liked the idea of access to free pot, so he quickly agreed. A bumpkin in many ways, Jacob didn't realize that the deal was Jeremy's true motive for coming into the store that day. Jacob later gave Jeremy a reggae CD as a gift. Thinking he was quite clever, Jacob eventually started putting some of his cut of the drug profits into the cash register at the store, to prevent the store from going under. Despite his profits from the illicit sales, he wanted to keep his job. It made him feel like a good guy, a clever guy. Jeremy just wanted to keep the location available for his shady dealings. The two became fast friends. Soon, the small pot business transformed into a full-fledged pharmacy of pills and powders that Jacob chose not to think too much about. It didn't take long for the two to become roommates. Jeremy thought this would make Jacob easier to monitor.

Every Tuesday morning, Jeremy's alarm clock rang at seven. He showered and was out of the apartment by eight, listening to headphones and carrying an old, gray backpack. He spent the day traveling by trains and buses. First, he stopped and picked up bialys and cream cheese from a local bakery that boasted the best bialys in Brooklyn. Then he visited his grandmother in a nursing home in Queens. When he arrived, she was always sitting in her room at the doily-covered table by the window. She wore a dress every Tuesday and was always waiting for his arrival. She asked a staff member to bring them some tea, and Jeremy fixed a bialy and cream cheese for each of them. They usually played cards or checkers. He stayed for exactly one hour, an hour that his grandmother looked forward to all week. He was her only visitor.

Three times a month, this visit was followed by a series of errands or other meaningless activities. But on the fourth Tuesday, he made his way to a tenement in the South Bronx. There, he emptied his backpack filled with money and refilled it with pills and powders. It was a long trip for a fast exchange. On his way back to the subway, he stopped at a small Puerto Rican takeout restaurant. He bought a large garlic chicken plate, a large order of rice and beans, and a large container of coconut drink. With his backpack on his shoulders and bag of food in his hand, he made the long trip back to Brooklyn to chow down with Jacob. Melville always smelled the garlic from his room. The next morning, Jacob took the backpack to the store, unpacked, and opened for business. This routine went off without a hitch until one cold Wednesday morning in March.

Tash had spent the night at Jacob's apartment. Although it seemed like she lived there, she normally went back to her dorm on Mondays and didn't return until Thursday night so she could attend her Tuesday and Thursday classes. This week, however, was Spring Break, and Tash wanted to spend it stoned at Jacob's. She wanted Lyric to stay too, but Lyric was growing tired of the endless cycle of getting high and coming down. She began to feel that the apartment was like a vortex that slowly sucked time before anyone could notice. Lyric was almost done with "up-the-ass Jeremy," as she had come to think of him, and used the school break as an excuse to get out of town with some of her friends. She was ready to sport a string bikini, guzzle margaritas, and go down on a random jock like the good old days. She wanted Tash to join her but Tash was living in another world.

Tash was usually able to pull it together enough to go through the motions of attending class, but she had become more of a squatter than a college student. And so, this was the first Wednesday morning that Tash found herself in Jacob's apartment. Jacob got up and ready for work as usual, trying not to wake her. As he was zipping up Jeremy's backpack, Tash rolled over and sleepily said, "Hey. What's going on?"

"I gotta go to work, you know that, babe. Go back to sleep. You can just crash here today, and we'll hang when I get back."

Tash was groggy but she rubbed her eyes and tried to focus on what was happening. It occurred to her that with Jacob at work, she would be stuck in the apartment all day with Jeremy.

"Wait! Wait for me. I'll come with you," she said, sitting up and stretching her arms toward the ceiling.

"Babe, that's sweet but I gotta go and you'll take forever. Besides, you'll be bored out of your mind," Jacob retorted while putting his jacket on.

Tash leapt from the bed, revealing a hot pink tank top and white cotton underwear. "I'll be ready super fast. I can hang with you in the store, and if it gets boring, I can bum around the Village. Besides, I need to stop by my dorm at some point to pick up a few things. Just hold up for a couple minutes."

Jacob didn't think Jeremy would be happy if Tash tagged along that day. He had been pissed when he had to share the takeout with her the night before, but looking at her and how sexy she was, he found it hard to say no and figured it wasn't a big deal. "You gotta hurry, I can't be late."

"No problem. Give me five minutes," she said as she pulled her jeans on.

Thirty minutes later, they were on the train with two coffees purchased from a street vendor. Despite rush hour, they managed to snag two seats when some yuppies got off. Tash leaned on Jacob's shoulder the whole ride. Sometimes she started to drift off, but a bump or announcement from the conductor always jarred her awake. Just before they arrived at their stop, Tash nodded off again, lost her grip on her coffee cup, and spilled it in Jacob's lap. He jumped up, screaming, "Oh shit!" Tash hopped up and tried to help. She found an old tissue in her pocket and manically wiped his pants, bumping into the other passengers as the train screeched into the station. She grabbed Jacob's coffee cup as they hurriedly tried to make their way off the bustling train. In all the commotion, Jacob left the backpack on his seat. He realized what he had done as soon as he was standing on the platform, watching the train go by. It happened so quickly. He could only stand there, with his heart racing.

"Holy shit, holy shit," he screamed. He threw his arms up in the air and then rested his hands on his head in disbelief.

Totally unaware, Tash asked, "What's wrong? Why are you freaking out?"

"The bag, the bag," he said, breathing heavily.

"You left your bag on the train?" Tash asked, rolling her eyes as if this was somehow an inconvenience for her. "Well, let's go find someone who works here and ask what you can do. They can probably call the driver or something, or maybe there's a lost and found or something."

Jacob just stood, staring down the dark tunnel that unfurled before him. It was crowded and loud, but he felt utterly alone. Everything was happening in slow motion. He could barely make out the words Tash was saying.

"Jacob, don't worry about it. I'm sure we'll get the bag back," Tash said, tapping his back. "Chill out."

"I'm dead. I'm so dead," he muttered.

"Come on, let's get out of here," Tash said.

"I gotta get to the store and call Jeremy."

"Why? Don't you think you should talk to someone here?" she asked. "Maybe they can get your bag."

"Come on, I gotta go and call Jeremy."

"Well, you can use my cell," she said, as she dug through her pocketbook.

"No, I'll call from the store. Let's get out of here. I'll explain on the way."

***

Jacob sat solemnly in the backroom of the store with the door closed. He was trembling when he picked up the phone to call Jeremy.

"Dude, it's me. Something happened," he said as soon as Jeremy answered.

"What is it?" Jeremy asked.

"I left the backpack on the train. It's gone. The bag is gone."

"What the fuck? You left the fucking bag on the train?" Jeremy shouted. "How the fuck could you do something so stupid?" he continued.

"It was an accident. Tash spilled coffee on me and I was distracted and it just happened," Jacob said desperately.

"Tash? What the fuck was she doing there? Does she know what's in the bag?" Jeremy furiously demanded.

"No, no. She was just coming to hang out with me. She doesn't know anything," Jacob said, but Jeremy suspected he was lying. "She told me to call the train station and see if they found the bag. Do you think I should do that? Maybe we can get it back," Jacob said.

"Yeah, that sounds fucking great. Call and ask for the backpack filled with drugs. Have you lost your fucking mind?" Jeremy bellowed.

"Well I just thought maybe they wouldn't have opened it," Jacob said. "You know, like a privacy thing."

"Are you fucking kidding me? You gonna take that chance? Ten to one someone reported a backpack on the train, and the goddamn bomb squad is down there."

"What do we do, man?" Jacob pleaded.

"Let me think. Just let me think for a minute." The only sound Jacob heard was his own labored breathing. Finally, Jeremy said, "Look, we have a few weeks. We have a few weeks to figure it out. Let's not do anything. Just work at the store today, and we can figure it out later."

"Okay, okay," Jacob agreed, still trembling.

"And don't fucking bring that bitch back with you, got it?" Jeremy said sternly.

"Yeah," Jacob said. They hung up and Jacob sat in silence, trying to will the room to stop spinning.

***

Jacob persuaded Tash to spend the night at her place, but it wasn't easy and she was pissed. He spent the day running through different scenarios of how this would all play out. He was able to convince himself that it would be all right. Everyone was entitled to a freebie, and this was theirs. It would be okay. That night when he got back to his apartment, Jeremy wasn't there. He waited in the living room for hours. Then, finally ready to go to bed, he walked past Jeremy's bedroom and had a frightening flash. He opened the door, and to his horror, the room was empty. It had been entirely cleared out. He opened the closet and every drawer, but there was no sign of Jeremy, no sign that he had ever been there. He just stood there wondering what he had done, what he had gotten himself into, and what he should do now.

Jacob spent the next three days getting stoned. At one point, he bumped into Melville in the kitchen. Melville asked why he wasn't at work and Jacob told him, "It's none of your fucking business." Tash was texting and calling incessantly, but he didn't respond to her either. He kept thinking that he had a month to figure it out. He just needed to stay put and think.

Then one day, he received a phone call on the landline. It went straight to the machine and he heard Jeremy's voice say, "Pick up the phone."

He flew off the couch and stumbled to the phone. "Hello? Hello? Dude, Jeremy, is that you?"

"Listen, you gotta get out of there."

"What do you mean? Where are you dude? Why'd you take off?" Jacob pleaded.

"Listen, you gotta get out of there."

"But we have four weeks, we have four weeks to figure this out," Jacob said.

"They watch the store. They know you haven't been there. They know there was no delivery. I don't know when they'll come looking, but it'll be soon. You gotta get out of there."

"But ... but we can explain. Can't we explain what happened and ask for a break or something? We can, like, pay it back or something, right?" Jacob asked frantically.

"You gotta get out of there," Jeremy said one last time before hanging up.

Jacob was motionless, holding the dead phone line with ringing in his ears. He could feel his blood coursing through his body but his mind was stuck. He was completely frozen. He hung up the phone, walked over to the couch, and searched for his cell. He sent Tash a text message.

```
Need 2 c u pronto. On my way.
```

He didn't wait for a reply before he grabbed a duffle bag and threw some random clothes and CDs in. He took an envelope of cash he had stashed under his mattress and left.

***

When Jacob arrived at Tash's dorm, he was in such a full-fledged panic that he could barely stop shaking. The desperation and terror in his eyes was the only reason Tash opened the door and let him in. She had planned to leave him out in the hallway begging to come in, only to be rejected. She spent the last few days livid at him, in such a bad way that she had not showered, left the dorm, or eaten anything more substantial than chips from the vending machine. She was strung out and pissed off at her boyfriend – a bad combination. But despite her mental state and her usually reliable preoccupation with herself, she took one look at Jacob, grabbed his hand, and pulled him into her room.

"What the hell is going on?" she asked while hugging him.

He pulled away and sat on her bed. "Where's your roommate?" he asked as he pulled a packet of cigarettes out of his pocket and tried to light one with trembling hands. (It took three matches before he was able to light it.)

"She's away; she's away somewhere for Spring Break. I told you that. Everyone is fucking away. I've been stuck here like a loser," she said as she sat down on the bed opposite Jacob. "You can't smoke in here. The Gestapo will come in and, like, throw me out or something," she continued.

"I thought you said everyone was away," he said anxiously while exhaling a big cloud of smoke.

"Yeah but like there are sprinklers or some shit, and some RA prick. You just can't, you just can't smoke here," she said rubbing her eyes.

He took another deep drag and then dropped the burning cigarette into a nearby Diet Coke can. It made a sizzling sound as the cigarette hit the flat soda.

Tash sat down next to Jacob. He put his head on her shoulder and softly said, "I need to crash here for a while."

"Yeah, okay. My roommate is coming back soon, I think tomorrow or the next day. Jacob, what's going on?"

"Nothing, I just need to stay here and figure some stuff out."

"Tell me what's going on. You're really freaking me out," she fumed. "And I'm still mad at you for ditching me."

There was a long pause, and Jacob started to cry. Tash was taken aback. Despite the fact that she was clearly ill-equipped to help anyone, she tried. She rubbed his back and in a much milder tone said, "It's okay. Whatever it is, it's okay. Tell me what's going on." And so he did. He told her everything.

They spent the next twenty-four hours brainstorming. Tash thought that maybe it wouldn't be so bad if he just went back to his apartment and then back to work. He could act as though he didn't know anything about it. When he refuted that idea, she suggested that he could explain what happened and work something out with whomever the drugs belonged to. She offered to try to get some money from her parents. She promised him that she was good at coming up with reasons for them to send money. He didn't think he could possibly get enough. She wanted to call Kyle for help, she trusted him, but Jacob made her swear up and down that she wouldn't tell a soul. By the next night, he was convinced that he needed to get out of town. But as they were falling asleep in her small bed, she muttered, "What about your brother?"

Jacob hadn't even realized that he had left Melville in the apartment. "Shit," he said. "Shit, I forgot about him. I was so fucked when I was leaving."

"Call him, tell him he needs to get out of there," Tash whispered.

"He won't answer the phone," Jacob said.

"Doesn't he have a cell or email or something?" Tash asked.

"No, he doesn't have anything and I told him to never answer the apartment phone." He paused and thought for a moment. "I'll try, I'll try in the morning. I'll shout into the machine and maybe he'll pick up."

Tash and Jacob didn't wake up until two in the afternoon the next day. Groggy and out of it, it took Jacob nearly an hour to remember that he needed to call his brother. He called the apartment at least half a dozen times, screaming into the machine for Melville to pick up, but he never answered. Melville was in the city, hanging out with Pete at the teahouse.

"Shit," Jacob muttered to himself.

Tash came out of her bathroom in a white robe with a towel around her hair. "It feels good to be clean," she said before noticing how distressed Jacob looked. "What is it?" she asked.

"I can't get a hold of Melville. I called like a million times but he won't answer. I knew he wouldn't. Fuck! Fuck!" he screamed.

"Hey, don't worry about it," Tash said, walking over to comfort him. "I'm sure he'll be fine. He didn't do anything, and he doesn't know anything. Don't freak out about it."

"I can't just leave him there, Tash. I mean, I can't just fucking leave him there. I don't know what's gonna happen," Jacob said, holding his head in his hands.

"Well, what do you want to do?" she asked as she towel dried her long hair.

"I gotta go back to the apartment, just to tell him to get out of there," Jacob replied.

"Are you sure that's a good idea?" Tash asked.

"There's nothing else I can do. I'll go there and watch the building to make sure there's no one weird hanging around and I'll go in fast and tell him to get out."

Without hesitation Tash said, "I'll go with you."

"No, absolutely not."

"I'm going with you. I have a bunch of stuff in your apartment. Besides, no one's gonna do anything to a girl. I'd be a good lookout or distraction or whatever if you need it."

Jacob was too worked up to think clearly, so he just said, "Okay, okay you can come, but we've gotta be fast. We're not gonna spend time packing all your stuff."

"Fine, I'll just grab my things while you get your brother. We'll be in and out in five minutes," Tash assured him.

* * *

Melville met Pete at the teahouse at eleven o'clock that morning. They drank coffee and Melville listened to Pete go on and on about an exhibit at the MoMA that he "must see." They grabbed a quick bite for lunch at a local deli where, as usual, they squabbled over the bill. Melville wanted to pay only for his tuna sandwich, and Pete wanted to split the bill down the middle. Then Pete said that he had plans and had to leave, so Melville headed back to his apartment by train. When Melville finally got home, he opened the refrigerator and took out a small bottle of Orangina. He flipped the cap off and walked into his bedroom, shutting the door behind him. He put his Orangina on his desk, took off his coat, and slung it over the corner of his chair. He lay down on his couch with his head propped up against the pillow and opened a book he'd retrieved from his desk. He left his shoes on.

He had been reading for about twenty minutes when there was loud knocking on the apartment door. He ignored it, assuming that Jacob or Jeremy would get it. Soon, the knocking turned into banging. Melville dog-eared his page and put the book down on his desk. He knocked on Jacob's door, but when there was no answer, he was sure that Jacob had forgotten his keys and had locked himself out again. He opened the door, expecting his brother. Two large men in black leather jackets shoved him into the apartment. He stumbled backwards but quickly regained his footing. In shock, he just stood there as they closed the door behind them.

"Where is it?" they demanded. "Where the fuck is it?"

Melville shook his head, having no idea what was going on or what to say.

"Come on guy, don't play stupid. We want our loot, and we want the candy shop open for business."

Melville just stood there shaking his head, which enraged the two men. One said to the other, "Do you believe this guy, playing stupid?" He turned back to Melville. "We want the candy shop open, you got it?"

When Melville didn't respond, the two men walked slowly toward him, forcing him to walk backwards. He fell back onto the round kitchen table, leaning as far back as he could while the two men towered over him. They were going to give him one last warning before they left, but Melville didn't know what was happening or what to expect. He reached backward and grabbed the first thing he could feel, a small bottle top from his Orangina. He lunged forward to jam it in one of the guy's eyes, but failed. He tried to run away. Confused, he ran into his bedroom and attempted to lock the door, but the two men pushed their way in.

One grabbed him and screamed at the top of his lungs, "What the fuck was that? What the fuck is wrong with you?"

Melville tried to push back, which caused the man who was holding him to throw him. As Melville tumbled through the air and over his couch, he had one clear thought: it was finally getting warmer in his little room. He was relieved. As he concluded this thought, he smacked his head on the corner of his desk and fell to the floor, lifeless. Blood poured out of the side of his head.

"Oh fuck, Marv. We were just supposed to get the store back open for business. Now we gotta fucking deal with this mess."

"He fell, he just fell," Marv said, shocked. "Well, let's clean this up and get the hell out of here."

The two men searched the apartment for something they could put Melville's body in. With little to choose from, they took comforters from the two other bedrooms, wrapped Melville up, and headed out. On the way out, Marv said, "We should make this look like a break-in." They broke a couple of chairs, flung the kitchen cabinet doors open, and jimmied the lock to the front door.

An hour later, Jacob and Tash arrived at the apartment. Jacob panicked when he saw the apartment door ajar. He pushed the door open, telling Tash to stay back. He walked in slowly and Tash followed, closing the door behind her. The place was in disarray, but he had left in such a hurry and haze that he thought he might have made the mess himself.

"Mel?" he called softly.

"I'll go grab some stuff from your room," Tash said.

"Mel?" Jacob said a little louder. He knocked on the door to Melville's room, and then twisted the knob. He slowly opened the door, hoping to find his brother lying on his couch with his headphones on. "Oh my God," he screamed, seeing the blood all over the desk. He ran over and saw a small pool of blood on the floor too. "Oh my God, oh my God. What have I done? What have I done?" he repeated over and over again. Tash rushed in and Jacob fell to his knees. "Look! Look at this. Oh my God," Jacob continued, now crying and rocking back and forth on the ground.

"Oh shit, Jacob," Tash said in a panic. "We gotta go. We gotta get out of here."

Jacob was inconsolable, so Tash put her hands on his face and forced him to look at her. "We've got to get the fuck out of here. Now Jacob, now."

"But … but, maybe we should call the police or, or …" Jacob had no words.

"What? Are you going to tell them what you think happened?" Tash paused. "Jacob, we don't even know what did happen. Maybe it looks worse than it is. And there's nothing you can do for him now. We've got to get out of here."

Wiping the tears from his face, he nodded.

"I'm gonna get my stuff from your room, and I'll try to grab some of your things too. You can't come back here, not ever. Maybe you should see if there's anything else you really need," she said as she left the room.

Jacob stared at the blood and then decided to take some of Melville's things in case Tash was right; Melville was all right. He grabbed a small milk crate from under Melville's desk, flipped it over, and put some things in it. He chose a stack of notebooks, some loose papers, and a few CDs from the desk. Then he went into his room and threw a jacket with a bag of weed in one of the pockets on top of the crate. Tash was standing with some clothes flung over one of her arms and a small backpack overflowing with Jacob's things. They took what they had and left the apartment in silence.

***

On the train back, Jacob sat with the crate on his lap, unable to control his shaking. Tash tried to comfort him by rubbing his shoulder, but he barely noticed. As they approached the city, Tash asked, "What are you going to do?"

"I've got to get out of here. I'm going to call Mel's best friend, Pete, and see if I can leave Mel's stuff with him just in case Mel is okay and comes back. But I've got to get out of here."

"Do you want to stay with me for a while until you figure things out?" Tash asked.

He shook his head. "I've got to get out of New York for a while." Tash didn't respond, but the look on her face showed that she understood. "Do me a favor," Jacob said as he turned to face her. "Will you look through the papers in here and see if you can find one with a guy named Pete's phone number?" he asked, holding out the crate.

"Sure." She put the crate on her lap. A minute later, she handed Jacob a coffee shop napkin with Pete's name and phone number scribbled on it.

"Thanks," Jacob muttered as he stuffed the napkin in his pants pocket and took the crate back. "I'll get off with you. Then I'm going to call this guy from a payphone and see if he can take this stuff."

"If he can't, I can keep it for you. Maybe you'll come back and you'll want to go through it all," Tash said sweetly.

"Thanks babe, but I don't think you should have anything that belongs to me lying around right now."

She nodded.

The train reached their stop. They stood on the crowded street, and Jacob put the crate down to hug Tash. They squeezed each other tightly.

"Look me up when you come back," she whispered to him.

"Yeah, will do. Take care of yourself. Get your stuff together so you don't, so you don't end up like ..."

Tash interrupted, "Yeah, I know." Then she pulled away and gave him one last model pose, throwing her arms up in the air and exclaiming, "New adventures! Don't let the party end!" She blew him a kiss and sauntered off. He picked up the crate, struggling to keep his overloaded backpack from slipping off his shoulder.

CHAPTER 18

Two hours later, Pete met Jacob at a local diner. Pete didn't know what to make of the frantic phone call, but when Jacob insisted they meet to discuss Melville's safety, he agreed. By the time Pete arrived, Jacob had been sitting in a booth beside the milk crate, drinking black coffee loaded with sugar for nearly two hours. The only reason he hadn't been asked to leave was that the place wasn't crowded. Although the two had never met, they recognized each other immediately. Jacob waved Pete over.

"Hey man," he said as he sat down across from Jacob. "Fuck, I know I don't know what you normally look like, but you look like hell, man," Pete said with his characteristic near laugh and no-holds-barred attitude. "So what's this all about? What's wrong with Melville?" Pete asked as he raised his arm to signal the waitress and mouthed the word "coffee."

After taking a few deep breaths, Jacob began. He told Pete everything and begged him not to repeat a word of it. Quite uncharacteristically, Pete sat quietly and mostly just listened. Each time the waitress came to refill their coffee, Jacob stopped talking. Blown away, Pete could only say, "Wow, wow. That's a mindfuck. Poor Melville. I can't believe it."

"I'm getting out of town tonight. I have some of Mel's things here, and I thought I would leave them with you, you know, in case. If that's all right. I don't know what else to do."

"Well, sure, sure you can leave them with me but don't you think you'd be better off leaving it with your cousin? Melville's probably more likely to call him, don't you think?" Pete asked.

Jacob looked puzzled. "We don't have any cousins. What are you talking about?" he asked.

"Your cousin. You know. Melville was always coming into the city to see him. That's how he and I would usually hook up and hang out, after he had visited his cousin. Are you two like step brothers or something?" Pete asked jokingly.

Jacob shook his head. "Dude, I don't know what Mel told you, but we don't have any cousins. Our parents don't have siblings. We don't have any family in New York at all. You must have misheard him or something."

Pete didn't know what to make of it, but he agreed to take Melville's belongings and wished Jacob good luck.

***

Prilly was just getting home from work when she heard her phone ringing. She let the machine get it but stopped in her tracks at the sound of Pete's voice. She knew she had the willpower to resist the urge to pick up the phone. If she did it once, she could do it again. But when Pete said that something really awful had happened to Melville and that he needed to speak with her, she gave in and picked up the phone. He begged her to come to his apartment. When she refused, he told her he thought Melville was dead and that he needed her. "Please, please Prill, please come over." She agreed. She changed into tight, dark blue jeans and a flowing, gray baby-doll top, fixed her makeup, and took a cab to his apartment. She arrived an hour after he had called.

She was excited, nervous, and unsure of what she was doing. Her hands trembled as she rang the buzzer. As she approached his apartment, the scene of so many heartbreaking and exhilarating moments, he opened the door, gave her a closed-mouthed smile, and said, "Come on in," in his sexiest voice. She sat on the chair by his desk and watched him open a bottle of wine in the kitchen.

"I think I remember you liked Chianti, right?" he asked.

"Actually, I like Cabernet," Prilly said.

"Oh, that's right," he said blushing. "Well this is fabulous. You'll love it. I'm sure it's better than what you normally have."

"Pete, what's going on? I didn't come for a social call. You said Melville might be dead. Were you exaggerating? What are you talking about? What do you mean *might*?"

He handed her a glass and then sat on his bed and took a sip from his own glass. He then told her about the call from Melville's brother, everything Jacob told him, and how he has a box full of

Melville's things, just in case. Prilly couldn't believe it. It was too awful. She suddenly felt ashamed of how she had treated Melville; she had always suspected he had a little crush on her.

As Prilly tried to process all of this shocking information, Pete got up and went to the closet. He took out a crate, which he placed on the bed. "That's it. Those are his things. Not much really, poor guy."

"May I?" Prilly asked, indicating she wanted to look in the box.

"Be my guest," Pete said.

As Prilly flipped through the papers (notes about book titles, flyers to local events, some backdated unpaid bills), Pete said, "You know, the weirdest part is something Jacob said to me. He said Melville didn't have any cousins, but that's why he always told me he was in the city. I would bump into him at the teahouse, and he'd tell me he had come into the city to see his cousin. I don't get it," he said shaking his head and taking another sip of wine.

"He was coming to see you. He must have been coming to see you and he felt embarrassed or something to say so," Prilly instantly said, now flipping through his notebooks and remembering how she had once seen him writing in one.

"Wow, you think so? Jeez. What a mindfuck. That's kind of sweet but also really sad, don't you think?" Pete asked.

"I don't know, I guess so," Prilly said. "Have you looked through these? It looks like he was writing a book or something," she continued, holding up one of the notebooks.

Pete shook his head. "I can't imagine it's very good," he said with a laugh. "I know it's terrible to say now, but Melville didn't have an original thought in his life. That's probably why he was so fascinated with me."

"Uh, huh," Prilly said, captivated by what she was reading and wanting to tell Pete he was a jerk.

"Listen, Prilly," Pete said, trying to get her attention, "I've missed you. I've missed you a lot and I think …"

Prilly didn't let him finish. "Pete, please. Don't. I only came because you said something horrible happened to Melville. Don't read anything else into it. I can't go there again."

"Ah, but you wouldn't have come if you didn't still have feelings for me. You know it's true. So it's silly to be stubborn about it …"

"Pete, I'm going to go. You seem fine and I'm not going to do this with you. I'm not. I just can't." She got up and turned to leave. Then she paused and turned back to face Pete. "What are you going to do with those things?"

"I don't know. I guess I'll just stick them in the closet," he said, shrugging.

"Well if you're just going to do that, do you mind if I take the notebooks? I'd like to read what he wrote. I can send them back to you if you want."

"Sure, sure, you can take them," Pete said. "You'll be disappointed, my dear, but suit yourself. Keep 'em."

Prilly removed the notebooks from the crate and headed to the front door. Pete followed her and put his hand out, shutting the door before she could walk out. She turned around, pressed firmly between Pete and the door. He leaned in to kiss her, but she turned her head. He pulled back, rejected. "I really hope Melville turns up and that he's all right," she said. Then she walked out of the apartment.

During the cab ride home, she experienced a slew of emotions. She felt sad for Melville, vindicated that Pete still wanted her, and both pride and pain at having to walk away. More than ever, the things he said and the way he said them showed her that he wasn't capable of caring about anyone except for himself. She knew that would never work for her. He was so arrogant, and for once, looking around that dingy little apartment, she couldn't quite figure out why. That night, she lay on her couch reading Melville's notebooks, which were a mix of memoir and fantasy with some mindless ramblings interspersed throughout. But there was a story in it all. It was a story about a shy and lonely man who longed to be all that he wasn't. She found it quite beautiful.

***

The next morning, Janice was brewing her decaf when Kyle came into the kitchen to grab an energy drink. "You're up early," she said, surprised to see him.

"Yeah, I'm meeting a friend for breakfast before school."

"Oh," Janice said, as she poured a cup of coffee. "Well, don't be late for school."

"Don't worry. I have a study hall first period."

"Who are you meeting? Sam?" she asked before taking her first sip of coffee.

"No, just a friend who was having some problems. She's better now, I think, and I'm just checking up on her."

"That's nice honey," Janice said. "Kyle," she called, as he was halfway through the dining room.

"Yeah Mom?" he paused and asked.

"It's nice how you look out for your friends. It's very nice. My mother is like that. That's all … I just wanted to say that."

Kyle walked back to her and gave her a kiss on her forehead. He smiled and left, hollering, "Have a great day," before shutting the front door.

She enjoyed another sip of her coffee and then noticed her Blackberry was vibrating in her suit pocket. She took it out and scrolled to her new emails. There was one from Prilly that read: "Janice: On my way to pick up the posters. See you at the convention center. Prilly."

Janice slipped her Blackberry into her pocket, leaned against the kitchen counter, and finished her coffee while admiring the ivory molding that framed the kitchen doorway.

BLUE

PART ONE

CHAPTER 1

That can't be right, Tash thought, squinting again to look at the time. "Shit," she said as she reached for the alarm clock. "Damn thing never works," she mumbled while placing it back on her nightstand. *I'm gonna be late again. I should hurry.* She rolled over before slowly stretching her arms and lazily dragging herself out of bed. Stumbling to her dresser and opening the top drawer, she rifled around for underwear before heading to the bathroom.

Twenty minutes later, wrapped in a towel after showering, she used her palm to wipe the steam from the mirror. *I look like crap. God, I hope I can cover those bags under my eyes*, she thought as she started to apply her signature black liquid eyeliner. *I'll use gray eyeshadow and make them smoky.* Realizing it must be getting late, she dried and straightened her long, dirty-blonde hair but skipped curling the ends to save time. Returning to her bedroom, she scoured her closet wondering what to wear before deciding on an off-the-shoulder, loose white tunic, a pair of skinny black jeans, and high-heeled black leather booties. Staring at herself in the mirror, she tried on four pairs of earrings, posing left and then right to fully view each option, before deciding on gold hoops. To match, she threw on her favorite gold, turquoise, and red evil-eye bracelet. *Coffee. I need coffee.*

En route to the galley kitchen, Tash stomped past her roommates' closed bedroom doors, clomping her heels without concern as to whether they were asleep. She got a bag of coffee and the nearly empty carton of milk out of the refrigerator, placed them on the counter, and opened the cupboard to get a coffee filter and her to-go tumbler, neither of which were there. She found her tumbler in the sink, dirty from the day before. *Fuck.* Turning back to focus on the coffee pot, she spotted a note sitting beside it. *There's nothing I dread first thing in the freaking morning more than these notes.*

Morning, Tash. Hope you didn't forget to turn the volume up on your alarm again and oversleep. I didn't want to wake you in case you had the day off. We're out of coffee filters and it's your turn to go to the store. I left my list on the back of this note. I can't cover for you this time so please go. Thanks. Have a nice day. Penelope

Tash flipped over the note and rolled her eyes. She started to leave the kitchen when she turned back, remembering to put the milk away. *Don't want the Gestapo after me for that again,* she thought. She headed into the common room, sans coffee, and looked around. *Where did I leave my bag?* The small loveseat was overflowing with random clothing, topped with her black blazer. *Hmm. Two pairs of men's shoes under the coffee table. Jason must have met someone. Good for him, but where's my stupid bag? Ah, there you are,* spotting her black bag hiding in the corner, with her keys and sunglasses conveniently lying on top of it. She scooped them up, put her dark glasses on, and headed out, double locking the door behind her.

"Hi, Mr. Collier," she said, passing her neighbor on the stairs.

"Good morning, Miss," he replied.

Despite the morning rush, she was able to hail a cab quickly. As the cab passed Washington Square Park, she stared at the chess players, already at it for the day. Soon she drifted into thoughts of the drama the day before. *Ray was a jerk, Jason was so right. He didn't deserve me. I'm glad I ended it.* As they pulled up to Alice & Olivia, Tash rummaged through her bag for cash before giving up and surrendering her credit card to the driver.

She flew into the store, quickly heading to the backroom before Catherine could open her mouth. Tash threw her arm up and hollered, "I know, and I'm sorry. My alarm didn't go off and blah, blah, blah."

"You're half an hour late, again," Catherine called after her.

"I know, I know, and I'm sorry," Tash said, rolling her eyes. As she hung her bag and blazer on a coat hook, Catherine continued to reprimand her.

"You need to get a new alarm clock then, because I…"

"I'll close for you tonight, okay? You can leave early; it's fine."

"You know if you left on time you could walk here and save yourself the cab fare. You probably lose at least an hour's wages by creating a situation in which you need to take a cab. And is it even faster with the morning traffic?"

As Catherine continued, Tash muttered under her breath, "Get off my ass, you bitch," if only to make herself feel better. She took a deep breath and headed to the Keurig machine to make some much-needed coffee. She plugged it in and flipped the switch, but Catherine exclaimed, "Don't bother. It broke yesterday." Tash squeezed her eyes shut, shook her head, and took another deep breath before forcing a smile onto her face. "Great, that's just great."

***

"I'm going to head out now, since you're closing tonight."

"Uh huh, fine Catherine. Have a good night," Tash said while leaning on the store counter and checking her phone. She was exchanging texts with Jason, reminding him to get them on the club list that weekend.

"Make sure you change the shoes and handbags in the window display. Last season's accessories go on sale tomorrow, so the newer items should be featured in the window."

"Uh huh," Tash said, without looking up from her phone.

"Okay, well, goodnight."

"Night, Catherine."

An hour later, after ringing up the final customers, Tash retrieved the new handbags and shoes from the backroom. She liked working on window displays because it was a chance to be creative and put things together in unexpected ways that were sure to perplex Catherine. Tash imagined the windows as still images from film, designed to convey a feeling as much as to display clothes. While there was a limit to what she could get away with, she pushed the bounds as much as possible. She didn't mind her job and loved working in SoHo, but window displays and the employee discount were the only aspects from which she derived genuine pleasure.

Once Tash was done putting accessories from the window onto the sale table, she gathered her things and locked up. With only a blazer on, she felt a chill. These early spring days were unusually warm but the evenings were still cold. *I should really walk home. I can't blow more money on a cab.* Desperate for a scarf, she stood on Greene Street rummaging through her slouchy leather hobo bag, which she carried everywhere despite its tendency to become a black hole in which she couldn't find anything. "Ah, there we go," she whispered as she pulled out a periwinkle scarf, which she double wrapped around her neck.

As the sky darkened, the SoHo lights seemed to shine at their brightest. Store windows screamed with flashing light bulbs, a frenetic attempt to command notice. Tash looked in the windows as she passed by, tempted by sale signs even though she was accustomed to them. These days, even New York City itself was on sale. Street vendors yearning to end their days well tried to entice her with sunglasses and other trinkets. When she smiled and shook her head, one guy screamed, "You look like Lindsay Lohan. You're dope."

"I get that a lot," she said with a mischievous smile.

As she crossed over into the Village, the restaurants and corner cafés were already bustling with people clamoring to sit outside. After a brutal winter, New Yorkers were ready to enjoy outdoor dining again. Waiters turned on heat lamps and uncorked wine bottles amid casual conversation and bubbling laughter.

Her feet sore, she slowed her pace as she passed Washington Square Park. As day turned to night, the park was the center of the world around her. People from all walks of life appeared. The parade of artists, writers, students, homeless people, drug dealers, professors, tourists, and countless others made it the perfect microcosm of the city itself, the dream and its shadow side. She overheard a group of preppy college students talking about social justice as they passed Harold, actively trying not to notice as he set up his sleeping bag on a bench. *Jerks*, she thought. *They're such posers.*

A year earlier, Tash had twisted her ankle racing to work one morning. A barrage of f-bombs flew out of her mouth. Harold, a witness to the accident, helped her to a bench and told her not to curse.

"Are you for real?" she asked.

"It's undignified," he replied. "Do you think you can walk?"

"Uh, yeah, but not in these shoes."

They spoke for a few more minutes before she decided to stumble back to her apartment to ice her ankle and change shoes. Since that day, she'd say hi to Harold when she saw him and stopped to talk with him at least once every couple of weeks, usually bringing him a cup of coffee and sometimes a donut. Powdered sugar was his favorite.

He once started to tell his life story and she interrupted saying, "It's cool, Harold. We don't have to do this. I don't need you to explain." He seemed relieved. Since then, their conversations were usually about how they were each doing that particular day. Although routinely chased away by the police, he always returned. On this night, she just waved as she passed him.

Only half a block from her apartment, she had the horrible realization that she was supposed to get groceries. Not willing to endure a lecture from Penelope, she passed her apartment building and headed to the corner grocer. After grabbing a hand basket and making a beeline to the freezer for some ice cream, she started searching for Penelope's grocery list. As she fumbled for the list, mumbling, "Ah, where is that stupid thing?" she heard a voice say, "Maybe you'd have better luck if you shut your eyes and put your hand in."

"Huh?" she queried, looking up at the six-foot-tall guy standing before her, dressed from head to toe in black. He had bleached blonde spiky hair, high cheekbones, a strong jawline, and a piercing through his right eyebrow that she thought was simultaneously cool and disgusting.

"You know, sometimes if you're looking too hard, you can't find anything."

"Uh, yeah," she said, staring into his evergreen eyes. *Oh my God, he's seriously hot.*

"Here, tell me what you're looking for and I'll shut my eyes and stick my hand in for you."

Raising her eyebrows, she said, "How stupid do you think I am? Maybe I should just go outside and scream, 'Somebody rob me!'"

He laughed. "Fair enough, but you try it."

Tash smirked and stuck her hand into her bag without looking. "Uh huh, here it is!" she exclaimed as she pulled out the small, crumpled paper. "That's uncanny."

"Sometimes you just have to concentrate less, you know?" he said. "What's so important, anyway?"

"Oh, it's just my roommate's grocery list. She's pretty uptight so I can't screw it up. You wouldn't believe the things she writes, like 'two organic red apples and flax seed powder,' whatever the hell that is. Anyway, I should probably get back to shopping."

He smiled and waved his arm, to indicate she could pass by. With only a few aisles in the small store, Tash bumped into him again in the produce section.

"Should I even ask what that's about?" she said while giggling, looking at the twenty or more coconuts in his basket.

"Oh, these are for a party I'm deejaying for a couple of friends over at NYU."

"They're serving whole coconuts?" she asked, mystified.

He laughed. "People try to get them open. It's like a drinking game kind of thing. It's pretty funny."

"Gotcha. Do you go to NYU?"

"No, I went to school in Chicago and moved to New York after I graduated. I'm a professional deejay. I'm just doing this party as a favor."

"So, what kinds of clubs do you spin at?" she asked.

"Uh, well, tomorrow I'll be spinning at the Forever 21 store in Times Square."

She smiled. "Well, do you get a discount at least?"

He laughed. "Didn't think to ask for that. So, what's your name?"

"Natashya, but my friends call me Tash."

"I'm Aidan. Do you live around here?"

"Just a block away. I share a place with two roommates."

"Pretty awesome area to live in, good for you."

"Yeah, well we're in like the only non-restored building in the neighborhood. Don't get me wrong, I love living here and it's pretty close to my work, but we're not in one of the swanky buildings with a marble entrance. It's more like splintery wood floors and a scary old-fashioned elevator that makes me want to take the stairs."

He smiled. "What's your work?"

"I work at a couple of stores in SoHo."

"For the discount, right?" he said with a smirk.

Tash laughed. "Well, nice to meet you but I've gotta finish up and get going."

"Sure, me too. Maybe I'll see you around. If you're not busy, stop by Forever 21 tomorrow."

"I have to work."

"Well, can I maybe get your number?" he asked.

"Why don't you give me yours instead?"

"Sure, that's cool." He put his coconut-filled basket on the ground and held out his hand. "Give me your phone and I'll put it in."

"You don't want me to have to search my bag again. Here," she said, handing him the note with Penelope's grocery list. "Do you have a pen?"

Aidan smiled and pulled a red crayon out of his pocket. "Don't ask," he said as he wrote his number on the little paper. "Here," he said handing it to her. "See ya."

"See ya," she said.

When she casually glanced around the store a few minutes later, he was gone. She brought her basket to the checkout. The cashier asked, "Did you find everything you needed?"

"Yeah, yeah I did."

***

Her feet aching and her arms overloaded, Tash felt like she was going to drop by the time she made it home. She dumped her handbag and keys on the entryway floor and swung the shopping bags onto the kitchen counter. She opened her new box of popcorn and stuck a packet in the microwave before putting the rest of the groceries away. She giggled to herself, thinking about the coconuts filling Aidan's basket. *I wonder if Jason is home.*

Tash met Jason Woo at a club a few years earlier. She was having trouble getting past the bouncers when Jason came to her rescue. His modeling career was just starting to take off thanks to landing a gig as Calvin Klein's first Asian male model. Both sarcastic and carefree, they bonded immediately and moved in together as soon as Tash graduated from college. Though they had a hard time looking out for themselves, they did a remarkable job of looking out for each other.

Tash was so lost in thought about Aidan's coconuts that she didn't hear Jason approaching.

"Hey," Jason said from the doorway.

"Oh, hey." She tossed him a bag of coffee. "Stick that in the fridge." As he put the coffee away, Tash said, "This too," and flung the loaf of bread.

"I can't believe you actually went shopping. Did Pen leave you one of her famous notes?"

"Yup," she said just when the microwave beeped. "Is she in her room studying?"

"She's not here. I think she had dinner plans with her study group or something."

"Seriously? She's unbelievable, making me do all this when she's not even here," she said as she opened the popcorn bag. Steam burned her hand and caused her to drop the bag on the counter. "Fuck," she mumbled.

"How is it you never learn not to open it that way?" Jason asked facetiously. "Here, I got it," he said. He grabbed a bowl from the cupboard and emptied the bag for her.

"You know if you leave it in the bag it's one less dish to wash. That's why I do that."

"Since when do you ever wash the dishes anyway?" he rebuffed, as he ate a handful of her popcorn.

"I don't know why she made me go to the store if she wasn't even gonna be home," Tash said as she threw the two empty grocery bags in the garbage.

"I know you can't relate, but some people actually plan ahead. She probably wanted breakfast."

"Oh, right, like you plan ahead," Tash jabbed, tossing a jar of maraschino cherries.

"You're lucky I caught that. What is it with you and these things?" he asked, sticking them in the door of the refrigerator.

"You know I love them. I can't help it," she said. "But listen, I kind of met a guy. I met him at the store while I was getting Pen's crap, so maybe it was meant to be."

"You met a guy? Ah, do tell," he prodded.

"Well from the looks of things this morning, I'm guessing you also met a guy, so you tell first." She opened the refrigerator and grabbed two cans of Diet Coke.

"Some lighting guy from the shoot. I kicked him out this morning."

"You're such a slut. Must be hard to be so irresistible," Tash bemused.

Jason smiled. "You would know. Come on, let's go curl up on my bed and you can tell me all about the guy you met. I hope he's better than Ray. I'm eating half this popcorn, by the way," he said, taking a fistful and heading to his room.

"Hey, that's my dinner!"

CHAPTER 2

Two afternoons a week, Tash worked at Anna Sui, which was directly across the street from Alice & Olivia. She was friends with one of the saleswomen, Isabelle, an aspiring actress who needed afternoons free for auditions and hooked her up with the job.

When the store was quiet, Tash was supposed to dust the glass display cases filled with jewelry and wallets or flatten old shoeboxes in preparation for the recycling company. Instead, she frequently used one of the tester nail polishes on the front counter to give herself a manicure. She loved how the bottles were shaped like a woman dressed in a black bustier. *The gold sparkle is definitely better than the silver*, Tash thought as she admired her nail lacquer. She leaned her elbows on the counter, blowing gently to dry her newly polished nails.

Her nails were still tacky when her phone beeped on the counter beside her. She peered over to read the incoming text from Jason:

> All set on the list tom night. But no shots for u tequila girl. Xx

She replied:

> Hey, any chance u could add one more? Xx

"Fuck, I smudged my nail," she muttered, scrutinizing her right hand as she waited for a response.

> For Coconut Boy I presume? Who's the slut now? Yeah, can do. U owe me. U pain in the ass. xx

Next, she texted Aidan, having saved his number the night before, just in case.

> Hey. It's Tash from the store last night.

Before she could put the phone down it beeped. *That's eager,* she thought.

```
Hey. So now I have your #. Setting up at
4ever21. Times Sq. = insanity. Can you
swing by?
```

She waited a minute before responding.

```
Gonna pass on the neon signs + mobs of
tweens. Must be good 4 your self-esteem
2 spin Katy Perry's greatest hits 4 the
kiddies. Bet the girls looove u.
```

Only a moment passed before her phone beeped again.

```
Ah, so I see we're already up to the
mockery part of this relationship. Ok
smart ass, u tell me. What's next?
```

As she started to laugh, she heard the annoying bell on the store door and the chatter of customers. "Please let me know if I can be of any help," she said unenthusiastically as they passed by.

She texted her response to Aidan quickly, smudging another nail.

```
My roommate got us on the list at Y tom
night. Can get u on 2.10pm.
```

"Miss, can you open this case please?" one of the customers hollered from the back of the store.

"I'll be right there, ma'am."

```
Cool. C u there. A.
```

Smitten, she leaned on to the counter to daydream when she remembered the customer in the back. "Shit," she mumbled as she jumped up and grabbed the shop keys from beside the register.

"On my way, ma'am."

***

Although she told Aidan to meet her outside the club at ten o'clock, Tash and Jason arrived at ten thirty. There were throngs of over- and underdressed bodies, fighting for their place behind the velvet rope, without realizing that even if they made it behind the rope there was little hope of actually getting into the club that night. Tash knew those hopefuls didn't stand a chance and she loved blowing past them, pretending her privilege was so grand it even prevented her from recognizing her special status. Jason was her ticket to that particular euphoria. Despite the mob scene, Tash spotted Aidan immediately, nonchalantly standing slightly outside of the crowd. With Jason in tow, she grabbed him and without a word spoken, the three waltzed into the club, with a mere nod exchanged between Jason and the bouncer.

They reached the main bar on the far side of the club before Tash stopped. With the music blaring, they stood close together and Tash shouted, "Aidan, this is Jason. Jason, Aidan."

"Hey man, thanks for hooking me up," Aidan said with an outstretched hand.

Jason shook his hand. "No worries." He then turned to Tash and said, "You all good?"

"Yeah, thanks sweetie," she said as she leaned in and pecked his cheek. "Go do your thing and I'll see you at home, or not."

"Later. Be good!" With that, Jason disappeared into the crowd.

Before Aidan could say anything, Tash asked, "So, do you want a drink?"

"Hello to you too," he said with a chuckle. "I'll get them. What do you want?"

"Tequila sunrise."

"That makes sense."

"What does that mean?"

"Tequila sunrise: hardcore but flirty. Totally you."

Tash smirked.

"Forgive me, I've bartended. You start to see patterns."

"So if I hadn't told you what I wanted, what would you have guessed?"

"Tequila sunrise."

Tash smiled. "Okay, very cute smart boy. Now go get my drink."

"You got it. And by the way, you look amazing." When Aidan returned with her drink, he said, "Cheers," and clinked his glass to hers.

"Cheers," she said before taking a gulp. "Wowza, that's strong. What's that?" she asked, gesturing to his glass.

"Club soda."

"Club soda? Just club soda?"

"Club soda with lime. I don't drink."

"Alcoholic?" she asked with a hint of hopefulness.

He shook his head. "Nope, just don't drink."

"You don't look like a straight edge."

"Well, then I'm already surprising you. That's good, right? I mean, for a girl who I bet gets bored easily."

She couldn't help but smile. "So when you're spinning at parties and coming up with crazy drinking games, you're stone-cold sober?"

"That's why my games are so good."

Tash nearly finished her drink as they looked around. There was a lot to take in. The club boasted a mammoth dance floor with platforms that people could jump up on when they wanted to be noticed, as well as bars on every side. Dozens of strobe lights and black iron chandeliers draped with crystals and purple light bulbs pulsed in sync with the techno music. Like Tash and Aidan, most people were dressed in black. Drag queens in long, sequined, jewel-colored gowns stood at the edges of the bars passing out cheap feather boas for twenty bucks a pop.

Aidan leaned over to Tash as she took another swig of her drink. "Is this a gay club? It's cool, I'm just curious."

"No, it's just gay-friendly," Tash said.

"Do you want to dance?"

"Sure." She grabbed his glass and said, "I'll ditch these. Be right back." She returned a moment later and soon they were on the corner of the dance floor, jumping, spinning, and swaying along with everyone. Aidan never took his eyes off her and every once in a while she smirked. They danced for hours, only taking breaks to use the bathroom or when Tash wanted another drink.

Late in the evening, when Tash returned from a trip to the bathroom, Aidan draped a white boa around her neck. She smiled and he said, "It gets better. Come here. Working in the deejay circuit has its advantages. And by the way, if you ever want to get onto a club list, I can hook you up."

He pulled her onto the dance floor, and within moments, a remix of ABBA's "Dancing Queen" came on. She finally broke down and laughed hysterically. Everyone around them jumped and cheered as loose feathers from all the boas flew in the air, falling around them like the sparkles in the snow globes she loved as a child. Tash pulled Aidan to her and leaned into him. They held each other and swayed as feathers landed in their hair.

***

The next morning, wearing black palazzo pants and a bra as she searched for a top, Tash heard a gentle tap on her bedroom door. She threw the clothes she was holding onto her bed and opened the door to find Jason holding two mugs of coffee.

"You're the best," she said as she snagged one.

Jason stood in the open doorway, scanning the room with a mischievous look on his face. "No Coconut Boy?" he queried.

"Oh shush. Come help me choose an outfit."

Jason plopped himself on her bed.

"What do you think of this?" she asked, holding up a sparkly top.

He shook his head, took a sip of coffee, and said, "I think I drank too much for that. The one over there is better."

She slipped on the simple white tank top he pointed to and stood in front of her dresser holding various hoop earrings to each ear. After she settled on the larger pair, Jason said, "Seriously, I expected you to steal my coffee for Coconut Boy. No sleepover? He was hot. Very Billy Idol in his heyday, but taller."

"I'm meeting him later."

"Wow, you didn't give it up on the first night. I'm impressed. You must like him."

"Oh shut up. I'm just not a slut like you."

"Yes you are," he said, sipping his coffee. "Ooh, speaking of sluts, Pen didn't come home last night."

"Oh please, she probably fell asleep at the library," Tash said as she applied her lip gloss. He laughed.

She sat on the edge of the bed, zipping up her black platform booties.

"So where are you meeting him?"

"I'm working a half-day and then meeting him at the MoMA."

"Wow!" he exclaimed, his eyes widening. "You must really like him to take him to your special place. Good for Coconut Boy."

"Please stop calling him that."

"Ooh, you reeeally like him."

"We just needed a place to meet, drama queen."

"Uh huh, sure."

"Oh screw you," she said as she leaned over and kissed his head.

"Screw you too, bitch."

She grabbed her purse, threw her hand up, and said, "Later, sweetie."

***

Aidan jumped up when he saw her. Before he could say anything, she blurted out, "Hey, I know. I'm sorry. I'm not always late, really."

"I already know that's not true," he said with a laugh. "No worries. Should we get tickets?"

"My membership will get us both in."

"Cool. Shall we?" he asked, putting his hand out.

"You're so corny, straight edge," she said as she took his hand.

They walked hand-in-hand. Aidan leaned over and whispered, "You know, your bullshit doesn't fool me, beauty queen."

She leered at him, but her eyes sparkled. As they headed up the escalator, she said, "Let's start at the top and work our way down. My favorite spot is on the second floor and I want to save it."

"If I'm worthy, right?"

"You're worthy."

***

The top floor boasted a special exhibit that paired the "blue" works of Picasso and Miró: paintings from Picasso's Blue Period and a sampling of Miró's greatest pieces, including his three-part masterpiece, Triptych Bleu I, II, III.

"Picasso is one of my favorites," Aidan said, "but the Blue Period is so dark. It isn't even just sad, you know, it's bleak. I'm not afraid of the dark side, but this is pretty far down the rabbit hole."

"Well, his friend offed himself and he was depressed."

"The people look like such sad souls, isolated and alone."

"I think it's their loneliness that makes them so wretched. I mean look at this one," Tash said, stopping in front of a portrait of a woman. "She's one of the prostitutes he painted. A rare moment of solitude. She probably wasn't alone much."

"But you don't need to be alone to be lonely, right?" Aidan said.

"True." They continued their tour, and when they reached the room devoted to Miró's Triptych Bleu, they stopped to take it in.

"It's amazing how one color can convey so many different emotions. Is there anything more cheerful than this? He was so playful," Tash remarked.

"I have to admit, I don't necessarily understand what he was doing, but I think it's awesome," Aidan replied.

"Yeah, it makes sense to me, but not in a way I can explain with words."

Aidan nodded, and then walked to the corner of the room to read the curator's notes. When he returned he said, "It says that Miró thought blue was the color of the unconscious and the surreal, like a dream state."

That's probably why it makes sense even though it like doesn't. You know? It taps into something that we get deep down."

"Totally," Aidan agreed.

"You know I never do that, look at what they write."

"Why?" he asked.

"It clouds how you see it. This might sound strange, but when I look at a painting and I start to get it, the images move, you know like a little film. It's like the film shows me what it means."

"That's not strange; it's awesome and I get it. I sort of have that with music. I see things, like objects or people doing something from a distance, and then I start to hear them."

She smiled. "Even when I was little, before I studied film, I did that."

"So if you don't read in museums, how do you know that Picasso's Blue Period was inspired by his friend's suicide?"

"I said I don't read the curator shit. I didn't say I don't read at all, genius."

Aidan blushed and looked down. "Fair enough, beauty queen."

"Okay, let's move it along," she said, taking his hand. He chuckled and they continued through the exhibit.

"I know a few things too," he said. "Did you know that Cézanne supposedly had at least sixteen shades of blue on his palette when he painted?"

"The guy who painted fruit?" she asked.

"Uh huh."

"Yeah, I knew that."

Aidan blushed and looked down again.

"But how about when he started painting skulls instead of apples and pears? Talk about dark. Maybe all that blue got to him after all," she said with a wry laugh.

"Yeah, maybe. Nothing gets past you. You know who should be known for his blue stuff? Chagall."

"I was never really into him. Did he use a lot of blue?"

"At the Art Institute in Chicago there are these amazing stained glass windows that Chagall created, cobalt blue with all sorts of symbols about America. They're pretty cool and there's always a flock of people standing in front of them."

"Aren't those in *Ferris Bueller's Day Off*? You know, in the museum scene?"

"Leave it to you to turn visual art into a movie," he said.

"I'm obsessed with all things eighties these days, especially movies."

"Cool. They kiss in front of the Chagall windows, Ferris and Sloane."

"She was so pretty. I wanted to be her in that time. I wonder what happened to that actress."

"She's got nothing on you. Funny how that kissing scene casually comes up in conversation, and we just happen to be in a museum and all."

"Okay, smart boy. Let's move it along."

By the time they reached the next floor, talk of art faded and they shared the details of their lives. Painting by painting, floor by floor, they talked about their childhoods, families, and what brought them to New York.

***

Tash learned that Aidan grew up in a small, middle-class suburb in the Midwest, in a home that his lower-middle-class parents struggled to afford. Although he clearly had a loving family, he was a misfit from an early age in a town that "prioritized football and God, in that order." In grade school he often found himself alone, lost in graphic novels and music, "imagining the beats of the music were footsteps, marching me away from that place."

He told her he was always the kid wearing headphones because they provided a protective bubble that no one could puncture. He lived in a sonic world when the real world let him down. Thanks to his height, which had him towering over many of the jocks, he was rarely bullied. Things changed in high school when his good looks and charisma propelled him into popularity with the girls. On several occasions when he was walking home alone at night after studying in the library, he was jumped by a group of jocks. They did little damage but always left a mark, like a fat lip or black eye. Despite his attempts to conceal his injuries or lie about their origin, his mother worried terribly and became critical of his gothic dress and "attention-getting" piercings. It put stress on his home life.

"Suddenly, who I was became a problem," he explained.

Tash asked, "If they only attacked you when you walked home at night, why didn't you just study at home or get a friend to walk with you?"

"Acquiescing to fear is a dangerous road. I guess I wasn't going to walk down it and give them that kind of control over me. I knew it would never be that bad. But you know what really got me? Every time they'd come after me, they'd call me gay. I know that it was a catch-all insult for those misogynist fucks, but come on. They're beating me up for fucking their girlfriends while they call me gay? Even as they hit me, I was laughing on the inside."

"They weren't very creative, that's for sure. Pathetic dicks."

"They said it so frequently that sometimes I wondered if they really believed it and they were just confused about why they hated me. Getting into the world of deejaying in Chicago was my way out of that small-minded crap. New York was the next stop. I'm making a name for myself on the circuit."

"Yeah, I kinda gathered that last night," she said, looking down sheepishly.

He smiled.

"Wanna hear something really messed up?"

He nodded.

"When I was in college, I studied abroad in Amsterdam."

"Don't tell me, you picked Amsterdam for the pot?"

"No, to work in the Red Light District," she said with a straight face.

He just looked at her.

"I'm kidding, God. I went to The University of Amsterdam for a semester because they have a kickass film studies program. Plus, you know, the pot."

He laughed.

"So I'm in Amsterdam during orientation and they set up all of these activities to help us get to know each other and the city and stuff. I signed up for a boat tour. A big-time feminist, Gender in Film professor took us. So we're on the boat and the automated guide is blaring out information like, 'look left to see whatever.' We all turn to see the famous thing, and there is this chick up against a wall, like my age, and this guy is screwing her. I mean, his pants are around his ankles and he's got her pinned against the wall, holding her wrists."

"Oh my God."

"But here's the messed up part: everyone just watches and the professor shouts, "He's fucking her! He's totally fucking her!" And we all just watched until the boat was too far away to see them anymore. To this day, I don't know if they were having public sex or if he was raping her. I can picture it clear as day and still don't know what to think. How could they all be so sure it was consensual, or did they just not care? Voyeuristic fucks. Sick. It was never mentioned again, not by the professor or anyone."

Aidan stopped walking, turned to Tash, and said, "That's really horrible."

"My point is that sometimes people don't know what to think about what they're seeing or feeling. They pick a reaction and go with it, even if it really doesn't make sense. It's all they're capable of. Even when they're right in the middle of it, sometimes they don't know. Like with those assholes who beat on you for screwing their girls while they called you gay."

He leaned in and gave her a soft, quick kiss on her lips. They continued walking, loosely holding hands, as if entirely natural.

***

As the escalator reached the second floor, Tash pulled Aidan along. "Come on."

"Wow, this is cool," Aidan said as they entered a large space with eight different parts of a film being projected onto the walls.

"Shh," Tash said, as she tugged him.

Cushions lined the edges of the room and large bean bags and pillows filled the center of the space. People were sitting all over the place watching the moving images.

Tash spotted an empty cushion in the far corner of the room and led Aidan there. From that vantage point, they could see most of the installments.

Tash leaned over and whispered, "It's this genius Japanese filmmaker. She won an international competition and got a huge grant when she was still in grad school. It was supposed run as a special exhibit, but that was over a year ago. It's like temporarily permanently here. It's about energy, about nature and humans. She filmed it in at least four Asian countries, and the images are incredible. It's the cinematography that I really love. Just watch. You'll get it."

People came and went, but an hour later, Tash and Aidan were still sitting there, leaning on the wall and each other.

Eventually Aidan whispered, "It's mesmerizing. I could stay here forever."

"Yeah, me too."

They looked at each other and he leaned in and kissed her. With his hand holding her face and beautiful images floating all around them, she felt entirely content.

***

The next morning, Tash awoke to realize she was cradled in Aidan's arms. She tried to wriggle her way out without disturbing him, but as soon as she moved, he sighed.

"Good morning," he said groggily.

She sat up and said, "Hey, sorry. I didn't mean to wake you."

"That's okay. What are you doing?"

"I need to shower."

"So you got what you want and now you're done with me. Is that it?" he asked sarcastically.

Expressionless, she turned to face him. "Yup, that's it."

"Come on, beauty queen," he whispered as he rubbed her arm. "Don't run away. Get back over here." He pulled her down and started tickling her while taunting, "Can you take it? Can you keep a straight face?"

Soon she was laughing hysterically. "I give in. I give in!"

He stopped tickling her and gently wiped her hair away from her eyes. "You're beautiful. Last night, well…"

Before he could finish, she leapt up and said, "Yeah, yeah, yeah, but without a shower and coffee, I'm gonna be a mega bitch."

He looked down and smiled coyly. "Coffee would be good."

Tash wrapped herself in her robe while Aidan threw on his T-shirt and boxers.

"Come on. Let's see if Jason's up and then you can meet my other roommate."

They passed Jason's bedroom and saw the door was wide open. "Looks like someone didn't come home last night," Tash muttered.

Just when they approached the kitchen, Penelope was catching her bagel as it popped up from the toaster. She fumbled a bit and dropped it on the counter. Tash wasn't sure if the bagel was hot or if they had startled her.

"Good morning, Tash."

"Hey. This is Aidan."

"Hey," Aidan said.

Penelope brushed her long, loose curls away from her face, adjusted her glasses, and nodded in acknowledgment.

"We were just gonna make coffee. Do you want some?" Tash asked.

"Oh, no thanks. I made this to take with me. I have plans and I'm already late."

Tash was no longer paying attention. She loaded a filter with coffee grounds as Aidan waited in the doorway.

Penelope wrapped her bagel in a napkin and scooted past Aidan.

"Nice to meet you," he called after her.

"You too."

Tash turned to Aidan and gave him an exaggerated eye roll. She opened her mouth but he put his finger against his lips and turned his head to watch Penelope leave the apartment.

The door clicked shut and Tash opened her mouth, but was again derailed when Jason came in.

"Hey," Aidan said.

"Oh, hey Aidan."

"I'm in here," Tash called. "We're making coffee. Want some?"

"No, I'm gonna crash for a while," he replied as he made his way through the small, crowded space.

"I need to go text my friend about something. I'll be right back," Aidan said before making himself scarce.

"See ya man," Jason said.

As soon as Aidan was out of earshot, Jason turned to Tash. "So, you and Coconut Boy must have had a good time yesterday."

"Oh, shut up you slut. What boy's heart did you break when you abandoned him this morning?"

"Well, at least I stayed until the morning," he said, opening the refrigerator.

"Yeah, what's up with that?" Tash asked.

"I had one too many shots and staying over just seemed easier."

She laughed.

Empty-handed, he shut the refrigerator and said, "Pen passed by me without even taking a beat for a hello. Where's she running off to?"

"Who the hell knows? Probably the library. You should have seen her face when she saw Aidan. It was so funny."

"He does look pretty fine in his skivvies."

"How much do you want to bet that Pen leaves me a note asking me to cover him up better? Little miss propriety."

"She's not that bad. Just remember, without her, you and I would need to be the grown-ups."

Tash smiled.

"I'm going to crash. Say goodbye to Coconut Boy for me."

"His name is Aidan."

He smirked. "Say goodbye to Aidan for me."

CHAPTER 3

Later that night as Tash lay in bed, Aidan's scent still on her sheets, images from the night before played in her mind. His eyes locked onto hers, his soft lips, and the firm press of his flesh, their bodies entangled. It was so good she could hardly remember it all, just a jumble of flickering moments and sensations etched in her memory. Over and over again, she imagined the feel of his touch and the look in his eyes. *Fuck. What's wrong with me? It was just good sex. Really good sex. Don't be one of those idiots who loses it because of an orgasm. Get a grip.* But no matter how hard she tried, whenever her mind quieted it was flooded with memories of how she felt lost in his eyes. Then, she had a surprising realization. *Shit, I don't usually open my eyes with guys. Why did we do that? What was that? New cardinal rule: no orgasms with open eyes. Messes with your brain.* She rolled over to go to sleep. As she drifted off, she pulled the sheets up high, clinging to the faint smell of him.

The next morning, she woke up to a text from Aidan.

Hey beautiful. When can I see u?

Not wanting to appear overly available, she showered, flipped through a magazine, and ate breakfast before responding.

No plans today.

Spinning at the H&M on 5th until 6. Meet me?

She laughed and thought, *I could use some tights anyway.*

Sure. Will be fun to see your groupies.

Tash arrived at H&M at five thirty. Aidan was set up just inside the store's entrance. Although he was wearing large black headphones and was engrossed in the music, he acknowledged her immediately with a wide smile. She made a funny face and he looked down, blushing. She pointed to the accessories on the far wall and he nodded, continuing with his work. No matter where she was in the store, whenever she looked back at Aidan, he had his eyes on her. Twenty minutes later, she returned with a small plastic bag containing her new tights and a belt. She walked over to Aidan, pecked him on the cheek, and sat on the edge of the display case near him. She sat back among the mannequins and watched nearly everyone checking Aidan out, girls and guys alike. While some women might feel insecure that a stream of people were admiring and even flirting with the person they're seeing, Tash reveled in it. *He can hold his own*, she thought.

Aidan gestured that he was shutting it down after one last tune. He transitioned from techno to a remix of "Dancing Queen." She put her hand on her chest, bowed her head, and laughed, overjoyed. When the song was over, he took his headphones off, turned to her and said, "I planned that one for you."

"Yeah, I sorta got that," she said, blushing.

"Want to make sure I keep surprising you."

You are, she thought.

Tash fiddled with her phone while Aidan packed up. Soon, he threw his backpack on and said, "Ready if you are."

As they headed out onto a bustling Fifth Avenue, Tash asked, "Where do you want to go?"

"Have you seen *Kinky Boots*, the musical?"

She shook her head. "But I do have a secret Cyndi Lauper girl crush."

He smiled. "I don't want you to think it's always gonna be like this because there's no way I can usually afford this kind of thing. A buddy of mine works on the show; he's been promising me tickets for ages and finally came through."

"Is he an actor?"

"Lighting guy. Nothing glamorous but it comes with perks. He called earlier and said if we get there fifteen minutes before the show, he has a couple of balcony seats for us. You in?"

"Fuck yeah."

"You know you have a real potty mouth," he said jokingly.

"Oh fuck, your Midwestern upbringing?"

He laughed. "No, I dig it. They say cursing is a sign of honesty."

"Well, don't believe everything you fucking hear."

"I'll keep that in mind, beauty queen. Come on, let's head down fifty-second to cut over," he said, grabbing her hand and guiding her.

On the way to Times Square, Tash teased Aidan about his "groupies." When they passed the MoMA, he gently squeezed her hand. They decided to stop at Aidan's favorite sandwich shop for a quick bite before the show, but as they got closer to the neon signs and Broadway lights, Aidan stopped against a building and handed his backpack to Tash.

"Hold this for a sec," he said as he unzipped it and pulled out his iPod and large headphones. "Put these on."

She looked at him quizzically.

"It's a new remix I'm working on. It's inspired by something I saw on the Times Square Midnight Moment – you know, the big arts campaign that uses the billboard space for digital art."

She nodded. "I've seen it."

"I want you to listen to it as you walk into Times Square."

She put the headphones on and Aidan pressed play before tucking the iPod into her pocket. He put his backpack on, grabbed her hand, and zipped towards the epicenter. Her heart raced as the music kicked in. Everything was vibrating: the ground, her skin, the neon signs begging for attention. She felt like she was racing through a film. Suddenly Aidan made a sharp right turn and pulled her into an old-fashioned sandwich shop. He took the headphones off her head and the clamor of human sounds in mundane conversation returned.

"You look flushed," he said. "What did you think?"

"Incredible rush. It was like you created the soundtrack for my energy mixing with the city's energy."

He leaned over and kissed her. "Come on, there are a couple of seats at the end of the counter."

They snagged the seats and Tash looked up at the menu board.

An older waitress with dyed red hair came over. "What can I get you?"

"You first," Tash said.

"Steak and cheese, no peppers please."

"Something to drink?"

"I'm good with water. Thanks."

"I'll have a grilled cheese and tomato on the challah bread and just water. Thanks," Tash said.

"I discovered this place when I had my first gig in the area. Killer sandwiches. We were lucky to get a couple of stools; it's usually packed so I have to eat on the go."

"Your music is really amazing. After that first drop, I felt like I took off. I don't know how else to describe it. It was like it injected me into the cityscape."

He blushed. "Thanks. After seeing that film installation at the MoMA, I knew you'd get it."

"Jason's the only other person I've taken to see that. Most people I know wouldn't appreciate it."

"You two must be really close."

"Yeah, he's my person, you know?"

"He seems chill. What's he like?"

"He's a really good guy, very smart. People see that he's hot and funny and miss out on all of his best qualities. He's so often the center of attention that people don't realize he holds back most of who he is. He's careful about what he chooses to let people in on."

The waitress returned and slid their plates in front of them.

"Always super fast here," Aidan said as he took a couple of napkins from the dispenser and handed one to Tash.

She picked up her sandwich and pulled apart the two halves, watching the cheese ooze. "This was my favorite when I was a kid. But I didn't know about challah bread until I came to New York." She took a big, uninhibited bite. "That's so good," she said as she chewed, the gooey cheese mixing with the buttery toast.

Aidan smiled and dug into his sandwich.

When they finished eating, the waitress dropped off the bill and Tash quickly took it. "I got this," she said and threw down some money. He thanked her and they headed to the show.

When they arrived at the theater, Tash stood in line while Aidan picked up their tickets at Will Call. They found their second-row balcony seats and marveled at their good fortune. Aidan offered Tash a program and she shook her head.

"Of course, you don't want to spoil it."

"Exactly."

They stood up to let an elderly couple pass by. The couple sat beside Tash, and the man asked his wife, "What's this about?" She replied, "It's about the gays, but it's supposed to be excellent." Tash shot a sideways glance at Aidan and they giggled discreetly at each other. Moments later, the lights went out. A wave of anticipatory energy flooded the room and the show began, instantly captivating Tash. By the final number, they were standing and clapping along with everyone else, including the older couple next to them.

"That was brilliant," Aidan said as they slowly made their way out.

"I knew from the opening number. Anything that starts with coveting shoes has to be good."

He raised his eyebrows.

"Kidding. I loved it."

When they stepped into the cool night air, Aidan asked, "What now?"

"Come to my place."

They walked to the subway station, still talking about the play.

Aidan said, "What was so beautiful about that was the message of accepting others as they are. So simple."

"Yet so hard," Tash said.

"Especially when we can't accept ourselves as we are. That's the real challenge, right?"

"I guess."

Soon they were back in Tash's bed, making love with their eyes wide open. They never spoke about their relationship, but after that night they became inseparable.

CHAPTER 4

Jason's life was a series of late night see-and-be-seen parties. Suddenly the "it" guy of New York, the city was his playground. He went to club openings, enjoyed backroom VIP treatment at his regular haunts, and was the person every guy and sexually confused girl wanted to take home. His lucrative and exclusive modeling contract made his time his own, other than occasional photo shoots, public appearances, and international trips for fashion shows.

Most days he slept in, ran a few miles, practiced yoga, and hung around the apartment reading until it was time to head out for the night. When Tash had time off, they snuggled in his bed, watching movies or marathons of their favorite talk shows. Sometimes they bummed around the city, shopping and checking out art galleries. When he suspected Tash's credit card bills were out of control, which was most of the time, he'd treat her to new shoes or accessories to discourage her from overspending.

Over the last six weeks, he spent many days hanging out with Aidan, who had basically moved in. Aidan worked at night so they had plenty of time together when Tash was at work during the day. They bonded quickly, sharing a love of *Monty Python*, sarcastic humor, and gently teasing Tash. Aidan was sensitive to Jason and Tash's close relationship; he knew when to pick up food or grab something from his apartment so they could have their alone time.

On this Friday, Jason woke up at seven thirty for a nine o'clock call time. It was his first solo commercial shoot and he stayed in the night before to get a good night's rest. Tash left him a note by the coffee pot that read, "You got this, rock star. xoxo."

Unfortunately, the subway was delayed. He arrived at the soundstage at nine thirty and was rushed into hair styling. After more than half an hour getting his hair to look naturally tousled, he plopped down in his makeup chair.

A short man with dark hair greeted him. "Hi, I'm Sam, and I'll be doing your makeup today."

"Hey," Jason replied, so busy texting that he didn't even look up from his phone.

"We're going to do a matte look today, nothing iridescent for commercial shoots."

"Uh, huh. Whatever, dude," Jason mumbled.

Sam pursed his lips in annoyance at the very moment Jason looked up to see himself in the mirror, catching Sam's expression. Sam blushed, clearly embarrassed.

"I'm sorry I was running late," Jason said.

"The talent is always late."

"There was a problem on the subway. I'm usually on time."

"Uh huh. That's fine. Please turn to your right," Sam replied.

Twenty minutes later, Sam sprayed a finishing shield on Jason's face and said, "You're all set. I'll go see if they're ready."

"Thanks, man."

When Sam returned, he said, "Wardrobe is waiting for you."

Jason stood up, slipped his phone into his pocket, and said, "You know, I'm a little nervous."

"Haven't you done this before?"

"Group shoots. Sometimes I was like the lead, but I've never shot solo."

Sam sneered. "You just have to stand there with your hands in your pockets and gaze off into the distance while a voiceover guy sells cologne. You'll be fine."

Jason was taken aback. It had been a long time since anyone had spoken to him that way. His face revealed his surprise, and Sam looked mortified, his cheeks reddening. Before either broke the silence, a frazzled-looking woman stormed over.

"Come on, come on. Let's get you in some jeans."

Jason followed her, but not without a glance back at Sam.

Throughout the day, Sam retouched Jason's makeup on set. With a crowd of people around, the bright lights burning and cameras rolling, neither said a word. As Jason was leaving the shoot five hours later, Sam ran up to him.

"Listen, I wanted to apologize to you. I didn't mean to be so rude. I'm very sorry."

"No worries, dude. I actually wanted to apologize to you."

"What for?" Sam asked.

"For not seeing you. When I first sat down, I was so preoccupied I didn't really meet you properly. I got us off on the wrong foot. I'm sorry."

"Uh, okay. Wow, uh thanks," Sam said, flustered.

Jason looked confused.

"I'm sorry. I don't mean to be, well, so incoherent. It's just that most people don't surprise me."

"Yeah, me either," Jason said before walking away.

***

"I can't believe you have to spend this long on the subway just to get anywhere. That sucks," Tash said, as the train roared into their stop.

Aidan smiled. "I use it as a chance to read or put my headphones on and get lost in new music. The subway has its own sound too, like the rest of the city. Sometimes I shut my eyes and feel the sound."

"I guess. You have a better attitude than me."

He laughed. "It's all I can afford, and as you'll see, it's not much. It's actually way better than my first crash pad in the city. I never would have brought a girl there, not even once."

"No offense, but I hate the subway. This would drive me nuts," Tash said as they exited the station.

"You do what you have to do. I'd kill for a place like yours. I still don't know how you manage to afford such a sweet place in that neighborhood."

Tash took in the sights and smells of the neighborhood. Many of the buildings were in decline but she admired the vibrant graffiti. Aidan greeted a few guys standing in line at a food truck.

"Who are they?" Tash asked.

"They live in my old building. Nice guys. Met them when I couldn't get my futon up the stairs. They helped. The little guy did some of the subversive street art you were checking out."

"Cool." They continued walking, but moments later Tash complained, "I can't believe you have such a long walk on top of that subway ride."

"We're almost there, beauty queen. The truth is, I would sacrifice anything to be in a major city – Chicago, New York, whatever. I just can't go back to the 'burbs and bullshit."

"Yeah, I still can't picture you in a place like that."

"Neither can I. I'd rather scrape to get by and be here in the middle of it all. Here I can just *be*. I'm not really into material stuff anyway, just people, places, and music. The deejay thing has its benefits too. I never pay cover charges."

"And you don't drink so you go out to the best places for free."

"Exactly."

"Pretty sweet."

"Okay, here we are," he said as he unlocked the door to a dilapidated walk-up.

Tash smiled.

"Don't worry; you don't have to start hanging out here. Thanks for coming with me. I just want to grab some clothes for tonight."

"Sure, but I don't know if I'm up to going to Brooklyn with you tonight. You'll be there late and I need to catch up on some sleep. You know I have to go to the store tomorrow morning."

"No worries. We can go for a bite and I can get you a cab before I head to the subway."

They entered the rancid-smelling building, and Tash followed Aidan to the stairwell. She put her foot on the first stair heading up, but he pulled her hand.

"This way," he said, leading her downstairs.

"You live in the basement?"

"Think of it as the ground floor."

She followed him into the tiny studio apartment, which was about the size of the small common room in her apartment, and she wondered if the bars on the windows made him feel more or less safe.

"Can you believe I have a weekend roommate?" he asked sarcastically.

"Uh no, I literally don't understand how that even works," she said, noticing one couch and no other places to sit.

"It was a bigger problem before I started seeing you. Couldn't swing this place on my own and my friend needed a place to crash on weekends because he's got a part-time job in the city. He pitches in a little rent and it's enough for me to get by. He used to sleep in a sleeping bag on the floor and I'd take the futon."

"Fuck," she said.

"When I have good gigs on the weekends I'm out all night anyway. Do you want a glass of water or something?"

"No thanks," she said, rifling through his shelves. "Wow! I can't believe you have all of these VHS tapes. I mean, that's crazy."

"When I first moved to the city, I went to this charity place to score some furniture and they had a working VCR for five bucks. You can still buy old VHS tapes for like a dollar online and at stores all over the Village, so I figured why not."

"How can you have the most modern laptop, headphones, and deejay setup and be watching freaking VHS tapes?"

"I spend my money on the things that matter. Plus the "be kind, rewind" stickers are hilarious. The retro thing is kind of rad."

"Oh my God, you have *Staying Alive*," she said. "Finola Hughes was so beautiful in this. I remember when Travolta's character, uh…"

"Tony."

"Yeah! He said that watching her dance was like watching smoke move. Brilliant line. Totally captures what lust feels like. But God, the rest of the thing was so cheesy."

"Come on, that was Travolta at his best. The soundtrack was killer for the time too."

She raised her shoulders and continued flipping through movies. "Is this any good?" she asked, holding up a tape.

"*Heathers*? Don't tell me you haven't seen it."

"Nope."

"It's great. Completely dated but great. It's the original *Mean Girls*, only darker. Total cult classic. With your eighties fascination I would have guessed that you knew it by heart."

"Wanna watch?" she asked.

He looked at the clock on the microwave before saying, "Sure. I could run to the takeout truck down the street and pick up dinner. We can watch it before I head to work."

"Cool. I'll wait here."

"What do you want from the truck, beef or chicken?"

"Just get me whatever the veggie option is. I never warmed to the idea of meat from a truck."

He smiled. "Yes, your majesty."

"Hardy har har."

Aidan returned twenty minutes later. The couch was set up with pillows and a blanket, and the small coffee table was cleared to make room for their food. Aidan smiled and said, "I see that my place brings out the domestic goddess in you. Very unexpected."

"Oh please," she said casually.

"Nah, it's cute. You wanted to make things nice. I dig it," he said with a sly smile.

She rolled her eyes and tried to blow him off but was given away by the ever-so-slight upward turn in the corners of her mouth.

While Aidan cracked open the soda cans, Tash opened the food containers and released the smells of the Middle East into the small space. "Oh no, they put peppers on yours," she said.

"Ah, you remembered I don't like 'em. No worries. I'll pick them out."

"I'll get it," she said as she scooped the peppers out of his container and into hers.

"Thanks for looking out for me," he said.

"More for me."

Aidan put the tape in the VCR and said, "The one bad thing about buying this thing used is that it didn't come with a remote. But hey, I'd probably lose it anyway."

"Not in this tiny place," she quipped.

"Touché, beauty queen."

"Wow, this is really good," she said as she took a forkful of her rice and veggie mixture. "Thanks for dinner."

"Sure thing. There's some pita in the bag."

"Cool," she said, reaching for it.

"Okay, so here we go," he said as the opening credits rolled.

Tash placed her food container on her lap and leaned into Aidan's shoulder. As the movie began, she nestled into him, her eyes lit up, and she declared, "Oh my God. The colors are brilliant."

CHAPTER 5

As Tash spooned coffee grounds into the filter, Jason crept into the doorway and said, "You're up early."

She dumped the grounds all over the kitchen counter. "Jeez, you startled me," she said.

"Sorry."

"Do you want some coffee?" she asked as she wiped the dark specks into the palm of her hand and threw them in the kitchen sink.

Jason shook his head. "No thanks. I'm going to try to catch a yoga class. Why are you up so early on a Saturday, and where's Aidan?"

"He was spinning at a club in Brooklyn last night. I was too beat to go and didn't want him to wake me up at like four in the morning, so he crashed at his place. Oh my God, I went to his place yesterday."

"Well it's about time."

"Oh, shut up."

"He said it's tiny. Is it awful?"

"Yeah, it's pretty heinous but we had a good time. He has an old VCR and all of these great movies. We watched *Heathers,* which was totally disturbed."

"Never saw it."

"*See*, he thought I was a freak for not seeing it before. I'll have to tell him that you've never seen it either."

"Well you are the movie maven."

"True. Anyway, I needed sleep last night. I have to go into the store for a couple of hours to deal with a shipment; Isabelle has a callback. He's meeting me there and then we're going out for a bite with Kyle."

"Ooooh, that's big! Introducing him to the one relative you actually like. What's next, a little walk down the aisle?"

"Oh shut up," she said with a roll of her eyes. "It's just lunch, drama queen."

Jason smiled. "You know I think Aidan is the bomb. I'm just teasing you."

Tash opened the cabinets in search of a travel mug. "So, rock star, how did your shoot go yesterday? And why weren't you out partying all night?"

"Um, it was okay."

"Uh, hold up," she said, giving her full attention to Jason. "Just okay? What happened?"

"It was fine. It's just that I was late because of a problem on the damn subway and some guy sort of said something to me about it."

"Who?" Tash asked.

"The makeup guy, Sam."

"Who gives a shit what the makeup guy said? He was probably jealous of you. I bet you could have gotten him in trouble."

"It wasn't like that. It was more of a misunderstanding. I was kind of rude to him but I didn't mean to be."

"So I think the pressing question is: why are you still thinking about this? Who cares?"

Jason didn't respond.

As she poured her coffee, Tash pronounced, "Ooooh, I seeeeee. This is about a boy. Shall we call him Makeup Boy? Will you be going down the Clinique aisle? Or going down …."

"Ha, ha, ha. Very funny. It's not like that at all. If you had seen this guy, you wouldn't be saying that. He was *so* not my type."

"Say what you want, but you're the one still talking about Makeup Boy." Tash grabbed her coffee and breezed past Jason, stopping to kiss him on the cheek. "Have fun at yoga," she whispered.

***

Tash looked up from the large cardboard box she was unpacking and noticed Aidan wandering around the store.

"Aidan, come here and help," she called from the door of the backroom.

"Hey, babe. Love the space of this store. The whole purple and black thing against the glossy cherry wood floors is badass."

"Hey. Hold this open," Tash said, handing him a large garbage bag.

Aidan sat on a small stool and held the bag as Tash stuffed it full of discarded styrofoam packing materials. "Why do they pack the shipments in this non-recyclable crap?" Aidan asked. "It's so retro, and not in a good way."

Tash sat on the floor, collecting errant Styrofoam bits. She looked up at him, clearly annoyed. "Think I know? Let's just finish so we can get the hell out of here. What time is it, anyway?"

Aidan looked at his phone. "Twelve fifteen."

"Shit, we're late. Let me just go to the bathroom," she said, tossing the full garbage bag aside.

They finished up at the store and headed to Café Borgia. The little SoHo staple was busting at the seams. Tash spotted her cousin sitting in the far right-hand corner. She slid into the booth next to Kyle, and Aidan took the opposite seat.

"I'm so sorry we're late," she said as she leaned over and hugged him.

He laughed. "I would expect nothing less. I know how you like to make a grand entrance."

"That's why it sucks; I was planning to be on time for once, but I got held up at work."

"It's good to know some things haven't changed."

She rolled her eyes. Noticing Aidan sitting there silently smiling, she said, "Oh sorry, Aidan, this troublemaker is my little cousin, Kyle."

"As usual, Tash forgot *she's* the troublemaker," Kyle said as he extended his hand.

"Nice to meet you," Aidan said, still smiling.

"What's so amusing ?" Tash asked.

"It's just fun to see someone else mocking you. Plus I think it's adorable that you always seem surprised you're late," Aidan said.

"I like this guy already," Kyle said as Tash shook her head.

They all laughed. A moment later, the waitress came over to take their lunch orders.

"The ham and cheese sandwich and a coffee, please," Kyle said.

"And for you?" the waitress asked Tash.

"A slice of today's quiche with salad and coffee, please."

"Same for me," Aidan said.

"It's not the same as the blintzes, is it?" Kyle asked Tash.

She shook her head.

"What's that?" Aidan asked.

"There's a diner Kyle and I go to. We always share a platter of cheese blueberry blintzes. They're outrageous. The coffee sucks, but they give you a plate of bagel chips and stuff while you're waiting."

"Except Tash eats the nasty cinnamon raisin bagel chips."

"I like them. Shut up."

Aidan smiled. "So, are you ever gonna take me for blintzes?"

"I don't know. We'll see," she said coyly.

After some small talk, their food was served. Kyle and Aidan scarfed theirs down. Tash teased them, saying, "What is it about guys and food? I mean, breathe!" While Tash leisurely nibbled on her meal, Aidan filled Kyle in on how they met. Tash interjected from time to time, insisting that Aidan was "infatuated the second he saw me." They talked about Kyle's life as a political science major at Columbia. When Aidan asked if he was seeing anyone, Tash proceeded to give him unsolicited dating advice. He wasn't having it. "Listen you, with those freaky exes; you are so not giving me advice." Aidan jumped in and insisted that he dish on her past beaus, and soon they were both teasing her mercilessly. Tash shook her head and smiled, giving in to the absurdity of it all. When the laughter died down, the conversation moved to shared interests in music and movies.

An hour later, they all threw down some cash and Aidan excused himself to use the restroom. With only a one-person unisex restroom available, they saw Aidan waiting in line across the café and knew they had a little time alone.

Tash opened her mouth, but before she could say anything, Kyle said, "Aidan is great."

She was surprised. "You never like the guys I date."

"First of all, they've hardly been guys – more like trolls," he said with a laugh.

She playfully punched his arm.

"None of the guys you've dated have been even remotely good enough for you. You deserve someone who gets you."

She smiled.

"Anyway, he's great. So here's hoping he doesn't dump you," he said as he burst into hysterics.

"Hey!" she said, again punching him in the arm. "You know me – I don't take things too seriously anyway."

"Maybe you should this time. What does Jason think of him?"

"He's in love with Aidan, but in a brother kind of way. You should see them together."

"Maybe Aidan is the roommate he always wanted," Kyle said through laughter.

"Hey! I'm gonna punch you harder next time."

"Okay, I surrender," he said, putting his hands up. "But seriously, if Jason and I both think he's good for you, maybe you should lean into it a bit."

"Let's worry about getting you a date before worrying about my boyfriend."

"Oh my God, you called him your boyfriend!"

"That's it, smarty," she said as she walloped him.

"Okay, okay, I'm moving on. How are your folks?"

"Fine I guess. I haven't visited in a while. What about yours?"

"Um, I guess they're all right."

"What is it Kye?"

"Probably nothing. They just seem, I don't know, like something's up."

"Well, didn't your mom start a new job as an agent or something? She's probably just really busy."

"Yeah, maybe. Anyway, they're fine. What about Jason, is his star still rising?"

Aidan returned and sat back down, not wanting to interrupt.

"He just had his first shoot as a solo model in a commercial. It's freaking crazy. I'm so happy for him. And I think he met a boy, although he says he didn't."

"When does he not have a new dude on his arm? That guy has game," Aidan chimed in.

"Don't say anything to him. It might be nothing and I don't want him to be mad at me."

"What about Penelope, how's she?" Kyle asked.

"She's had a low profile lately, hardly ever home. No annoying notes."

"Low profile? I'd say more like downright mysterious," Aidan said. "I've probably seen her two or three times and I've barely left your place for weeks."

"She must be there more often than that," Tash said.

Aidan shrugged.

"Is she dating someone?" Kyle asked.

"I doubt it. I think she's just really busy with school and she visits her dad a lot and stuff. She's most likely spending her nights curled up to a library book. You know, the dusty, big-word kind she likes so much."

"You used to be good friends."

"Yeah, that was before we lived together."

"You lived together in college."

"I was abroad like for half of that year. She didn't have enough time to get on my nerves."

"She's a sweetheart; you should be nicer to her. Grad school is probably stressful, too," Kyle said.

"You see sweet, I see uptight," Tash said.

Kyle shot her a stern look.

"Yeah, yeah, yeah. I'll make an effort. Okay gentleman, ready to go?"

They left the café, hugging each other on the street outside before Kyle took off in one direction and Tash and Aidan in the other.

***

Tash and Aidan spent the next few hours wandering from SoHo back to the Village. They looked in store windows and stopped in art galleries.

"Come here," she said, pulling him into a gallery featuring Andy Warhol prints.

"Warhol was ahead of his time," Aidan said as they walked through the gallery.

"I know. Can you imagine what he would say about reality television?"

"He predicted it. I don't think he'd be surprised in the least," Aidan said.

"Uh huh. I love the Marilyns," she said, stopping in front of one of Warhol's most iconic pieces.

"Of course you do, beauty queen."

"Shut up," she said, playfully punching his arm. "I saw a documentary about her in college. Did you know when she talked to reporters she used to say, 'Would you like me to be her for you?' or something like that. She knew Marilyn was a character she created."

"Or one side of her personality," Aidan suggested.

"Exactly. It was like she was able to hold on to both Norma and Marilyn."

"But kind of fucked up if she never integrated them, right? I mean, living as two people instead of one whole person can't be easy. Maybe that's why she..."

"Oh don't even say it. I never believed she killed herself."

He smiled. "Neither did I, but that doesn't mean she was happy."

Tash shrugged.

"That's what was so brilliant about Warhol. He captured the lie and shoved it in everyone's face, decorated in bright, psychotically happy colors."

"Can I tell you something?" she asked, turning toward him.

"Of course."

"You know how some people have this romantic notion of New York in the 1920s?"

"Uh, rich white people might."

"Shut up," she said, punching his arm harder this time.

"I'm just kidding. Yeah, I know what you're talking about. People who read a lot of Edith Wharton or whatever."

"Well, I have this romantic notion of New York in the 1980s. I think that's why I've been so obsessed with the films lately. My medium has always been film; it's how I connect with different times and ideas."

Aidan smiled. "You always light up when you talk about film."

She shrugged. "Anyway, I have this love of New York in the 1980s, you know when the Mary Boone Gallery was the hottest place in SoHo, not a freaking H&M or whatever. The time of Warhol and all of those pop visionaries."

"You know who I love from back then? Basquiat. Nobody blurred graffiti and art like that before he did. He was exposing the lie too, I think, but in his own way. I think the bullshit is really what killed him."

"Totally. I'm telling you, when Mary Boone closed her SoHo gallery and opened on Fifth Avenue, something died forever."

They smiled at each other and finished their tour of the gallery.

Once outside, Tash bought a black fedora from a street vendor. "How do I look?"

"Too cool for school, beauty queen."

"You're so lame," she teased, before grabbing his hand and continuing their stroll.

They were a few blocks from Tash's apartment when Aidan received a text message.

"Hey, a couple of my friends are in the neighborhood and they invited us for a drink. You up for it?"

"Sure."

A few minutes later, they sat down on the patio of a local Italian restaurant with Aidan's friends Jaime and Stu, both of whom Tash liked instantly. Jaime's black hair, black sundress, combat boots, and row of silver-studded earrings gave her a gothic look. Tash knew her appearance was just one facet of her personality when she greeted them ironically with, "Hello, happy shiny people." Jaime grabbed Aidan's arm. "Did you see the cover of *The Economist*, with the belly flop? Hysterical. Reminded me of what you said about Republicans."

Not only did her outgoing personality contrast her gothic look, but Tash suspected she was wickedly smart. *I like her*, she thought. Tash pegged her as late twenties, maybe early thirties.

"Jaime works as a satirist for an art and culture magazine and freelances on the side, so we're always talking about art and politics," Aidan said, filling Tash in. "She got her master's in journalism at NYU, actually."

"Oh, Jaime, there's something on that seat. Let me get a napkin for you," Stu said as he raised his hand to get the attention of a waiter.

He's a sweetheart. And God, he's even taller than Aidan. He could be a basketball player, Tash thought.

"Stu works as a personal assistant, so he's used to taking care of people," Jaime said.

"Who do you work for?" Tash asked Stu as he wiped Jaime's seat.

"I work for a New York celebrity," he said.

"But due to a confidentiality agreement, he's not allowed to reveal any details," Jaime added.

Tash's eyes lit up.

"Oh, don't be impressed," Jaime said. "He's basically a manservant."

Stu winced. "I can't even disagree. It's true. It's sad and true."

"You guys seem like an old married couple," Tash said.

"Oh he wishes, but we're just roommates," Jaime said.

"Yeah, if only she had a penis," Stu said.

"And if only you had boobs!" Jaime added. They all dissolved into a fit of laughter.

Tash fit in as if she'd known them for years. Before long, they were on their second carafe of the house red, sharing fried calamari and a bread basket. Aidan couldn't stop smiling, and Tash was having a great time.

Jaime said, "So Tash, Aidan tells me you studied film at NYU."

"Yup."

"Did you ever have Professor Mercer?"

"Oh, I totally did. I signed up for some semiotics class, having no idea what it was. God, that was so boring."

"I took a class with him too; it was awful. It sucked because it was the only class I took in the film department but I didn't realize what it really was either. It killed my elective space."

"Did you like NYU?" Tash asked.

"Loved it. Of course, I'll still be paying off my student loans when I'm in the retirement home. I love my job but my salary is truly pathetic. That's why I have to share a place with this one," she said smirking at Stu. "What about you? Did you like NYU?"

"Yeah. I partied too much the first couple of years, so my folks didn't get their money's worth. Once I settled in, I loved the classes for my major. I'm really into avant-garde film studies and there were some amazing professors. I was constantly going to hear speakers outside of class and going to film screenings, especially senior year. You know, all the perks that aren't for your grade. I just loved it all and couldn't get enough."

"You should think about going to grad school and doing something with it."

"I thought about going for an MFA in cinematography. Maybe. I don't know if I could do the school schedule thing again."

Aidan chimed in, "I know you could do it and I think it would be awesome for you. You have an amazing eye and it's obviously your passion."

She shrugged and changed the subject.

Before they left, Tash and Jaime went to the restroom together.

"It's so great to finally you meet you," Jaime said as they fixed their lipstick.

"You too."

"He talks about you all the time."

"Really?"

"Oh yeah. He won't shut up about you. He told us he met a beautiful girl who was smart as hell, and that we'd like her because she doesn't let him get away with anything."

Tash smiled.

Soon they were all standing in the street, saying their goodbyes and making plans to attend an animated short film festival the following month. Aidan took Tash's hand and they headed in the direction of her apartment.

"Your friends are pretty cool," Tash said.

He squeezed her hand. "Yeah, they're good eggs."

She giggled.

"They're sharp too. You know, Jaime was on point. You should do something in film. Is it a money thing, not going to grad school?"

"No, my parents can pay to send me."

"Damn. You're so lucky."

"I guess," she said dismissively.

As they approached Washington Square Park, Tash noticed Harold sitting on his favorite bench. A man walking past him flicked a cigarette butt, nearly hitting Harold's foot. *Jackass*, she thought.

"Follow me," she said, leading Aidan over. "Hey there, Harold."

"Hello, Natashya. Isn't dusk extraordinary tonight?"

Tash smiled. "Harold, this is Aidan."

Aidan put his hand out and Harold nodded, sparing him the physical contact. "Nice to meet you, young man. I've noticed you around."

Tash looked at Aidan, "Harold is my buddy. Sometimes we have coffee together in the mornings."

Aidan smiled.

"We gotta go, but I'll try to bring donuts on Monday if it's not raining."

"That would be lovely."

"Goodnight," Tash said.

"Nice to meet you," Aidan said.

Harold tilted his head down and blinked his eyes tightly.

As they walked away, Aidan said, "So what's his deal?"

"I don't know his story. Told him he didn't have to tell me. He's just my friend, sort of. I don't like people mistreating him. Sometimes I bring him coffee and stuff on my way to work. That's all."

Aidan stopped in his tracks, looked Tash in the eyes, and said, "I love you."

"Don't be so dramatic," she blithely said.

"I love you, beauty queen. You know I do."

She smiled. "Let's get out of here, you big sap."

He took her hand and they headed down the street.

***

After washing her face and slipping into an oversized t-shirt, Tash jumped on the bed next to Aidan, who was reading a novel.

"Uh, well hello there, beautiful."

"Listen, it's no big deal or anything, but do you want to see my final film project from college? It's experimental and I couldn't really achieve what I wanted to, but…"

"I would absolutely love to see it," he said softly.

Aidan beamed and Tash fidgeted as they watched it on her laptop. At one point Aidan said, "I love what you did there, with the swirling colors."

"Thanks. See, I had this idea that since cinematography is basically defined as painting with light, that I would mirror that here. I couldn't fully realize the idea, but…"

"But I totally see where you were going. I can actually hear it, like music."

She smiled.

When the short film was over, Aidan said, "You're talented. Truly. I'm so impressed."

"It's kind of my thing I guess. It's the only thing I've ever really been into," she said as she put her laptop away.

"What's your vision? I mean, if you could create something in the film world, what would it be?"

"I always wanted to bring the true pop art sensibility to contemporary film, but not in a cheesy or expected way. You know, something fresh and cutting edge."

He nodded. "Come here."

He put his arm out and pulled her to him. He wrapped his arms around her and whispered, "Thank you for sharing that with me."

She had never felt so close to anyone, and just for a moment, she leaned into the feeling and his embrace.

***

The next morning, Aidan was pouring some orange juice when Penelope came into the kitchen.

"Oh, hey," Aidan said.

"Hi," she said as she set the coffee pot.

"I finally get to see the invisible roommate," Aidan said jokingly.

"I'm not that exciting I guess. Not like Tash and Jason."

"Not at all. I didn't mean it that way. You're just out a lot."

Penelope continued tinkering with the coffee pot.

"I hope you don't mind that I'm here so much," Aidan said.

She shook her head.

"Tash said that you're in graduate school. What are you studying?"

"Art history."

"Oh, wow. Cool. Is that how you and Tash became friends?"

"Uh huh. I think she would say that even in art, she's all about the beautiful and fun parts. I like the boring history. Someone has to, I guess. It's not exciting to most people." Before he could respond, Penelope said, "I'm going to get ready while the coffee is brewing."

"Oh, sure," Aidan said.

She stopped and turned around. "I forgot to let Tash know the monthly bills are on the mail table. I broke everything down so she can just leave me a check. Would you please let her know?"

"Sure."

Tash was busy trying on possible outfits for the day when Aidan returned with two glasses of juice.

"Hey, what do you think of this?" Tash asked as she spun around causing the fringe running down the seams of her white shirt to sway.

"Cute. Very *Urban Cowboy*," he said as he plopped down on her bed. "Oh, before I forget, Penelope said she left your bills on the mail table."

"You talked to her about the bills?"

"All she said was that she divided them up."

"Oh," Tash said as she searched her drawer for matching socks.

"It's kinda nice that she takes care of the accounting stuff for you guys."

"Yeah. She lives for that stuff."

"I still don't know how you can afford this place."

Tash, now more serious, turned to face him. "Jason and Pen pay more than I do. Obviously Jason can afford it and Pen has money from her family. I'm not a mooch. I pay, just less than them."

"That's cool. I didn't mean to make you feel bad. I guess I'm two for two and it's not even noon."

"What?" Tash asked.

"I think I kind of put my foot in my mouth with Penelope."

"Whatever. Don't stress. She's hard to talk to these days."

"Maybe the universe is telling me to close my mouth today. Come here, beauty queen."

"No way. I just got ready and you'll mess me up."

"You're such a girl."

"Yeah, I am."

"Come on," he said. "Just come sit with me. I won't mess you up."

Tash pursed her lips and conceded. Aidan put his hands out, and when she leaned in to take them, he pulled her down, flipped her onto her back, and started tickling her.

"I knew you would mess me up," she squealed through laughter.

He stopped tickling her, brushed her hair from her forehead, and said, "Nothing could mess you up. To me, you are extraordinary."

He kissed her gently. All the while her mind was haunted by a single thought: *You don't really know me.*

PART TWO

CHAPTER 6

Penelope Waters was born in Boston. Her father, Ted, came from an affluent family with deep New England roots and became a corporate attorney because "it was expected." Her mother, Mallory, held a bachelor's degree in finance from Harvard, but pursued a career as a pastry chef because, "Living life means following your dreams." As a child, Penelope was overjoyed to see her mother on the cover of *Boston Magazine*, noted as the most revered pastry chef in the area.

Penelope inherited her father's gravitas. Both were reserved, studious, and above all, serious. Mallory was the opposite. For instance, when she whipped up Penelope's favorite cream puffs, she glazed the tops and smooshed them in rainbow sprinkles.

"Mom, aren't cream puffs supposed to be plain?" Penelope asked.

"There is no such thing as 'supposed to be.' Besides, everything is better covered in sprinkles," she replied.

"Dad, she's being silly again," Penelope complained.

Ted smiled. "She can't help it. Her spirit is as light and airy as those little pastry clouds," he said before popping one in his mouth.

When Penelope spent too much time hunched over her desk, Mallory barged into her room and dragged her outside to look up at the stars. She didn't let her return to her studies until, with pinky fingers hooked, they made a wish together. Secretly, Penelope wished to be more like her mother; despite her ambivalence about "frills," she always kept her hair in long brown spirals, like Mallory's.

When Penelope was seventeen years old, her mother was killed in a car crash. She died instantly, as did the driver responsible, who had been texting. The lightness left their house that day. Although she and her father believed Mallory was in heaven, their shoulders permanently slumped and they never once looked up at the stars.

At Penelope's high school graduation, her father told her that he'd quit his job, sold their Beacon Hill brownstone, and was moving to Vermont to open a bed and breakfast. *He's given up on life*, Penelope thought. While packing her room, half in boxes for storage and half in bags for NYU, she was overcome by waves of guilt. *How can I abandon my dad? He seems irreparably damaged.* As guilt shook her confidence in her decision to forge her own path, she found the old *Boston Magazine* with her mother on the cover and remembered how Mallory always encouraged her to be braver and to find herself. *I need to be more like my mother, more fearless.* Mustering all her strength, she lifted herself from the gravity of grief and headed to New York City.

With a major in art history and minor in French, she excelled academically, but was less successful socially. During the first few weeks of freshman year, almost everyone left their doors wide open, popping into each other's rooms, jumping on each other's beds, and quickly forming friendships to carry them through their college years. Grief-stricken and out of her comfort zone, Penelope smiled politely as she walked through the dormitory corridors, but rarely spoke to anyone other than an occasional "excuse me" as she passed groups of friends overtaking the narrow space.

Her roommate was from New York. She spent most nights in her boyfriend's room, also an NYU student, and weekends at home, leaving Penelope on her own. When she saw groups of friends crammed in someone's room, laughing loudly, she wished she could start over again. She berated herself over the time a few girls invited her into their room for a horror movie marathon. With an assignment due the next day, she had hesitated. One girl said, "Don't worry if it's not your thing," and all Penelope could do was smile and walk away. *What's wrong with me?* she wondered as she walked back to her empty dorm room, closing and locking the door behind her as usual.

During her junior year, she took an elective in French cinema. Each Thursday night, students were required to attend a film screening. One night, at a screening of *Betty Blue*, Penelope noticed Tash arriving ten minutes late. As Tash scanned the dark room for an empty seat, Penelope moved over, gesturing for her to take the aisle seat.

"Thanks," Tash whispered.

Penelope smiled. "Do you want me to fill you in?" she whispered back.

"Nah, it's one of my favorite movies."

At the end of the screening, Tash turned to Penelope. "So, what did you think?"

"The score was beautiful."

"Is that all?"

"Betty was so self-destructive. Do you think they ever had a chance?" Penelope asked.

"No one in love has a chance," she said with a smirk.

Penelope looked at her blankly.

"I mean, we're each alone, right?" Tash added. "The love illusion just makes people lose their shit." As Penelope wondered if that was true, Tash followed up with, "I'm meeting some friends for a drink. Do you want to come?"

"Oh, it's already pretty late and…"

"You can't be that lame. Come on, live a little."

Remembering the price of hesitation, she responded, "Okay. Just for a little while."

Once at Jelly Belly, a local bar, Tash introduced Pen to a group of girlfriends who were busy rating all the guys in the bar. Penelope sipped a soda while the others slammed the bar's famous Jell-O shots. Supporting a staggering Tash, Penelope got back to her dorm at three in the morning and she didn't care. When Tash slurred, "Thanks. I should really party less and do more of the school thing," Penelope thought, *And I should do the opposite.* They became fast friends, sharing class notes, attending film screenings together, and offering each other honest advice. Penelope became Tash's excuse when she wanted to forgo the party scene for a quiet night in, and Tash became Penelope's passport to the American college experience she had only seen in movies. They roomed together senior year.

One night, Tash met Jason at a club when she was having trouble getting in.

"Screw you! I'm on the damn list. Maybe you should look again," she was yelling at the bouncer. Out of the blue, with a wink from Jason, she was in.

"Thanks! My friend was supposed to get me on the list but I guess she fucked up," she said once they were inside.

He smiled. "No sweat. You're gorgeous – you would have better luck flirting than screaming."

"Yeah, I tried that. Asshole said he had a girlfriend. Like I care. I just wanted to get in."

Jason laughed.

"So, you're pretty connected to just waltz in here like that," she said with a coy smile.

"Honey, I don't play for your team. But nice work with the flirting. I totally want to buy you a drink."

They loved each other immediately. Tash introduced Jason and Penelope and they all became friends. When Tash was getting ready to graduate, she and Jason made a plan to live together.

"Come on, Pen, move in with us," Tash cajoled.

"Yeah, we need a grown-up," Jason added.

"Grad school is going to be hard. I'll need a quiet place to study and I don't want to cramp your style."

"We need you, Pen. Don't worry, we'll behave," Tash said.

At first, the three spent a lot of time together hanging out in their apartment, watching movies or reality show marathons. They all squeezed onto Jason's bed with Tash in the middle, and laughed for hours at corny rom-coms. Tash threw her arms up and melodramatically reenacted the ridiculous "you're the one" speeches, as she called them. Jason mused that if they only had more gay storylines, it wouldn't be so cliché. Then he and Tash stood up, created new characters, and played out the climax scene. They didn't stop until Penelope's giggle morphed into a hearty laugh. Over time, such instances were fewer and farther between. As Jason's star rose, he spent more time going to clubs. Tash loved tagging along, but Penelope studied during the week and often traveled to Vermont on weekends. Tash and Jason's bond grew and Penelope felt increasingly lonely.

By the end of their second year in the apartment, Jason was famous throughout the city, Tash was spending every free moment with Aidan, and Penelope was quietly trying to finish graduate school.

Having completed her last semester of classes, Penelope planned to use the summer to finish her thesis. She had uncharacteristically fallen behind. She claimed to have gotten held up trying to pick the perfect topic, something intellectually interesting that her committee would approve. Everyone accepted this excuse as it affirmed their assumptions about her. The truth was something no one would expect.

***

I'll deal with it today, once and for all, Penelope thought as she stared in the bathroom mirror, searching for herself. *This can't continue. I wasn't thinking. I have to get out before anyone gets hurt. How could things get so complicated?*

She finished getting ready and jammed a few overdue library books into her backpack. Noticing the cover of one book about the Greek goddesses, she wondered, *Why did I pick this of all topics for my thesis? I miss being smart.*

Tash and Jason were cuddling on his bed as she passed his bedroom. Without meaning to, she stopped outside the partially open door and listened.

"Meet us there at ten. There's a bigwig club promoter coming to meet with Aidan and he needs good energy."

"You're relentless. I told you I should stay in tonight. We're shooting at a bunch of outdoor locations tomorrow and there's an early call time."

"Sleep during the day and just come for one drink. I'm not relentless, I'm restless. It's not just Aidan, I need you there. He's being really clingy and I need a…"

"You don't need me. He's not clingy, T. Come on, what gives?"

"His 'I love you' stuff freaks me out. What does he even know about me?"

"He knows what matters. Stop letting the past mess with your head."

"What if…"

Penelope caught herself eavesdropping and quickly scampered out of the apartment. The warm air caressed her face as she stepped onto the street. *It's a beautiful day. Too bad I'll be stuck inside.*

Soon she was at her regular haunt, the library, where she planned to spend the day working on her thesis. As soon as she sat down and opened her laptop, her phone beeped with an incoming text.

```
Meet me?
```

After inhaling slowly, she responded.

```
Tonight. At the library now. Need to
concentrate on work.
```

She slipped her phone into her backpack and started reading. Stopping only once to go next door for a veggie wrap and smoothie, Penelope worked all day, taking such copious notes that her fingers hurt from typing. While her thesis focused on representations of Persephone, she became increasingly tired and began running searches on some of the other Greek goddesses. An amateur blog about Penelope, her namesake, captured her attention. The blogger described Penelope as faithful and loyal, suggesting she not only married a hero, but was herself a hero. It was no wonder she was her father's favorite. *That's it. I can't take it anymore. My dad would be so disappointed.*

As she switched her computer off, a librarian passed by. "Can I return those books to the stacks for you?"

"Yes, thank you," she said. She pulled her phone out of her bag and sent a text.

```
Leaving the library now. Meet me.
```

The response was almost instantaneous.

```
On my way.
```

The library seemed to stop time, concealing the day from the night. By the time she left, the sky was dark. *I wonder if Tash convinced Jason to go out with her. They always have so much fun.* She hailed a cab and was on her way, with all of her thoughts redirected to the impossible task ahead.

As the driver pulled up to The Plaza, she remembered the first time she saw it. *Just like in the movies*, she thought. Although not materialistic or interested in the city's ever-changing hotspots, this New York landmark had once taken on a mythic quality in her imagination. She could still hear her mother reading the *Eloise* books to her, and their family movie nights often featured scenes at The Plaza. Suddenly feeling ashamed for having denigrated her childhood memories, she climbed out of the cab and marched into the hotel with conviction. *I will end it.*

***

Tash arrived at the club at ten thirty, half an hour late to meet Aidan who was already waiting inside. Wearing a sparkling black mini-dress and matching high heels, she looked like a movie star. Her hair was pimped out in perfect loose curls and her severe makeup was capped off with cherry red lipstick. Her style was all at once soft and hard, just like the dreamy trip-hop music swirling in the industrial club.

She made her way through the large industrial space featuring exposed pipes contrasted with a perimeter of lush black leather sofas. The blaring trip-hop music and soft blue lighting around the bars set the mood. As she scanned the room both for Aidan and random celebrities, a tall, dark-haired guy dressed head to toe in Gucci offered to buy her a drink. Before she could respond, Aidan was beside her.

"Another time," she said to the guy as she turned to Aidan.

"Fending off your suitors already? Not surprised. You look amazing," he said.

"Well, that'll teach you not to wait for me outside."

"This place is pretty sick, isn't it?"

Tash nodded. "I guess. It's kind of nineties wannabe."

"The music is pretty sexy. And see that roped off area over there?" he said, pointing to a mezzanine level.

"Uh huh."

"That's the VIP area. We have a private table waiting for when Tony and his crew arrive. It's pretty sweet."

"Not bad," she conceded.

"I heard there are some reality stars hanging around, so that should make it worth your while."

"Really? Who's here?"

Aidan laughed. "Don't know. But when you see them you can tell me all about it."

"Okay, smartie. How about you buy me a drink already?"

After a strong cocktail and half an hour of dancing, Tash pulled Aidan close to her and said, "I have to go to the bathroom."

"Sure. I'm going to wait at the table. Tony should be here any minute. Meet me there. You're on the list."

He leaned in to kiss her on the cheek, but she pulled away too quickly.

This is interesting, Tash thought as she entered one of the unisex bathrooms. After relieving herself, she waited for a sink and mirror.

"Damn girl, you're hot," said a young guy who reeked of beer.

When she raised her eyebrow in response, he adopted a more hostile tone. "Can't you take a compliment?"

She turned to face him and said, "Thank you. All right?"

"You don't have to be a bitch. You're not all that, you just look easy. Thought you might do me in a stall. Fucking cunt," he said before stumbling out of the restroom.

"That guy's just a dick," a nearby woman said. "Don't let him get to you. Girls have been turning him down all night and he's not taking it well."

"Thanks," Tash said as she slipped her lipstick into her purse.

As she turned to walk away, the woman called after her. "Hey, come here."

"Yeah?"

The woman pulled a tiny plastic bag filled with white powder out of her Jimmy Choo clutch. "Do you need something to take the edge off?"

Tash stared at the little bag. At first, she was offended. *What the hell? Do I give off junky whore vibes?* But her outrage morphed into temptation. As she contemplated her choices, the woman pulled out another little bag.

"I also have some X if that's more your thing."

A chill went up her spine. Flashes of a horrible night from years earlier surfaced – she had woken up in a boyfriend's bed with him and his roommate, fearing what happened to her while she was unconscious.

"I haven't done that shit since college and I don't plan to start again," she said firmly before leaving the bathroom.

Despite her swagger, she was rattled. She leaned against a wall for a moment before heading to the bar and downing a shot of tequila to calm her nerves.

By the time she got up to the VIP section, Aidan was having an intense conversation with a group of people. When he didn't notice her approaching the table, her mind spiraled. *Fucking great. Maybe if he were a gentleman he would have met me downstairs. Now I have to chat it up with these tools. Can't believe Jason didn't even come. If...* Her thoughts trailed off as Aidan saw her and waved her over, scooting over on the semi-circle leather couch to make room for her.

"Everyone, this is my girlfriend, Tash," he said.

Everyone smiled and nodded. The man directly across from her extended his hand and said, "I'm Tony. Nice to meet you."

"You too," she said.

As the group conversation resumed, Aidan whispered in her ear, "You were gone a while. I was getting worried you ditched me."

"I was dealing with a douchebag in the gross bathroom."

"What happened?"

"Maybe if you had come with me you would know." Aidan looked stunned. Tash said, "Whatever, don't worry about it. It's not a big deal."

Tony redirected Aidan's attention. "Aidan, tell me more about your ideas for themed party nights."

Aidan squeezed Tash's hand and resumed his conversation with Tony. A few minutes later, the waitress stopped by. Tash ordered a shot of tequila, which she slammed back the second it was served.

As the night progressed, Tash became increasingly bored listening to Aidan talk music with Tony and his entourage. Despite his promises, there were only a couple of D-list pseudo-celebrities there, but none of them interested her. Desperate to shake things up, she coyly looked over at Tony and gave him a half smile, catching his attention.

"Aidan, I think your lovely girlfriend might like to dance."

"Oh," Aidan said, jarred. "I'm sorry Tash, are you fed up with music talk?"

"No, but I would like to dance," she said as she stood up.

Aidan started to slide toward the edge of the booth, but Tash looked at Tony, extended her arm, and said, "Shall we?"

"Well, how could I resist such a beautiful woman? Aidan, you don't mind do you?"

"No, man," he said, clearly dumbfounded.

Aidan watched as Tash and Tony walked down to the main dance floor, where she led him to the center stage, pulled him close to her, and danced seductively with him for nearly half an hour to Hooverphonic remixes. She was so tipsy that he had to hold her up a few times but she refused to return to the booth. Aidan watched from the mezzanine. When they came back to the table, Aidan jumped up and said, "I think I should probably get Tash home."

"I think Tash can decide when Tash should go home," she slurred.

"Are we good, Tony? Can we follow up by email?"

Tony nodded.

"See you, man," Aidan said as he took Tash's hand to leave.

When they reached the front door of the club, she pushed his hand aside and said, "I don't like being manhandled."

"What the hell is your problem?"

"I don't have a problem."

"The one time I need you to do something for me so that I can make a good impression and land a job, you get wasted and flirt with the club promoter? Are you kidding me?"

"This is just who I am."

"No, it's who you're afraid people think you are."

"Leave it alone," Tash mumbled.

"It or you?"

"Same difference."

"No, it's not the same. What is *it* anyway? What's wrong with you? Just tell me," Aidan pleaded.

"I'm getting a cab. You can come with me or not," she said as she tottered outside.

"I want to make sure you get home safely," Aidan said.

Neither said a word in the cab. At one point Tash thought he was going to say something so she opened her window and stuck her face into the breeze.

When they got to her apartment, Tash walked in but Aidan stood outside the door.

"Are you coming in or not?" she asked in an irritated tone.

"I don't know. We need to talk but I think you should sleep it off first."

"I'm not drunk."

"Yeah, right."

"We can't talk here. Jason is probably sleeping. He has a big day tomorrow. Come to my room."

Aidan followed Tash in, locking the door behind them. When they got to her bedroom, she sat on her bed to take her shoes off. Aidan leaned against the bedroom door, arms crossed.

In a quiet and calm voice he asked, "What was that tonight, with Tony? Why did you do that?"

She shrugged. "I was bored."

"You were bored? Big freaking deal. You weren't the center of attention for all of five minutes, but that doesn't mean you have to go crazy. You're so damn narcissistic, but it's all bullshit. There's more to you behind this wall of crap."

She didn't respond.

"Fuck, that's it. I can't take it anymore," he said, wringing his hands.

"Then leave."

"Don't you get it? I don't want to leave. I want to be with you but you need to confront your stuff."

"I'm not your fucking project."

"Everyone has stuff to deal with. Stop pretending. Let me in."

"I'm fine the way I am."

"Really? Let's examine things. You went to NYU to study film, which you're passionate about, but you work as a part-time sales clerk instead. Do you know how many friends I have that pounded the pavement to do something in the arts, and reluctantly took jobs as waiters and bartenders because they couldn't make anything happen? And you don't even know if you have to because you never even tried to pursue the one thing you actually care about. What is that?"

Shocked, she jumped up and shouted, "You're not my fucking family."

"Yes, yes I am. I'm your family right now. Me, Jason, even Pen, we are your family in every way that matters. They might be willing to let you float by for now, but not forever. That's not anger, so don't warp it in your mind. It's love. But you can't handle love, right?"

"You're talking out of your ass. My life is just the way I want it to be."

"I doubt that. You have some bullshit idea about who you are so you created a persona to match it, but it's all crap."

"Just get the fuck out."

"I must be getting close to something real, is that it?"

"You don't know what you're talking about," she insisted.

"Let's take your big obsession with the eighties, for example."

"I like the movies. So what?"

"Look a little deeper. It was all about big hair, big shoulder pads, and McMansions. But all of those big things covered up big lies. AIDS, inequality, all of it. Sometimes I think *you* are like the eighties. The quarterback shoulder pads don't fool me. What's behind all the lip gloss?"

"You're seeing things that aren't there. I like to party so I keep things simple."

Aidan shook his head. "I'll never get through to you."

"Just go. We're done."

As she heard the words come out of her mouth she gasped a little. She looked at Aidan to see what he would do.

"You hurt me tonight. Do you get that?" he asked softly.

She didn't know what to say, so she said nothing.

"I would let it go if I wasn't convinced it will happen again. Until you confront your demons, I know I'm only ever going to get glimpses of the real Tash, the one that hides in the MoMA film room and befriends a homeless man. The other version of you, what you show everyone else, she's just a shadow. I'm not willing to chase a shadow anymore."

Tash looked down.

Aidan pulled a copy of *Looking for Alaska* off of her dresser. "I know you've read this half a dozen times," he said, waving it around. "But you missed the point. Smoking to die isn't cool. It didn't make the character fun and mysterious. It's sad. Not romantic sad, just pathetic sad."

Tash looked perplexed.

Aidan put the book down and walked over to her, kneeling on the floor in front of her. "Listen to me. I love you as you really are, but you can't sit on the sidelines anymore."

She shook her head and turned away.

"You live at the edge of living, terrified to go after anything you actually want. Or even to figure out what you want. Why don't you think you're worth taking a chance on? If I do, why don't you?"

She looked him directly in the eyes, and said, "Stop your psychobabble and get out my apartment. We're over."

He stood up and looked at her, giving her a chance to take back her words.

"I never loved you. Get out."

He turned and left the room, gently shutting the bedroom door behind him.

A few minutes later, Jason knocked on her bedroom door.

"I'm so sorry; did we wake you up?"

"Don't worry about it. What happened?"

"It's over. I told Coconut Boy to leave."

"Sweetie, I know you're upset, but don't call him that. His name is Aidan."

CHAPTER 7

Penelope opened her eyes at the crack of dawn. *This comforter is like a cloud*, she thought, knowing it would be the last time she'd wake up there. She quietly shimmied out of bed and got dressed. As she grabbed her backpack and started walking to the door, a voice called behind her, "You're sneaking out?"

Pausing at the door, she turned around and said, "I meant what I said. I can't do this anymore. It's not who I am. Please don't contact me again."

"But…"

"But nothing. You're married and you know it's much worse than that."

"You know my marriage isn't real. As for the rest of it…"

"Please, I never should have let this continue once I learned everything. We both know it's well past time."

"Look, I know we weren't meant to last forever. But I'm concerned about what I have brought to your life. If I had known. I feel like I put you in an impossible situation and that wasn't my intention."

"You didn't."

"Penelope, please don't regret anything. You're very special and I'm grateful that you reminded me of what I was missing. I care deeply about you."

Penelope tilted her face shyly downward. "I'm grateful to you too. You'll always be my first, well, my first everything. But I need to move on and do what makes sense. Goodbye, Richard."

***

As Penelope left the hotel, she noticed the gardeners watering the bright red flowers that flanked the entrance. She was overcome by memories of the flowers at her father's bed and breakfast. On her way home, she thought back to that first day and everything that had happened since. She hoped that by remembering it all she could achieve closure.

It all began with a dreaded trip nearly one year ago during her summer break. Penelope was visiting her father for a week in Stowe, Vermont. As she pulled into the driveway of the large, refurbished Victorian, she wondered how she would survive a full week. While it was a magical place for those seeking a romantic getaway, for Penelope's father, it was a hideaway.

Throughout college and graduate school, she never scheduled Friday classes. This allowed her to visit for at least one long weekend each month, but full weeks were harder to bear. As she sat in her parked car, dragging her feet on going inside, she thought about how fatigued she felt after those long weekends. Tash once suggested that she "stop going so much because it's too far away and lame."

Penelope had responded, "He needs me. Since my mom, you know?"

Tash never mentioned it again. As Penelope sat there, she wondered if things would be different had she confided in Tash about how hard things really were. Lost in her thoughts, she didn't notice her father until he tapped on the car window, startling her. After catching her breath, she smiled at him and popped her trunk.

"Hey, Dad," she said as she emerged from her car.

Already leaning into the trunk to collect her luggage, he mumbled, "Hi, honey."

As they walked into the house, her father remarked, "You seemed deep in thought."

"Just a long drive."

"Well, come on in and have a snack. I just put the afternoon refreshments out in the library."

"Okay. I'll unpack and come down."

"Here," her father said, handing her a key. "I had to put you on the third floor this time. It's a full house all week."

Penelope nodded as she took the key. She followed her father up the dark mahogany staircase, smiling politely while passing an elderly couple on their way down. As she entered the small room that featured a rickety canopy bed and flowered wallpaper, she felt envious of her friends who were returning home for the summer to their own bedrooms.

"I'll just put these here," her father said, placing her suitcase and backpack on a bench at the end of the bed. "This one is heavy," he continued, gesturing at the backpack.

"I have a lot of reading to do for school."

"Aren't classes over for the semester?"

"It's for my thesis. I'm supposed to present a proposal to the committee in the fall."

"Ah. Well, get settled in and I'll see you in a bit."

As he closed the door, she had two thoughts. *He forgot to hug me. This room is stuffy.*

***

Half an hour later, Penelope sat in the library sipping a glass of lemonade. Guests roamed about, occasionally stopping in to pick up a cool drink or a maple scone that paled in comparison to her mother's. Soon her father found her.

"Let's sit down and catch up," he said.

"Sure. Do you want to go sit outside on the porch swing?"

"Okay."

Penelope followed her father outside, glass of lemonade in hand.

As they sat on the swing it swayed, as if mimicking the unease they felt, but it soon steadied with their weight.

"So, the business is going well?" Penelope asked.

"We've been booked solid every weekend since the season began, and we're quite busy during the weeks as well. There was a lull between the end of the ski season and the start of summer, but that's normal."

"Uh huh," Penelope said, in an attempt to show she was paying attention.

"I've been toying with the idea of doing some kitchen renovations. We'll see. How's that lemonade? I squeezed it myself."

"Oh, it's good," Penelope said, taking a sip of the overly tart beverage.

"So, how are things in New York?"

"Pretty good."

"The apartment?"

"It's great. I spend a lot of time hanging out with my roommates. You remember that Tash is a big movie buff so we have a lot of movie nights. Kind of reminds me of when I was little."

"I still wish you would've gotten the other apartment, in the building with the doorman. New York isn't safe and you shouldn't get complacent."

"It's fine, Dad, really. You shouldn't worry."

"What about school?"

"Everything's good. I just have to finalize my thesis topic and get it approved. I've narrowed it down to representations of the Greek goddesses in contemporary art, but it's still too broad. Tash thinks I should focus on Persephone because she's kind of a rebel, but I'm leaning more towards Demeter, her mother, the goddess of the earth and harvest. Do you know the story about how she made the land desolate and barren each winter out of grief? She…"

"Honey, I have to run inside and check on the laundry machine. A guest needed it earlier, and, well, it doesn't matter. You stay here and enjoy the fresh air. I'll see you at dinner."

As he jumped up, the swing again swayed, this time taking longer to steady.

Penelope went to her room, where she napped and read before joining her father for a late dinner after he was done attending to his guests for the day. The dining room was only used to serve breakfast, and Ted avoided sullying the table linens by eating in the outdated kitchen instead, even when Penelope visited. He was able to fake his way through a couple of breakfast classics for his guests, but he was such a poor cook that after a year of eating frozen dinners he hired a local woman to deliver homemade, family-style meals once a week. This week it was roast beef, something neither he nor Penelope particularly enjoyed.

"Her roast turkey is top notch. The sides too. I should have asked her to make that for your visit," Ted said, noticing Penelope moving the food around on her plate.

"It's fine, Dad. I'm just not very hungry."

Although he was making an effort, Penelope was preoccupied with her greatest fear: she would have to accept her father as he now was, a man she hardly knew in a place she hardly belonged.

The next four days passed, each undifferentiated from the ones before. Penelope woke up at five o'clock to help her father prepare breakfast for the guests, which they served from six to nine, followed by an hour of cleaning. Then she read, drank afternoon lemonade, napped, read some more, and ate roast beef with her father, which, like their strained conversation, became increasingly difficult to digest. On the fifth day, everything changed.

***

The howling winds the night before forced her to shut her window, so Penelope was scarcely able to sleep at all in her stuffy room. She dragged herself down to the kitchen at five o'clock to find her father desperately searching in the cabinet under the sink.

"Morning, Dad. What are you looking for?" she asked sleepily.

"Flashlights. I can't find enough for all the guests."

"What? Why do we need flashlights?"

"The forecast changed overnight and the storm they thought was going to miss us is heading this way in full force. Hurricane winds, torrential downpours, and lightning are expected to start mid-afternoon," he said as he moved on to the pantry.

Penelope poured herself a cup of coffee, unbothered. "We probably won't lose power, Dad."

"I just want to be prepared. Check the freezer for batteries."

"The freezer?"

"They last longer there."

After locating the needed flashlights and batteries, Penelope and her father proceeded to make, serve, and clear breakfast. Penelope created emergency kits with flashlights and bottled water for each hotel guest, just in case. Concerned that the quickly dropping temperatures would make the place unseasonably chilly, Ted built a fire in the library fireplace. Penelope set out a platter of marshmallows and skewers to make the storm fun for the guests.

From that point on, Penelope's day was no different from the days before, except the comfort she felt listening to the teeming rain outside. The conversation with her father was limited to weather reports he was reading on his smart phone.

Claiming he was exhausted from the long day, Ted retired immediately after dinner. Penelope washed the dishes and then searched the freezer for something sweet. She found a carton of Neapolitan ice cream tucked away in the back and opened it to discover the chocolate was gone. *It figures*, she thought. There was a frost-covered block of strawberry and vanilla left. After scraping away the freezer burn on the top, she put the rest in a bowl, grabbed her book, and went to curl up in the armchair by the fireplace. She was taking her last bite of ice cream when the bells on the front door rang out. She walked to the opening of the room and saw a well-dressed, middle-aged man standing in the entryway, dripping from head to toe.

"Can I help you?" she asked.

"I hope so. I have a vacation house about two miles away and we lost power. My back-up generator died after an hour. I usually only come up here during ski season and I guess I neglected to have the tank filled. I need a room for the night," he said, as she noticed the puddle he was creating as he stood there.

"Uh, my dad said all the rooms are filled but I can go wake him up and ask," she said.

"I wouldn't want you to do that. I'll find someplace else."

As he started to leave, sloshing with each step, Penelope said, "It's too dangerous to drive. Please come in and I'll get you some towels to dry off and a cup of tea or something. You can sit by the fire. I can fix the couch for you if that would be okay for the night."

"I wouldn't want to put you out."

"No, it's fine. Just stay put and I'll be back in a jiffy."

Penelope returned a few minutes later with a stack of towels and some bedding. "Here, take off your coat and dry off with these."

As she fitted the couch with sheets she said, "You'll be toasty in here by the fire. Can I get you some tea or coffee?"

"Tea would be lovely if it isn't too much trouble."

"No trouble. Are you hungry? We have some leftover roast beef, which I have to confess isn't very good. There are also some scones and muffins."

"Just the tea. Thank you."

Penelope returned ten minutes later holding a silver tray with a full tea service and a small plate of chocolate chip cookies.

"I found these in the cookie jar, in case you changed your mind and wanted a snack."

"Thank you. Do people really have cookie jars?" he asked.

"I guess people in Vermont do."

"I sense you're not from here?"

"No. I'm originally from Boston but I go to graduate school in New York City, at NYU. I come up here to visit my father from time to time."

"I live in the city as well. Normally, I only come up here with my son during the winter to ski."

"What brings you up here now?" she asked as she poured him a cup of tea.

"Truthfully, the short version is that I'm unhappy at home and wanted a change of scenery."

Pleasantly surprised by his candor, she asked, "What would the long version be?"

"An earful."

"I have time," Penelope said. "Uh, that is if you want to talk. I'm sorry, I'm being horribly rude. I've forgotten my manners altogether," she said, jumping up.

"Not at all."

"I should let you warm up and get some rest."

"Please, stay. Here, join me for a cup of tea," he said, lifting the teapot.

Penelope smiled and sat down.

"Do you take sugar or milk?" he asked.

She shook her head.

"What's your name?" he asked as he handed her the teacup.

"Penelope. And yours?"

"Richard."

Penelope took a sip of tea and said, "I don't want to pry, but you said…"

"That I'm unhappy at home."

She nodded. "I'm a good listener, that's all."

"Well," he said with a sigh, "where to begin?"

Over the next hour, Richard told Penelope that his twenty-year marriage was a sham. He revealed that he went out on a few dates with his wife because he was "never a ladies man and lacked the experience to know that indifference was a red flag." When she became pregnant and insistent on having the child, he felt marrying her was the right thing to do.

He explained, "I look back and see that I had other choices, but shall we say, appearances are very important in my family. At the time, it seemed easier to marry her and try to create a life together. Foolish."

Penelope listened sympathetically, thinking how lonely he must be, and how in her own way she could relate. She realized that she hadn't felt this connected to anyone in a long time.

She asked, "Have you ever thought about ending the marriage?"

He nodded. "I could never bring myself to do it though. I used to justify staying because I focused on my son and trying to keep his home together. The truth is that I feel sorry for my wife. We don't have any relationship to speak of, not even a friendship, but she's had a troubled life. The shell of the marriage is somehow important to her."

"And for you?"

He chuckled and shook his head. "I'm not used to people asking how I feel. Well, for me the shell is just what a shell is: empty."

"I'm sorry," Penelope said, unsure of herself.

"Please, don't feel sorry for me. My life has mainly been about my career and there's no one to blame for that but myself. The truth is that I'm probably not an emotionally giving person. Maybe the real reason I stayed all these years is because there is a part of me that is more comfortable with the façade. I don't know if I'd be any good at the real thing."

"Don't you want to find out though?" He smiled but before he could respond, she said, "Oh God, I'm sorry. That was inappropriate."

"No, don't be sorry. It's a thought I've had myself. That's really why I'm up here. I needed to escape to somewhere other than my office for a few days. You're remarkably easy to talk to. Believe it or not, I'm usually quite reserved."

She smiled. "Me too. I'm a good listener though."

"You also sound like quite a romantic. Is there someone special back in New York?"

"Oh, no, not at all. I mean no to both. I'm not seeing anyone and I'm not much of a romantic. I mean, I just never prioritized that stuff, but…"

"But?"

"My parents were very much in love, so maybe there's a part of me that at least believes that kind of movie love is possible. But it's not for me."

"Why not?"

She paused and set her teacup on the silver tray. "Would you like something stronger than tea? I think there's a bottle of brandy around here somewhere."

"Yes. Thank you."

Penelope returned a few minutes later with two brandy snifters.

"Cheers," they said as they clinked glasses.

"That's good," Richard said as he took a sip. "You know, the amber color is a bit like your eyes."

Penelope blushed.

"I'm sorry. I don't mean to make you uncomfortable."

"You didn't. I'm not used to people noticing things like that. Most people just see my glasses and don't even know what color my eyes are."

"You're very beautiful. I'd imagine there are guys your age lined up for you."

"Hardly," she said as she took a swig. "I'm sort of invisible to most guys, which suits me just fine."

"You were saying that before, that you're not a romantic."

"My mother died when I was in high school and it destroyed my father."

"I'm sorry. Was she ill?"

"No, it was a car accident – some reckless person, texting. My dad became a different person overnight. A shell of who he used to be. I guess I don't want to open myself up for that kind of hurt."

"Take it from me: avoiding love doesn't spare you from pain. At a minimum, it creates a slow but persistent numbing that might be worse than actual pain."

Penelope took another sip of her drink. "I've been focusing on my studies anyway."

"That's right; you said you're in graduate school. Why did you pick New York?"

"I wanted to change my life I guess. Take more chances. But I haven't really changed like I hoped."

"Change is hard. What are you studying?"

"Art history."

They talked for hours about art, literature, and mythology. Richard was well-versed in every subject that came up, which he chalked up to "a good education." They batted around some of Penelope's thesis ideas and Richard suggested she read the work of Sarah Cohen, a feminist historian who has written about the goddesses in modernity. When Penelope asked how he was familiar with her work, he hesitated a bit before saying, "My wife has taken me to some book events."

"Oh," she said, unable to conceal her irrational disappointment. After a moment passed, Penelope said, "It must be really late."

Richard looked at his watch. "God, it's after two. I shouldn't have kept you so long."

Penelope stood up. "I should let you get some rest. I have to be up in a few hours to help my dad with breakfast. Please join us whenever you wake up."

Richard stood up and put his hand out.

Penelope extended her arm in anticipation of a handshake, but instead he took her hand and clasped it in his. They stood for a moment, the only noise the last crackles from the dying embers of the fire.

"Well, goodnight," she said.

"Goodnight." It seemed as though he wanted to say more, but he didn't.

Penelope went to her room where she lay wide-eyed, wondering what had just happened and trying to understand what she was feeling. *He's so average looking and he's old; why am I thinking about him? He's obviously having a midlife crisis. But he has kind eyes, and he seemed to get me – really get me – and I think I got him. What was that?*

After a sleepless night, she rolled out of bed at five o'clock and headed down to the kitchen. *Dad must have slept in. Wonder what he'll say about Richard sleeping on our couch*, she thought as she started the coffee pot. She noticed that the two brandy glasses had been cleaned and placed in the drying rack, so she walked into the library to check on Richard. He was gone. The bedding was folded neatly, and atop it, she found a note.

Thank you for your hospitality and for listening. Forgive me for overstepping, but my failures have opened my eyes and so I want to offer you some advice. Open your heart to somebody, someday. They will be very lucky. You deserve all life has to offer. Richard.

She smiled as she held the paper, the faint smell of last night's fire still in the air.

"Penelope, there you are," her father said from the doorway. "I saw you started the coffee. You look tired. Did you get any sleep or did the wind keep you up too?"

"Uh, no. I didn't get much sleep."

***

Two months later, Penelope was crouching on the floor of the Fifth Avenue Barnes & Noble looking at Moleskine notebooks when she heard, "Penelope?"

She looked up to see Richard. She smiled as he reached his hand out to pull her up, her skin sparking when it touched his.

"Hi, Richard."

"Buying a notebook?" he asked.

"Oh, yeah. It's a start-of-the-semester ritual. I pick a different color each time."

"It's reassuring to know people still buy non-electronic notebooks."

"What about you?" she asked, sheepishly.

"I just left a meeting nearby and stopped in to get a birthday card for my sister."

Penelope smiled softly. "I wondered if I'd ever see you again. Every time I visit my father and someone walks through the front door, I look to see if it's you, which I know is stupid because you have a house down the road and…"

"It's not stupid. I've wondered if I would see you again, too."

"You left in the middle of the night. Was your power restored?"

"Actually, I drove back to the city."

"In that awful storm?"

"I wanted to do it before I lost my nerve."

"To do what?" she asked.

"Change my life."

She paused before asking, "And did you?"

He looked down and shook his head. "My wife lost her job. If you asked her, she would say that she made a career change, but that's par for the course. Her career was all she had. We're two of a kind that way. It wasn't the right time."

"I'm sorry."

"Don't be. You helped me more than you know."

Penelope smiled. After an awkward moment, she said, "Well, I guess I should buy my notebook."

"Are you in a hurry? Maybe you'd like to get a drink or a bite to eat. I owe you for the tea and brandy."

"Oh, well, uh…" she stuttered.

"It's all right if you'd rather not. I hope this doesn't sound strange but I felt a connection with you that I haven't felt before, so seeing you again is remarkable."

"I felt the same way."

"Shall we then?"

"Yes. Let's," she said without hesitation.

Penelope helped Richard find a suitable birthday card, after which he insisted on buying her new midnight blue notebook. As they stepped onto a bustling Fifth Avenue, Penelope asked, "Where should we go?"

"We're a few blocks from The Plaza. The Rose Club has a great wine list. Have you been there?"

She shook her head. "Would it be pathetic to say that I was obsessed with the *Eloise* books as a child? I've always hoped for an excuse to go there."

He smiled. "The Plaza it is."

***

They lifted their champagne flutes. "Cheers!" they said in unison.

"So, what do you think? Does it live up to your expectations?" he asked.

"It's just like the movies, especially the lobby. Although my fantasy was more hot chocolate than champagne."

He laughed. "Well then, since we're writing our own script anyway, shall I order us a bite to eat?"

"Sure."

"It's a special day. How about caviar?"

Penelope nodded.

After Richard ordered, Penelope asked, "Why is it a special day?"

"Because I saw you again."

She blushed and looked down, hiding behind her long curls.

"And it's your first time at The Plaza."

She smiled.

For the next hour, they talked about their favorite books and films set in New York. Both workaholics, neither spent much time taking advantage of all the city has to offer. They vowed to push each other to work less and play more. Then Penelope came up with an idea.

"What if we meet up once in a while to see the places from our favorite books and movies? It could be a way to explore the city with new eyes. Since you brought me here, I feel like I should return the favor."

Richard smiled. "Your plan reminds me of something I might have seen in a movie."

"*Breakfast at Tiffany's*. They explore the city by taking turns doing things one of them has never done before. My idea is a spin on that."

"It's a deal."

The waiter came to remove their empty champagne bottle and Richard said, "I should probably take care of the check and get you a cab."

"Okay."

As they stood at the cabstand, Penelope felt morose. *Will I really see him again? What is this? Does he feel something too? Is there something between us?* She contemplated asking him but couldn't bring herself to be so direct. She took a deep breath to say goodbye when Richard said, "It feels like fate running into you today. I hope I can see you again. Another landmark from the movies, as you suggested?"

"Sure," Penelope said softly.

"Should we exchange numbers?"

She nodded.

A moment later, a cab pulled up. They both seemed unsure of what to do so Richard hugged her and she gave him a peck on the cheek. On the way home she mused, *Was it really fate? Do I even believe in that?* When those thoughts faded, the warmth of their embrace lingered.

For the next three days, she checked her phone incessantly, something she had never done before. Disappointed with each confirmation that there was no missed call or text, she eventually decided, *I'm being impractical. He's older. He's married. He was just being nice. Let it go.* On the fourth day, she received a text message:

> It was wonderful to see you the other day.
> I can't stop thinking about it. There's
> a showing of Breakfast at Tiffany's at

```
The Paris a week from tonight at 7. It's
not exactly a landmark but it does seem
like fate. Would you like to go? Maybe
we could go for a hot chocolate after. R.
```

Penelope felt exhilarated as she texted back:

```
I'd love to.
```

She spent the next week consumed by anticipation and worry. *What have I gotten myself into?* When Friday came, Penelope laid potential outfits all over her bed. She tried on jeans with several different t-shirt and blazer combinations, overcome by disappointment each time she looked in the mirror. *If I want to be less serious and have more fun, I need to change it up. I just need to get outside of myself.* After spending an hour trying on everything in her closet, she settled on a simple white sundress, far more frivolous than her daily attire. On her way out the door, she panicked and grabbed a blue cardigan, rationalizing that she didn't want to be cold.

She arrived at The Paris and was relieved to see Richard waiting for her, tickets in hand.

"You look lovely," he said as he handed her a ticket.

"Oh, thank you," she said, hoping he wouldn't notice her sweaty palms.

They stepped into the crowded line of moviegoers, slowly making their way into the sold-out theater. Penelope's heart raced; she wasn't sure if it was the crowds, Richard, or both. As the smell of buttered popcorn wafted into her nostrils, she stole a glance at Richard. *With just one change, the familiar can be made unfamiliar.*

"What about over there?" he asked, pointing to two seats in the dead center of the theater.

"Perfect." Other patrons stood up to let them wriggle into the row, so he took her hand and led her to their seats. After some small talk about their days, the lights went out. They sat in the glow of the screen, and Penelope made a conscious decision to let go and lose herself in the movie, something she wasn't accustomed to. By the end, she had a palpable lump in her throat. Unable to speak, she turned to face Richard and smiled, teary eyed. He gently rubbed her hand.

After they made their way outside Richard said, "The Plaza is right here. Should we go for that hot chocolate?"

Penelope nodded. *Could he be what I was waiting for? Maybe this is my chance to change my life.*

They entered the grand lobby for the second time, and Richard took her hand.

He pointed and said, "I think the hot chocolate is over there."

"What if we get room service instead?" Penelope's words surprised even her. *Who am I? I can't believe I said that.*

He nodded. "Stay here for a minute."

He returned a few moments later with a room key. They held hands during the impossibly long elevator ride, each watching the changing numbers as if afraid to look at each other.

They entered the room in silence and stood next to the bed, still holding hands. Richard stroked Penelope's cheek, leaned in, and kissed her. He took her sweater off and the strap from her sundress slipped off her shoulder. He touched her shoulder and she felt a shiver. They made love that night.

When she awoke the next morning, she suddenly wondered, *Was that a one-night stand? My first time can't be a one-night stand in a hotel. I think I feel different. Everything feels kind of different. Or do I just want it to?*

Richard looked over and said, "Good morning. Did you sleep well?"

"Uh huh."

Richard caressed her face and she averted her eyes.

"What is it? What's wrong?"

"You're married. I'm just wondering if you do this kind of thing often."

He shook his head. "I promise, not once in all of these years. And I didn't mean for this to happen with us, but I'm glad it did. Are you?"

She nodded.

"How about I order some breakfast and we can decide what landmark we're going to visit next?"

She was surprised that he'd thought of their plan.

"Remember? We said we'd see the sites from our favorite books and films."

"I remember," she said.

Over the next several months, they visited the Empire State Building, Central Park, and Times Square. Penelope particularly enjoyed going to museums together so she could teach Richard about the origins of the paintings and their historical significance. They saw *The Woman in Gold* at the Neue Galerie and Van Gogh's *The Starry Night* at the MoMA. While standing before Van Gogh's masterpiece, she realized it was the closest she had come to looking at the stars in years and she felt grateful. After their outings, they always returned to The Plaza, which had become "their place." Since Richard didn't appear to have any worries about going out with her in public, she chose to forget that he was married.

She spent increasingly less time with her roommates, who were busy with their own lives and didn't seem to notice. Her schoolwork suffered a little and her thesis proposal was past due, but as a lifelong overachiever, she felt entitled to a break.

Everything changed on Valentine's Day. Penelope was approaching her apartment after class, trying not to slip on the veneer of frost covering the sidewalk. To her surprise, she saw Richard standing outside of her building. He looked startled to see her.

"Penelope! What are you doing here?"

"You're not here to see me?" she asked, bewildered.

"No. Is this where you live?"

She nodded. "What are you doing here?"

"I'm taking my son Kyle out to dinner, but he wanted to stop by his cousin's place to drop off a gift. She recently broke up with someone and he wanted to make sure someone gave her a Valentine's gift."

Oh my God. It can't be, she thought, trembling.

"That name never meant anything to me before, but…" she mumbled incoherently.

273

"What are you talking about, Penelope? Do you know Kyle?"

"What's your niece's name?" she asked with dread.

"Natashya."

"Oh my God."

"You know her?"

"Tash is my roommate and she's going to kill me."

***

Over the next few months, Penelope started to unravel. For the first time in her life, even when she hunkered down at the library, she was unable to concentrate. She was racked with guilt, exacerbated every time she saw Tash, who was more protective of Kyle than anyone. Terrified she would confess the affair and ruin everyone's lives, Penelope avoided Tash, which meant avoiding Jason as well. Their movie nights and roommate talks became a thing of the past. Worse, Tash and Jason didn't seem to miss her. Penelope felt utterly alone. Richard was the only person she could talk to, which made ending it with him seem impossible. Now afraid to be caught together in public, they saw each other less frequently and only at The Plaza.

It all came to a head as the spring slipped into summer. Richard insisted that it was time to tell his wife. "We can't go on like this. You're too afraid to go anywhere and this feels wrong."

"Please don't. If you do, Kyle will surely find out and then it's only a matter of time before Tash finds out. We haven't been terribly close recently, but she's probably still my best friend. If she hates me, Jason will too. I will lose everything."

"Kyle won't find out. My wife would never tell him and neither would I."

"You don't know that. Besides, I don't want to be the cause of a marriage ending, whether it's a good marriage or not."

"You're not the cause. I've wanted to do this for a long time, since before we met."

"We should split up, just end things. Then you can do what you want and it will have nothing to do with me."

Richard shook his head. He looked broken.

"I'm ashamed I didn't end this sooner," she said, unable to make eye contact.

"Listen to me. I won't do anything, and you don't either. Let's just take some time and sort things out. See where the chips fall. Please."

Emotionally drained, Penelope agreed. In the coming weeks, she tried to pull herself together and look at things rationally. She hoped to make progress on her thesis but was entirely too preoccupied. Then one day Richard texted to say that he wanted to see her. She knew when she left the library to meet him that she would end the relationship once and for all.

As the cab pulled up to her apartment building in the early morning light after her last night with Richard, she had one thought: *Should I tell Tash?*

CHAPTER 8

Oh shit, Jason thought as he approached the Battery Park set and saw Sam at the makeup tent. *I wonder if he still thinks I'm a jerk. Tash would have a field day with this. I hope she's okay.*

"Hey," Sam said as he pulled out a folding chair for Jason.

"Hey, dude. Uh, I mean Sam. Hey, Sam."

Sam smiled as Jason silently berated himself. *What's wrong with me? He's just the makeup guy. Don't let him rattle you.*

"They want to get started as soon as possible in case we go long. So Tanya here is going to do your hair while I do your face. Your makeup! While I do your makeup," Sam said, looking flushed.

"Cool. Hi, Tanya," Jason said with a nod. *Hmm, Sam seems nervous. He remembers. I can almost hear Tash saying that he's probably worried you're going to get him fired.*

Soon they were doing the first set-up. Distracted with thoughts of Tash, Jason had trouble finding his light. He required repeated direction from the photographer. Sam noticed and requested they stop the shoot for a moment, pretending he needed to fix a stray eyelash on Jason's face.

When he got close to Jason, he whispered, "You seem a little off. Are you okay?"

"My best friend is in crisis, broke up with her guy last night. I'm preoccupied, I guess."

"Remember, you're the star. Tune it all out."

"Thanks, Sam."

Jason regrouped and was soon in the zone. He was egged on as the crowd of bystanders grew, necessitating the crew to put up more barricades. At the command of the photographer, Sam ran on set to do touch-up work.

"You're on fire now!" he said to Jason.

"Thanks, and for earlier too."

Sam smiled. "People are standing around, waiting for your autograph."

277

"Really, dude? I figured people stopped to see if anything looks exciting and they don't even know what it is."

"I heard some of them say your name. They know you," Sam said excitedly.

Jason smiled, but then caught himself, afraid to appear arrogant.

"You're all set. I'm jumping out."

"Cool. Thanks, Sam."

After another hour of shooting, they broke for lunch.

Jason bypassed the catered food and headed straight to his makeup chair. The rest of the crew ate their lunch together. Noticing Jason alone, Sam put his half-eaten tuna sandwich down, grabbed two bottles of water, and headed over to Jason.

"Thanks," Jason said as he took the water Sam offered.

"I'm sorry about your friend. I hope she's okay."

"She's going through some stuff and kind of fucking up her life, but she needs to figure it out for herself."

"Hopefully she will. Maybe you can nudge her in the right direction."

"You know what's funny is that we watch movies together all the time. She's one of my roommates. We watched *Desperately Seeking Susan* like a week ago. You know the old Madonna flick, back when people thought she'd always be ahead of the trends?"

Sam nodded.

"The big scenes all take place here in Battery Park, and now I'm here."

"Yeah, that's right. I watched it online a few years ago. What I remember most was Roberta, the desperate housewife, you know before there were desperate housewives. God, she was so lonely in her sad, orgasm-free suburban marriage."

Jason laughed. "At first it seemed like it's all about Madonna's fabulous lace bustiers and sequined boots, but then I wondered if each of us really has a person we would chase around the world, you know, like the Susan character. That one person you can't quite forget... Jeez, listen to me. Sorry. I guess I'm still thinking about my roommate."

Sam smiled. "So, are you one of those models who doesn't eat? They're going to call you back soon."

"Just not during shoots. Nerves."

Sam smirked.

"What?" Jason prodded.

"It always surprises me when guys like you get nervous."

"Guys like me?"

"Guys who've had it easy."

"Wow, that's a big assumption."

"I keep putting my foot in my mouth," Sam mumbled before backtracking. "I just meant that you seem like you have every reason to be confident."

"It's not like I've had any training for this. I never planned on becoming a model. Some guy approached me at a yoga studio. Turned out he worked for one of the biggest agents in the business. I didn't really know what I was in for."

"Is that regret? Seems like you have a pretty huge opportunity."

"No regret. I'm just saying I get nervous. Pretty sure one of these days, these people are gonna figure out that I don't belong here."

"I doubt it. You're a rising star."

"I'm a token, an experiment."

Sam looked perplexed.

"The only thing they like about me is my skin color. I'm just a trend that hasn't gone out of style yet, you know?"

"God, I feel like a jerk."

Jason laughed. "I'm not saying you should feel sorry for me. I have a sweet gig and I'm enjoying it. But it is what it is, you know?"

Sam nodded. "I bet people underestimate you."

At that moment, the photographer's assistant came to the tent to fetch Jason. As Jason walked back to the set, Sam called after him.

"What you asked before, about each person having someone they can't quite shake – I think we do, if we're lucky."

Jason smiled.

***

The shoot moved to the South Street Seaport and eventually the Circle Line Ferry, continuing until dusk, when the photographer finally lamented that there was no more usable light. Jason was ready to leave when he noticed Sam packing up.

"Sam, thanks again for everything today."

"My pleasure. You smashed it. And I hope your friend is okay."

"Would you, uh, that is if you don't have plans, would you like to go grab a bite to eat?"

"Are you asking me out?"

"Yeah," Jason replied.

"Well, I usually don't date models. You know, models always hang all over the makeup guys," he said, before bursting out into laughter.

Jason sighed.

"I was just kidding. I'm sorry. My timing is seriously off. Yes, I would love to go out with you, if you still want to."

Jason nodded.

"You must be starving. What are you in the mood for?"

"Ever since we talked about that movie, I've been craving Chinese food. Remember the scene where they get wasted and eat takeout on the roof?"

Sam smiled. "Chinatown it is."

***

"Do they really say that?" Sam asked as he took his last sip of hot and sour soup.

"Oh yeah. Sometimes I even hear the crew gossiping about me and they always say 'That one, the Chinese one.' And I'm like, my mom is Japanese and my dad is Korean. On what planet does that make me Chinese?"

"That's awful. Maybe it's the price to pay for breaking the stereotype."

"Most of the time I feel like a huge sellout. I've never said that to anyone before. I know it's a bullshit job and I let them use me, but it's such an easy way to make serious bank. To be honest, I don't know what I would have done if this hadn't landed in my lap. Most of my friends are struggling to make ends meet. Some had to move back home, couldn't survive in the city."

"I hear that. I lay awake some nights wondering how I'm going to pay my bills. My apartment is three hundred square feet and I can't afford it. The interest on my debt from my cosmetology program keeps growing and it seems like I'll never get ahead of it. I keep waiting for it to get just a little easier, but it never does."

"Why do you stay in the city?"

"It's oxygen. Survival. I'd do anything to stay here. You have to understand, I'm from a small town in Missouri where you lived in fear if people even suspected you were gay. I walked down the street with people following behind me, saying that they hoped I died of AIDS."

Jason listened intently, not taking his eyes off of Sam.

Sam continued, "I dreamed of making my way here someday. Cliché, I know, but for me New York represented more than a safe place; it was an idea, a concept. You know, the way America is an idea as much as a place. New York represents possibility. That idea got me through a hell that others didn't survive. As soon as I could afford a ticket, I left all that shit behind. Beating after beating, threat after threat, I found a way to survive. But I think if I gave up on the idea of New York now, well, I wouldn't survive that."

Jason outstretched his arm and put his hand on Sam's. At that moment, the waiter delivered the bill.

"Let me get this," Jason said as he snatched it up.

"I didn't mean…"

"I invited you out," Jason said.

As they left the restaurant Sam asked, "So now what?"

"Now how about you take me home to your tiny apartment?"

***

The next morning Jason woke up to the smell of French vanilla.

"I made coffee," Sam said from the galley kitchen. "Are you hungry or are you in a hurry?"

Jason thought for a moment. "Not in a hurry at all. Now come here and give me a kiss."

Sam prepared omelets while Jason showered. Over brunch they talked about photographers they like, the benefits of work travel, and books, discovering they both have an interest in architecture and design. Before Jason left, he invited Sam to a club opening the following night. Although he seemed surprised by the invitation, Sam agreed to meet him there.

When Jason got home late that afternoon, he bumped into Penelope.

"Hey, Pen."

When she turned, he could see she had been crying.

"Are you okay?" he asked.

"I'm fine," she sighed before closing the bathroom door.

Jason redirected his focus on Tash and knocked on her door.

"Come in."

He opened the door and walked right over to the bed, sitting on the corner.

"Hey sweetie," he said.

"Hey."

"You might want to get out of bed and start the day."

"I called out of work. I'm tired."

"Do you want to talk about what happened with Aidan?"

"No."

"There's something wrong with Pen. She looks like she's been crying all night. Do you know what's going on?"

Tash shook her head.

"Weeeeelll, then we can talk about me. Do you want to hear about the shoot?"

Tash sat up, leaning against the wall. "Wasn't that yesterday? Are you just getting back?"

"Uh huh. Remember that guy I met? Sam?"

Tash thought for a minute. "Makeup Boy?"

"We went out last night after the shoot and I stayed at his place."

"And you're just getting back now? Did you take downers and sleep all day?"

"No, he made me brunch."

"You stayed for brunch? Wow, so does this mean ugly sex is as hot as they say? You know, because they like try harder or something?"

"He's not ugly. He has great eyes, among other things."

"Oh my God," she said, perking up. "You actually like him!"

Jason smiled brightly.

"That's great, honey. But just remember, we're all tomorrow's discards. I wouldn't get too heavy."

"Sweetie, you have to call Aidan."

PART THREE

CHAPTER 9

"Since you're actually on time this morning you can help me open the shop."

Fine, oh passive aggressive one, Tash thought. "What do you want me to do?" she asked from the customer couch she was slumped in.

"Clean the jewelry case. A customer's child got fingerprints all over it yesterday."

She rolled her eyes and sluggishly made her way to the backroom to get the cleaning supplies. Moving a Windex-soaked paper towel in circles over the glass case, she was completely detached from herself. Lost in rote movements and absent of discernible thoughts, she didn't realize that she was wiping the same spot on the counter over and over again. When Catherine called, "Tash, I'm opening," she was jarred back into the moment. *Great, another thrilling day begins.*

Inundated with the morning rush, Tash immediately started assisting customers. She was good at sizing people up and when she was attentive, customers were captivated by her. To them, Tash was the living embodiment of the confident, effortless style they were hoping to buy. When a young woman in a miniskirt came in, Tash pointed out each skirt in the store, explaining how flattering the cut is. Once in the dressing room with a pile of skirts, Tash assembled mix-and-match outfits and suggested additional pieces. "You look hot in that," she said, her standard phrase of encouragement. Her skills and charisma landed her the considerable sale.

Catherine said, "You know, you're very good with customers when you make an effort. If you made a bigger commitment to the store, you could be assistant manager someday."

"Thanks," she said, half-heartedly. *Then I can be just like you. Holy shit. I didn't think I could feel worse today.*

Deflated from the prospect of turning into Catherine, she returned to assisting customers. She rang up sales, issued store credits, answered calls, and ran back and forth from the register to the dressing rooms to the storeroom and back again. It was an utterly normal day.

When Catherine left to pick up lunch, Tash wandered aimlessly around, looking for an outfit to rehang or a display in need of adjustment. She thought about rearranging the new arrivals up front but didn't want to spur a lecture from Catherine. So she meandered back to the counter, her usual place for slouching and counting the minutes. Normally engrossed in making plans for her evenings, time moved far slower now that she was spending her nights alone at home. *It can't only be 12:05,* she thought as she glanced at the clock. *The days are getting longer. I wish there was at least a window display to create.*

Just when she thought she couldn't be any more bored, customers walked in. Like a switch going off in her mind, the ring of the door chime propelled Tash into a fantasy. In her mind's eye, the store suddenly turned into the scene of a musical. Everything was transformed into Technicolor and she envisioned herself screaming and then breaking out into dance and song. Customers became backup singers and mannequins swayed from side to side.

"Miss, do you have these pants in a smaller size?" a customer asked, instantly closing the curtain on her fantasy musical.

"Yes, ma'am. I'll go check in the back," she said.

Fuck, what's wrong with me? It's like I'm in a Björk video. God, who directed that video? It was so different than... fuck, snap out of it, she thought as she hit the side of her head.

She returned with the pants to find even more customers milling about. Soon Catherine returned and took charge, assisting the wealthiest-looking customers while Tash fetched different sizes from the back, cleaned out dressing rooms, and offered bottles of water to bored men waiting for their wives. The hours passed slowly.

She breathed a sigh of relief when it was finally time to clock out. On the walk home, she barely acknowledged the street vendors trying to catch her attention, too lethargic to offer a smile or even a sarcastic word. As she crossed over from SoHo into the Village, the city transitioned from work to play, with the sounds of friends meeting filling the air. The only thing Tash could concentrate on was crawling into bed and watching TV, her new nightly ritual that had taken the place of the club scene. As she approached Washington Square Park, she noticed Harold wrapping something around his ankle.

"Oh, hello Natashya."

"What's wrong with your ankle?" she asked, staring at the purple, swollen appendage.

"Had a little tussle," he said with a wince as he tried to wrap it with an old navy-blue bandana.

"Did someone do this to you?" she asked in outrage.

He shook his head. "A lovely young lady like you shouldn't worry. I'm fine."

"You need ice on that. Hang on and I'll run to the store."

"You needn't…" he tried to call after her but she was already on her way.

When she returned, she sat on the bench next to him and opened a plastic bag to reveal ice, baby wipes, and an Ace bandage. She opened the container of wipes and held it out.

"I thought it would be smart to clean it first," she said.

"Thank you," he said as he used one to wipe the dirt from his swollen ankle. "You didn't have to go to all this trouble. I can get by."

"I know," she said. "Do you remember the day we first met? I had twisted my ankle."

He nodded.

She opened a soda cup filled with ice. "It was the only way I could get some," she said. "Don't worry; I got some napkins we can put the ice in."

He offered a close-mouthed smile.

As he held the makeshift ice pack against his injured ankle, Tash quietly said, "Harold, I don't want to pry, but…"

"The time has come?"

She looked at him, uncertain of herself.

"Yes, you can ask me. Go ahead."

"How did you end up here?"

"I wish I could tell you the story you want to hear: a fairytale about the perfect life that unraveled because of one tricky bend in the path I didn't see coming. The career that toppled, the love of my life I lost, the children I miss. I long for that beautiful lie. But Miss Natashya, I have no such story."

"I'm sorry. I didn't mean to…"

He put his hand up. "I do not wish to be a cautionary tale for anyone. But if my story were told, it wouldn't be one of someone who lost it all, rather, someone who never wanted anything to lose."

Tash looked down and tried to make sense of what he was saying.

"I am quite content, most of the time," he said, returning his attention to his ankle.

She stood up and smiled. "Don't wrap the bandage too tightly. It should fit comfortably. You might want to save the rest of the wipes, you know, for whatever. There's a sandwich and a bottle of water in the bag."

"Thank you, Natashya," he said as he continued tending to his injury.

She took a few steps and considered saying something more, but decided against it and headed home. She dropped her bag inside her front door and dragged herself to the kitchen. She took a tub of Campbell's chicken noodle soup from the cabinet and stuck it in the microwave. As it cooked, she grabbed a Diet Coke and opened a jar of maraschino cherries, popping a couple directly into her mouth. She bit into the cherries, releasing their sugary liquid, and thought about how much she'd always loved them. When the microwave beeped, she stuck her soda under one arm and retrieved her soup and a spoon.

Both of her roommates' doors were closed. Jason must be out with Sam again, and Pen's probably locked in her room. When she got to her room, the floor covered with dirty laundry, she made space to put her food down on her nightstand before changing into her sweats. She crawled into bed, searched the sheets for her remote control, flipped on the TV, and started eating.

Afraid of bumping into Aidan at a club and too depressed to go out with friends, this had become her new nightly ritual. Jason spent most nights out with Sam, and although he invited her to join them many times, she didn't want to be a third wheel. Without plugging into the city's energy at night, her days felt longer and increasingly monotonous.

When he was home, Jason sat on her bed while she got ready to go to work in the mornings. She lived vicariously through his stories.

"I took Sam to a film screening at the SoHo House last night."

"What film?" she asked, searching for a clean tank top.

"I don't know. Some docu-whatever about eating disorders. It was a charity thing and my agent put me on the list."

"Kind of sketchy to send models to promote eating disorder awareness or whatever."

"Yeah, I know. Aaaaanyway, Sam is great in those places. He can talk to anyone and a lot of A-listers know him from work."

"Uh huh."

"I know it's early…"

"In the morning? Yeah, it is!" she said with a snicker.

"No, early in the relationship, smart ass," he said, tossing a wet towel at her.

"Okay, jeez, I'm listening. Early in the relationship for what?" she asked, still searching for a top.

"To think it might be something. It's good for me to be with someone like him. Someone, um, down to earth."

"First of all, it's not early in the relationship by your slutty standards; it's shockingly far into it."

He laughed.

Second, he's so lucky to have you. Seriously."

Jason smiled.

"Shit, now I'm gonna be late for work again. Help me find a shirt."

***

"Tash is always in and out of relationships. They never last, but she's sort of a love junkie…"

"Or maybe a love seeker," Sam suggested.

"Yes! You nailed it," Jason agreed and took his hand as they walked into Minetta Tavern. Recognizing Jason, the hostess immediately showed them to a reserved section of the bar. "We have a nice semi-round in the dining room ready when your friends arrive."

"Thank you," Jason replied as he and Sam hopped on barstools.

"This place is cool," Sam said, looking around. "You'd never expect this when you walk in."

"They have the best high-end cheeseburgers in the city," Jason said.

"You eat burgers?" Sam asked skeptically.

"Once in a blue moon."

"You never finished telling me about your roommate and her relationship drama."

"Actually, what I wanted to tell you was more about me, well, us I guess," he said, putting his hand on Sam's thigh.

"I'm listening."

"This is the first time I've done the healthy relationship thing. It's amazing. *You're* amazing, Sam. You're good for me."

Sam put his hand over Jason's hand and smiled softly.

"Listen, we're having a great time, but it isn't too heavy, right? I mean, we're keeping it light?"

"Uh, yeah. Of course. We're just having fun," Jason stammered, trying to cover his confusion.

"I mean, I'm not seeing anyone else. How could I? We're always together. But it's meant to be a good time. We're on the same page, right?"

"Definitely," Jason said.

Their friends arrived just in time to rescue Jason from the uncomfortable spotlight. Sam leapt off his stool to give them hugs while Jason sat thinking, *Not too heavy? Keep it light? What exactly does he mean?*

As the group settled in at their table, Jason excused himself to use the men's room. He splashed cold water on his face, wishing he could go back in time and wash the heart off his sleeve.

***

A few weeks later, Tash received a text from Kyle asking her to meet for lunch. She was reluctant because she didn't want to talk about

Aidan, and Kyle could always tell when she was in a bad space. But it would be nice to see him, so she agreed to meet at their favorite diner the next day.

"Damn! I'm perfectly on time and was hoping to surprise you by beating you here for a change," Tash said as she hugged Kyle.

"You get credit for being on time," he said as they slid into the booth.

The waitress tried to hand them oversized laminated menus, but Kyle stopped her. "We actually know what we want: two coffees and a platter of blueberry blintzes to share, please."

As the waitress walked away, Tash said, "She's new, not like the other dinosaurs here. She looks like she's our age. God, that's depressing. Can you imagine working here?"

The waitress returned with their coffee and a plate of complimentary bagel chips. As they fixed their coffee, Tash asked, "What's been going on?"

"Summer kind of sucks. I'm living back at home, which is a major drag.

"That blows," Tash said as she searched for a cinnamon raisin bagel chip.

Now that my mom is a literary agent, she's working for herself so she's always home."

"That totally sucks."

"Yup."

"Does she like being an agent at least? Being your own boss sounds cool."

"She was pretty stoked that she landed a big deal for one of her clients. Some unknown guy, Pete Rice. His book is called *The Lost Notebooks* and she got him a deal with Random House. I guess it's her first big score. We got Chinese food to celebrate, which was lame."

Tash giggled.

"There's definitely something up with my parents though."

"You said that when I saw you last time."

"Being at home, I'm certain. It's obvious. I don't know what happened but they don't talk at all. I mean, not a word. It's creepy."

"No offense, but they've always been kinda messed up."

"Yeah, I know."

"So, you seeing anyone?" she asked.

Kyle shook his head.

The waitress interrupted to deliver their blintzes with two small plates for sharing. They each took a blintz and a dollop of sour cream. Kyle asked, "What's been going on with you?"

"These look really hot," Tash said as she cut into a blintz and watched the creamy filling ooze out.

Kyle put his fork down and looked intently at Tash. "Okay, what's wrong?"

"Why do you think…"

He shook his head. "Just tell me."

"Aidan and I broke up."

"When?"

"A few weeks ago," she replied before taking a bite of her blintz.

"What happened?"

"It's a long story," she said with a full mouth.

Kyle continued staring at her, tilting his head slightly as a means of gently prodding her.

She eventually threw her fork down. "Fine. It was stupid. I drank a little too much and danced with some guy at a club and it caused all of this drama."

"Some guy?"

"Some club promoter Aidan was kind of interviewing with."

"Oh, Tash."

"Whaaat? Don't 'Oh, Tash' me. He totally overreacted and said all of this awful stuff to me."

"Like what?"

"Crap about how I hide behind a persona like I'm fake or something. And how I'm wasting my life and don't go after my dreams."

"Well?"

"Well what?" she snapped.

"Hey, I love you but it sounds like he's just calling you on your shit, right?"

She didn't respond.

"And getting drunk and dancing with the club promoter? Really?"

"Why are you judging me and taking his side?"

"I'm always on your side. You know that. But what you did at the club isn't who you are, so what's really going on?"

"What are you talking about? You know better than anyone how I am when I'm out having fun."

"That's how you used to be; it's not who you are now. And for the record, I never thought that was how you were when you were truly having fun. I always thought that's how you acted to *look* like you were having fun."

"Sometimes it's hard to tell the difference," she said softly.

"Listen, I remember the assholes you dated in college, and I remember how they treated you. Aidan seemed really different, like he gets you."

"Wait," she said with a laugh. "You never like the guys I date."

"Exactly."

***

As she walked home in the summer heat, the foul smell of garbage permeating the air, she replayed Kyle's words. *It's not who you are. Then who the hell am I?* she wondered. The rumble of the subway caused the ground beneath her feet to vibrate and she was reminded of the sound of film spinning in the old projection rooms she visited during college. She started to imagine her life, frame by frame, whirling in front of her. Lost in thought as she walked down Macdougal Street, she paused when she noticed the rare music store an old boyfriend worked at was out of business. With Kyle's words still ringing in her ears, she saw a new series of images from a horrible New Year's Eve years earlier.

Drunk and high on pot and ecstasy, she and her boyfriend passed out in his bedroom after a party. She awoke the next morning, naked and lying between him and his lecherous roommate, with no memory of what happened, nor any doubt. It was unfolding again before her eyes in a series of visceral flashes. Pulling the dirty sheets up to her chin to cover her cold body. The stale smell of pot and cigarettes in the air. Pretending to sleep while he lay there. Chills going up her body but feeling too afraid to move to get her clothes. Trying not to even breathe. The lump forming in her throat, moving into her chest, like a vice getting tighter and tighter. Exhaling when he finally woke up and left the room.

As the flashes came faster and faster, she quickened her pace, as if trying to outwalk the images. But she couldn't outpace them. She remembered frantically searching in her pocketbook for cab fare to get home, only to realize that he had also stolen from her. *He took whatever he wanted.* The intense humiliation. Wondering, *Why do I care about cab fare? What's wrong with me?* She shuddered as she remembered boasting to her friends about what a "killer party" it had been, too afraid to say the truth aloud. The physical hurt. The wretched soreness that worsened the next day. The unbearable fear that it would never get better. The worry of disease.

Deep in thoughts she was trying to escape, she approached Washington Square Park and didn't notice Harold until he spoke to her.

"Hello, Ms. Natashya," he said.

She stopped to chat, still breathing rapidly. "Oh, hi, Harold. How's your ankle?"

"Better. Haven't seen you in a few weeks," he said.

"Been busy. I'll bring you coffee soon."

"Lovely. And your young man? Haven't seen him around here lately."

"Oh screw you!"

CHAPTER 10

Every day for the next week, Tash looked for Harold on the way to and from work, hoping to apologize. Twice she brought donuts but there was no sign of him. *He's been gone a long time. Even when they run him off, he's usually not gone this long. I wonder if he's okay,* she thought. *I shouldn't have been such a bitch.*

She gave up on finding him for the moment and went home. She tossed her bag toward the common room love seat and watched it land on the floor. She left it, intending to head to her room, but wound up standing in Jason's doorway. He was lying on his bed and watching old cartoons.

"What are you watching?" she asked with an attitude.

"*Rainbow Bright*. She's amazing, and she's totally gay!"

Tash smirked. "I think rainbows used to be just rainbows."

"No way. I'm telling you, totally gay. Anyway, I needed something upbeat."

"Well, you picked the right thing. Why? What's up?"

"Relationship stuff. I don't know. I may be misreading something. Trying not to think about it and just chill."

"I hear that," she commiserated.

"There's a new cable station that shows marathons of the old eighties cartoons. You would love it! Beats the crap out of the stuff they make now. This shit is seriously inspired."

She shook her head. "Whatever. I'm going to make popcorn and chill in my room. You want some?"

He shook his head.

Tash went to the kitchen for a Diet Coke and tub of microwave popcorn before going to her room. She changed into her most worn-in cotton pajamas and crawled into bed, propped up against pillows. She cycled through the channels, searching for something to watch. She came across the end credits for *Rainbow Bright* and was curious enough to stop. *Jason's a trip. Too funny,* she giggled. Before she could change the station, *Jem and the Holograms* came on, catching her attention.

The aesthetic is fantastic, she thought, instantly riveted. *What a dope look. Such great colors. God, imagine this aesthetic in a live-action suspense flick. It would be like pop noir. J was right. This stuff is inspired.* After acclimating to the fashion and vibe, Tash became immersed in the story. The idea that one woman had two distinct personas, the glamorous Jem and the responsible, orphan-raising Jerrica, resonated deeply. *They keep acting as though Jerrica is real and Jem is an illusion, but they're both real. That's why Rio loves them both. He's kind of a douche, cheating or whatever, but he can't help it. Together, Jem and Jerrica are like the perfect woman. No wonder their superhuman, cyborg savior is named Synergy. Brilliant.*

She watched the *Jem and the Holograms* marathon for hours, relating to the two-persona lead character more than any real person she had ever known. They shared a bond. All night her thoughts vacillated from Jem to her conversation with Kyle. She kept replaying his words, "It's not who you are. That's how you acted to look like you were having fun." Every time there was a scene with Rio, she transposed Aidan's face on his. Eventually she fell asleep, with the glow of the television beaming like a halo around her face.

***

The next morning, she woke up to find her popcorn spilled across her bed and onto the floor. The television was still on and playing the final scene of *The Last Unicorn*. As Tash wiped the sleep from her eyes, the mythical creature admitted how she now lives with regret because she had to give up the man she loved to save herself. Tash sighed, searched for the remote control, and turned the television off. As she rolled out of bed, she stepped on some popcorn, making a crunching sound. She grabbed her robe and walked out into the hallway, peeking into Jason's room, where he was asleep on top of the sheets.

"Hey, what's up?"

"Sorry. Didn't mean to wake you."

"It's fine," he said as he rubbed his eyes. "You look tired. Come sit," he said, propping his pillows up and stretching his arms.

"I didn't get much sleep last night. Don't laugh, but I flipped on that cartoon station and they were running a marathon of *Jem and The Holograms.* I kind of binged on it."

"I wouldn't laugh. She's outrageous. Truly, truly, truly outrageous," he said with hearty laughter.

Tash grabbed a pillow and smacked him in the face with it. "Can I tell you something that will make me sound crazy?"

"Always."

"I kinda related to Jem, a lot. It's like she has this fun persona that this guy is attracted to, but it's not the only thing she is. She's a totally different person too."

"Yeah," Jason prodded.

"It made me think about Aidan. He said I hide behind a persona and need to figure out who I really am. And Kyle said something like that too. I think, I think…"

"Do you remember when we watched *Desperately Seeking Susan*?"

"Yeah."

"Well Sam and I were talking about it and I had a realization. They were in their twenties. Roberta, the Rosanna Arquette character stuck in a bad suburban marriage, she was our age. It's just the shoulder pads and makeup back then that made everyone look forty."

"And?" Tash probed.

"The movie is really about her trying to figure out who she is, not who people say she is or who she thinks she's supposed to be. It got me thinking that there's this time in your twenties, you know after college or whatever, but before whatever is supposed to happen actually happens."

"Before you figure your shit out," she said.

"Before you figure out who you are and what you're doing. Nobody tells you what the hell to do after school. It just feels like being suspended in air or something."

"Totally."

"I think it's like a period of time you have to struggle through to get to where you want to go."

Tash smiled.

"What?" Jason asked.

"It's like our Blue Period. Your friend doesn't have to off themselves. We kill off parts of ourselves; we have to. It's not really about grief or sadness, just being sort of lost," she said.

"But lost on the way to somewhere. Don't forget that. If we say goodbye to some version of who we are, it's only to become a better version."

"Jason, can I tell you something?"

"Anything."

"I fucked up. I miss Aidan."

"I know," he said, leaning over to hug her.

"I love him," she whispered in his ear.

"I know."

She pulled away and wiped tears from her eyes.

"Call him," Jason said.

"I will. But I think I need to do something for myself first. I may need to go out of town for a few days. Don't tell anyone, okay?"

He nodded. "But only if you text me every day so I know you're all good."

She smiled. "Love you."

"Love you back."

CHAPTER 11

As Jason was shaking the Lucky Charms box, hoping enough bits were stuck in the corners that when freed, he'd have enough for breakfast, Penelope came into the small kitchen. She opened the refrigerator and stared at the nearly bare shelves.

Jason put the cereal box down in defeat.

"Can you grab the milk?" he asked.

Penelope passed the milk cartoon, which contained a few last drops. He watched them drip into his crumb-lined bowl. Jason stood and ate the two bites of cereal before saying, "Pen, wasn't it your turn to go to the store?"

"I'm sorry. I forgot."

"That's not like you," he said, putting his empty bowl on the counter.

She shrugged.

"Pen?"

"I'll go to the store today. I'm really sorry."

"I don't care about the groceries. We can get takeout. I'm worried about you. What's going on? Whatever it is, you can tell me."

She took a deep breath and looked behind her to make sure they were alone.

"Tash isn't here. She had to go out of town for a few days," he assured her. "Pen, what is it?"

"Promise me you won't tell anyone."

"I promise."

"That includes Tash, especially Tash."

He nodded. "Okay, but why especially Tash?"

"I had an affair with a married man."

Jason's jaw dropped. "Holy shit!"

"Jason!"

"I'm sorry. But holy shit! That was literally the last thing I thought you were going to say."

"There's more."

Jason's eyes widened.

The man, the man I had a relationship with. I didn't know it at the time, but he's Tash's uncle, Kyle's dad."

"Holy shit!" he bellowed. He put his hand over his mouth and shook his head. "Sorry, oh God, I'm so sorry, Pen. It's just *that* is actually the last thing I thought you were going to say."

She looked down and shook her head.

Jason walked over and put his hand on her shoulder.

"Come on, let's make some coffee and sit down. You can tell me how this happened."

Soon Jason knew the entire story, from their initial meeting in Vermont to the "fateful" meeting months later, and everything that followed.

"I had no idea how hard your visits with your dad were. I'm so sorry. I feel like I got preoccupied with work and going out and wasn't paying attention. I guess I haven't been the best friend to you."

"It's not your fault. I never said anything. I think it made me too sad."

"Honestly, we both thought you were completely together, like a model citizen visiting your dad all the time and working so hard in school."

"I guess I kind of was for a while, but it was never easy," she said.

"Can I ask you something personal?"

She nodded.

"Were you in love?"

She shook her head. "I don't think so. I think I was just lonely more than anything and I wanted to change my life. It all just kind of happened. For a while, it felt comfortable. It makes what I did so much worse. I mean, if we weren't really in love there was no excuse."

"If you weren't in love, and you broke up, why are you struggling so much? I don't mean that in a judgmental way; I just mean I've noticed how upset you've been lately. Some days it looked like you were crying in your room. Are you crying over him?"

"No. I've been depressed and ashamed. Once it was over, letting him go didn't even hurt. It should have hurt, shouldn't it?"

"Isn't it better that it doesn't hurt?"

She shrugged. "I've been terrified that Tash will find out and hate me. On top of everything, I let school slide to be with him. Now, the one thing I was always good at is also a mess. I'm overwhelmed."

Jason leaned in and hugged her, gently rubbing her back. "It will be okay," he whispered.

"Thanks," she said as she pulled back.

"First of all, the school stuff will work out. You can get yourself back on track with some of those long library days you love. And as for Tash, I doubt she'll find out. But I do think you should tell her. It will make you feel better. Plus, I'm pretty sure she'll be glad to know you're human like the rest of us."

"You know how close she is with Kyle. I messed up his family."

"I doubt she'll see it that way. It's up to you. Tell her or don't, but either way you have to let it go and move on. I know this is new territory for you, but people fuck up all the time. You have to rebound."

"Once my classes ended, I think I was kind of in a free fall. After my mom died, I went to college and then straight to grad school. I did what I knew how to do: school. Being a student is so easy. There is always more you can study, more you can read, to fill the time. When my classes ended, I had to start figuring things out on my own. That's when I met Richard. I thought it was fate but he was really just something to fill my mind and my time. I needed somewhere to be, someone to meet, and something to focus on. I mean, why do you guys think I always handle all the household bills and everything?"

"Because you don't want the electric turned off and you're the only real grown-up here."

She smiled. "There is that. But I also need predictable ways to fill my days. I need a structure that I understand, which I realize makes me sound pathetic. But I mean, without classes to attend or a family to go home to, what am I supposed to do?"

"You're already home, and you're with your family. I'm your family. Tash is too, in her own, dysfunctional way."

"You don't have to say that."

"I mean it. I know we can be pretty self-absorbed, but that doesn't make us feel like family any less. Isn't that part of what life is?

303

Creating your own place in the world, with your peeps, even if they're a mess."

She giggled. "Thanks. I guess I needed a reminder."

"How about we get out of this funk by going out? How does a movie sound?"

Penelope nodded. "By the way, where's Tash?"

***

After canceling on him the day before to spend time with Penelope, Jason met Sam at an Italian restaurant in Tribeca, promising to "make it up to him." As he approached the restaurant, he saw Sam waiting outside.

"Do they have a table?"

"I was thinking we could sit at the bar for a drink," Sam said.

"Sure."

They sat at the nearly empty bar and savored the smell of garlic bread wafting in the air.

"You won't believe all the drama going on right now," Jason said as he focused on the cocktail menu. "My roommates are both going through some seriously screwed up stuff with guys. I promised I wouldn't say anything, but…"

"Yeah, that's what your text said. Listen…"

"Do you want to share a carafe of the house red wine or should I just get a glass?"

"Jason, I need to talk to you," Sam said solemnly, placing his hand on the drink menu.

Jason put the menu down and swiveled his barstool to face Sam. "What's up?"

"You and I have had a fun time together, but…"

Jason's jaw dropped. "Oh my God, you're blowing me off."

"I wanted to tell you in person. I just don't see this going anywhere."

"I don't get it," Jason said, mystified.

"We talked before, you know, about keeping it airy. I was coming out of a relationship when we met. I was flattered when you asked me out and, well, I never thought it would go anywhere. I'm not looking for a serious thing right now."

"So you used me to get over someone else?" Jason asked, trying to process what was happening.

"Not intentionally. But yes, you helped me move past someone else and now I think I need to be on my own for a while," Sam said, putting his hand on Jason's.

Jason was silent.

"Let me guess, no one has ever broken up with you before?" Sam asked.

"Ah, no. But I've never really done the exclusive thing before. It never occurred to me that if I wanted to be with someone, he might not want to be with me. God, that makes me sound like a jerk. I don't mean it that way."

Sam laughed. "I know you think that you were slumming it with me or doing some noble thing by dating someone so obviously beneath you."

"No, not at all. I thought we had a connection," Jason said, hurt. "Is that how little you think of me?"

"I'm sorry. That came out all wrong. I always trip over my words with you. Maybe I should go."

"Wait. Why did you make me come here to meet you? Why not just call?"

"Because I suspect that when you end things with someone, you just take off and leave them wondering. I wanted to show you it doesn't need to be that way. I don't mean to be condescending, but…"

"But what?"

Sam stood up. "I should go. Despite what you may think, I've enjoyed every minute with you. It was a lot of fun."

Fun? Is that all anyone thinks I'm good for?

Sam turned back to Jason. "For what it's worth, I wish you great success in figuring out how to use your platform to achieve what you really want."

As Jason watched Sam walk away, he thought, *Why is he so damn lovely? It would be so much easier to hate him if he were an asshole.*

When Jason got home, he headed straight for Penelope's room and tapped on the door.

"Yes?"

He opened the door and said, "I just got dumped. I'm inconsolable."

"Oh, no. Come sit. I'll get a carton of sorbet and you can tell me what happened."

"Can we skip the sorbet and order a pizza instead?" he asked as he flopped on her bed.

"Of course."

***

A couple of days later, Tash returned. She wheeled her suitcase past Jason's room, peeking in to find him watching talk shows.

"Hey."

"You're back!"

"Yeah. What did I miss?"

"Oh sweetie, we had our own drama for a change."

"What's wrong? Why the *Sally Jessy* reruns?"

"Sam broke up with me."

"Oh, honey. Let me go put my bag away and I'll be right back for cuddles. We can talk about what an ugly douche he is."

Jason smiled. "Glad you're back."

***

As Tash finished sending a text, she turned to find Penelope standing in her doorway.

"Oh, hey Pen. I was just going to go check on Jason. He's pretty upset."

"Yeah, I know all about Sam. Listen, I really need to talk to you. It's important."

Tash widened her eyes, waiting.

"I've been working myself up to this and I'm afraid if I don't..." She trailed off.

"Is this about the bills? I promise I'll get you my share."

She shook her head. "No. It's just that, well, I wasn't going to tell you but Jason thought I should and, well…"

"Pen, I was just on a plane for like six hours. What is it? Spit it out."

"You may want to sit down for this."

Tash sat on the edge of her bed and Penelope told her everything, avoiding unnecessary details.

"Ewww! Gross," Tash said, squeezing her eyes shut in disgust.

"I'm so sorry, Tash. I had no idea who he was. I would never do anything to hurt you or anyone you care about."

"I'm not mad at you," Tash said.

"You're not?"

"No. I'm shocked and grossed out, but not mad. You didn't know, and it's not like I've never slept with the wrong guy. At least now I see why Dick is short for Richard."

"Are you going to tell Kyle?"

"No way. Listen, his parents have a totally screwed up marriage anyway. You probably did them a favor. I mean, if he wasn't getting it for years, you gave him what he needed. Otherwise he'd probably leave my aunt. She's a total whack job."

Penelope took a deep breath. "I've been such a wreck, terrified you'd never forgive me."

"You worry too much. But what the fuck did you see in my uncle? He's so totally unappealing, except that he's rich, but you don't care about that stuff."

"He was nice to me. He listened to me. I guess it was sort of like a fantasy. I've always been good at reality but I wanted an escape so I let myself believe it was fate. I've been kind of lost, trying to figure out where I fit in."

Tash smiled knowingly. "Don't worry. I get it. It's your Blue Period."

"My what?"

***

Tash and Penelope joined Jason in his bed, sandwiching him in the middle.

"Cheer up, J. I mean, how long was it going to last with a makeup artist anyway? He knows all of your flaws," Tash said.

Jason sighed. "I know. I just can't believe he dumped me. And I ate pizza, like the really greasy delivery kind!"

"How could you let him eat that?" Tash scolded Penelope.

"He needed comfort. I didn't think a healthy fruit snack was going to do the trick."

Jason and Tash burst into laughter.

"Pen, you made a joke!" Tash exclaimed.

Penelope shook her head.

"Maybe all the sex with my nasty old uncle loosened you up!" Tash continued through laughter.

"Oh, shut up," Penelope said, burying her face in her hands.

"Seriously, Jason, can you believe our virtuous little roomie was going all around town screwing someone?"

Jason laughed. "She's not a girl anymore."

"Honestly Pen, we thought you'd be chaste forever. If it weren't for who you did it with, I'd be impressed!"

Penelope grabbed a pillow and hit Tash in the head.

Jason, now hysterical, chimed in with, "Well, this took my mind off Sam."

As the laughter subsided, Penelope said, "I really missed this. You know, hanging out together."

"Yeah, sorry I've been so wrapped up in my own shit," Tash said.

"We love you for that, honey," Jason said.

Penelope nodded. "Hey, so where were you anyway, Tash?"

"First I visited my parents for two days to beg for some money and then I flew to LA. Listen, guys. I have big news."

***

That afternoon there was a knock on Tash's bedroom door. She opened it and came face-to-face with Aidan.

"Jason let me in. I got your text."

Her eyes lit up. "Thanks for coming over. Come in," she said, closing the door behind him.

"Do you want to sit down?" she asked as she sat cross-legged on her bed.

"I'm good here," he said, leaning against the door.

"You never called or texted, not even once," she said.

He raised his eyebrows.

She sighed. "I know, I know. It was on me."

He lowered his chin.

"Listen, I'm sorry about that night, how I acted."

"You really hurt me."

"I know. I wish I could take it all back."

"Tell me why. What was really going on?"

She took a long, slow breath. "I've never had a relationship where someone treated me well, until you. I guess I self-sabotaged. Maybe you were right and I don't believe I deserve good things."

"Did something happen that night?"

"Some guy in the bathroom basically called me a whore and then someone offered me ecstasy."

"Assholes."

"No, you don't understand. A few years ago, I probably would have screwed that guy, and I would have taken whatever crap I could get my hands on, to party. I was a mess and I didn't care."

"So it's good because it shows how you've evolved," Aidan said supportively.

"You don't understand. Back then I did a lot of bad stuff, and bad stuff happened to people, including me."

Aidan sat next to her on the bed. "We're not responsible for everything that happens to us."

"I feel like I brought bad shit on myself. It's hard to shake that," she said.

"Then don't shake it. Deal with it head on, and then let it go."

"Aidan..."

"Yeah?" he said as he took her hand.

"I missed you so much."

He smiled brightly. "That's all I was waiting for, beauty queen."

She looked down, blushing. "Harold is missing. I saw him a couple of weeks ago and I snapped at him. I was having a horrible day and now he's missing and the last thing I said to him was mean."

"I'm sorry. Maybe the cops chased him off and he'll come back."

"Maybe."

"So are you coming or going?" Aidan asked, gesturing to the suitcase.

"Both, actually."

He knitted his brow.

"Aidan, you were right about so much. I was stuck, afraid to take a chance on myself. I don't want to be bored or restless. I want to go after things."

He smiled.

"But you weren't right about everything. I am a person who likes to have fun and to be carefree. That's not an act; it's a part of who I am. If you can't accept that…"

He squeezed her hand. "I love that about you. Always have. I mean, I'm a deejay for a reason. I like the lighter side too."

She leaned in and kissed him softly. He took the back of her head in his hand and returned her kiss with passion. "I love you. You know that, right?" he asked as he pulled back, centimeters from her face.

She nodded.

"So you never told me, what's with the suitcase?"

"One of my professors always promised to hook me up with an internship at Paramount Studios. I finally took him up on it and flew to LA for an interview. They hired me on the spot."

He smiled. "That's amazing."

"It's actually a pretty crappy job and I'll mostly be getting people coffee, but if I'm going to have a crappy job I figured it should be where I can meet people who can teach me."

"That's awesome," he said.

"My bigger plan is to go to grad school and get my MFA in cinematography. I want to make films or at least do something related to film. I missed the application period but I'm going to apply for next year. UCLA has a kickass program. Even if I don't get in, there are a bunch of schools in the area."

Aidan looked down. "That's really great. Truly," he said softly.

"I was thinking: I know you're established here, but if you could move from Chicago to New York, can't you go from New York to LA?"

He looked at her, grinning like a Cheshire cat.

"I mean, there's a huge deejay scene in LA, right? At the very least, there must be a Forever 21 or frat party you can spin at. What do you think?" she asked with a smirk.

"Well, they do have coconuts there."

She smiled.

"Do you remember?" he asked.

"I remember."

FILM

PART ONE

CHAPTER 1

Tash used her palm to wipe the steam off the bathroom mirror. *Damn the LA sun. Are my freckles actually getting bigger?* She began rubbing foundation on her face, followed by blush, highlighter, her signature black liquid eyeliner, and mascara. *My eyes look fierce*, she thought, staring at her reflection. *I wish I hadn't agreed to work for Monroe today. At least I can party tonight.* After curling the ends of her perfectly straightened, long hair, she headed to the bedroom to get dressed.

While rifling through her underwear drawer, she noticed her favorite Polaroid of her, Jason, and Penelope in their old New York apartment. *Jason was so funny with that old-school camera. I miss him. Both of them.* Never one to display her vulnerability, she tucked the photo safely back at the bottom of the drawer. From her closet, she selected black leggings, a light gray tunic with strategically placed cutouts, and black gladiator sandals. She got dressed and looked herself over, putting on small, gold hoop earrings. *Something's missing.* She surveyed her closet. *Aww, perfect. Haven't worn you in ages*, she thought as she snatched her favorite black fedora, bought that day on Macdougal Street in New York, when Aidan first said, "I love you." The hat always reminded her of that day. Running her fingers along the rim, she wondered why it had been so hard to say I love you in return. *I did love him*, she lamented, placing the hat on her head. She took a final glance in the mirror. *Now I'm ready.*

Grabbing her slouchy black leather bag, she searched for her sunglasses and car key. Finding neither, she scoured the dresser. *Shit. Where's the key? I hate that you can't get anywhere in LA without a car. Must be on the mail table.* As she approached the small table by the door, she spotted her sunglasses, car key, and latest rejection letter. She slipped the glasses on her head and stared at the folded paper. *Don't do it, Tash*, she warned herself, but it was too late. She picked up the letter and began reading. *Dear Ms. Daniels, We regret to inform you that you have not been chosen to receive our screen writing grant.*

317

With the highest submission rate we have ever received… blah, blah, blah. Same shit, different day. At least when these jerks reject me, they don't tell me everything that's wrong with my work, unlike those film festival scumbags. Whatever. She crumpled the letter, tossed it in the trash, and headed out.

* * *

"Stop honking, you assholes," Tash muttered. *Why does anyone think they can get anywhere quickly in this town? I hope Monroe isn't pissed if I'm late again. I still can't believe I came to LA and all I'm doing is this personal shopping crap. At least when I worked retail in New York I wasn't stuck in gridlock. Monroe's life is a trip though.* Tash remembered the day they met, over a year ago. She was rummaging through a post-holiday sale accessory table at a store on Rodeo Drive, searching for the perfect bangle bracelet. A striking woman with platinum hair, who Tash pegged for mid-forties although she looked much younger, came out of the dressing room wearing an ankle-length, ivory dress. The saleswoman scurried over.

"I'm just not sure it's flattering on me. What about the color?"

"It's very sophisticated," the saleswoman assured her.

Tash snorted.

The woman turned to her. "Excuse me, Miss. I don't want to bother you, but what do you think of this dress?"

"It's fine," Tash said, returning her attention to a seventy-five percent off jewelry bin.

"Please, I usually shop with friends or my assistant, but she recently quit to get married. I need an honest opinion. It's for a dinner party."

Tash dropped a handful of earrings and turned toward the woman. "That color is horrible on you. You have flawless skin; I'd actually kill for your complexion, but that dress washes you out. And you're swallowed up in fabric. It makes you look matronly and you're obviously hot, like, really hot."

The woman blushed. "It's an upscale event."

"Unless that's code for old lady event, you should show some skin, tastefully. Hang on, I'll find you something," Tash said.

"I'm a size…"

"Six, I know. I worked retail for a couple of years."

A moment later, Tash returned with a knee-length black crepe dress with three-quarter length flouncy silk sleeves. She held it out and said, "Before we waste any time, do you have good legs?"

"Well, uh…" the woman stammered.

"Veins or no veins? Just be honest," Tash said.

"No veins. I have nice legs."

Tash handed her the garment. Minutes later, she emerged from the dressing room, beaming.

The saleswoman ran over. "Oh, that looks great on you too. You could wear anything."

Tash rolled her eyes. "That's much better. You look ten years younger. And it's on sale," she said, smirking at the saleswoman. "Well, enjoy your party," she said, returning her attention to the sale table.

The woman extended her hand. "My name is Monroe Preston."

"Nice to meet you. I'm Tash, Tash Daniels."

They shook hands and Monroe said, "Please give the salesgirl whatever you were looking at. My treat."

Tash laughed. "That's okay."

"Please, I insist," Monroe said.

A little later, as they were checking out, Monroe handed her a small bag with the three gold bangles Tash selected.

"Thanks for the bling."

"My pleasure. It was wonderfully refreshing to have someone tell me the truth."

"I get that," Tash replied.

"You mentioned you've worked in retail?"

"Yeah, but I haven't done that in a while. I moved to LA to work in film, well, whatever, it's a long story. I had an internship at a film studio, but quit when my boss tried to feel me up. It was kind of a regular thing, but I finally had enough."

"That's awful. You couldn't report him?"

"Who would care? He was someone. I was no one."

"I understand how it works," Monroe said, wistfully. "What are you doing now?"

319

"You know those studio tours?"

Monroe nodded.

"I drive one of those trams. It's beyond awful, but it's all I could get. I'm really a filmmaker, though, and a writer. Aspiring, anyway. I have a short film that's almost done. I'll be submitting it to festivals and stuff."

"If you could use a flexible part-time job, I'd like to hire you as my personal shopper."

"Oh, I don't know."

"I'll pay you extremely well. More than you earn now."

Tash bit her lip and gave Monroe the once-over. "You know what? I'll do it. If I have to drive that tram one more day so tourists can take pictures on the *Friends* couch, I might explode."

"Splendid! Do you have time right now? I have a couple of hours before my Kabbalah class and I need shoes. We could stop for lunch. This calls for a champagne toast," Monroe said.

Tash smiled. "I'm in."

The two got along smashingly from that day forward. Monroe was never short on money; Tash was never short on candor.

***

Miraculously, Tash arrived at Monroe's estate on time. She was immediately buzzed through the security gates. Although she detested Beverly Hills, she thought the Spanish-style mansion set behind palm trees on a perfectly landscaped property would be an ideal film location. It was impossibly Los Angeles and reeked of throwback Hollywood glamour. Some days Monroe opened the door herself, looking like a movie star from the 1940s or '50s. Her resemblance to Marilyn Monroe was uncanny, and like her idol, Tash learned that she had changed her name to fit the big life she imagined for herself. On this day, Henry, the butler, let her in.

"Hey there, H," Tash said.

"Hello, Miss Daniels. Mrs. Preston is in her dressing room."

"Thanks," Tash said, flying up the grand staircase.

Tash walked right into Monroe's bedroom and through to her dressing room. Monroe, wearing a white silk robe, was seated on a pink leather ottoman, looking through a stack of shoeboxes.

"Oh, hi Tash. I'm glad you're here. I want to donate some of these to charity, but I'm not sure what to hold on to. And the clothes you ordered have arrived. Also, I have three events this weekend to prepare for."

For the next two hours, they sorted shoes and Monroe tried on outfits while Tash styled them with accessories. As Monroe had come to expect, Tash wasn't shy about assessing each look or admonishing a store for sending pieces Tash hadn't preapproved. When Monroe tried on a gray silk halter dress, Tash abruptly said, "Uh, no. Just no. You're not going to a party at the Playboy mansion." Monroe giggled. No one spoke to her that way and she adored Tash for it.

By the time they were done, Monroe had all her looks for the weekend selected, two garment bags full of items for Tash to return, and several shoeboxes designated for charity. When Monroe told her to take any of the shoes she liked, Tash selected a pair of black Prada heels. Monroe was half a size larger, but for shoes like that, Tash would stuff them with cotton balls to make them work.

"Okay, so I'll take these with me. I know you want to start planning the gifts you need for next month as well as the hostess gifts for your garden lunch. Would you like me to stop by on Monday?" Tash asked.

"I'm having a little something done on Monday. Can you come at lunchtime on Tuesday? I'll have the cook prepare something for us. You can bring your swimsuit if you want to take a dip before you leave."

"Sounds good. And whatever you're doing Monday, just remember: less is more."

Monroe smiled. "You're such a sweetheart," she said, hugging her.

On her way out, Tash turned and said, "Don't forget, Band-Aids on the back of your heels Saturday night. Those shoes aren't broken in."

"I'll remember. Thank you, Tash."

Tash winked and headed out, carrying the garment bags and her new shoes.

***

After spending hours in traffic to return Monroe's unwanted garments on opposite sides of LA, Tash stopped at home for a quick bite and to get ready for the night. Decked out in a t-shirt style, black sequin mini-dress and her new Prada heels, she headed out again. She noticed her neighbor Darrell going into his apartment. He was carrying canvases under his arm, the white cloth stark against his dark skin. She waved and he nodded in return. *Quiet dude*, she thought.

She arrived at the club at ten o'clock, after easily finding a parking space.

"Yo, T," a bouncer called as she bypassed the long line.

"Hey, Jimmie," she said as he unlatched the rope, letting her in.

She walked into the mammoth space, lit with blue lights. Electro house music was blaring and the whole room of beautiful people pulsed like an excited heartbeat. As she wiggled through the crowd on her way to the bar, Texas gently touched her arm, his shaggy, blonde hair brushing the front of her face. "Well hey there, Tash," he said in his southern drawl.

"Hey, Texas. I'm in desperate need of booze. Catch ya later, okay?"

"Sure thing," he said with a tilt of his chin.

He's sweet and I don't mind the flirt, but I'm so not in the mood tonight. She approached the bar and without a word, Leo handed her a tequila sunrise.

"You're the best bartender in LA," she said, taking the drink. She took a sip while scanning the room. Lu, her best friend in LA, spotted her and was already sauntering over. Tall with short blonde hair and dripping with it-girl charisma, Lu stood out in the crowd. Tonight, she was wearing black leather pants and an old Depeche Mode tank top that showed off her toned arms. Tash watched as every lesbian and bi woman in the place checked her out.

"Hey, baby," Tash said.

"Hey, babe. This place is on tonight," Lu said.

"You're lookin' good. Very butch-chic."

"You know it. I'm digging your vibe, very Liza Minnelli meets pole dancer."

"Good one, baby. Prowling for some poor girl to hook up with?" Tash mused.

"My own personal Jesus," Lu said with a laugh.

"You're a heartbreaker," Tash teased.

"Speaking of, your little southern admirer is here," Lu said, grabbing Tash's drink and taking a gulp.

"Oh yeah. He's already made his presence known."

Lu smiled.

"You working tonight?" Tash asked.

Lu nodded. "Yeah, I'll go take over for your boy so you can have some time. Give me another hit of that first."

Lu took another sip of Tash's drink and they both started walking toward the deejay platform.

"See ya later," Lu said.

Tash waved and looked up. With his headphones on and working his sound, Aidan had never been sexier. He looked straight at her, grinning from ear to ear.

She smiled and mouthed, "I love you."

CHAPTER 2

Lu's alarm sounded at eight o'clock in the morning. Too exhausted to open her eyes, she felt around for her phone and turned it off. *Damn. This schedule is killing me. I can't wait to sleep tomorrow. Better get my ass out of bed before I pass out again.* She slithered up to a sitting position and forced her eyes open, the crust in the corners acting like glue. She yawned, long and slow, and then shook her head, trying to wake up. *I'm cold*, she thought, grabbing a pullover hoodie off the floor and putting it on as she shuffled out of bed. "Damn!" she hollered, stubbing her toe on the laptop she left on the floor. She rose again, only to trip on a pile of clothes as she tried to make her way to the galley kitchen of her studio apartment. She set up the coffee pot, accidentally spilling some grounds on the counter, which she brushed into her hand and dumped into the coffee maker.

As the coffee brewed, she leaned on the counter and shut her eyes. The alarm rang again, startling her. "Fuck. I must have hit snooze," she grumbled. She noticed five unread texts: four from women she met the night before, each making sure she had their number, and one from Tash, promising to see her that night. She responded to Tash:

> Thanks, babe. But dude, if you need tonight
> w/your man, no worries.

When the coffee machine finally beeped, she filled a mug and her to-go tumbler. She placed the tumbler next to her sunglasses on her small, two-person table, so that she'd remember it. With the mug in hand, she headed to the bathroom, slurping the steaming coffee on the way. "Well, that's a look," she said upon seeing herself in the mirror, hair matted to one side and bags under her eyes. *Please let the hot water be working*, she prayed, flipping the shower on. *Fuck. It's ice cold again.*

***

325

Lu arrived at the juice bar to find the typical Saturday line out the door, and her two younger coworkers frantically trying to keep up.

"Oh Lu, we're so glad you're here! It's been like this since we opened. We're running low on prepped veggies," Amanda said.

Too tired to risk slicing off her finger, Lu responded, "I'll take over at the register and you can do prep." She made her way behind the counter and switched off with her coworker.

After three hours taking orders for kale and carrot smoothies, the morning and lunch rushes were over and one of Lu's coworkers clocked out. The juice bar had been quiet for ten minutes when Lu told Amanda, "It's cool if you take your break. I can handle it on my own for a bit."

Finally alone and still wiped out, Lu leaned on the counter and rested her eyes.

"Um, excuse me," a soft voice said.

Lu opened her eyes to see a woman in her early twenties standing before her. "Oh shit," she mumbled. "Sorry. I was really spent. It got so quiet I must have nodded off. Hope I wasn't drooling."

The woman smiled. "That's okay. I'm sorry I woke you. Late night?"

Lu noticed how inconspicuously beautiful she was: wavy auburn hair, green eyes, and a freckled, porcelain face. "Uh, yeah, late night. I'm a deejay and I was working. I got, like, four hours of sleep."

"Wow, a deejay. That's really cool. Too bad you can't do that full-time."

Lu grimaced. "Uh, yeah. Too bad for me."

The woman blushed. "That came out wrong. I'm so embarrassed! I always say the wrong thing," she said, biting her lip. "I just meant it must be hard having a day job and a night job."

"Yeah, it's hard, but who doesn't have it hard, right?" Lu replied.

She smiled awkwardly. "My name's Paisley."

"I'm Lu. Well, Paisley, you must have come in for a juice or smoothie. What can I make for you?"

"Oh sure, right. I wanted a smoothie – something sweet. What's good?"

"The Tropical, Mango Sunrise, and Strawberry Star are all sweet."

"I'll go with the strawberry one, please."

A few customers came in while Lu made the drink.

"Here you go," Lu said, handing her the pretty pink concoction.

Paisley unzipped her purse, but Lu stopped her. "It's on me, since you had to wake me up and all. Plus, I was a giant grump."

"Oh, that's okay…"

"It's no problem. Enjoy," Lu said.

"Well, thanks. Uh, I hope you get to rest when you get off."

"No can do. I'm working at Club 47 in Hollywood tonight. I'll crash tomorrow."

Paisley started walking out, sidestepping her way to the door, looking at Lu.

"What can I get you?" Lu asked the next customer. She tried to focus on his order, but she couldn't help but glance over to watch Paisley leave.

CHAPTER 3

Tash slowly opened her eyes, squinting to avoid the bright sun. Aidan was already awake, smiling at her, his bleached hair in spikes. "Hey, beauty queen," he whispered.

She looked into his evergreen eyes and gently touched the piercing on his right eyebrow. "How long have you been up?"

"Just a few minutes. It's almost noon."

"Shit," she mumbled.

"Doesn't matter. We have the day to ourselves. Plenty of time," he said, cuddling closer to her.

"Don't forget we're going to that club in West Hollywood tonight. It's Lu's first time headlining there on a Saturday. It's a big deal for her."

"Tonight? Really?"

"Yes, really. I promised. We need to support her," Tash said.

"I work with her all the time. She won't care if we're there, trust me."

"You don't want her to think you're a jerk, abandoning her now that you're almost famous. Plus, it'll be fun."

"I thought we might do something quiet, just the two of us," Aidan said.

"I don't do quiet."

Aidan laughed. "Okay, you got me there. I'll make some coffee and breakfast and then we can figure out the day. Your choice. Maybe the Getty, or the beach. Soon it'll be too hot. Gotta say, I won't miss that."

Tash rolled to her side, sat on the edge of the bed, and slipped her robe on. "I'm just gonna have a yogurt, but coffee would be good."

Aidan leaned toward her, putting his hand on her back. "Hey…"

She leapt up. "The Getty Center," she called back. "I'm jumping in the shower. Bring me coffee when it's ready, okay?"

"Yeah, sure."

Tash went into the bathroom, put her hands on the sink, and dropped her head forward. She looked up, confronting her reflection. *No, Tash. Don't be pathetic. You're fine.*

***

Tash and Aidan sat on the crowded tram heading up to the Getty Center. It was their favorite place in LA. They had taken this ride many times, but today she noticed people staring at them. Aidan had his headphones on, lost in the beats of his future. Tash looked out at a landscape that not long before they feared would be lost to a wild blaze. She looked at Aidan with thoughts of the past and the future, place and space, swirling in her mind. Aidan squeezed her hand, thrusting her into the present.

They disembarked hand in hand. As expected on a cloudless Saturday, the grounds were teeming with locals and tourists.

"We were lucky to get a spot in the garage," Aidan said.

"Uh huh. We always have good parking karma. I'm starving. Let's grab a bite."

"Actually, I made a reservation at the swanky restaurant," Aidan replied, raising his eyebrows.

Tash contorted her face.

"I made it weeks ago, in case we wound up here today. When you were in the shower, I called to push it back. They're holding a window table for us, but we're about fifteen minutes late so we should hustle."

"We usually grab something to-go and sit on the lawn," Tash said.

"Yeah, but I thought this should be special. Besides, we can finally afford nicer things. We can walk around outside after. Cool?"

Tash shrugged. "Sure."

Soon they were sitting in the far corner of the dining room, windows on all sides, overlooking spectacular mountain views.

"Wow, they really gave us the best table in the place," Aidan said.

Tash smiled. "You should probably get used to that."

Aidan opened his mouth, but before he could respond, a waitress came over to take their drink orders.

"Could you do us a favor and take a photo of us?" he asked, handing over his phone. Returning his attention to Tash, he whispered, "I want to remember how beautiful you look today."

"You're such a cheeseball," she quipped.

After taking a few shots, the waitress returned his phone and said, "I don't want to bother you and come off all fangirl, but could we take a picture? I love your music."

Aidan blushed. "Thank you. Of course."

He stood up and the waitress retrieved her phone from her pocket and handed it to Tash. After taking a couple of pictures of them, Tash returned her phone, adding, "I'll have a glass of prosecco."

"A seltzer water for me, please," Aidan said.

As she walked away, Tash smirked at Aidan. "At least I can say I always knew you were hot shit, even back when your big gigs were an H&M store and keggers at NYU."

Aidan looked down and laughed. "It's surreal. Whoever thought that someone like Calvin would happen to hear me and that it would snowball into all of this."

"Imagine what it'll be like when your record drops. Aside from your club groupies, most people have only heard your single and you're already a badass at the star table."

"Luckily, I'll be on tour when it streets, too busy to let it distract me. I still can't believe Calvin asked me to open on his US leg."

"I believe it. Your music is dope. I thought that even before I knew you could also sing and play like every freaking instrument." She paused to take a sip of water before continuing. "And you've got that *thing*, anyway. That thing people want to be around."

Aidan reached across the table for her hand. "As long as you want to be around, I'm good."

"You're such a sap," Tash teased.

The waitress delivered their drinks and took their orders. After she left, Tash said, "It's great we're not totally busted anymore. Living in that dump in the boonies was super depressing. I'm way happier in Venice Beach. Using your advance for a down payment on the condo was genius, but now that money is gone. You're getting paid squat on tour if you can't sell your CDs, and like, who buys those anymore? And you won't be getting your regular club money."

"What are you saying?" Aidan asked.

"We're not flush," Tash replied.

"Babe, it's just lunch. And you know I've never cared about money. I want to make music, live my life. I'm cool with having just enough to get by, always have been. You're the one who relentlessly wants more. The way I see it, we caught a huge break. Let's roll with it."

"*You* caught a huge break," Tash muttered.

"Hey," he said, reaching across the table again. "You're talented and passionate. It's going to happen. It just might not be how you expect. That's the trick: being open to whatever way it comes. And it's not like you haven't done anything these past three years in LA. You rocked all those classes and actually made your short film and it's the bomb. No one can take that away from you."

Before Tash could respond, their food was served.

Aidan focused on his plate, cutting into his chicken. After a long silence, he gently said, "You will make this happen, but you gotta find happiness in the work itself again. The rest doesn't matter as much."

"Easy for you to say," she quipped back, taking a bite of her beet salad.

"Hey, you know I've always felt that way. For me, it's all about making music. I'd be happy spinning at a college party like the old days. Everything else is sparkle, as you would say."

"It's different in film. You need money and connections. There's no frat house version. Without funding, it's impossible to keep going. I can't hit my folks up again. I've done everything I can but all I have to show for it is a pile of rejections."

Aidan's face twitched.

"What's that look about? What could I have done differently?"

"After the internship…"

"Don't even fucking start," she shrieked, dropping her fork. "You'll never know what it was like working for that perv."

"Babe, I know. He put you in a horrible position. I still want to smack the hell out of that guy. It infuriates me. Leaving was the right thing, I just wish you could have found something else in the industry."

"Like what? Like giving freaking studio tours? There was nothing else." Tash picked up her fork and took a bite of salad. "You know I ordered this with the dressing on the side. Our waitress must have been too preoccupied making eyes at you to hear me."

"Do you want me to get her and ask them to make you a new one?"

Tash shook her head. "It's fine."

They sat for a moment and Aidan started eating. Tash took a deep breath and looked directly at him. "I'm sorry. I don't want to ruin the day. It's just…"

"Tell me."

"It's really hard. I mean, I could barely fund *Pop Candy* and it's only seven minutes long. And it was rejected from every short film festival I submitted to. Getting into a festival would have helped with the screenwriting grants for the full-length version, but it doesn't look like that's happening either. And…"

"Yeah?"

"And you're leaving," she moaned.

"It's only for the summer. Just a couple of months. I asked you to come with me or meet me on the road."

"You know I can't. Monroe has that Magic Manor thing and I have to do a ton of shit for her. Summer is her big event season."

"This morning you said that you didn't want Lu to think I was abandoning her. You know I'm not abandoning you either, right?" Aidan asked.

"Yeah, I know. It's fine. I'm good on my own. But I could kill you for planning a huge birthday bash for me and not showing up."

"If we didn't have a show that night, I would fly back for it. In a heartbeat."

Tash smiled. "Chill, it's cool. It's just that being dateless at your own birthday party is kinda sad. Plus, with the whole eighties theme we were supposed to go as Jem and Rio. It was gonna be rad."

"Don't worry. My buddies at the club are all over it. I've planned every detail and it's not going to be even a little sad. I'm pumped, actually," he said, smiling widely and laughing. "It's gonna be sooo you. Truly, truly, truly outrageous. You'll love it."

Tash smirked.

"It's gonna be sick, but the summer is more than one night. Try not to get too wrapped up in Monroe's stuff. Don't forget that you took that job to leave time for your film work."

Tash rolled her eyes. "Being rejected doesn't fill as much time as you'd think."

"Remember, be open to whatever form it comes in. That gallery was interested in showing your film. That could be another path."

"Yeah, but I blew them off. Fucking kills me now. At the time, I was so focused on festivals. Everyone in the classes I took said that's the way you do it, that I'd never get future backing for the longer version unless I went that route. But if you're not the professor's pet student, you don't get the support you need for that either."

"There's more than one gallery in town. For that matter, there's no reason you can't pitch to New York galleries, or Boston, Chicago, or a fishing village in Maine. Just sayin.'"

Tash furrowed her brow.

"Okay, well New York at least. My point is that it's truly a piece of art. I mean, it's stylized, totally pop noir like you intended. The black and white with those eighties pops of color – I think it's brilliant. Films like that can do well on the art scene. You know that better than anyone. That's what you said years ago when you first had the idea, before the people here got in your head. Maybe you should let it be what it is and not worry about what it'll lead to. Carve your own path."

"Maybe. Sometimes I think I should just bag it all. I don't know if I want to put myself out there again."

"It's tough, I know, but I remember how happy you were working on it. Even when it wasn't going perfectly, and even during those brutal editing months, you were alive. Just do me a favor and promise you'll think about it."

"I'll think about it," Tash said, reaching her arm across the table. Aidan rubbed her hand.

"I love you," he said.

"I know."

CHAPTER 4

Aidan and Tash circled the block, looking for a parking space.

"Man, everyone's out tonight. Our luck may have run out," Aidan said.

Tash lowered her visor to check her makeup in the mirror. "Just valet."

"It takes forever to get your car when you valet."

"Not for you. They'll totally get your car first and you know it."

"Yeah, I'm not into cutting in front of everyone."

Tash rolled her eyes, flipped the visor up, and turned to face him. "Don't be lame. Besides, you're on the list like everywhere we go. It's the same thing. Ever notice all the people standing in line?"

He laughed. "Can't argue with that. I'll double back around to the front."

"Ooh! You don't have to," Tash said, pointing to a car pulling out.

"Our lucky streak continues," Aidan said.

Minutes later, they were walking toward the club. Tash was wearing black cigarette pants, a white sequin camisole, and black high heels, her long hair curled into large ringlets at the bottom and her lips stained red. Aidan was wearing tight, black leather pants and a white T-shirt with a peace sign. At six feet tall, he was hard to miss, and together, they were impossible to ignore. Tash grabbed his hand as they strolled past the long line of hopefuls waiting for entry. When the bouncer waved them in, Tash grinned and squeezed Aidan's hand. He looked down, smiling like a schoolboy.

They walked into the intimate, moody club. The venue boasted garnet red walls, a large, black, mirrored bar, a VIP room with black leather couches partly obscured by the bar, and to the right, the dance floor. They spotted a few casual friends they knew from the scene and made small talk. Everyone wanted to shake Aidan's hand or was smiling in his direction. The manager invited them for a drink in the VIP room, but they declined. Lu was on the deejay platform, spinning for the crowd on the dance floor. Aidan raised his hand to get her attention. She smiled and pointed at him and back at herself.

"I think she wants you to make a guest appearance," Tash said.

"This is her night. I'm here to be with you."

"Oh look, she just held up two hands. I think she wants you to join her in ten minutes."

Aidan gestured to Lu, and she nodded in confirmation.

"Told ya so," Tash said.

Aidan blushed. "Well, at least I can get you a drink before she puts me to work."

"Damn straight."

***

Tash leaned on the bar, sipping her fruity drink and watching Aidan join Lu on the platform. Lu took the mic and turned the music down. "Hey, I'm takin' a break because I've got a treat for you. Before he heads out on tour, our friend, the kickass A-A-Aidan, is gonna jump up here and do his thing."

There was thunderous applause as the music swelled and Aidan appeared on the stage. With a fist bump to Lu, he put on her headphones and they swapped places. "Glad to be here, LA! Let's do it," he shouted, to more applause.

Lu pushed through the crowd toward Tash when someone touched her shoulder. She turned to see Paisley.

"Uh, hey there," Lu said.

"Paisley, from earlier today."

"Yeah, I remember," Lu said.

"Your music is great."

"Uh, thanks. I'm surprised to see you here."

"Oh, well you mentioned you were working here tonight, and I'd never been, and I thought, well, I thought…"

"It's cool. So, what do you think of our little spot?" Lu asked.

"I like it. When I got here and saw the line, I didn't think I'd get in."

"Sorry about that. If I knew you were coming, I'd have put you on the list. Come to think of it, how did you get in?"

"I gave the bouncer a hundred bucks."

Lu's eyes widened. "Yup, that'll do it."

"So, that guy's your friend?" Paisley asked, gesturing toward Aidan.

"Yeah, you know his music?" Lu asked.

Paisley shook her head.

"Guess you're not into the club scene. He's kind of a superstar around here."

"I'm not really a late-night person," Paisley said, biting her lip.

"What are you into?" Lu asked.

"Theater. I teach drama at a private high school."

"Very cool."

Paisley smiled.

"Where's the school?"

"Malibu. It's right down the road from me. I actually went to school there so it's kind of like I never left high school, which probably sounds a little pathetic. I guess I never really left home either. I'm crashing in my parent's guesthouse."

"You're from Malibu?" Lu asked, her eyes wide again.

"Yeah, why?"

"No reason. Just never thought people were actually *from* Malibu. But hey, teaching drama is dope."

"Yeah, I'm off for the summer now."

"Sweet deal. Do you have a summer gig?"

"No, I try to keep it chill. I do a lot of hiking, I hang out on the beach quite a bit, and my friends and I see a ton of movies."

"That reminds me, I was actually heading to the bar to meet someone."

"Oh, uh…"

"My best friend. She's into film too. The dude deejaying is her BF. They came here to support me tonight and my only chance to connect is while he's covering for me."

"I totally understand. Of course you should go see your friend."

Lu smiled. "You gonna hang?"

Paisley nodded.

"Cool. See ya," Lu said, brushing her hand as she walked away.

***

"So, my drink is almost empty. Did you get lost on the way?" Tash teased.

"There's this chick, Paisley..."

"Yeah, I totally saw. She's pretty."

Lu blushed.

"Oooh, you like her."

"She's probably psycho. I met her at the juice bar today and she just showed up here."

"How did she know where you'd be?"

"I kind of told her."

Tash rolled her eyes.

"It wasn't like that. I was making small talk."

"You're one of the most private people I know. Intel like that doesn't slip out, not from you. I call bullshit."

Lu scrunched her face. "You're such a bitch," she said before laughing.

"She's hot and she's into you. It's not complicated."

"But she's so girly. She ordered a strawberry smoothie. Who orders strawberry past the age of ten?"

"I eat maraschino cherries out of the jar," Tash said.

"Yeah, I know. It's weird."

Tash made a face.

"I didn't want to have to tell you this, but she's from Malibu. Malibu! She's like a real goody-goody; it's written all over her. I'm not feeling that."

"She looks comfortable in your world tonight," Tash said, nodding toward the other side of the club.

Lu whipped around to see Paisley dancing with abandon in the middle of a group of vinyl-clad strangers. Her cheeks reddened.

"Aww... Lu likes a girl," Tash mocked.

"Forget about me and the goody-goody girl. What about you and your guy? Why the hell are you here tonight? Shouldn't you be spending this time alone together?"

Tash's face fell.

"Babe, it's only like two and a half months. He'll be back before you know it."

"I know. Just didn't want to do the dramatic last-night thing. It's such a downer."

Lu rubbed Tash's arm. "Try to have a good night. This club has one of the sickest vibes in the city."

"I always think this place is so un-LA. It's missing the sanitized, canned happy thing."

"Funny, that's why I think it's the *most* LA of all the clubs I play; it's the underbelly, you know?"

Tash shrugged.

"Well, I'm gonna run for a bathroom break and then relieve your man. Get another drink and try to have fun."

"Yup, I'm the party girl," she said sarcastically.

"I'm off tomorrow if you want to hang after he leaves. Just need some shut-eye first. Text me."

Tash nodded.

"See ya, babe."

"Bye, baby."

***

Tash and Aidan got home at two o'clock in the morning. Tash kicked off her heels and announced, "I'm gonna get ready for bed."

"I'm starving. You want eggs or something?" Aidan asked, grabbing a fistful of Lucky Charms cereal.

"Sure. Sunnyside."

Tash shut the bathroom door and stood still for a moment, breathing deeply. She changed into her robe, put her hair in a ponytail, and washed her face. When she emerged from the bathroom, Aidan called, "Food's up."

Tash plopped down opposite him, crossed her legs on the chair, and sprinkled a little salt on her eggs. She dunked a piece of toast in the yolk, watching it ooze around her plate.

"You're gonna miss my late-night meals," Aidan said, crunching into a piece of buttered toast.

"I'll manage."

"Try to eat something more than cereal and soup from a can," he said with a laugh.

"Hey, I can survive on potato chips and cheese doodles if I have to," Tash joked.

Aidan smiled. "I know you can take care of yourself. I guess I'm just really gonna miss taking care of you, too."

After eating and brushing their teeth, they got into bed and turned off the lights. Aidan lay behind Tash, wrapping his arms around her. "It's really late," she whispered. "You don't want to miss your flight tomorrow."

"Okay, beauty queen. Sweet dreams."

"Good night."

***

Lu unlocked the door to her apartment and let Paisley in. "It's a mess. I wasn't expecting company."

"That's okay. Your place is really cute," she said, looking around. "I like your posters."

"Thanks. Got them all from indie music stores back in the day. Most of them are limited edition promo posters that I begged them to give me when they were done with them. They actually toss most of those."

"That's cool," Paisley said, inspecting an old Cocteau Twins poster.

"Thanks for sticking around the club all night. I hope you weren't bored out of your mind."

"I had a great time. I liked watching you work. You get really intense."

"Speaking of, I'm kind of sweaty and gross. I'm gonna take a quick shower, okay? Help yourself to a beer or water or something."

Paisley smiled.

Lu closed the bathroom door behind her, quickly taking her clothes off and tossing them in the corner. She flipped the shower on. *Please, let it be hot. Ah, yes!* She jumped in and let the water beat on her head, streaming down her body. Her eyes were shut when she felt hands slip around her waist. She opened her eyes to find Paisley in the shower with her. Lu gently touched her face and leaned in to kiss her.

***

Just before dawn, Tash rolled around in bed. When she turned to face Aidan, he put his hand on the back of her head.

"Hey, you," he whispered.

"Hey."

They stared into each other's eyes for a long moment. Tash moved closer to him, gently caressing his forehead. He pulled her head to him and they began passionately kissing. Soon they were making love, with eyes wide open. After, Tash nestled into Aidan. "You smell good," she whispered, before falling asleep cradled in his arms.

A couple of hours later, the alarm woke them both.

"Shit, I gotta get moving," Aidan mumbled.

"Do you want me to make coffee?" Tash asked.

"Nah, I'll grab some at LAX. I'm gonna hop in the shower."

He leapt up and headed to the bathroom. Tash scrunched up the sheet, pulling it to her chest, and closed her eyes.

The next time she awoke, Aidan was sitting on the edge of the bed, softly saying, "My ride's gonna be here in five."

Tash groaned. "I'll throw on sweats."

"Stay in bed."

"No. Hang on," she said.

Aidan got up and retrieved a pair of sweatpants and an old NYU sweatshirt. Tash dragged herself out of bed and slipped them on.

"Okay, let's roll," Aidan said, grabbing his supersized duffel bag and backpack.

Tash scooped up her keys from the mail table and followed him out. Aidan's friend was already waiting for him at the curb. He loaded up the car and turned to Tash.

"You should've let me drive you," she said.

"It would be a waste of your time. Enjoy the day and having the car to yourself this summer. I'll text or FaceTime you when I get there."

"Have a good flight."

"I'll miss you so much."

"Yeah, me too. This is really a big deal for you; have the time of your life. Don't worry about me."

"You're gonna have a great summer, too. Keep working on your film stuff. And stay out of trouble."

Tash rolled her eyes.

"I love you," Aidan said.

Tash smiled, tilting her chin forward; a silent me too.

Aidan got in the car and looked out the window. Tash stood there and watched the car disappear down the street.

As she walked back toward the apartment complex, she saw Darrell leaving his apartment, pulling a wagon loaded with paintings. She waved and he nodded in acknowledgment.

Shoulders slumped, she entered her quiet apartment, dropped her keys on the table, and shuffled into the bedroom. She took off her sweatpants and crawled into bed, pulling the covers up. She inhaled deeply. *It still smells like him.*

CHAPTER 5

Lu's eyelids flitted open and closed, like a butterfly scrambling to take flight. She saw flickers of Paisley, bathed in sunlight, each time her eyes opened.

"You passed out. You must have been really wiped," Paisley said.

"Yeah, I slept hard," Lu muttered. "What time is it?"

"It's almost two."

"Damn," Lu mumbled, stretching her arms and pulling herself up to a sitting position. "I'm sorry if you felt kept hostage. You could have bailed."

"That's okay. I snagged one of your books about the East Village in the 1970s and '80s."

"Cool stuff, eh?"

"Totally. I'll have to maybe borrow it to finish, if that's okay."

"Sure," Lu grumbled through a yawn. "You must be starving," she said, her own stomach growling.

"I had a granola bar. I hope you don't mind. I wanted to make you something to eat, but…"

"Yeah, haven't been to the store in a while."

"If you're busy and you want me to go…"

"No, not at all," Lu said, reaching for a shirt on the floor. "Maybe we can grab a bite. There's an all-day breakfast place nearby."

"Breakfast every hour, it could save the world," Paisley said.

Lu furrowed her brow.

"It's the lyric of a song."

"Ah, yeah. Old Tori Amos, right?"

"Uh huh."

"Cool. I like the musical free association."

Paisley smiled.

"So, you up for some chow?"

Paisley nodded.

"I'm gonna run to the bathroom. Hang tight."

When Lu re-emerged, her hair was damp and she was humming.

"Well you're bright and shiny," Paisley said, seated on the edge of the bed with the book open on her lap.

"Yeah. My mind's been all blocked up for days and it finally feels clear."

Paisley stood up as Lu walked over, the book falling to the floor. Lu took her hand and said, "And last night…"

"Yeah, last night," Paisley said softly, biting her lip. They stared at each other before Paisley took a deep breath and continued, "Well, I guess you must be hungry."

Lu touched the side of her face. "Food can wait."

***

Paisley was still scouring the laminated menu when the waitress came over.

Lu leaned in. "Do you know what you want?"

"You go first," Paisley said.

"I'll have the sausage breakfast sandwich and a coffee," Lu said. "The sausage here is homemade. It's awesome," she said to Paisley.

"Uh, can I please have an egg white omelet with spinach, no dairy, with fruit and coffee?"

"Toast and home fries? Comes with," the waitress queried.

"No, thank you."

"I'll have hers," Lu said, handing her both menus. She then turned her attention to Paisley. "I'm starving."

Paisley giggled and coyly tilted her head. "Well, I guess I'm kinda to blame for that."

Lu smiled. "You're blushing."

Paisley looked down, her cheeks getting redder by the minute.

"This place is kind of great, huh? Totally kitsch."

"Uh huh," Paisley responded, still blushing.

Lu reached her hand across the table, but before she made contact the waitress delivered two cups of coffee. "Ah, thank you!" Lu said, immediately dumping cream into her cup. She held out the creamer.

"Oh, no thanks. I drink it black."

Lu gulped her coffee. "Lactose intolerant? I noticed you asked for no dairy in your omelet."

"I used to be vegan. I still try to keep as close to vegan as I can, but I do eat eggs sometimes. I know it's such an LA cliché. It's my mom; she's a total 'paint with all the colors of the wind' hippie and raised me that way."

"Is it totally gross to you that I ordered sausage?"

"Not at all. I'm not like that."

Lu sipped her coffee again. "So, your mom is a hippie living in a Malibu estate. How'd that happen?"

"She was in the music business, a producer, big in the nineties. She got in early on a lot of things and developed really nurturing relationships with a bunch of musicians. They were loyal to her. Grunge, hip-hop, the folk singer renaissance, she had a hand in everything. She spends most of her time now doing yoga and gardening."

"Wow," Lu said, her eyebrows raised. "That's dope."

"My mom's great, really supportive. We're close. I know it's sorta lame, but she's my best friend. She's from Newport Beach and grew up in this very white-bread, corporate kind of family. Not super rich, but upper-middle class. She was like this Bohemian chick that didn't quite fit in. My dad is a hippie at heart, but he's a computer geek and hit it big in tech. They're two of the mellowest people you could ever meet, but they've had these massive careers in intense industries. That's how they ended up in Malibu."

The waitress delivered their food, with the toast and home fries on a separate plate for Lu. Lu picked up her sandwich and took a bite. She moaned as she chewed. "Sorry, this is so good."

Paisley smiled, taking a bite of her cantaloupe. "What about you?"

"What about me?" Lu asked, taking another bite.

"You're not from LA. I'm guessing you came here for the music scene."

Lu nodded as she took a forkful of home fries.

"Where are you from? Where else have you lived?"

Lu chugged her water. "I'm from the Midwest, which felt like the middle of nowhere. Lived in Seattle before I came here. It was pretty cool."

"How'd you end up in Seattle?"

"My girlfriend at the time, Jenna. She was a couple of years older than me and was moving to the Pacific Northwest. Totally granola. She wanted to go to Portland to live on a commune or some shit, but I convinced her to go to Seattle instead. I figured it would be easier to get into music there."

"Was it?" Paisley asked, taking a bite of her omelet.

Lu shook her head. "I worked in a coffee shop. I was just buying time before I could make it here."

"What about Jenna? She didn't want to come?"

"We broke up. I left her, actually."

"Oh," Paisley said, taking a sip of coffee.

"I was never serious about her like she was about me. Don't get me wrong – she was a beautiful person." Lu paused and then added, "Honestly, she was a getaway car."

"What were you trying to get away from?"

"Everything," Lu said, picking up her sandwich and taking a hearty bite.

***

Tash looked at her newly organized closet and shook her head. *I should have some outfits ready to go for days that I'm running late.* For the third time that afternoon, she removed every hanger from her closet, piling clothes on her bed. This time, she paired some pants and tops together on a single hanger. She then rifled through her jewelry drawer, taking out necklaces and bracelets to hold up against each outfit. After a long process of trying each piece of jewelry with each outfit, she wrapped the selected jewelry around the hook of each hanger. She then rehung everything in her closet, beginning with outfits on one end and single items on the other. After reviewing her work, she made a few final adjustments, grouping similar colors and similarly weighted clothes. She felt proud of herself but then inadvertently glanced at

Aidan's side of the closet and sighed. *I should start on my dresser*, she thought.

Half an hour into organizing her underwear drawer, her phone beeped with a message from Lu.

```
Hey. Slept half the day. Wanted to check
in. What are you up to?
Color coding my bras
Fuck. I'm coming over. You have food there?
A little
Booze?
Yeah
See you in an hour
```

***

Lu showed up at Tash's with a grocery bag in one hand and a glittery cardboard tiara in the other. She held out the tiara.

Tash smiled as she put it on.

"I figured you could use a little sparkle," Lu said, walking past her toward the kitchen.

"I'm really fine," Tash said.

"Great, then you can help me make dinner."

Tash followed Lu into the kitchen and watched her unload spaghetti, crushed tomatoes, garlic, broccoli, maraschino cherries, and mini marshmallows.

Tash grabbed the jar of cherries and simpered. "But what's up with the marshmallows?"

"They're my thing. I usually indulge in private. I'll be weird with you."

Tash smiled.

"Oh, totally random, but I saw your neighbor, that painter dude, on the pier a few days ago."

"Darrell. Yeah, he sells his art there sometimes, 'til the cops chase him away. I saw him this morning with a wagon full of paintings, probably heading there."

"His stuff is pretty haunting. The eyes in the faces, like *wow*. What's his story?"

"I don't really know. He's kind of a loner."

"Hey, I need a large pot with a lid and a sauté pan," Lu said, poking through cabinets.

"Down there," Tash said, pointing.

"Great," Lu said and she retrieved the items. "Do you have a colander to drain the pasta? And where do you keep olive oil and spices?"

"Oil and spices are over there," Tash said, pointing again.

Lu perused the selection of spices and dried herbs. "Nice spread, all organic."

"Aidan's kinda into cooking," she replied, as she grabbed the colander from an upper cabinet.

"You heard from him?" Lu asked, as she filled the pot with water.

"Got a text when he landed. He sent me a cheesy picture we took at the Getty yesterday."

"Cool. Open a bottle of wine and then you can help me peel garlic."

***

Tash swirled the spaghetti around her fork, using a spoon. "This smells so good," she said, before taking a big bite.

"It's one of the few recipes I've mastered," Lu said, sipping her Merlot.

"It's got a kick. You're such a badass, even in the kitchen. It's really good," Tash said, dragging a piece of broccoli through the extra sauce on her plate.

"Chili flakes. You know me, I like a surprise," Lu said.

"Oh hey, speaking of surprises, what happened with that chick last night, the goody-goody girl?"

Lu's face turned red.

"Oooh, you can't even speak," Tash teased.

"I'm chewing," Lu said, covering her full mouth with her hand.

Tash shook her head. "Come on, give me the dirt."

"She came home with me and…" Lu trailed off.

"And?" Tash prodded.

"I jumped in the shower because I was gross from work…"

"Oh my God, she surprised you naked in the shower?" Tash asked, her eyes like saucers. "I told you she looked at home in your world. Not such a goody-goody, huh?"

Lu laughed. "Uh, yeah, she did," she said, looking down and smiling. "It was amazing. We just clicked, you know? We had this intense chemistry. And then today, again…"

"You are beet red!"

"I didn't expect to like her so much. She's such a sweetheart, really soft, you know? She's into art and she loves the outdoors. It's been a while since I've felt this, if ever, really. Caught me off guard."

Tash smiled.

"We went to Mandy's for a late breakfast and…"

"Yeah?"

"I don't know. She wanted to do the whole 'tell me your life' thing. No surprise, her life has been all shades of rosy. Like seriously freaking perfect. It's just not me. Plus, I mentioned Jenna and probably scared her."

"You never tell anyone about Jenna."

"It was nothing. She asked me where I lived before, that's all. I have her number, but I'm not sure. I don't have time for a big thing. She's definitely not the casual type."

Tash dropped her fork, rested her chin in her hand, and stared at Lu.

"What?" Lu asked, taking a sip of wine.

"Look, I get it. I do, more than you know. But she's hot and you have a connection. Let go of your shit and see what happens."

Lu shrugged. "Speaking of letting go of shit, what's with the spring cleaning?"

"Slept late after he left. Felt like staying home. At least I got something done."

"Fair enough. You working tomorrow?" Lu asked, before taking a bite of pasta.

"Monroe is having 'something done,' so she doesn't need me until Tuesday."

"Not what I mean. You working tomorrow?"

Tash poured more wine in both of their glasses.

Lu tilted her head, sympathetically. "Look, I get it. Maybe more than *you* know. Do you want to talk about what's really going on here?"

"No. Do you?" Tash asked.

Lu took a sip of wine.

Tash stood up. "I'm gonna get more sauce, it's really good."

CHAPTER 6

Tash usually sped through Monroe's neighborhood, but today as she drove down the palm tree lined streets of Beverly Hills, she slowed down to take stock of each home. *That one's a garish monstrosity. What are they trying to prove? You're rich, new money, we get it. Ew, the next one's even worse. Why do the super rich have such bad taste? Oh, that one's pretty sick. Great throwback vibe. I can imagine the kind of person that lives there. Probably someone from the industry, a director from back in the day or a once-upon-a-time red carpet darling. Being a washed up star must be a mindfuck. And they all fall or fade. To get something you've chased, to live the dream, knowing it won't last and then having that truth come to pass. Maybe it's not an industry suited to happiness, just the pursuit.* Her thoughts turned to her own pursuit of happiness. *Can't believe I lost all of yesterday vegging in bed. I should be making movies, not watching them. Aidan would give me so much shit. What's my problem? I'm sliding back into who I used to be. Didn't think I'd ever go back. Fuck. Snap out of it, T. Get back to it. Okay, a couple of hours with Monroe and then when I get home, I'll work. I just need to get into it again.*

Tash's thoughts settled as she pulled into Monroe's driveway. She hopped out into the blazing LA sunshine to see Henry standing outside, speaking with the gardener.

"Yo, H," Tash called.

"Good afternoon, Miss Daniels. You'll find Mrs. Preston by the pool."

Tash waved as she walked around to the back of the estate. She spotted Monroe in the distance on the upper terrace, dressed in a white sundress, large white hat, and black sunglasses. She was seated under an umbrella at one end of the long teak table, reading as usual.

Tash walked on the pathway along the pool's edge, past the red, yellow, and purple flower beds, and then up the stairs to the sprawling terrace that ran along the backside of the estate. As she approached, Monroe looked up from her book and smiled. Tash immediately noticed her lips were poutier than usual. *Ah, so that's what she did.*

"What are you reading, another Oprah pick?" Tash asked, as she took a seat.

"It's supposed to be one of those soul-enriching books. It's on the bestseller list, but so far it's nothing more than clichés and empty platitudes, as far as I can tell at least."

Tash smiled, thinking that Monroe was much wiser than most people probably assumed.

"How was your weekend? Did the clothes work out for your events?" Tash asked.

"I received compliments all weekend, especially on that jumpsuit. I never would have chosen that without you, but you were right, it was so comfortable. You have such a good eye. I've always loved to dress up, but I never had a real knack for fashion."

"You're getting there," Tash said. "You could do this on your own."

"People keep asking who my stylist is. Is it terrible I don't want to share my secret?"

Tash laughed. "I'm all yours."

A member of the kitchen staff brought over a tray carrying their lunch: two pristine butter lettuce salads topped with avocado and crab salad and garnished with fish roe, a mineral water for Monroe, and a diet cola for Tash.

"Thank you," Monroe said. "I remembered how much you enjoyed the crab puffs the cook made. I thought this would be refreshing on a hot day."

"Looks great," Tash replied, taking a bite of the tarragon-laced crab.

"How was your weekend?" Monroe asked, sipping her water.

"Uh, it was all right. Aidan left to go on that tour, so…"

"That's right! It's exciting what's happening for him. He's really made it. I was talking with one of my girlfriends and she knew his music, her son is a fan. I may have to ask you for an autographed picture or something someday."

"Sure."

"I have to confess: I looked online and wow, he's gorgeous. What a jawline. He looks like he was born for this. He has that indescribable *thing*. Your lives must be changing so quickly."

Tash sighed.

"Oh dear, I'm sorry. You must miss him."

"Yeah, I miss him, but I'm cool with him doing what he needs to do." She paused before continuing, "It's really his life that's changing, not mine."

Monroe took a breath, looking at her sympathetically. "I've had to come to terms with some things about Bill's world over the years. When a studio head is in the room, no one else is. It's about power. They all want something from him."

Tash put her fork down. "Can I ask you a personal question?"

"Yes."

"You look like a star, truly, you're crazy beautiful. I always wondered if you came to LA to be an actress or something."

Monroe smiled ever so slightly. "I wanted a grand life, more than anything. Of course, it was just a fantasy, but I was headstrong about making it happen. When I was a teenager, I watched a lot of eighties nighttime soap operas. The fashion and opulence blew my mind. My mother and I argued about them; she didn't care for those shows and we only had one television."

Tash smiled. "That's so funny. I'm obsessed with eighties pop culture. Love it. It influences my work."

"Then you understand the allure. I also watched old movies and fell in love with the stars of the 1940s and '50s. I mean that in the truest sense. Deeply in love with them. I guess I developed an idea of old Hollywood meets contemporary glamour, or at least what was contemporary at the time. I knew I'd get myself here, come hell or high water, to the land of palm trees and silver screen dreams." With a giggle, she added, "Mind you, I had no real talent or even passion for acting, but I thought it would fall into place if I could only get here."

"Did it?" Tash asked.

"I was living with a bunch of girls, models who were all waitressing or doing odd jobs on the side. I modeled for a bit. I didn't have much luck because of my body type. Thin was in and I was too voluptuous. All I could book were lingerie shoots. It wasn't glamorous in the least. The adult industry was interested, but that wasn't for me. Eventually, I gave up and took a job as a hostess at a chichi industry restaurant. One night, a VIP came in with a large group. You could tell he was important because everyone fawned over him. It sounds naïve, but I was drawn to him because of his sweet eyes. The most powerful man in the room had the gentlest eyes. He was taken with me too. He asked for my number that night, but I said no."

"Why?"

"I was so young, only twenty at the time. He was twice my age. I thought he was out of my league and I didn't want to be his girl of the week. My mother had warned me about that sort of thing and that sort of man. But he pursued me for weeks and eventually I said yes. It was a whirlwind romance and we got married ten months later. No one thought it would last, which I can understand, but here we are a quarter of a century later. We had a connection. It was easy. He always says I bring him joy, which is strange to me," she said, her eyes distant.

Tash cocked her head. "In a way, that kind of reminds me of my relationship with Aidan. We both like the lighter side of life. We gel."

Monroe smiled, pensively.

Tash continued, "What about acting? Since he's in the film industry, did you ever ask him to get you a part or an audition or something?"

"Never. Because of him, I met everyone. When I was young, many offered me small parts or representation. I always said I wasn't interested. I was tempted once, in the very beginning. We were at a party and I met the man who owned Guess. He asked me to do a test shoot. He said I looked like a modern-day Marilyn Monroe and he wanted me to be their next model. Guess girls became very famous at that time. I admit getting a little swept up by the idea."

"You didn't pursue it?"

Monroe gazed down and then looked confidently at Tash. "Our lives were busy with professional commitments, and Bill thought I would enjoy charity work, which turned out to be mostly hosting parties. I took some classes, too. Sculpture, watercolors, I even took theology and philosophy in a continuing education program." She stared into the distance for a moment before continuing. "And I was adjusting to all of it, which took time. This life, even though I wanted it, I suppose it isn't natural for me. I had never known a world like this.

Just getting rid of my southern accent took ages, and it still creeps in a bit." She paused again for a moment before concluding, "Besides, I never had any real talent, just a dream for something glamorous."

Tash looked around at the house and grounds. "Seems like your dream came true."

"Hmm, I suppose it did. Funny how things are often different than we imagine. We never know what form our dreams will take."

"Yeah, I've actually been thinking about that a lot lately."

Monroe smiled and sipped her water. "What about your short film? I didn't realize it was influenced by the eighties."

"Yeah, it's black and white with eighties-inspired pops of color."

"You haven't mentioned it in ages. Did you screen it at festivals?"

Tash shook her head. "That didn't work out. I've been hoping to write a feature-length version, but…"

"I'd love to see it sometime, your short film," Monroe said.

"Sure. I'll bring it by. Well, should we start on the garden party gifts? I have some ideas I think you'll like."

***

Lu picked up the cutting board to wipe off the carrot peels. She dropped the carrots into the bin and then started on the beets. Amanda turned around from the register and hollered, "Strawberry Star and Tropical Blend up next."

Lu's heart raced. She turned to the counter, but it was just a couple of kids. She made the drinks and then tried to wash the stains off her hands before saying, "Hey, Amanda, we're low on kale. If you can handle it up here for a minute, I'll go back and clean some."

"Okay."

Lu made her way to the backroom, gathered a pile of kale from the refrigerator, and threw it on the counter. She grabbed her backpack and took out her phone. She shut her eyes, shook her head, and then texted Paisley:

> Hey. Sorry I didn't call yesterday. Busy.
> I'm off tomorrow. Wanna go for a hike or
> hit the beach?

She slid her phone into her pocket and started cleaning the kale. Ten minutes later, her phone beeped.

> Let's go for a hike. Should I pick you up
> at 10? I'll pack snacks.

Lu smiled. *Damn, she's too sweet.*

***

Tash got home at the end of the afternoon, threw her keys on the entry table, and walked into the kitchen. She opened the refrigerator and mindlessly scanned the contents. Not really hungry, she opened the maraschino cherry jar and popped one in her mouth. The sweet, squishy burst soothed her.

She went into her room and changed into sweats and a tank top. Her laptop was on her dresser, taunting her. *Get your shit together.* She climbed into bed with her computer. Waiting for it to boot up, she thought about Monroe. *She has everything people dream of, but there was something in her eyes, like she wonders what else she could have had, wonders where she'd be had she gone for that modeling job. Hard to imagine her life could be any better than it is. I guess we all have many lives: the one we live and the ones we might have lived.*

Staring at her desktop, she looked at her grant application folder, her writing folder, and the link to her film. She hovered the mouse over each one as a lump formed in her throat. *Fuck it*, she thought, slamming the laptop shut. She fetched the remote control from the nightstand, flicked on the television, and nestled under the comforter. *His smell is fading.*

PART TWO

CHAPTER 7

Monroe Preston had slept peacefully virtually every night since her wedding day. It didn't matter whether her husband was traveling or lying beside her in one of their many homes, free from the anxieties and to-do lists that kept most people spinning in their own heads, she shut her eyes each night and quickly drifted off to sleep. Until tonight.

Monroe lay awake nearly all night, her silk nightgown soft against her one-thousand-count sateen sheets. Something indiscernible wasn't quite right, or perhaps, she feared, she wasn't quite right. Listening to Bill breathing, she stared at the ceiling thirty feet above. She remembered being a young girl, lying awake in bed and counting the glow-in-the-dark stars she stuck on her ceiling, dreaming of her big life and no longer being Jenny Anne Foster from the south of nowhere. Suddenly, the county talent show flashed before her eyes.

"Mama, do I look all right?" she asked, twirling in front of the mirror, examining her silver sequined dress.

"You look like tinsel sparkling under twinkly lights. Lucky thing I'm good with a needle and thread, isn't it, since you love to dress up? Come on now, grab your baton. They're gonna call you next."

Moments after her performance she ran backstage, where her mother was waiting with open arms. "Now I warned you to practice more." She sighed before continuing, "Don't feel too bad, Jenny Anne. Everyone drops the baton sometimes."

"I don't feel bad, Mama. Did you hear the applause? They loved the dress you made me. It sparkled even brighter under the stage lights."

"Well of course they loved it. Who doesn't like tinsel in twinkly lights, sweet girl?"

With a slight snore, Bill rolled over, interrupting her thoughts and flinging her into the present. When he was settled, she let her mind wander back to how it felt standing center stage, and then to her mother's words. "You look like tinsel sparkling under twinkly lights."

That's all I wanted, Mama, to sparkle in Tinseltown. And here I am. But nothing is quite as I imagined.

***

Even when Bill was in town, Monroe rarely saw him in the morning. His car always picked him up hours before she'd rise. So, when he tried to slip out of bed, quietly as usual, he was surprised when she whispered, "Good morning."

"Did I wake you?"

"I've been up for ages." He started to walk toward their master bathroom when she said, "Did I tell you Tash's boyfriend got a record deal?"

"Wow. That's great."

"He's on tour," Monroe added, sitting up.

"Uh huh," Bill replied, walking into the bathroom.

"He might really make it. Isn't that something?"

"Uh huh," Bill mumbled.

"Bill, I was thinking about the funniest thing," she hollered.

"Come in here," he replied.

She slipped on her silk robe and sashayed to the bathroom doorway. Bill stood at the marble vanity, brushing his teeth.

"I was thinking about that offer I got to model for Guess. Do you remember that?"

He switched his electric toothbrush off and turned to face her.

"I remember. Seems like another lifetime. What made you think of that?"

"Oh, I don't know. Tash asked me if I'd wanted to be an actress. We were chatting about why I came to California."

"With regret or nostalgia?"

She blinked and shook her head. "Do you ever wonder what it would have been like if I modeled or acted?"

"You hated modeling. When we were dating, you told me such horror stories."

Monroe shrugged. "I suppose that's true. Well, acting then. A lot of people offered me things when we were first married. Remember? You discouraged it."

Bill crinkled his face. "I remember the offers. You never seemed interested. You told me you'd never even been in a high school play."

"Yeah, I guess."

He put his toothbrush down and folded his arms. "What's going on? Do you wish you had…"

"I'm being silly. I didn't act, you're right. I was just wondering 'what if,' I guess."

Bill walked over and kissed the top of her head.

"I'll let you get ready for your day," she said, closing the bathroom door.

***

An hour later, alone again, Monroe looked in the bathroom mirror, inspecting her freshly washed skin. After spraying her face with hydrating mist and gently rubbing in SPF moisturizer, she examined her newly plumped lips, pouting and releasing several times before concluding they still appeared natural. She couldn't shake her conversation with Tash. *It's been years since I've thought about those early days in California. I do wonder how things would be different if I had gone to that test shoot, or taken one of those other roles. Bill is right, though. I didn't have any real interest after I met him, just a curiosity or fantasy. And now that I've seen the other side, what their lives are really like, celebrity has lost its luster. I hope Tash is all right. She must be afraid her boyfriend will leave her. Maybe she's afraid of having to choose between his dream and hers. Or that his dream will eclipse hers, slowly becoming her own, before she can notice. Our choices always have shadow sides. Like I told her, dreams never come to us quite the way we expect.* Fluffing her platinum hair with her fingers, she remembered the first time she and her best friend Lauren tried to dye it, at the age of fifteen.

"My mother's gonna kill me if I ruin the towels."

"I'll help you clean up. Jenny Anne, you're gonna look like a movie star. You're already the prettiest girl in school," Lauren said.

"Do you really think I could be a movie star?"

"Definitely!"

"Oh, I don't know, there are lots of pretty girls. But it sure would be exciting to be famous and have everything you ever could want. To have people admire you. Don't tell anyone, but I've been thinking about changing my name to something that stands out, just like Marilyn Monroe did."

"I bet you'll look just like her when your hair is done."

"Maybe I should call myself Monroe. You know, as my first name."

"That's so cool. You should do it. Change your name as soon as you're eighteen and then go to Hollywood. Maybe I can be your assistant or makeup artist or something, if we're still friends," Lauren said, adjusting her wire-rimmed glasses.

"Of course we'll still be friends!"

"Oooh, the timer! Let's wash your hair."

Twenty minutes later, as she finished blow drying her hair, disappointment set in. Lauren tried to console her. "It's not exactly what you wanted but it's not that bad. It's kind of auburn-ish."

"It's not blonde like the woman on the box at all. I don't know what we did wrong. It's still dark brown, but now it has a reddish glow. It's awful," she whined.

Lauren comforted her as best as she could, reminding her she was still the most beautiful girl she had ever seen in real life.

Months later, after saving every penny she earned from her new after-school job at a local grocery store, she went to the fanciest salon in three counties where she learned it wasn't simple to go from dark to light hair. Her wish would take time and money. After a few visits, she gazed into the salon mirror to finally see the hair of her dreams reflected back at her.

"Oh wow!" she exclaimed, catching her breath. "I look like *someone*, you know," she said, earnestly.

"Everybody is someone," the stylist replied flatly.

"Uh huh," she muttered, admiring her transformation.

She bounded home to show off her new coif. Her mother wasn't impressed.

"Jenny Anne, most girls would kill to look like you just the way you are. You don't need to keep doing these things to attract attention."

"Mama, I want to stand out, to be in the spotlight. Don't you ever imagine a glamorous life? That's what I'm going to have. My life will be grand, you'll see."

Her mother leaned closer and gently touched her hair, grimacing. "You're young. You'll have different priorities someday."

"Like sewing until my fingers bleed, just to scrape by? Like sitting alone night after night in a house with more paint chipped off than is left on?"

Her mother, who always had a quietness, looked at her sharply.

"I'm sorry, Mama. I didn't mean it like that. But was your dream really to sew hems and make dresses for other women? Don't you want a closet of dresses of your own, and fabulous parties to wear them to?"

Her mother softly said, "Fancy dresses and parties don't make people happy. Taking care of yourself by doing something simple and useful is nothing to feel ashamed about. You'll see that someday."

"Then why are you so lonely?"

"One thing's got nothing to do with the other," she muttered.

"You don't think I'll make it, that I'll get out of here and do something special."

Her mother shook her head. "You don't hear a word I say. Going, going, going to some big and glitzy life, that's all you ever think about. You don't even act or sing. All you've ever done is baton twirling, and that was only because you liked the costumes I made for you. You didn't even practice. Glamour alone isn't a goal. It isn't a life. You're already plenty special, but I wish you'd get your head out of the clouds, Jenny Anne. Life will disappoint you."

Defiantly, she replied, "Lauren's mom invited me for dinner. They want to see my new hair. I have to go or I'll be late."

"Wipe off some of that makeup first. I don't want her parents thinking I'm permissive. Besides, you're plenty pretty without it."

Monroe continued fluffing her hair, wondering whatever happened to Lauren. *She was so sweet. I feel bad that I never called after I moved.* She glanced at her vanity, covered with top-of-the-line cosmetics, and thought of her mother. She looked over at the small, framed photo she kept next to her wedding photo. "Funny thing is,

Mama, you were right. I bet you'd love that. When you go to bed at night, you wash it all off and have only yourself. I still wish you would have lived long enough to see my life. The thing is, my head was in the clouds because I wanted to be up there with the stars. Nothing wrong with dreaming, Mama. Only bad part of dreaming is waking up. The details start to slip away, and you can try to catch them, to remember, but eventually they fade to black."

***

As she did each morning, Monroe grabbed the book off her nightstand to take to breakfast. She was midway through Sarah Cohen's latest tome and was eager to keep reading. Although she had a full day planned, she uncharacteristically meandered around her house, admiring the exquisite art that lined the walls. She stopped in front of the Andy Warhol rendition of Marilyn Monroe. Bill had bought it at auction for her thirtieth birthday. It was the best present she had ever received. *He said everyone would be famous in the future. Wonder if he ever said anything about being near the famous. It's not quite the same thing, is it Mr. Warhol? And what about you, Marilyn? Poor, haunted Marilyn. It's not so easy to be two people, is it? It's like being no one at all. What did Hollywood do to you? Did fame help you escape Norma Jeane? I guess it wasn't as glamorous as you hoped. I do wonder, though, were you truly and deeply unhappy or did you just wake up one day feeling somehow outside of the moment and outside of yourself?* She ran her fingers along the frame and suddenly had a thought that was entirely new to her. *Could it be that I'm living the shadow side of my own life?*

With this question lingering in her mind, she strolled downstairs and into the sun-kissed breakfast room. The cook promptly served her usual breakfast: Italian roast coffee, fruit, and a soft-boiled egg.

"May I get you anything else, Mrs. Preston?"

"There are some fashion magazines by the pool. I'd like to flip through them before Tash arrives, if you don't mind. Thank you."

The cook set off to retrieve the magazines and Monroe picked up a sterling silver teaspoon and started tapping the top of her egg. As it cracked, her mind veered to her early days in LA and one particularly terrible modeling job. She and another model were in a small backroom the size of a closet. It reeked of bleach and she wondered if it had been the scene of a crime. Monroe leaned against the wall, changing into lingerie two sizes too small when the photographer started screaming for her. The other model warned, "He's impatient." She touched Monroe's shoulder, "He's feely. Watch yourself." Monroe's anxiety grew as she hurried to the set.

"Get on the bed," he snapped.

Anxious but afraid to be perceived as difficult, she sat on the edge of bed.

"Lie on your side."

In a flash, he had her flat on her back. She stared at the cracks in the popcorn ceiling as he hovered over her, his body odor permeating the air.

"On your knees," he barked.

She lifted herself up and he put his camera down beside her.

"Your bosom doesn't look right," he said, placing his hands on the underwire of her bra and manually adjusting her breasts.

Humiliated and wondering why none of the others in the room – assistant, makeup artist, hair stylist – intervened on her behalf, she withstood the manhandling. The other model glanced at her, but quickly averted her eyes. At the end of the shoot, embarrassed and afraid to end up alone with him, she quickly changed and ran out of the building, tripping on the cement stairs and bloodying both knees. When she got home and told her roommates what happened, they just shrugged and insisted "that stuff happens all the time" and she was "lucky it didn't go further." One of the girls, who she suspected was jealous of her, suggested it wasn't surprising because she "looks like a Playboy model" and "only does lingerie jobs, which everyone knows is code for something else." After that experience and repeated pressure to pose nude, she quit modeling. Determined to make LA work if only to prove her mother wrong, she took a job as a cocktail waitress, until months later her friend helped her score a hostess position at a high-end restaurant. Within eight months, she met Bill. As she sat in the breakfast room of their estate, she remembered the moment they met, when he'd stumbled on his own name, unable to take his eyes off her.

She smiled, still able to feel the warmth emanating from him. *He's such a kind and generous man. I've been bathed in his light nearly my whole adult life. I'm luckier than I ever imagined, aren't I?* Lost in thought, she was visibly startled when the cook returned with the magazines.

"I'm sorry, Mrs. Preston. I didn't mean to sneak up on you."

"Oh, that's okay. I don't know where my mind was."

The cook placed the magazines in front of her. "May I get you anything else?"

"I have everything I could want."

CHAPTER 8

"Fuck," Tash grumbled, realizing she was out of coffee filters. *I need caffeine.* As she created a makeshift filter using a paper towel, she remembered her days in New York with Jason and Penelope. *Pen always got so annoyed when I forgot to pick stuff up. Never thought I'd miss her so much. And Jason, oh my God, Snapchat isn't enough. I gotta go to New York and visit him.* As the smell of coffee began to waft through the air, her thoughts turned to her New York college days. *God, I was with some sketchy dudes back then. I was so messed up. Funny thing, as gorgeous as he is, I probably wouldn't have given a guy like Aidan a real chance back then; he's too nice. I would have driven him away, not believing he was for real. Hell, I still almost did that. Can't get over that I thought that loser Jacob was cool. What the fuck, Tash? Asshole thought he'd share me with his lowlife friends, whether I consented or not. Scumbags.* She shuddered, wanting to clear her mind, and snatched her phone for a distraction. There was a text from Aidan.

Hey, beauty queen. I know you're sleeping, damn time zones. Wanted to say I miss you. FaceTime me tomorrow before 2 my time if you can.

Yeah, I miss you too, she thought, before replying with smiley face emojis. The coffee maker beeped and she filled her mug. *Fuck, there are grounds in it. I used to be good at this.*

***

Tash arrived at Monroe's with a sample invitation from the calligrapher. Monroe held the invitation up to the light and said, "I love how they've made the lettering on the top look like it's disappearing."

"Yeah, it came out great," Tash replied.

"Did I tell you it was my idea?" Monroe asked.

Tash shook her head.

"So, I was hosting a small dinner party for a few of Bill's employees. They were all making suggestions for the studio's anniversary party, typical stuffy parties and tired red-carpet themes. Sometimes people in the industry side of the business forget what it's all about, what draws people here, why we're still mesmerized when we sit in dark theaters, watching larger-than-life people on the screen and imagining our own lives."

Tash smiled, knowingly. "What do you think it is?"

"Magic. And that's what I told them. It wasn't meant as a suggestion, I was just thinking out loud. I said it should be a celebration of movie magic. And what better place to do that than Magic Manor, to put a fun, childlike spin on it?"

"I love it," Tash said.

"It's going to be the social event of August, the whole year really, but very exclusive. We're inviting studio executives and a select few of the actors, writers, and directors from our biggest, award-winning films. I emailed the calligrapher the final guest list this morning."

"Sounds fantastic."

"The studio is handling most of it, but there are still details for us to work out, including the gift bags and, of course, my outfit. I want to get everything settled for the rest of the summer as well. I hate to impose, but can you work some extra hours over the next few weeks? Bill and I decided to spend a couple of weeks at the Santa Barbara ranch house, and I want to make sure everything is taken care of before we leave. You'll have two paid weeks off while I'm away. Possibly more if I can convince him to stay longer."

"No problem. I could use something to keep me busy anyway."

Monroe smiled compassionately. "Okay, let's get started. I clipped some magazine photos. What do you think about a black, strapless gown?"

They worked for a couple of hours before Monroe had to leave for her weekly appointment with an astrologer.

"It's a scorcher today. With your boyfriend away, if you're not in a rush, you should take a dip in the pool and relax before you go," Monroe said.

"Oh, thanks, that's okay."

"I insist. Someone should enjoy the pool. If you don't have a bathing suit, you know we keep a variety for guests. Everything is in the pool house."

"I actually have a suit in my car, but…"

"Splendid! Stay as long as you like. I'll see you the day after tomorrow, once you've picked up the samples for the gift bags."

"Sounds good. And if you really don't mind, maybe I'll take you up on your offer."

"Of course. Please do."

Monroe's safari-themed pool house featured bamboo floors, brown and green wallpaper, and chocolate-colored wicker furniture. Tash slipped into her apropos leopard-print bikini and gold aviator sunglasses. *Not bad*, she thought, posing in front of the free-standing, full-length mirror. "Wow, look at these suits and sarongs," she whispered, admiring the large rack of designer swimwear carefully arranged for guests. *Wonder how many celebrities have worn these*, she thought, brushing her hands across the garments. *Monroe has some life*. She sprayed sunscreen all over herself and headed outside. Henry was waiting.

"I took the liberty of placing towels on that chaise under the umbrella," he said, pointing. "There's a diet cola on the table and I put several floats in the pool. Please let me know if I can get you anything else."

"Thanks, H. You're the best," she said, patting his back as she passed by.

"You're quite welcome, Miss Daniels."

Tash sat on the edge of the pool, her feet soaking in the warm, aqua water, her eyes focused on the majestic estate. She imagined what it would be like to live there. She always felt for those born in America, there were two versions of the American dream: the worker's version and the dreamer's version. This was the dreamer's version. This was where improbability kissed reality, sparking like a firework and casting an iridescent film over everything it touched. The glistening estate was merely a grand symbol of a dream realized. Tash was captivated. She took her sunglasses off, slid into the pool, and waded over to the bright pink flamingo float. *This is the life*, she thought, hoisting herself up onto the hot plastic bird. *A tequila sunrise would make this moment perfect. I should hit the club tonight, get back into the swing. Maybe Lu's working.*

After floating around for twenty minutes, she was parched and disembarked from her flamingo with a head-first dive. Gently gliding underwater all the way to the stairs, her mind cleared. She sauntered over to the chaise, casually reclined, and sipped her soda. *Too bad I don't have my iPod. I'll just chill for a bit and then head out*, she thought, closing her eyes. *This is so relaxing*, she mused, as she drifted off to sleep.

Soon, Tash was dreaming that she was walking down Abbott Kinney Boulevard in Venice Beach. Although she knew the stores well, they all looked different. Two mannequins in a window slowly began moving their heads toward each other. "This is weird. It's like a Björk video. What's in the next window?" Grass was springing from the floor, working its way up the mannequins' legs. "That's strange." She walked on. There was a large television in the third window, projecting Aidan's face.

"What are you doing, beauty queen?"

"Aidan?" she asked.

"Look everyone, it's my muse," he bellowed.

"Wait, what are you saying?" she pleaded.

She pressed her hands and face against the glass.

"Love you, beauty queen. Gotta go."

"Wait, Aidan!"

Static.

Her heart racing, she continued walking, quickening her pace, but soon feared she was slipping through the ever-widening cracks beneath her feet. She slammed her body against the next store window and caught her breath. Turning her head, she saw her reflection, frightened and undone. There was a Help Wanted sign that read:

Wanted: beauty seekers
Positions to fill: countless
Hours: time is slipping by

"Time is slipping by?" As she said the words aloud, the crack in the cement below her feet widened more. She prepared to leap over it, and then took flight. In midair, her stomach dropped. Tash's body shook violently and she woke up like a bolt.

"Huh," she mumbled, trying to acclimate herself. She sipped her watery cola before noticing the position of the sun. *Shit. I must have been asleep for a while.*

***

Dazed from sitting in rush hour traffic and troubled by her peculiar dream, Tash didn't notice Darrell standing outside her building smoking a cigarette until he called to her.

"Hey there," he said.

"Oh, hey. Did you hit the pier today?" she hollered.

He shook his head. "There's a time to sell and a time to create." She smiled.

"You know the time to sell, right?" he asked.

She shrugged.

"When the rent's due."

She laughed half-heartedly and waved goodbye.

There's a time to sell and a time to create. Hmm. Bet he never gets creatively blocked. Feeling down, she took a shower and then looked in the mirror, debating whether she had the energy to go clubbing. *I'm spent from the sun,* she concluded before changing into sweats and a tank top. Her laptop sat on her dresser, taunting her. She grabbed it and switched it on. The seconds it took to boot up felt impossibly longer than the seconds before. There was a slowness to time that recalled her dream. *My muse? Is that what he said?* By the time her desktop loaded, she decided that she was too tired to work and flipped it off. *I'm kinda hungry.* She scoured the kitchen for something to eat. Settling on a tub of Campbell's Chicken & Stars soup, she stuck it in the microwave. Soon she was carrying her soup and a Diet Coke to her bedroom where she turned the TV on and slid into bed. She flipped through the stations and landed on *Purple Rain. Ooh good, it just started.* She blew on her soup before eating a spoonful. *Wonder what'll be on after this.*

For the next few weeks, Tash followed the same routine: running errands, working with Monroe, who seemed increasingly tired, swimming and sunning, texting Aidan to avoid FaceTime, staring at her film files without opening them, contemplating going to the clubs, eating soup from a tub, and watching movies. Eventually, she stopped turning on her laptop altogether.

***

Lu and Paisley had become inseparable. They went hiking, spent lazy afternoons at the beach, and strolled around farmer's markets. Paisley hung out at clubs while Lu worked. Every night they went back to Lu's, and every morning they awoke entangled in each other's arms. Paisley invited Lu to meet her friends a couple of times, but Lu cited work as an excuse not to go. One Friday morning before they got out of bed, Paisley asked again.

"So, you're off tomorrow, right?"

"Yeah. What do you have in mind?" Lu asked, sliding her hands down Paisley's torso.

Paisley giggled. "Well, *that* of course, but I was thinking of you coming somewhere with me tomorrow night."

"Where?"

"To a midnight screening of *The Rocky Horror Picture Show* in West Hollywood. It's this thing my friends and I do the first Saturday of every month. It's my only night owl thing, well, before you came along."

"Seriously?" Lu asked.

"You're not a drama nerd or a film geek so you may not get it, but yeah, it's actually really fun. You've seen it before online or something, right?"

"No, never did."

"Seriously?!" Paisley exclaimed, leaning back to register her shock.

"Okay, now I feel lame."

"No, I'm just surprised, that's all. So, you up for it?"

"I guess, sure."

Paisley smiled brightly. "You can dress up, but you don't have to."

"Uh, okay."

"Could you meet me there? I always go early to see my friends and stuff."

"Sure. Maybe I'll ask Tash to come if that's cool. Since you've been occupying all my time, I haven't really talked to her. I feel bad about it. She's having a hard time with the whole Aidan thing, even if she won't admit it," Lu said.

"Definitely. Bring her. It's about time I meet her. I'll leave tickets for you both at the box office. And I was thinking one more thing."

"Oh yeah, what's that?" Lu asked softly, touching the side of her face.

"Maybe after, you could come grab a bite with my friends."

Lu inhaled and looked into Paisley's eyes, her hand still on her face. "Yeah, I can do that."

CHAPTER 9

"It's usually not so tough to find a spot around here," Lu said.

"I'm telling you, my parking karma is totally fucking shot," Tash moaned, as she and Lu drove down the same street for the third time.

"Go down a couple of blocks before you circle this time," Lu suggested.

"Look at how many homeless people there are. Those tents must be crazy hot this time of year," Tash said. "It's really depressing."

"Yeah, it's gotten a lot worse in the past few years."

"Did I ever tell you about Harold, the homeless dude I was kinda friends with in New York?" Tash asked.

"Don't think so."

"Like I brought him coffee and doughnuts sometimes and we'd talk. He hung out in Washington Square Park near my apartment. The NYU kids treated him like crap. Maybe I thought I was better than them. But I probably wasn't."

"What do you mean? What happened to him?" Lu asked.

Tash sighed. "Not sure. I was having a bad day once and I was kind of bitchy to him."

"Nah, not you!" Lu joked.

"Hardy har har. Anyway, I never saw him again. Suddenly, he wasn't there, like he vanished. It bothered me for a long time, wondering what happened to him. And then I started to think about how I called him my friend, but it's not like I invited him over or ever actually helped him get his life together. Maybe I was just nice to him to make myself feel better."

Lu was about to respond when she spotted a driver getting into their car. "Over there," she hollered. Tash pulled up, waiting with her blinker on. The driver of the other car seemed to be in no rush to leave.

"Hurry the fuck up," Tash grumbled.

"Chill, we have time," Lu said, as the car slowly moved out.

Tash pulled into the spot. They hopped out into the steamy night air and started walking toward the theater.

"Thanks for coming with me. I was sort of surprised you wanted to," Lu said.

"Uh, what do I love most in the world?"

"I don't know. Your hair?"

Tash winced. "Very funny."

"Film. You love film."

"Yup. Besides, I haven't gone anywhere except work in weeks. Been hibernating. It's probably good you dragged my ass out." Then Tash looked more carefully at Lu. "What's with the blue jeans and button-down shirt? You look so cleaned up."

"Paisley said to dress up."

"Uh, dumbass, she meant to dress as one of the characters."

"What?"

"Oh my God, I still can't believe you've never seen this before. At a lot of screenings, people dress up like the characters in the film. They even act out certain parts, like jumping up in the aisles and doing this dance, 'The Time Warp.' It's like a whole thing."

Lu shook her head. "Christ."

"It's fun. You'll see."

"Am I too dressed up?" Lu asked.

"Yup, but it's fine. No one who goes to these things is judgmental. They're like a misfit cult or something."

"Be careful what you say. You were pretty into it when I invited you," Lu said with a laugh.

"I'm a film junkie and Rocky Horror has had the longest theatrical run in history. Of course I'm into it. Besides, I want to meet your girl."

"She's not my girl," Lu said, looking down at her feet. "Well, I guess she is, but don't say that kind of stuff in front of her, okay?"

"I thought you were really into her," Tash said.

"I mean, she's amazing. She's such a good person. Too good, you know? I just don't know if I'm ready to do the whole relationship thing."

Tash chuckled. "I thought lesbians were all about the love at first sight, 'let's get a place together' thing."

"I'm not that kind of queer."

Before Tash could respond, they bumped into the end of a long line of people waiting to get into the theater. The line was wrapped around the corner, and most people were dressed in campy makeup, wigs, and costumes.

"This is so weird," Lu whispered.

"Chill, you'll see. But please tell me we're on the list or something," Tash said.

"Yeah, Paisley said to go straight to the box office window."

***

"I don't see her anywhere," Lu said, scanning the crowded theater.

"Relax and sit. We're dead center. She'll find us," Tash said.

The red velvet seat creaked as Lu sat down. "Give me your purse so I can save the seat next to me." Tash handed over her purse and Lu placed it beside her. "So, you've been busy working for Monroe?"

"Yeah, but she's going out of town tomorrow. I'll have a couple of weeks off."

"Cool. Doesn't Aidan's record drop soon?"

Tash thought for a moment. "Wow. Yeah, midnight tomorrow, actually. I've been so preoccupied I lost track."

"Since your boss and your guy are both on the road, why don't you come to the club tomorrow night? Haven't seen you there in a while. The party isn't the same without you. Do it for LA."

Tash giggled. "I haven't really been in the mood, I guess."

"Get back out there. Put on one of your killer outfits and let loose. I'm working the late shift the next couple of nights."

"Damn, you're gonna be dragging."

"I'm almost used to it," Lu joked.

Suddenly, the lights went out. The audience started pounding their feet and cheering.

A woman asked Lu to move the purse so she could sit. When she said it was the last open seat in the theater, Lu begrudgingly gave in.

"I don't understand where Paisley is. It's not like her to flake."

"Don't worry. She must be here. She'll find us after," Tash whispered.

"Listen, think about what I said. You're a club chick. Be who you are. Maybe it feels like A's space, but it isn't."

Tash offered a half-hearted shrug and then whispered, "Yeah, thanks. Now focus. You're gonna love this."

Lu rolled her eyes.

The film began. As an image of red lips appeared on screen, reflecting light onto the faces of the faithful audience, Lu waited in anticipation. When the opening wedding scene began, a troupe of actors ran in from the wings and began acting out the scene in front of the screen.

Tash squeezed Lu's wrist and whispered, "This is the bomb. Some theaters have volunteer casts that act out the whole thing live. Never got to see that before."

Lu smiled and then noticed Paisley among the wedding guests. She was wearing a lavender skirt suit and white hat. In unison with the running film, she caught the wedding bouquet.

Lu whispered, "That's Paisley."

"Oh my God. She's Janet."

Lu shrugged.

Tash leaned closer and whispered, "She's totally making fun of her goody-goody image. Brilliant. Just watch."

Enthralled by what was unfolding, Lu couldn't take her eyes off Paisley.

Soon, Brad and Janet were walking in the rain toward a mysterious castle. With a folded newspaper over her head, perfectly wide-eyed, Paisley mouthed along, "There's a light…"

A smile began to creep onto Lu's face.

When "The Time Warp" started to play, everyone in the theater jumped up to participate. Tash showed Lu how to follow along.

Before long, Paisley was stripped down to her white bra and slip, childlike barrettes still clipped in her hair. Lu's smile brightened. During the climactic sexual liberation scene, when Paisley began throwing her head back and mouthing, "Touch-a, touch-a, touch-a, touch me. I want to be dirty," Lu, utterly mesmerized, smiled so wide it morphed into laughter. In that moment, with the glow of the screen reflecting on her face, Lu gave in to her feelings. She looked at Paisley and the cinematic images projected behind her and had one clear thought: *Damn. I love this girl.*

***

The lights came on and people started making their way out of the theater. Lu checked her phone and saw a text from Paisley:

```
Need to change real quick. Will meet you
in the lobby.
```

Lu and Tash waited as the rest of the audience filed out. Tash, obviously captivated by the building, was looking all around.

"This place is dope. I love these old, restored theaters. There's so much history. This one's super gothic. Imagine the premieres that took place here back in the day. I bet it was raunchy in the eighties."

"Yeah, it's cool." Lu was visibly nervous.

"What's with you?"

"Paisley was really something, huh?"

Tash nodded. "She's hot. And she definitely has a good, ironic sense of herself. I dig her."

"Yeah, me too," Lu said.

Tash smiled. "Lean in."

"I'm kinda getting that message," Lu conceded.

Soon, Paisley and four of her castmates were skipping into the lobby on what one called "a post-show high." After introductions, they walked to a nearby all-night diner. Paisley explained it was their after-show tradition.

At the diner, everyone ordered eggs, pancakes, or pie, except for Lu, who opted for a meatloaf sandwich at everyone's urging. The group of vegetarians was oddly thrilled someone could finally honor Meatloaf's performance in the film. As she bit into the sandwich and gravy dripped on her hand, Lu said she was "glad to sacrifice for the group." After an hour and a half of lively conversation, raucous laughter, and comfort food, Lu sat with her arm around Paisley, her belly and heart both full.

***

"Thanks for driving us, Tash," Lu said as they pulled up to Lu's apartment building. Paisley leaned forward from the backseat to peck Tash on the cheek. "It was great to finally meet you," she said.

"You too," Tash replied.

"Maybe I'll see you at the club tomorrow night."

"Yeah, I'll try," Tash said.

Paisley and Lu hopped out of the car, but Lu leaned back into the open passenger window. "So, you'll come tomorrow night?"

"Probably."

"Okay. Thanks for tonight. It was actually really fun."

"Yeah, your girl is great."

Lu smiled. "Yeah, she is."

CHAPTER 10

"Monroe, is there anything you'd like me to put in the car?" Bill called from the bedroom.

Monroe stared in the bathroom mirror, wondering if the dark circles under her eyes were as pronounced as she feared, or if they were like her heartbeat, louder in her own mind. She took a deep breath before responding, "No thank you, darling. Henry already loaded my small travel bag and my books."

"I need to make a quick call. I'll meet you at the car."

"Be down in a minute."

Even that brief exchange depleted her energy, so she sat perfectly still, taking deep, purposeful breaths. She plucked a tube of concealer off the vanity, rubbed the porcelain-colored goop on her fingertip, and gently dabbed it under each eye. She sat for another moment, vacantly gazing at the mirror before sauntering into her bedroom to fetch her beige Hermès handbag and oversized, black Chanel sunglasses. At the last minute, she rifled through her nightstand and removed an unopened prescription for valium. With the bottle tucked safely in her handbag, Monroe headed out. She stopped at her beloved Warhol, almost involuntarily, and cocked her head as if trying to see the brightly colored image from a new perspective. *Marilyn, I read something you wrote, something about how you felt life coming closer. Had it been further? Had you been removed from your own life? Is that what Mr. Warhol saw? Is that what he was trying to show us?*

Her daydream was interrupted when Bill called from the bottom of the staircase. "We should get on the road before the traffic picks up."

She smiled ever so slightly at the painting, slipped on her sunglasses, and hollered, "Coming, darling."

***

Bill turned north onto the 101, flipping through the stations on the radio.

"Oh, leave that on," Monroe said, as Billie Holiday's voice oozed through the speakers.

"Looks like an easy ride today," he said.

"You should have taken the driver so you could relax."

"It's my only chance to drive. If I had my way, we'd be in one of the convertibles."

"Oh Bill, you know the wind and sun are too much for me."

"That's why I leave one of them at the ranch house. We can just do a short, local drive when we're there. It's an excuse for you to put your hair up in one of those silk scarves I bought you in Paris."

"Mmhmm," Monroe sighed.

"Maybe you should try to take a nap. It's been weeks since you've slept properly. I don't remember you suffering like this since before we got married, after your..." he trailed off.

"Yes, I know."

"Back then, your doctor prescribed something. Maybe..."

Monroe interrupted. "Yes, I already got something, just in case."

"Hopefully you won't need it. A change of scenery will do you good. Riding always knocks you out, and the horses will be happy to see you too."

She turned toward him and smiled faintly. "I think you're right, darling. Perhaps I'll close my eyes for a bit."

"When we get to Ventura, should I stop at that produce stand you like?" Bill asked. "We could get greens for your smoothies and maybe some melon for breakfast."

"All right," she muttered, her eyelids becoming heavier. As Billie Holiday warbled her last note, Monroe shut her eyes.

I should remember to get kale and spinach. Oh, and cucumbers. I always forget the cucumbers. Bill wants melon. Perhaps they'll have nice cantaloupe. He loves cantaloupe. Suspended somewhere between sleeping and waking, her thoughts drifted to the supermarket where she worked at as a teenager. She remembered the day she quit, at the age of sixteen, as if it had just happened.

Her twenty-two-year-old manager, Tom, a tall, skinny man with dark hair and sparse stubble on his short chin, called her over the store intercom.

"Jenny Anne to the stockroom."

She headed straight to the stockroom, glad to have a break from bagging groceries, a job that made time move slower than the little turtles Lauren raced with her brother. Tom was already in the small, dank room, holding a clipboard. A crate of honeydew melons sat atop a stack of boxes.

"These melons need to be shelved," he said.

"Sure thing," she replied, wriggling past him in the cramped space. She placed her hand on a melon when she heard the clipboard drop onto the small table beside them. Suddenly, she felt him standing behind her, not a centimeter separating them.

"Those melons should be ripe," he said, his voice lower than usual.

"Uh huh," she mumbled.

He placed his hand on the melon she was touching, his body now pressed against her.

"You've been here for almost a year, right?" he asked softly. "Feel that melon. When something's ripe, it starts to smell different. When you bite into it, the sweetness drips from your mouth."

Her heart thumping, she said, "I'm all set here. I got it on my own."

"You sure you don't need my help?" he whispered, still pressed firmly against her.

"I'm all set," she replied, trying to control her shaking.

He stepped back. "When you're done with those, you can go on your break."

She inhaled, holding her breath until she was certain he was gone. She shelved all the melons, collected her backpack from her locker, and walked out of the store as if she was taking her break. She never went back, not even to get her last paycheck.

By the time she got home, tears were streaming down her face. She cleaned herself up before her mother got home from work, not wanting to upset her after a long day and afraid she might blame her "attention-getting" appearance for the incident. At dinner, she casually announced she quit her job because it had nothing to do with what she wanted to do in life. For weeks, she and her mother argued about it, her mother insisting "life isn't just made up of things we like." Lauren was the only person she confided in. After that, whenever her mother sent her to the grocery store, she took two buses to go to the store two towns over.

Every night, as she lay in bed counting the Day-Glo shooting stars on her ceiling, she dreamt of a life far away from minimum wage, managers, and buses. Sometimes she'd picture herself on the cover of Vogue and she'd imagine Tom, old and ugly, bagging groceries and looking at stacks of magazines adorned with her face.

***

As they pulled away from the produce stand, Bill turned the radio back on. Sinatra came through the speakers. "Ah, this is perfect for the scenic part of the drive," Bill said.

Monroe smiled. "You're so old-fashioned. I do love that about you."

Bill laughed. "I've been blessed with good taste."

Monroe giggled. "I love the coastal part of the trip." She gazed past Bill, the deep blue water of the Pacific glistening in the sun. "The water in California always sparkles," she said softly.

Bill turned the music up and Monroe watched the water as if it were a film where the past and present met. Her husband provided the soundtrack. Her eyelids once again became heavy, but she fought to keep them open.

It always sparkles, she thought. *I'll never forget the first time I saw the Pacific. Vast and glorious, just like I imagined my future would be.*

She landed in LA with less than a thousand dollars in the bank and everything she owned crammed into two suitcases. She had hustled, mailing her semi-professional headshots to various modeling and talent agencies, the latter offering no response. However, she had meetings arranged with three modeling agencies and was told if she was signed, they would help her get settled and send her on go-sees to clients right away. Confident that she could make big things happen for herself, she ignored her bank balance and hailed a cab at LAX. When the cabdriver asked, "Where to?" she handed him a slip of paper with the address of a cheap motel she had booked. He warned her, "Be careful. That's a rough area."

"That's okay. I won't be there long. Oh, and sir, can you drive by the Pacific? I've never seen it before."

"It's out of your way and will cost you more."

"That's okay. Please take the longer route."

***

When the Prestons arrived at their home away from home, they were promptly greeted by their housekeeper, who ran outside to help them. Bill handed her the cardboard box overflowing with fresh produce.

"Oh my, these berries are beautiful," she said. "I'll get these into the house right away."

"Thank you," Bill said, as he retrieved Monroe's bag from the trunk. "Feeling better? You dozed off in the car."

"Yes, a bit better."

"Shall we head inside?"

Monroe nodded. "I think after we settle in, I'll go to the stables, see the horses. Perhaps I'll go for a short ride."

Monroe changed into her riding clothes in her bedroom. She noticed the small, framed photograph of her mother on her dresser. Her mother was young and uncharacteristically wearing a party dress. It was Monroe's favorite photo. She picked it up and smiled. "Oh Mama, you were beautiful. Strange how you spent your life making party dresses for other women, but never for yourself. You never did care much for fancy clothes or makeup, but you didn't need any of that. I'm sorry I thought you were plain or simple. You weren't, were you?"

She gently placed the frame back on the dresser and sat on the edge of the bed, thinking about the day she called her mother boasting she'd been signed to a modeling agency.

"Mama, I don't understand why you aren't more excited."

"I told you, I'm happy for you if this is what you want."

"They set me up with an apartment with a bunch of other girls. They think I'd be good at print work, and I have go-sees all week."

"Go...?"

"Go-sees, Mama. They're like auditions."

"The thought of you parading around for them and being judged – judged on your God-given body..."

Monroe rolled her eyes. "It's not like that, not really. Besides, if I book some jobs, I'll be able to take another stab at talent agencies, maybe try my hand at acting."

"I just don't know how anyone could be happy like that, being rejected all the time."

"Mama, did you ever think that some people just are happy, and even if they're not, they're trying to be?" After a long silence, Monroe changed the subject. "What about you, Mama?"

"Oh, well, I'm fine. I'm the same."

"How's work?"

"The same as always."

"Have you gone to play cards at Elaine's?"

"I've been too tired." She paused for a moment. "Jenny Anne, we should hang up. This call will be very expensive for you."

"Maybe someday we won't have to worry about that. I'll call you next week."

"Call after seven when it's less expensive."

"Yes, Mama."

"And Jenny Anne, if you're happy, *truly* happy, that's all a person can hope for, I suppose."

"I'll call next week. Wish me luck. Bye, Mama."

All these years later, Monroe could recall every detail of that conversation. *Was dressmaking in that small town really your ideal life? I remember the stacks of unpaid bills, and you, sitting alone every night, eating reheated casserole and watching game shows. Weekends spent cleaning the house or doing odd jobs. Oh, I wish I knew what your dreams had been. You must have had some, even if you held onto them tightly. Or was it that you let them go too easily?* Her thoughts shifted to her mother's words about happiness: "If you're happy, *truly* happy, that's all a person can hope for." She began to wonder about her tone. She tried to remember how she sounded. *Were you mournful? Was I too preoccupied to truly hear you? Oh Mama, were you ever happy? If you were, when did your happiness end? When did life slip farther away?*

***

Luke, the stablehand, had prepared Monroe's favorite horse, Captain, in case she wanted to go for a ride. As she mounted the beautiful animal, his coat the color of dark chocolate with creamy white splotches along his gait, she whispered, "Oh Captain, how I've missed you."

"I took him out for a walk so he's ready for whatever you have in mind. I'll be here when you get back," Luke said.

Monroe nodded and then gently pressed on her horse. He began walking. There was little that brought Monroe the peace and joy she felt with her horses. She'd spent twenty-five years searching for meaning in religion, spirituality, astrology, mythology, self-help, and countless fads that had quickly come and gone, but she felt most centered when she was riding. It cleared her mind. But today, she couldn't focus on the horse, the breeze, or the sunshine. She couldn't quiet her mind. She began to wonder why she felt out of sorts these past few weeks, unsettled, and outside of the moment.

Bill adores me. Our lives are perfect. I have more freedom and glamour than I ever could have envisioned. What's wrong with me? Her mother's words came barreling into her mind. *"Glamour alone isn't a goal. It isn't a life."* She remembered when she called her mother to announce her engagement and the argument that ensued.

"Why are you always so negative? You're never happy for me."

"That isn't true. I just don't want to see you throw your life away. You're too young, you barely know him, and my God, Jenny Anne, he's too old for you."

"Stop being so provincial. He's not old, he's accomplished."

"And what will you accomplish in your life?"

"Do you know how many girls would kill to marry someone like Bill? Do you know how lucky I am?"

"You need time to find out who you are and what you can do for yourself. There will always be men who want to take care of a girl as pretty as you."

"Then why were you alone your whole life?" she shrieked. "Working till your fingers were raw, sitting alone at home and crying at night. Don't you think I heard you, whimpering, crying yourself to sleep?"

No response. When what seemed like an eternity had passed, Monroe softened her voice. "I'm sorry, Mama. You know I'm grateful for everything you did for me. I just want you to be happy for me. We're different, that's all."

"Jenny Anne, I hope you find what you're looking for. Call me next week."

"Bill is gonna buy your airline ticket for the wedding. He'll take care of everything. Don't forget, it's just a couple of months away."

"I'll talk to you next week."

"Bye, Mama."

Embarrassed by what she had said and preoccupied with planning a whirlwind wedding, she didn't call her mother for three weeks. When they finally spoke, her mother was quieter than usual, distant. Things that would usually provoke an argument got no reaction at all. Her mother's response to everything was, "that's nice," which was how she always spoke to others, but never to Monroe. Feeling guilty, Monroe assumed her change in demeanor was because of the hurtful words she had spoken weeks earlier.

Three days later, a police officer called to inform her that her mother had been killed in a car accident. Her car veered off the road, slamming into a tree. Monroe was devastated. Instead of flying her mother out to California, Monroe and Bill flew in for the funeral. After the service, she hosted mourners in her mother's home. The next-door neighbor, Elaine, walked over and hugged Monroe tightly. Elaine and her mother sometimes stopped at each other's homes for coffee, to play cards, or with a bowl of soup if one or the other was sick.

"I'm just so sorry, Jenny Anne. I always knew of your mother's troubles, but if I had thought…"

Monroe's eyes widened. "What are you saying, Elaine? It was a car accident."

Elaine took Monroe's hands. "It was a clear night and there were no skid marks. No other cars. You've always been such a firecracker that you kept her going, kept the flicker of fight alive in her. But once you were grown… I'm sure you knew… she always had such a sadness about her. She…"

Monroe squeezed her hands and released. "Thank you for coming."

Monroe didn't sleep for weeks. Bill suggested postponing the wedding, but she refused, saying, "Life is too short." He couldn't argue.

As she rode her horse, the afternoon sun beating on her face, she thought about every word her mother spoke in those final phone calls, trying to compare them to all the words she had spoken before. The words were like an avalanche threatening to overtake her mind. She squeezed her calves and heels and her horse began to gallop. *"You need to find out who you are. Glamour alone isn't a goal. Fancy dresses and parties don't make people happy. Life will disappoint you. You look like tinsel sparkling under twinkly lights."* Desperate to outrun the avalanche, she applied more pressure and screamed, "Go, Captain." He began galloping at full speed, the wind pushing against her skin, pushing against the words.

CHAPTER 11

Tash was walking home from her favorite neighborhood boutique, swinging her shopping bag back and forth, when her phone rang. She flipped her sunglasses onto the top of her head and smiled as Lu's name flashed on the screen.

"Hey baby, what's up?"

"Just checking to see if you're comin' tonight."

"As a matter of fact, I just bought the fiercest little dress."

Lu chuckled. "You go, girl."

"Since when did you get so formal? Why not text?" Tash queried.

"Didn't want you to dodge me."

"As iiiiiif," Tash said, exaggerating the word.

"Glad to hear you're back to your old smart ass, it-girl self."

"Well, someone has to save the LA club scene from the monotony of the reality star brigade and their Z-list groupies."

"That's the spirit!" Lu exclaimed.

"I'll see you tonight. Ciao, baby."

"Ciao."

***

With her favorite eighties playlist blaring and a towel wrapped around her freshly showered body, Tash applied a final coat of hot pink lipstick. She stepped back and puckered her lips, blowing her reflection a kiss. *I need some extra pizazz*, she mused, adding a streak of silver glitter eyeliner above her signature black liquid liner. She batted her long, false eyelashes. *I've still got it.*

The Smiths' "How Soon Is Now" swirled in the air as she strutted into her bedroom and plucked the last couple of pieces of popcorn from the microwave bag on her nightstand, eating them one by one. Her new, sparkling silver dress was hanging on the back of the door. She slipped the slinky mini on, placing the spaghetti straps on her freckled shoulders. *Where are my strappy silver heels?* she wondered, scouring her closet. "Ah, you were hiding! Guess I haven't worn you in a while."

Sitting on the edge of her bed to buckle her shoe straps, she glanced up and saw the picture she and Aidan took on their first day in LA. Hair in a ponytail and makeup-free, she had tried to shield her face, but Aidan insisted on capturing the start of their adventure together. It was the only picture she'd ever put in a frame. She paused to examine their goofy smiles, then grabbed her purse and headed out.

＊＊

Tash's mood had plummeted by the fifth time she passed the club, searching for a parking space. Circling the block in larger and larger loops felt like a less-than-subtle metaphor for her life. She feared her luck had simply run out. What was once within reach felt further and further away. Everything had always fallen neatly into place, but now nothing quite fit. Even her shoes felt too tight. Lost in her own troubles, she barely noticed the people camping out merely blocks away from the club. When they eventually caught her eye, she realized they were getting closer each month: the truth encroaching on the lie. *Must be more of them. Fuck, it's sad. It's like the fires springing up in the canyons, getting harder to control, harder to keep at bay. They're warnings that there's no such place as paradise, because there's always a shadow side. People here like everything to be airbrushed. They like their pretty pictures. Everything is filtered.* As a yellow Aston Martin zoomed past her, likely carrying fellow club-goers, she was confronted with multiple realities. Her complicated relationship with LA blurred at the intersection of her waning dreams and the stark reality that her life was indeed privileged.

By the time she found a parking spot, she was vacillating between rage and despair, but no longer sure why. Determined to shake it off and have a fabulous night, she turned her attention forward, ignoring everything in the periphery.

Reinvigorated, she breezed past the line of beautiful people. The bouncer ushered her over and unlatched the rope. As she passed through, he called, "How's A? You think he'll ever come back?" Her body clenched, but she turned, smiled at him with a shrug, and then walked into the packed club.

Tash wriggled her way through the crowd, slowly making her way to the bar. She stood for a couple of minutes before Leo handed her a tequila sunrise.

"You're slipping! Your arm's usually out before I make it over," she hollered over the noise.

"I know. Epic fail. Wasn't expecting to see you; you've been MIA. We all figured you went on tour with A after all."

"Nope. Just been busy. But I'm back," she said.

"And hotter than ever, but don't tell your man I said that."

She winked at him and held up her glass. "Cheers," she said, taking a gulp.

Leaning against the bar and steadily sipping her drink, Tash surveyed the room. It was full of the usual suspects. Lu was on the deejay platform, flaunting her favorite vintage David Bowie T-shirt and black leather pants as she rocked her sound. Paisley was holding her own on the dance floor. They were exchanging looks. *Wow, never thought I'd see the day. Lu's totally in love. It's great.* Just then, Lu glanced over, smiled brightly, and cocked her head. Tash held up her arm to say hi in return. Several people asked her to dance and offered to buy her drinks. Despite relishing the attention, she declined, gesturing to the one in her hand. Paisley came over and they chatted for a while. As Tash was finishing her second drink, a tall guy with a chiseled face and midnight-black hair sidled up to her.

"You're the most drop-dead beautiful woman here tonight. You know that, right?" he asked in a sexy English accent.

"That's quite the line," she said.

"Ah, I'm gutted," he said, grabbing his chest. "I did want to impress you, but I can tell that's no easy task."

The corners of her mouth turned up in an almost imperceptible smile.

"Take pity on me and have a dance?" he asked.

She gave him the once-over, took the last sip of her drink, and nodded. With electro-techno beats guiding the way, they made their way onto the dance floor. Tash danced freely, happily losing herself in the moment. After fifteen minutes, her dance partner leaned in and said, "By the way, my name is Liam."

"I'm Tash."

"Oh, I know who you are," he shouted over the music.

Puzzled, she leaned in closer. "What do you mean?"

"My friends told me you're A-A-Aidan's muse. Don't worry, I know you're taken. I'm a musician and I was just hoping some of that good luck might rub off on me."

Repelled, she stepped back. Bodies whirled all around her, but Tash was perfectly still.

"Oh, I'm sorry. I didn't mean to offend you," Liam said.

"No problem. I need a break. See ya," she said, as she walked away.

His muse? Just like that fucking dream. Is that how people fucking see me now? Her internal rant continued all the way to the restroom where she intended to regroup. She tried to calm down, but her mind was flooded with warring images of herself – those projected from others were indecipherable from her own. She wanted to be carefree and strong, but another part of her wanted to run home and crawl into bed. *Fuck that. And fuck Aidan for putting me in this situation. I should be able to have a good fucking time.*

Determined to "have fun" no matter what, she made a beeline for the bar and ordered a third drink. Halfway through her drink, Texas appeared.

"Hey there, pretty lady," he said, running his fingers through his shaggy blonde hair.

"Hey, Texas. How ya been?"

"Can't complain, can't complain. Missing you, of course. Where you been hiding out?"

"Not hiding, just busy."

"Well, I sure am glad you're here tonight. This place is stuffed to the gills with rich kids blowing their trust funds."

"Yeah, nothing stays cool around here for long," Tash groaned.

"I don't want your boyfriend to kick my ass, but I must say, holy smokes you're looking mighty fine."

"Well he's not around these days, so I wouldn't worry about it."

"In that case, you want to finally grace me with your presence on the dance floor?"

Just as she was about to respond, Lu announced another deejay was taking over while she took a short break.

"Sorry, Texas. My friend is coming over. Later, okay?"

"Sure thing, pretty lady. Find me."

Tash watched as he walked away. Lu leapt off the platform, said something to Paisley, and then made her way to the bar.

"Damn, girl! You weren't kidding. You look amazing," Lu said.

"Thanks, baby. You're looking like a total boss, as usual."

Lu shrugged sarcastically. "Well, you know, I gotta represent. You having a good time?"

"Trying," Tash said. She inhaled deeply, but before she could elaborate, the deejay made an announcement, and they both turned to listen.

"Hey everyone! It's midnight, and that means our very own A-A-Aidan's album has dropped." Thunderous applause. He continued, "This is my mix of our boy's single. To your feet, LA!"

Aidan's music swelled and the club was electric. Lu slowly turned to Tash.

"Well, bottoms up, baby," Tash said, raising her drink and downing what was left.

"Hey, you. Take it easy or I'll have to carry you home. My place isn't big enough for three."

"Goddamn it," Tash muttered.

"I was just teasing," Lu said.

"No, it's not that. I'm so stupid, I fucking drove here. It was force of habit, I guess. I always drive and then Aidan drives us home. You know he's a straight edge."

"How many have you had?" Lu asked.

"A few," she replied, playing with the straw in her empty glass.

"Leave your car and Paisley and I will drive you. We'll get your car tomorrow."

"I don't wanna stay all night," Tash whined.

"So Uber it. Paisley will take you to get your car tomorrow."

"Yeah, I guess that will work. Thanks," Tash mumbled.

"Listen, I gotta go to the bathroom and see Paisley before I jump back up there. Promise you won't drive?"

"Scout's honor," Tash said, doing the sign of the cross over her chest.

"Uh, yeah, that's so not from the Scouts. Definitely don't drive."

Tash smiled. "I promise. Go have a good set. Big shoes to fill," she slurred.

Lu winced. "See ya, babe."

"Later."

***

Two hours and two more drinks later, Tash was dancing with Texas when she began to lose her balance, falling into him with increasing regularity.

"Well there, pretty lady. Maybe you need a little break," he said.

"Yeah, maybe I do," she replied.

She tottered over to the bar, occasionally stumbling onto him. He lent a hand as needed. Paisley spotted Tash's inebriated stumbles and came over.

"Tash, do you want me to call an Uber for you?"

"I don't want to leave my car here. Can't get another ticket," she slurred.

"I only had one drink, hours ago. I can drive you in your car if you want," Texas said.

"How will you get home?" Tash asked.

"Uber. No difference to me if it's from here or your place."

"Paisley, I'm gonna go with my good friend Texas, here. We go way back," she said, patting his chest.

"Okay, drink a glass of water and take something for your head when you get home," Paisley said.

Tash nodded, grabbed Texas by the arm, and they headed out into the night.

***

A few minutes later, Paisley was hanging out on the deejay platform with Lu. Lu leaned over and asked, "I saw Tash leave. Did you get her a car?"

"Her friend offered to drive her."

"What friend?"

"Some guy, Texas. She said they're good friends."

Lu shook her head. "He's just a dude that has a monster crush on her."

"Oh my God, is she unsafe?" Paisley asked in a panic.

"Probably only from herself. Oh Tash, what are you doing?" she mumbled.

***

The task of finding Tash's car wasn't made any easier by her poor memory or the fact that she was having trouble balancing in her heels. When they eventually got in the car, Texas asked for her address, which she was miraculously able to communicate along with directions. He opened the windows and she complained, "My hair's gonna get all messed up."

"I think the fresh air will do ya some good," he replied. "How about some tunes?"

"Okay," she said.

He turned the music on and the sounds of the eighties came storming through the speakers. He lowered the volume and said, "Dig the throwback tunes."

"Yeah, me too, or I used to," she mumbled.

"Something bothering you, pretty lady? I got the feeling you were maybe trying to escape a little tonight."

Tash sighed. "Let me ask you something, Texas. Why'd you come to LA?"

"Came to sunny Los Angeles to get away from my family. Woulda gone clear across the country, but I love the warm weather. The big ole Pacific beckoned. Figured I'd take up surfin'."

"You an actor or something?"

"No way. I work at a Mexican restaurant. Saving for a food truck with one of my buddies."

"Wow, Texas. You know, you may be the perfect guy. You're the only person I know who's not here for the bullshit."

"There's no bullshit about you either, I'd reckon."

"Ha! You'd be wrong."

"Havin' a dream don't make it bullshit. Like my food truck. It may not happen, but ain't nothin' wrong with working for it."

"Hmm. Yeah, I guess," she mumbled.

When they arrived at Tash's apartment building, Texas parked the car and they both got out. He handed her the keys.

"Thanks, Texas. You're a nice guy. Such a nice guy," she said, nearly falling onto him. "And you're so good looking. Have I told you that?" she asked.

He blushed and cocked his head. "Can you make it into your apartment?" he asked.

"You've been flirting with me for ages."

"Uh, yes I have. Pretty hard not to. You seen yourself?"

Tash smiled. "That's just what I mean. You always make me feel good. But…"

"But you're definitely drunk and I'm pretty sure you still have a boyfriend. So, if you're okay to make it in, I'm gonna keep on being a nice guy, even though I'll kick myself tomorrow."

She gave him a long look, smiled, and said, "See ya, Texas."

"See ya, pretty lady."

A few minutes later, Tash finally stumbled into her apartment. Dropping her keys on the floor beside the entry table, she made her way to her bedroom. She plopped onto her bed, unbuckled her shoes, and flicked them off. Her feet were throbbing. She took off her dress and slipped on a tank top she found on the floor. *I need to lie down, but if I fall asleep with all this crap on my face, I'll regret it.* Resisting the urge to fall over on the bed, she forced herself to the bathroom. *Music. I need music so I won't pass out.* She flipped her eighties playlist back on, and Duran Duran's "Save a Prayer" filled the room. She listened to the words, staring at her reflection, and thinking about how shamelessly she flirted with Texas. Smeared eyeliner, sweat marks on her face, and a pit in her stomach were all reminders that she had nearly fallen to a new low. She pulled off her false eyelashes and took a long, hard look in the mirror. *I can't believe I came home with Texas. What the fuck was I thinking? If he wasn't such a stand-up guy, what would have happened? I'm such an asshole sometimes. And Aidan. Fucking Aidan. He put up with so much shit with me when we first hooked up. He deserves better. I'm not good enough for him.* As she looked at herself with disdain, her eyes began to well up and tears flowed down her face. She just stood there, drunk and crying. Finally able to catch her breath, she washed her face and raised her gaze to the mirror, patting herself dry. Puffy eyes, freckled skin, and regret stared back at her. She dropped the towel on the floor, shuffled into her bedroom, and collapsed into the bed. She grabbed Aidan's pillow and clenched it tightly until she fell asleep.

CHAPTER 12

Tash woke up late morning, her mouth dry and head throbbing. She grumbled as she opened her eyes, the light piercing her brain. In desperate need of Advil, she dragged herself out of bed and stumbled to the bathroom. Glimpsing herself in the mirror, she recoiled, all the night's foibles etched on her bloodshot eyes and puffy face. She opened the medicine cabinet, retrieved the bottle of Advil, and popped four into her mouth. She turned on the faucet, cupped her hands to collect some water, and then threw back the pills in one gulp. With the medicine cabinet still flung open and pill bottle on the sink, she stumbled back to bed. *Sleep. Please let me fall back asleep until my headache is gone.* Despite the sharp pain emanating from her temples, deep exhaustion won out and she drifted back to sleep.

Tash opened her eyes again at noon, grateful to find that her headache had abated. She wanted to go back to sleep to avoid facing the day for as long as possible, but her stomach growled and she realized she was too hungry to sleep. She got out of bed and lumbered to the kitchen. Aidan's box of Lucky Charms was on the top of the refrigerator. She grabbed the box, stuck her hand in to scoop out some cereal, and hopped onto the counter. Munching on the sweet morsels, she pictured Aidan, standing in his boxers, pouring cereal into a bowl, and then grabbing a fistful to eat dry. Her eyes welled with tears. "No Tash, not again. Not now," she said, wiping her eyes. She finished the cereal, hopped down, and tossed the box in the recycling bin. "Pull yourself together and just do it for him," she whispered. "He can't see me like this. I can't fuck things up for him. Don't be selfish, Tash. Not to him."

She walked into the bedroom, sat on the edge of her bed, and reached for her phone on the nightstand. With the phone gripped tightly in her hands, she took a deep breath, and then, feeling together, called Aidan.

"Hey, beauty queen!" he said.

"Hey, superstar. Congratulations! I can't believe your record is out."

"Yeah, me neither."

"How do you feel?"

"Well, I'm trying to be chill about it with everyone else, but between us, I'm pretty pumped."

"You should be. It's freaking awesome," she said, pausing for a moment before adding, "I'm so proud of you. I really am." As she said these words, she knew she meant them and she felt a twinge of relief.

"Thanks. You know, it goes both ways."

His words hit Tash like a dagger to the heart. She slumped over and inhaled deeply, intent on holding it together. Eventually, Aidan filled the silence.

"I wish you would have FaceTimed so I could see your gorgeous face."

"Believe me, I'm sparing you. Partied a little too hard last night."

"Ah."

"They gave you a huge shout-out at the club. Everyone's really happy for you."

"That's sweet. Glad to hear you went out. From your texts, I get the feeling you've been laying low. You getting any work done?"

"Not really, but I will. You know how tricky inspiration can be."

"Sure do. That's why we can't wait for the muses to visit, we have to chase them."

Hearing those words, Tash couldn't keep the tears back any longer. She sniffled a bit and softly said, "Yeah, I know. I will."

"Are you okay?" he asked.

"Uh huh."

"Really? Because I have no interest in moving backward."

She sighed. "You know I can't keep things from you. I did something kind of stupid last night and I feel like crap."

"How stupid?" he asked, his tone sharper. "Something that can't be undone?"

"No, I stopped myself because," she hesitated, searching for the words before concluding, "because that's not who I want to be."

"Then let it go. We all screw up, but we can't let our mistakes define who we are. Focus on who you are today. Today is what you have."

Tash smiled, wiping the tears from her cheeks.

"I'm pretty lucky to have you," she said.

"You are," he said with a laugh. "Get out in the LA sunshine today. Hit the Getty or the beach."

"Yeah, that's probably a good idea."

"So, how's everything else? Who was spinning at the club last night?"

"Lu, and oh my God, she's totally head over heels. Remember that chick, Paisley, I told you she was sleeping with? Well, they're going strong and I've never seen Lu like this before. I think this might be it for her, although she'd never admit it."

Tash and Aidan continued talking for ten minutes. After they hung up, Tash jumped in the shower, determined to wash away the last night, the last few weeks, and the last residue of who she used to be.

***

"Rise and shine," Lu said, gently stroking Paisley's arm. "I made you breakfast in bed."

"What?" Paisley mumbled, as she opened her eyes.

"I made you breakfast in bed," Lu repeated. "Well, I guess it's more like brunch in bed. It's almost one o'clock."

"Yeah, but the sun was up by the time we went to sleep," Paisley countered, slowly sitting up with a yawn. "How long have you been up?"

"Hours. Couldn't sleep," Lu said as she placed a tray in front of Paisley.

"Uh, yeah, I see that. I can't believe you made me breakfast."

"It's nothing fancy, just oatmeal with strawberries and coffee," Lu said.

"It's perfect. Thank you," Paisley said, taking a sip of coffee.

Lu smiled.

"Why couldn't you sleep? Are you worried about Tash?"

"She's having a really tough time. That's what last night was about."

"Have you heard from her?" Paisley asked, taking a bite of oatmeal.

Lu shook her head. "She'll text me when she's ready. I don't want to push her. We have an unspoken understanding."

Paisley looked at Lu, wide eyed. "Is it all about missing her boyfriend?"

"It's about her feeling like he's on a rocket to the stars and she's stuck on the ground. They actually moved here for her, so she could break into filmmaking. She's faced a lot of roadblocks, a lot of disappointments, and a lot of bullshit, you know? And suddenly, out of nowhere, he's catapulted into the stratosphere and he wasn't even trying." She paused before adding, "And she feels guilty."

Paisley furrowed her brow.

"She feels guilty because she knows she should support him, but the truth is that a part of her resents his success."

"And what about you?" Paisley asked.

"What about me?" Lu replied.

"Is it hard for you?"

"I mean, if I'm really honest, yeah. Aidan is the nicest guy in the world, truly, and he's big time talented. Don't get me wrong – I'm happy for him. But I've been here a lot longer and it's frustrating because as a woman on the circuit, these things just don't happen. Like, *never*. Guys see talent in other guys. They see them as their buddies and they want to go on the road with them. There's no fairness in it, and that always gets to me. And it's not like that kind of success is even my dream; I really just love the music. But it's tough knowing it could never be me."

"I'm sorry," Paisley said.

"Don't be. It's all good. I've just gotta keep reminding myself that the music is what matters."

Just then, Lu's phone beeped. She grabbed it to see a message from Tash, which she read out loud.

```
Hey. I'm fine. Texas was a perfect
gentleman. Sorry if I worried you.
```

"I'm so relieved. I would have felt awful if something happened to her," Paisley said.

"Me too."

Paisley ate a heaping spoonful of oatmeal with a slice of strawberry. "Mmm. This is so good. How come you're so sweet?"

"I'm not. I guess you bring out the best in me."

***

Tash walked along the beach, holding her flip flops as the water rushed over her feet. Looking across the vast cobalt sea, a sense of abundance began to take hold. Mesmerized by the water, she walked farther than planned and soon found herself at the Santa Monica Pier. *Well, why not*, she thought, deciding to take a stroll down the pier.

Children holding soft-serve ice cream cones that melted down their arms walked past her, couples took photographs with selfie sticks, and the famous Ferris wheel slowly spun against the cloudless sky. Craving something sweet, she bought pink cotton candy, indulging in a few sugary bites before tossing it. After a caricaturist tried to convince her to have her portrait done, she decided she'd had enough of the boardwalk. She turned to leave and saw Darrell sitting on a stool with a small painting at his feet, his dreads pulled back in an elastic.

"Hey, Darrell. How's it going?"

"Can't complain."

Tash picked up the painting of a woman's face painted in shades of blue; her eyes were haunting. It was reminiscent of a Picasso and Modigliani hybrid. "Nice work."

"Thanks. Sold a few other small ones today. Funny how the same painting that sells for thousands in a gallery is only worth about sixty bucks on the street." He chuckled. "I'm thinking about calling it a day, it's pretty hot in the sun," he said, beads of sweat dripping down his face.

"Can I give you a ride? My car is a few blocks down."

"That would be great. Thank you."

Darrell folded the legs on his stool, picked up his painting, and they headed home. During the ride, he asked about her work and Tash told him about her short film. As a fellow artist, and one who'd been working at it a bit longer, she realized he might have valuable insights and could help her brainstorm.

"I think I got distracted by the Hollywood thing and how people play the game. Even when I was taking classes, if you didn't follow a certain path, the professors wouldn't throw their weight behind you and you couldn't get into the festivals. My work is artistic," she explained. "A gallery was interested in screening my film, but I blew them off. I was stupid."

"Which gallery?" he asked.

"Patty Price's gallery down on..."

He cut her off. "I know the place. Patty is cool. You should stop by and see if she's still interested."

"Yeah, maybe," Tash said. "You know of any other good galleries?"

"When I first came here, I checked them all out. The scene here didn't exactly welcome me. It was happening for me in New York; I was a part of two group shows in SoHo, and there was this art dealer who hooked me up with high-end clients. Hoped it would translate here, but LA is a fickle place."

"Tell me about it. Fuck. Why'd you leave New York? Sounds like you had it made."

Darrell laughed. "Life happens, you know? Choices have to be made. Come to my place and I'll show you my work."

"Sure," Tash said.

When they arrived at their building, Tash followed Darrell into his apartment, a spacious studio that smelled like turpentine and was overflowing with paintings. Every inch of wall space was covered, and stacks of canvases lined the perimeter of the room. Darrell's life clearly revolved around his art. Half the paintings were of the same subject: a forlorn, dark-haired woman with haunting eyes. Tash stood before one piece, studying it.

"That's Sara, my girlfriend," Darrell said.

"Oh, I didn't know..."

"She's the reason I'm in LA. We lived together in New York for three years. She's a poet. We had wonderful conversations about art, philosophy, religion, all the big ideas, while we worked. I did most of the talking, but she would listen to me, sometimes for hours, encouraging me to go on. She was always quiet, but then one day, her quietness seemed to take hold, like she retreated into herself. Soon she was completely mute and it was as if her beautiful eyes had filmed over."

"Oh my God," Tash mumbled.

"We tried different medications. Nothing worked. I think that shit made her worse. She was from California and I thought the warm weather might help."

"Did it?"

"When her parents saw how bad she was doing, they had her committed to an institution. I'm not even allowed to see her. They blame me for everything."

"That's awful. I'm so sorry," Tash said. "Can I ask why you didn't move back to New York, if it was better for your career?"

"When she's released, I need to be here. This was our last home together."

"How long has it been?"

"Five years. But she'll come back, one day, when she's ready. She'll come back to herself and back to me. I kinda think she's taking a time out from the noise and composing a really long poem. And I'm lucky – I have my art to keep me busy until she's ready to share her beautiful voice again."

Tash smiled.

They said goodbye and Tash headed to her apartment. She grabbed her laptop and plopped onto the bed. She hovered the mouse over the link to her film and clicked on it. For the first time in a long time, she watched her own film.

CHAPTER 13

The day after watching her film, Tash woke up with a fire in her belly. *Be fucking brave*, she told herself. She made a pot of coffee and began an online search for art galleries in Los Angeles, San Francisco, and New York. She decided to start with the local galleries. Adept at using her charisma as currency, she figured her chances were better if she could pitch her case in person.

She visited every gallery and artist cooperative on the list. Some gallerists shooed her off and said that they don't accept "unsolicited works," others said they weren't interested in film work, and some claimed their calendars were booked for years. A couple agreed to watch her film and "let her know." Tired but determined, she sat in her car outside of the last place on her LA list: the Patty Price Gallery. Tash started biting her nails, desperately trying to muster the courage to face Patty, the one gallerist who had loved *Pop Candy*, and the one who Tash had naively blown off. *Be brave. Be fucking brave*, she told herself as she hopped out of the car.

She walked into the gallery. It was her favorite space in LA, with dark wood floors, high ceilings with exposed pipes, and white walls meticulously displaying large, abstract artworks. Tash felt it was the only gallery in LA that had the "it factor" that the New York scene possessed in spades. A young woman with short brown hair was sitting at the desk. Tash walked right over, shoulders back and head high.

"Hi. My name is Tash Daniels and I met with Ms. Price about a year ago. She was interested in showing my short film. I was hoping she might consider it again. Can I leave a message for her?" she asked, handing her a one-page resume.

A voice from behind called, "That won't be necessary."

Tash turned to see none other than Patty Price walking toward her, with her signature dark-rimmed glasses, red lipstick, and perfectly pin-straight, brown bob.

"Patty, it's wonderful to see you. I don't know if you remember me, but my name is Tash Daniels and…"

Patty cut her off. "I remember. You had a film. Seems like forever ago. You know how quickly the art world moves."

"Uh, yes, I do. Listen Patty, I want to apologize for not taking you up on your generous offer to screen the film. At the time…"

Patty put her hand up. "No need to explain. It wasn't right for you. It's your art. I get it."

"Well, that's the thing. I've reconsidered and I was wondering if you might be willing to give me another chance. If you'd just watch it again…"

"I'm booked solid for the next two years. We have your information on file. Thanks for stopping by." Patty abruptly turned to her assistant and began talking.

Tash quietly said, "Thank you," and left.

Although disappointed, Tash kept her spirits up. *Nothing ventured, nothing gained. Be brave.* She also knew that while many people could open or close doors, she was the architect of her own life. Her art and her happiness were in her hands. The weight of that responsibility finally felt like something she could handle, and for the first time, she embraced it.

The next day, she called all the out-of-town galleries on her list. Monroe texted that she decided to extend her trip, so Tash spent the next three weeks making lists of galleries in other cities, researching funding opportunities, and writing. Not quite ready to write her full-length script, she played with ideas. It was thrilling to be back in the creative zone, both planning and experimenting, finally working toward something. Most days she'd forget to eat until her stomach started grumbling in the late afternoon.

The day before Tash's birthday, Monroe returned. Tash stopped by to review final details for the upcoming studio anniversary party. When Tash met her poolside, she noticed Monroe looked run down. They discussed party details, but as their meeting wrapped up, Tash felt compelled to express her concern.

"Are you feeling okay? You look a little tired," Tash remarked.

"Oh, you're sweet to ask. I haven't been sleeping well, but I'm fine."

Monroe quickly changed the subject, giving Tash a pair of gold earrings from Tiffany's and the next two days off to celebrate her birthday. Tash beamed at the sight of the earrings, thanking her profusely.

"It's my pleasure. Wear them well."

"If that's all," Tash said, standing up.

Monroe smiled. "Oh, before you go, I wanted to remind you to pick up the silver pens from the engraver by the end of the day, for the studio party gift bags."

"No problem. I'm heading home to do a few things, but I'll get there before they close."

Tash picked up her Tiffany's gift bag and turned back to Monroe. "Are you sure you're okay?"

"Nothing a little sunshine and sleep can't fix," Monroe said. "Maybe I'll do a face mask. That always helps."

Tash smiled. "Go for it."

***

Running late to make it to the engravers, Tash was frantically searching for her keys when her phone rang. "Fuck, I don't have time for this," she grumbled, but looked to see who was calling anyway. It was a local number that she didn't recognize. Thinking it might be the engraver or one of the other vendors for Monroe's upcoming party, she answered.

"Hello, this is Tash."

"Tash, Patty Price here."

"Oh, hi Patty," Tash said, her heart racing.

"Listen, I'll cut to it. You've probably seen that story on the news about the English video artist arrested for child porn."

"Uh…"

"Well, he was supposed to be a part of a group show starting in two weeks. Apparently, his love for video production was more varied than any of us knew."

"Wow, Patty. That's awful."

"Yeah, well it worked out for you. We were going to show one of his short films in our media room. Now there's a slot open. I know

I wasn't that receptive when you came by, but your work would fit right in. Truth is, I love your film, have since you first showed it to me. Talent is what matters. And you had the chutzpah to come back here. I figure women like us should stick together."

"Thank you. I don't know what to say."

"Say yes. I'm in a rush, dealing with the nightmare of redoing all the signage, flyers, and media announcements."

"Yes. Of course. Thank you."

"My assistant will email you the details. Make sure you're on time for setup, I don't want any problems. And spread the word about the show."

"Okay. And Patty, really, thank you for this."

Tash hung up the phone and jumped up and down. *Did that just happen?* She leaned against the wall and inhaled deeply, wanting to savor this moment, the culmination of many small, unspoken acts of bravery.

CHAPTER 14

After yet another restless night, Monroe crawled out of bed and dragged herself to the bathroom. She stood in front of the mirror, examining the ever-darker circles under her eyes. Her arms felt heavy and her movements were lethargic, but she reached for her toothbrush anyway. Robotically brushing her teeth and washing her face, her only thought was how desperately she longed to sleep. Too exhausted to read, she left her book on her nightstand and headed down for breakfast. She stopped in front of her Warhol, captivated by Marilyn's expression. *Hmm. Today is August fifth, Tash's birthday. Isn't that the day they found your body, Marilyn? How your death must have shattered the myth people cling to, that a perfect life exists. But it wasn't about them, it was about you. I do wonder what happened. Perhaps you were you just so tired, tired of all of it, that you decided to sleep forever. Maybe it was subconscious. We'll never know, and yet, I feel I understand somehow.* She stood for a moment, blankly staring at the painting. *I should wish Tash a happy birthday.*

***

After spending the day watching her favorite films, a birthday tradition, Tash treated herself to Chinese takeout in bed. She maneuvered some lo mein out of the box, tipped her head back, and sucked down the noodles. There was something comforting about the feel of chopsticks between her fingers and a takeout container on her lap. It reminded her of late nights in New York watching TV in bed with Jason and Penelope. She smiled, grateful that her life was no longer about forgetting but remembering. Before long, she had finished the last spring roll and it was time to get ready for her party.

Thinking it would be a downer to dress up like Jem when Aidan wasn't there to be Rio, she had decided to go as Susan, the title character from *Desperately Seeking Susan*. She put her favorite playlist on shuffle, laughing when Foreigner's "Urgent" came on. Opting to go big or go home, she gave her makeup an eighties vibe with heavily shadowed eyes, rosy cheeks, and rouge-stained lips. She styled her hair in large ringlets at the ends, admiring herself before getting dressed. Decked out in black pants, a black bustier, sparkle boots, and several strands of rhinestones and faux pearls, she looked like she stepped right out of the film. As she admired herself in the full-length mirror, her phone beeped. The driver Aidan hired was waiting outside. *Time to get into the groove*, she thought, winking at herself before grabbing her purse and heading out the door.

***

Tash arrived at the club to see a line around the corner and many people dressed up in eighties attire. There were two signs outside that said, "Come Party '80s Style," and a third directing birthday party guests to the VIP entrance. Tash headed to the VIP door where she was given a wristband for drinks. "Happy Birthday! Have a blast," the bouncer said. She smiled and walked inside. Immediately, her group of friends and the club regulars cheered. Tash blushed. The entire place was decorated with neon twinkly lights and streamers. The bar was running a special on "Tash's Tequila Sunrise," and a half-naked male model was passing out feather boas. Tash smiled hard. *Oh, Aidan. I can't believe you remembered that night in New York.*

As she made her way through the crowd, friends wished her a happy birthday, and soon, strangers did too. Texas was among the well-wishers. He tipped his head and said, "Happy Birthday!" She tipped her head in return, put her hands on her heart, and said, "Thank you. Really, thank you." He smiled and walked off. Tash continued to the bar, where she was promptly handed a cocktail. As she was chatting with the bartender, someone tapped her shoulder. She put her drink down and turned around to see Jason. Her eyes lit up, her jaw dropped, and she started screaming, "Oh my God! I can't believe you're here! I can't believe you flew in from New York! Oh my God!"

Jason laughed and pulled her to him. They hugged each other tightly for so long it was as if time stopped. When they finally released, Tash had tears in her eyes.

"I could fucking kill you," she said, smacking his chest. "My makeup is gonna be a mess."

He laughed. "That's the price you pay for my presence. But get your shit together, we don't want to make a scene."

"I can't believe you're here. I'm so happy!" As Tash sniffled, trying to pull herself together, she got a better look at Jason. He was wearing a shiny purple blazer and had matching purple spray layered over his black hair. "What's with the purple?"

"Aidan said you were coming as Jem. I'm your Rio. But I see you're doing the Madonna thing instead," he said, taking her hand and twirling her around. "I dig it."

"Aidan told you?" she asked, searching her purse for a tissue.

"He called me as soon as he found out he had to miss your party. He bought me a plane ticket and put me up in a hotel so I could surprise you."

"I can't believe he did that," Tash said, dabbing her eyes, careful not to smudge her makeup.

"Yes, you can."

Tash looked down, smiling. "Yeah, he's the best."

"So, I need a drink and then we dance."

Tash nodded. She wiped her nose, stuffed the tissue in her pocket, and got Jason's drink. They clinked glasses.

"To you being more fabulous than ever!" Jason said.

"And to you being here," Tash added.

"Cheers and Happy Birthday, T," Jason said.

"Cheers."

A-ha's "Take on Me" came on and everyone in the club cheered. Tash patted Jason's chest. "Oh my God. I love this song so much. Too perfect."

"Yeah. Aidan really outdid himself," Jason said, scanning the room.

"Speak of the devil," Tash said, retrieving her vibrating phone from her pocket. "He's calling."

"Hey there," she said loudly over the music, pressing her fingers to her free ear to block out the sound.

"Did my present arrive?"

"He's here. I can't believe you did this. I was so surprised."

"That was the plan, beauty queen."

"It's the best present I ever got."

"Aw, shucks," Aidan said, with a laugh. "So, tell me, how are you?"

Tash inhaled deeply. "Slowly learning that life is okay."

Aidan laughed. "That's my girl. Get back to your party. Tell Jason he's the man."

"Yeah, I will." She paused before saying, "And Aidan, thank you."

After Tash hung up, Jason took her hand and led her to the dance floor. They danced for twenty minutes before taking a break to get some water. Engrossed in conversation, they were startled when Lu and Paisley joined them. Lu was dressed in black leather pants and a white T-shirt. She claimed to be an eighties singer but Tash heckled her for looking practically the same as she always does. In contrast, Paisley went all out. She was dressed as Rainbow Brite, complete with rainbows painted on her cheeks, arms, and legs. Jason took one look at her and said, "See, Tash? I told you Rainbow Brite was gay!" They all laughed.

They spent hours drinking, dancing, and laughing. At one point, someone put a white feather boa around Tash's shoulders. She stood in the middle of the dance floor, surrounded by her friends and hundreds of bodies in motion, feathers flying in the air and lightness in her heart.

***

Monroe slipped on her favorite gray silk nightgown and matching robe, and tied the sash around her waist. She opened her nightstand drawer and retrieved the unopened prescription bottle. Sitting on the edge of her bed and rolling the bottle in her hand, it occurred to her that she felt no emotion whatsoever. No sadness, or despair, or grief held her hand. Exhaustion was her only companion. She was done. After moving the bottle from one hand to the other, over and over again, she tucked it into her pocket. She got up and wandered through her house until she found Bill in his office, hunched over the desk.

"It's so late, darling. Why don't you come to bed?" she asked.

"I'll be there soon enough. I have to get through these papers first," he said, gesturing to the stack on his desk.

"Goodnight, Bill. I love you. Truly, I do," Monroe said, before gently shutting the door behind her.

She bumped into Henry on her way back to her bedroom.

"Goodnight, Henry," she said softly.

"Goodnight, Mrs. Preston. Oh, I forgot to tell you that Miss Daniels left her short film here yesterday. She said you had asked to see it."

"Oh, that's right. I did promise her," she mumbled to herself. Then she refocused on Henry. "Maybe I'll watch it now. I know it's late, but would you mind putting it on for me in the screening room?"

"Certainly, ma'am," Henry replied.

Monroe settled into one of the raspberry-colored velvet seats in their lavish private screening room. Henry switched the lights off as the film began. Light from the screen flickered on Monroe's face as the opening credits rolled. Shot in black and white, the camera zoomed in on two young people on a city rooftop in the middle of the night. They were laughing and running across the roof, bits of paper swept up in the breeze. A burst of hot pink leapt off the screen, followed by eruptions of turquoise and purple. Monroe leaned closer. The corners of her mouth trembled and a smile began to crawl across her face. She leaned closer and let the glow from the screen wash over her. Her smile morphed into laughter and tears flooded her eyes. As her smile grew and her laughter became louder, the tears flowed harder. Her face was drenched by the time the closing credits rolled. She sat, soaking in a feeling she couldn't quite name, a feeling she knew was connected to life itself.

Henry returned and flipped the lights on. "Shall I close the room for you before I retire to bed?" he asked.

She wiped her face with her palms and turned to face him. "No. Henry, please get Bill right away. Tell him there's something he must see."

PART THREE

CHAPTER 15

Lu woke up to find Paisley's arm slung across her chest. Careful not to wake her, she gently maneuvered herself out of bed. As she searched the floor for a T-shirt to slip on, she noticed rainbow paint smeared across her chest and legs. Her hands were sticky, so she looked and discovered more paint. *I told her not to do the face paint*, she thought, although she couldn't help but laugh. *Definitely need strong coffee today.*

Still groggy, she shuffled to the kitchen. Given the demands of her day and night jobs, paired with an unpredictable sleep schedule, it was the smell of coffee that helped denote the start of a new day, whether at seven in the morning or two in the afternoon. So, she ignored the paint on her hands in favor of starting the coffee pot. After hitting the brew button, she went to the bathroom and got a look at herself in the mirror. Her hair was matted on one side and there was a multi-colored streak – red, orange, yellow, green, and blue – on her face. "Well, that's a new look," she mumbled.

She flipped the shower on, praying it would be hot by the time she finished brushing her teeth. She swished mouthwash around until her teeth gleamed. Stepping into the shower, she breathed a deep sigh of relief. The water was hot. She rubbed the bar of soap in her hands until it lathered, and then she scrubbed the rainbow splotches in a circular motion. The colors started to meld together, creating a light film of color all over her body. It dawned on her that she was quite literally covered in Paisley. Suddenly, the paint felt like more than an amusing annoyance. It was getting harder to tell where she ended and Paisley began. This made her uncomfortable. She didn't want to think about it, so as she had done for most of her life, she focused on the task at hand and pushed the distressing thoughts to the far edge of her mind. She took the bar of soap and vigorously rubbed it directly on her body, watching the colors trickle down until they circled the drain. When the water ran clear, she could breathe again.

Lu emerged from the bathroom, drying her hair with a towel. Paisley called from the kitchen, startling her.

"I just poured myself a cup of coffee. You want some?"

"Fuck," Lu grumbled, having just pulled a muscle in her neck.

"You okay?" Paisley called.

"Yeah, just a neck strain. It's fine."

"Coffee?" Paisley asked again.

"Yeah, please," Lu replied, tossing her towel in the corner. "I thought you'd still be asleep. Did I wake you?" she asked, before taking a seat at the small table.

"The smell did. You know there's paint on the handle of the coffee pot?" Paisley took the milk out of the refrigerator to splash some in Lu's mug.

"Yeah, it pretty much got everywhere."

Paisley bit her lip. She handed Lu a mug of steaming coffee, taking the seat opposite her. "Uh, yeah. Sorry about that. Guess I kinda went overboard."

Lu smiled and blew on her coffee before taking a sip. "That's okay. It's sweet you went all out for Tash. Besides, it's a reminder of a fun night. Better than a hangover, eh?"

Paisley giggled. "I hope Tash had a great time. It seemed like she did."

"She definitely did. I think she spent most of the summer dreading her birthday. It's hard to celebrate when you feel low, but she's doing a lot better. I can tell. Having Jason there meant the world to her."

"I guess I was sort of dreading it, too. I mean, not the party, per se, but just that it's a marker of time. I've been thinking about how the summer's almost over." Paisley looked down, as if searching for the words. "I start teaching again soon."

"That's right," Lu said. "I almost forgot."

"Yeah, well, the thing is I won't be able to be on your schedule anymore. I mean, I'll be working during the day, so I won't be able to go to clubs as much and you know always crash here."

Lu silently sipped her coffee and Paisley continued.

"I mean, I can come on the weekends, but…"

"Look, I get it. This summer has been amazing, but you need to get back to your life."

"Well, I wouldn't exactly put it that way. You're obviously a part of my life. A big part. But things will change." She looked at her feet, something obviously on her mind.

Lu slipped her hand into Paisley's hand and asked, "What is it?"

"Come to my place tomorrow. My folks invited us over for brunch. They've been dying to meet you."

Lu pulled her hand away and shifted back in her seat. "I'm not so great with parents. Never been into the whole family thing."

"They're not like that. You'll like each other; they're cool. My mom's really into music. And they're important to me, so I want you to know each other. Besides, if you met them, maybe you'd be more comfortable staying at my place sometimes. I'm sure you've avoided it because of the whole parents thing. You'll see that the guest house is actually really private. That way, when I'm teaching, we could maybe go back and forth."

Lu inhaled and took another sip of coffee.

"It's just brunch. I promise, you'll like them."

Lu looked down, squirming in her seat, and then looked up at Paisley. She noticed the flecks of aquamarine sparkling in her eyes, the brown freckle on the tip of her nose, and the soft pink indent at the edge of her upper lip: the beautiful rainbow of Paisley's face of which she never tired. "Yeah, okay. I'll come to brunch. I have to open the juice bar, but I can take off at eleven."

Paisley crinkled her face into a silly smile as her cheeks reddened. She put her mug down and leaned forward to kiss Lu. Then she jumped up and said, "I'm taking a shower."

Lu continued drinking her coffee, wondering what she had gotten herself into. Paisley was thinking about the future, and what's more, how their futures were tied together. Lu was fiercely independent, "an island," Tash always joked. She had never allowed herself to need another or to be needed. The idea of a family being more than a random group with whom meals and homes are forcibly and temporarily shared was foreign to her. She had no interest in spending time with family, including her own, whom she visited once a year on Thanksgiving out of obligation and spoke to on the phone only a few times more. Although she periodically flirted with feelings of guilt for her lack of interest in people she described as "good folks who did their best," those thoughts were few and far between. She rarely thought of them at all.

As she listened to the water from the shower, Lu wondered what she would tell Paisley's parents about herself. She hated answering questions about her upbringing. Her peers simply accepted her as Lu K, hot LA deejay, but older people always asked her "real" name. She never understood why people were so interested in something she felt had nothing to do with who she was. What a boring question.

Lucille Kowalski grew up in Cincinnati in a nuclear family hovering on the edge of the middle class. They were impossibly ordinary: her father, a sales clerk; her mother, a nurse; her older brother, a high school hockey player; and Lu, a misfit. To Lu, it seemed they were all dwelling in the same space without rhyme or reason, random cohabitants. The only real time they spent together, aside from holidays and annual back-to-school shopping, was at the dinner table. Lu's mother insisted they eat together every night, at six o'clock on the dot. Lu sat at the rectangular, Formica table each night to eat a dinner that didn't taste quite right and make small talk that didn't sound quite right.

For as long as she could remember, she had a passion for music, although for years there was little she could do about it. Her school offered music classes, but they were full of uninterested kids clanging away on bongos and tambourines. When she was twelve, her grandparents gave her a small, preprogrammed keyboard designed for kids. She played with it every day, finding ways to push it beyond its bounds. At the age of thirteen, her parents indulged her with weekly piano lessons, but without the ability to practice at home she never got far, and they eventually decided it wasn't worth the money. When she began high school, she realized how limited her exposure to music had been, mostly rock, pop, and classical. At fourteen, she discovered other kinds of music: electronica, trap, hip-hop, trip-hop, and techno. She loved anything with an interesting beat. She became fascinated with creating and digitally altering music. When she attended her first high school party, some kid's older brother was deejaying. He wasn't merely playing existing music, but rather, creating his own mixes.

A new world opened to her. She wanted to learn everything she could about music production and deejaying. She begged her parents for a laptop, deejay turntables, a mixer, and other basic equipment, but they said it was too extravagant. They always paid for her brother's sports equipment. It felt terribly unfair. Was it because she was a girl? Was it because her interest was somehow less valid? Did they not take her seriously? These questions haunted her. She concluded that a girl with a dream is on her own in the world. She spent the next year mowing lawns and babysitting, even though she was ill-suited for the latter. By the time she was fifteen, she had hobbled together the equipment she needed, all second-hand, and began the long road of self-education.

Lu studied her family during the long silences at dinner. She was taller than her mother, lankier than her father and brother, and looked as out of place as she felt. One night, as she swirled the tuna casserole around her plate, it dawned on her: *I must be adopted.* The thought brought instant relief. Suddenly, she had an explanation; she didn't feel like one of them because she wasn't. The next time she was home alone, she searched the cobweb-filled attic for some proof of her lineage: a baby blanket with another name, a stack of unopened mail from her birth mother, or her real birth certificate. When she didn't find anything, she crept into her parent's room and rifled through their drawers. The only noteworthy things she discovered were a secret stash of Oreo cookies her father was hiding and a stack of poems tucked away in her mother's underwear drawer. The poems were in her mother's handwriting, although she had never known her to have the slightest interest in the arts. That was the first and only time she ever thought her mother's life may not have been as boring as it seemed.

After coming up empty on her search, the question of her origin festered. One night at dinner, after her father told her brother to rake the leaves that weekend, to which her brother merely grunted in response, Lu couldn't hold it in anymore. She looked around the table and blurted out, "So, am I adopted or something?"

Her mother casually replied, "What a strange thing to say."

"That's not an answer," Lu said, more convinced than ever.

Her brother laughed. "I wish you were adopted so we could send you back."

Lu ignored him and pressed her mother. "So, am I? It's okay, I just want to know."

"No, you're not adopted. Why on earth would you say that?" her mother replied.

"Because it's the only thing that would explain it, explain us. Haven't you noticed that we don't have anything in common? Not a single thing!"

"I don't understand. We're a family. Is this about that band you want to see?" her mother asked.

Her father sighed. "Not that again. It's past your curfew and that part of town isn't safe."

Lu shook her head. "I told you, it's not a band. It's an open mic night. I want to perform. If I'm gonna do something in art or music, I need experience."

"Maybe you could be an elementary school music teacher," her mother said.

"If she's going to be a teacher, she should teach math or history. That's more stable," her father added.

Lu sat in disbelief before shouting, "What are you talking about? I don't want to be a teacher!"

"Well, you don't need to decide now," her mother said.

Lu opened her mouth, but knew there was no adequate response. These people had no idea who she was and they never would. She looked around the table and silently screamed: *How the fuck can I be one of you?*

The next day, Lu stopped at the cheap hair salon in their local shopping center and got her hair cut very short, "edgy," as she instructed the stylist. That night at dinner, her brother said, "You look like a boy." She replied, "And you look like an idiot." Her parents never said a word, as if they hadn't noticed the loss of ten inches. Lu knew they were too uncomfortable to acknowledge it and so they ignored it. While she had never uttered the words out loud, Lu considered that to be the day she boldly and unapologetically came out, both about her sexuality and musical career path. From that moment on, she considered herself a free agent, free from the pretense of caring about other people's expectations.

Two weeks later, she snuck out to go to the open mic night. She paid her brother twenty dollars to cover for her. When it was her turn on stage, she recited a spoken-word poem she had written for the occasion, set to music. The poem needed work, but her delivery and sense of musicality were compelling. Even at the age of fifteen, she possessed the charisma to command attention. She was invited to come back. And so began her years of performing in coffee shops, bookstores, bars, and anywhere else that would give her a stage. She met older artists and musicians, some of whom were catty, which taught her to always watch her back. Others became friends "from the scene," although sensing there was somewhere bigger and better in her future, she tried not to get too attached. She frequently found herself in sticky situations. Some nights, drunk men heckled her, other nights they hit on her. These encounters forced her to learn how to negotiate personal safety. One night, a man followed her to the bus stop, making lewd comments. She eventually whirled around and said, "Look buddy, it's not happening. I like girls." He got right in her face and started screaming homophobic slurs, his spit hitting her cheeks. He threatened to "give it to her good," claiming that "a real man would fix you." She was terrified but did her best to hide it, jumping on the first bus that came by. She thought about asking the bus driver for help, but was unsure if she could trust him either. She concluded she was on her own and could no longer risk certainty about people. From that night on, Lu wore her distrust like armor, even when it was exhausting and lonely to do so. She learned to carry herself with attitude and confidence at all times. At the urging of a twenty-something gay man she befriended at a slam poetry event, she began seeking out LGBTQA-friendly venues. She felt an uncomfortable mixture of gratitude for these safer spaces and resentment at the need for them. They made her world at once bigger and smaller. Over time, she developed her persona as Lu K and built a small and loyal following.

When she was seventeen, her brother left for college and her mother began working the night shift. So ended family dinners. This worked well for Lu, who was busy living her authentic life, one her parents didn't care to know about. After a string of casual encounters with girls from school, she met Jenna at a club when she was eighteen.

Lu cared for her but could never truly match Jenna's feelings, but when Jenna prepared to move across the country, Lu jumped at the chance to go with her. She left Cincinnati determined to find her people, even though she was equally determined not to need them.

This all came rushing back as she drank her coffee and thought about meeting Paisley's parents, and then as she thought about Paisley, her softness and goodness. Eventually, she heard the shower turn off. *Fuck, I need to get out of my head. Coffee, I need more coffee.* She slurped the last bit in her mug and got up for a refill, stretching her neck, still strained from earlier when Paisley startled her. *Damn*, she thought. She searched the cabinets for Advil, but the bottle was empty so she settled for another cup of coffee. When she put the pot down, she noticed her hand was sticky again. She looked to see a rainbow splotch in the middle of her palm.

CHAPTER 16

Monroe's eyelashes were stuck together, with thick layers of crust in the corners. She wiped away the crust and slowly opened her eyes. She couldn't remember the last time she felt so rested. It was as if she had slept for days. She turned to look at the clock on her nightstand. It was almost noon. She stretched her arms, reached for her silk robe, and sauntered into the bathroom. When she saw her reflection in the mirror, she thought, *I know you.* Then she glanced at the small picture of her mother. She picked it up and whispered, "I think I know you too, Mama. Rest well." As she moved to put the photo down, she heard a slight rustling noise and realized she still had the pill bottle in the pocket of her robe. She retrieved the bottle and confidently tossed it in the trash. After freshening up, she grabbed the book on her nightstand and headed to the breakfast room. On her way, she bumped into Henry.

"Good morning, Mrs. Preston, or perhaps I should say good afternoon."

"I can't believe how well I slept, Henry. I feel marvelous."

"Shall I have the cook prepare your usual breakfast or would you prefer lunch?"

"Perhaps an egg white omelet and we'll call it brunch."

"Very good, Mrs. Preston. Shall I bring your book?"

"Thank you, Henry," she said, handing him the book.

Henry hurried off to inform the cook. Monroe strolled through her home, absentmindedly humming. This time, when she stopped by her Warhol, she saw it with fresh eyes.

Oh Marilyn, thank you for helping me to see. I finally understand what you meant, about life slipping further away. Some of us use glamour as armor, or perhaps as a mask. Others of us prefer to dwell in isolation. No matter the path, we can never hide from ourselves. We can't stop the feelings in all shades of light and dark. She stood for a moment and then smiled, mischievously. *I'm glad Mr. Warhol captured this part of you, the smile just a bit too bright. He was clever. Rest well, dear Marilyn.* Monroe walked away knowing she had finally made peace with something that could not be named and knowing that the painting that had once captivated her would now take on a welcome ordinary quality.

She practically floated into the breakfast room. She poured herself a cup of coffee and picked up her book, left on the table for her. Before she could open it, the cook walked in and presented her meal.

"This looks delicious. Thank you," Monroe said.

"May I get you anything else?"

"My cell phone, please. I must have left it upstairs." *I need to get in touch with Tash right away.*

***

"Oooh, this is so Cali," Jason said, as he took his seat on the patio at Café Gratitude.

"Yeah, it's kind of hot today but I knew you'd want to sit outside. It's *the* it spot. I once saw Jennifer Lopez here."

"How'd she look?"

"Flawless, of course. She was wearing a short, gold, tunic-style dress, and I would have killed to know what brand of highlighter she was using. Her cheekbones, like *wow*."

"Forget the celebs. Look at the waiters. My oh my," Jason said, lifting his dark sunglasses to get a better look.

"You're such a slut," Tash joked.

"Uh huh," Jason said.

"I can't believe you're moving in with your boyfriend. That's so grown-up. But I can see you haven't lost your wandering eye," Tash said, as Jason strained his neck to look at the waiter.

"Looking is good. Keeps us healthy. It's like yoga for the libido."

Tash laughed. "I do have to admit the waiters here are seriously hot and they have this chill, Zen thing going on that makes 'em even hotter."

"Speaking of," Jason said softly as their waiter approached.

"My name is Brock and I'll be taking care of you today. Welcome to Café Gratitude. Have you dined with us before?" he asked as he filled their water glasses.

"I have," Tash said.

"It's my first time," Jason said coyly.

Tash rolled her eyes.

"Welcome. Would you like to hear today's question?"

"Absolutely," Jason said.

"Today's question is: In what ways are you growing? I'll give you a few minutes with the menu and check back."

As he walked away, Tash shook her head. "You are positively shameless."

"Brock. His name is Brock. I mean, *hello*. God, I love LA."

Tash giggled. "I missed you so much."

"Me too."

"We're not really answering that lame question, are we?"

"Hell no. I just wanted the pretty man to stay at the table longer. Okay, so what's good here?" Jason asked, picking up his menu.

"It's totally vegan, but the food is amazing. They have great pressed juices and smoothies you'd love. They do breakfast 'til one on the weekends and I know how you love brunch."

"Oh my God, I love the names of things."

"Yeah, when you order something, they'll compliment you based on the name they've given the food you order. Like if I order a muffin, he'll call me beautiful. It's so LA."

"Do you ever order based on what you want the hot waiter to say to you? I totally would," Jason mused.

Tash laughed. "I'm not as hard up for compliments as you are."

"Yes, you are."

Tash crinkled her face.

"The doughnut is called holy. That's adorbs," Jason said. "Isn't there some nineties song that goes something like 'you'll never gain weight from a doughnut hole?' Kind of heavy for brunch, huh?"

Tash shrugged.

Soon, Brock returned to take their order. "What can I get you, Miss?"

"I'll have an Arabica coffee and the superfood granola, please."

"You are courageous and powerful," Brock said.

Jason smirked.

"And for you?"

"I'll have the energy juice and the buckwheat flax pancakes, please."

"Would you like to add berries or cashew whipped cream?"

"Let's live a little. I'll add it all," Jason replied.

"You are succulent and open-hearted," Brock said.

Jason smiled. "Indeed I am."

Brock grabbed their menus and walked away. Tash shook her head. "You are so bad. And since when do you eat carbs?"

"I'm treating myself. I mean, cashew whipped cream. How could I pass that up? Damn, I love LA. I can't believe you don't."

"I never said that."

Jason took his sunglasses off and placed them on the table. "Oh, please. It's me."

Tash looked down.

"Tell me."

"I don't want to be a downer," she replied.

"Sweetie, I didn't come all this way for fake talk."

"It's been a really big adjustment. In the beginning it was great, but then..." she trailed off as Brock returned with their drinks.

Jason took a sip of his green juice. "Come on, how could you not love this?" he asked, holding up the glass.

"Gross. It looks like sludge."

Jason laughed, but then his expression turned more serious. "What happened? Was it the dead ends with your film? If they don't get it, screw them. You're ahead of your time."

"Not being able to make anything happen was depressing, but then... God, I feel like a piece of shit for even thinking it..."

"When Aidan got a break, it was hard as hell and you wanted to pull your hair out. Metaphorically, of course. Your hair is fab."

"You know how much I love him and how talented he is. I mean, if anyone deserves..."

Jason interrupted. "You don't have to do that with me. I get it. Aidan's awesome. We all love him. Not the point. You can want good things for him and still feel that it's not fair."

"Thanks. I guess I really needed to say it out loud to release it."

"What about Lu? Can't you talk to her about this?"

Tash raised her eyebrows. "Are you kidding me? She's been working the LA club scene way longer than Aidan. It's tough for her too. Tougher than she'd admit."

Jason took another sip of his juice. "How's the summer gone while he's been away?"

"Honestly, I wasted most of it. I just couldn't try anymore. I couldn't keep putting myself out there just to be rejected. But then I decided, *fuck it*. Regardless of what happens, I'm going to make art. That's how I got the show I have next week. I crawled my way back to myself."

"Which is freaking amazing," Jason said. "See? The waiter was right; you *are* courageous and powerful."

Tash blushed.

"I guess we answered that inane question-of-the-day after all. Sounds like you're growing in lots of ways."

"You too, sweetie. I mean, a full-time man and a full-time job. That's a big change! I'm so proud of you for starting your own interior design business. You're gonna crush it. And you never looked better."

Jason smiled. "And Pen! She was always a grown-up, but now that she's getting married, I mean, like wow. And he's so perfect for her. You'll see at the wedding next summer. He's really nerdy and loves talking about dusty old history things. They're adorable together."

Tash smiled. "Just as long as she doesn't make me wear something awful at the wedding."

"Oh, honey, you're fucked for sure. I'm picturing pink taffeta, hopefully with lots of ruffles."

Tash shook her head and laughed. "You're such a shit. I can't believe you have to head back tomorrow."

"I know, the price of having an actual job. Modeling was so much better."

"Well, on the plus side, you never would have ordered pancakes when you were modeling, and I'm totally taking a bite."

Just then, Brock delivered their food.

"This looks great," Jason said.

"You go ahead. I'm gonna check my phone quickly, to see if Aidan's tried to reach me."

Tash had received a text from Monroe.

```
Hi Tash. I'd like to invite you to the
studio's anniversary party. Please buy
yourself a fabulous gown and put it on
my account. It's only a few days away,
so tell them any alterations need to be
done immediately. Use my name. I'm sorry
for the last-minute notice. I do hope you
can come.
```

Tash was stunned. Monroe had never invited her to an event before. She slipped her phone back in her purse and looked at Jason.

"What?" he asked, with a mouth full of pancakes.

"Uh, so how do you feel about spending the afternoon helping me pick out a designer gown?"

CHAPTER 17

Lu pulled up to Paisley's parent's home, her heart racing from the stress of being nearly twenty minutes late. She cranked the air conditioning in her car, afraid she'd sweat through her shirt and have pit stains when she met Paisley's parents. The sight of the modern, oceanfront mansion did nothing to calm her nerves. As she sat in her car, berating herself for wearing a button-down shirt and trying to catch her breath, the front door to the house opened. Paisley flitted over, her white sundress blowing in the breeze. Lu jumped out of the car.

"I'm so sorry. The line was out the door today and my replacement was late. I changed as quickly as I could and motored, but the traffic was epic."

Paisley smiled. "Don't worry about it. You're not that late. And you look great, but you didn't need to dress up."

"Is it too much?" Lu asked nervously, as she made sure her shirt was tucked in.

Paisley giggled. "You're perfect. My folks are out back. Let's cut through the house to join them and then I can take you around to my place after we eat."

Lu nodded and followed her. They walked into an enormous entryway that opened to an even more enormous living space. Everything was white and airy. The far wall was made entirely of glass, offering an expansive view of the cobalt sea from the moment you entered the house. Even after years in LA, Lu believed that places like this only existed in movies.

"Holy shit," she muttered.

Paisley giggled. "The view is pretty rad, huh?"

"Uh, yeah. You could say that."

"Come on," Paisley said, taking her hand.

They walked to the other side of the room and stepped through the sliding glass door onto the patio. The back of the property boasted a long infinity pool overlooking the Pacific. There was a row of lounge chairs facing the pool, a firepit and bar to the left, and a large table to the right, where Paisley's parents were seated under umbrellas. They casually stood up as Lu and Paisley approached.

"Mom and Dad, this is Lu."

Lu stuck her hand out. "So nice to meet you, Mrs...."

Paisley's mother interrupted. "Please, call me Ivy."

"And I'm Paul," Paisley's father said, outstretching his hand.

Lu smiled. "I'm so sorry I'm late. I had trouble getting out of work and then the traffic was terrible."

"Don't worry about it. We're enjoying the beautiful day," Ivy said. Lu noticed how much Paisley resembled her. Ivy was taller and thinner, but they had the same coloring: hair, eyes, and complexion.

Paul was a slight man with light brown hair and glasses. "The traffic gets worse each year," he said, sitting down.

"Shall we?" Ivy said, indicating they should all take a seat. "You know, sometimes I think that when Paul retires, we should pack up and move to the mountains to get away from all the congestion here. Maybe Montana. It's beautiful there."

"She says that, but she could never leave the ocean," Paul said with a smile.

"He's probably right," Ivy conceded. "I've been spoiled. There's nothing like doing yoga on the beach. I don't know if I could give it up."

Lu smiled. "Your home is spectacular."

Just then, a staff member came over with carafes of freshly squeezed orange and grapefruit juice.

"Theresa, this is Lu," Paisley said.

"Nice to meet you," Lu said.

"Can I get you coffee or tea?"

"Coffee would be great, thank you."

"For me too, please, Theresa. Oh, and Lu takes milk," Paisley said.

Lu glanced at Paisley, thinking that no one had ever really known her well enough to remember her likes or dislikes before.

Ivy turned to Lu and said, "Please help yourself to some juice, if you'd like."

"I got it," Paisley said, picking up the pitcher of orange juice and pouring some for Lu and then for herself.

"Thanks," Lu said, taking a sip. "Wow, that's delicious. Sweeter than what we've had in the store lately."

"Paisley told us you have a part-time job at a juice bar," Ivy said. "I'm a big juicer. I do a detox at least once a month."

Lu smiled. "Yeah, I've been there for years. I'm the assistant manager. But honestly, it's just a way to pay the bills."

Ivy grinned. "Yes, we've heard you're a gifted deejay. I think it's admirable to do whatever it takes to live as an artist. I could tell you stories about famous musicians I've worked with who walked dogs, washed cars, and bussed tables to make ends meet. That's how you know the real artists: their willingness to work hard because they have to find a way for their art. It's just in their soul. It's a beautiful thing to be around that energy. That's what drew me to the music business."

"You'd be surprised, but it's the same in the tech world, at least for the real creatives who tinker in their parents' garages because they've got some wonderfully bonkers idea they can't let go of no matter how many times they fail. Some people breathe invention and they've just got to spend their lives discovering and creating," Paul said.

Lu smiled, nodding along. It hadn't been five minutes and she already felt that these people saw her, understood her, and what's more, they embraced what mattered most to her. She felt more at home with them than she ever did with her parents. She liked them.

Theresa and another staff member returned with coffee and brunch: an eggless vegetable frittata, fruit salad, and a mesclun salad with tahini dressing.

Once everyone was served, Lu said, "This looks great."

"Most of it came from my mom's vegetable garden, even the herbs."

Paul chuckled. "Be glad it doesn't come from Paisley. This one couldn't keep a cactus alive. She could kill weeds."

"Dad," Paisley whined.

"It's true," Paul insisted, taking a bite of salad.

Paisley turned deep crimson.

"You've always been wonderful with animals, but your dad's right. You didn't inherit my green thumb," Ivy added.

Paisley rolled her eyes. "At least I'm good with bunnies."

Ivy laughed. "You'll always have bunnies."

Lu loved the playful banter. It was clear they were all connected in a special way.

"So, tell me more about your music, Lu," Ivy said. "When did you begin developing your sound?"

They spent the next hour eating, talking about music, and gently teasing Paisley. Ivy was a fount of knowledge about music, and Lu loved listening to her stories about the industry. She thought she'd never stop laughing when Ivy told her about a party at which two members of the Rolling Stones were almost thrown out because someone thought they were homeless people who wandered in off the street. Ivy also knew what the industry was like for women. She said, "It's always tougher for women. If there's ever anything I can do for you," but Lu quickly declined and moved the conversation forward. Paul was equally disarming, just as Paisley had described. In meeting them, she understood Paisley better. They all made sense together. As comfortable as Lu felt with them, there remained a small, nagging discomfort. She fit easily into their dynamic. Things never came easily. She didn't know how to trust it.

**

"You can see it's a lot cozier than the main house" Paisley said, waving her arms around.

"It's great," Lu said. "It's kind of dope to have a two-room house."

"When I was in high school, I begged my folks to let me live here. They wouldn't let me, but my friends and I would sneak in here whenever it wasn't being used. Once I caught one of the guys from Aerosmith in here with a half-naked model. That's a funny story. I was banned from the guesthouse for months. I know I need to move eventually, but it's been great to finally be allowed to live here."

Lu smiled.

"Take a load off on the couch. I'm just gonna grab us some water," Paisley said.

Lu plopped down. She picked up an art book from the coffee table and started flipping through it.

"You should take my mom up on her offer, if there's ever anyone you want to meet or something," Paisley hollered.

"That's really nice of her and all, but there's no way I would ever ask her for a favor."

"She doesn't mind. She loves helping musicians. If you're too shy to ask, I could do it for you."

Lu put the book back on the coffee table. "No way. Please, don't."

Paisley walked over and handed her a glass of water before taking the seat next to her. "Okay, but I don't see what the big deal is."

"Can we just drop it?" Lu asked.

"Yeah, sure," Paisley said. She tilted her head toward the book Lu had been looking at. "Someone gave me that because the Hockney on the cover reminded them of this place. I don't really see it though. To me there's something unbelievable about his work. It's all surface."

"Yeah, I was never a huge fan, but I can see the resemblance. I mean, this place has a sort of hyper-real, picture-perfect quality."

Paisley giggled. "Yeah, it's kind of a postcard. But what's inside is real. So now that you've seen it and met my folks, can you picture yourself spending some time here?"

Lu squirmed. "The thing is, Malibu is way too far from work for me."

"Yeah, and your place is far from my work."

"Yeah, it's a drag. You know the crazy hours I work. I can't be on the road all the time."

Paisley huffed and shook her head. "I'm not suggesting we always stay here."

"I just don't see how I could ever really come this far."

"Of course you don't. That would mean you'd have to consider someone other than yourself."

"Excuse me?" Lu bellowed, leaping up.

Paisley took a deep breath, steadied her nerves, and then looked up at Lu. "You don't care if it works between us. You can take it or leave it."

"That's not fair," Lu said. "I'm here now."

"When I told you that school is starting soon and things would have to change, you assumed that meant we were over. And you didn't even care. I mean, that was your first thought. You made it pretty clear. And I..."

"What?" Lu asked.

"I can't do it anymore. We don't want the same things. I want to find a way to make it work, to make us work, and you don't even care if we break up. You won't meet me halfway and I can't keep doing it for both of us and hoping or pretending."

"If that's how you feel, maybe I should go."

"Yeah, I guess maybe you should."

Without hesitation, Lu walked out the door. Her heart was racing again, but this time with an overwhelming feeling of regret. Too proud or perhaps too afraid to deal with these uncomfortable feelings, she scurried to her car and headed home.

For the next three days, she focused on each task at hand, whether it was peeling carrots at the juice bar or spinning at the club. Yet no matter how hard she tried to push Paisley out of her mind, she kept slipping in.

CHAPTER 18

Tash finished washing off the green face mask she applied to make her skin luminous. She was patting her face dry when her phone beeped. There was a text message from Lu.

> Hey. You're probably getting ready for that fab Hollywood thing, so no sweat if you don't have time. Just feeling meh. Text if you have a minute.

She immediately dialed Lu's number.

"Hey," Lu said. "You didn't have to call. I know it's a big night for you."

"The driver's not picking me up for two hours. What's going on?"

"Do you think I'm really screwed up?"

"Define *really*," Tash joked.

Lu let out a small laugh. "It's like I'm standing at a precipice and I want to take the leap, I really do, but I'm afraid of…"

"Of smashing to the ground and shattering into a million pieces?"

"Thanks for the vivid image!" Lu joked. "But seriously, what if I crash?"

"Yeah, that could happen. But what if you fly?"

Lu sighed.

"Listen, I get it. I do. You've gotta do what feels right for you. I just know from experience that being the invincible cool girl takes a toll. It's a lot easier when we have people who get us so we can let our guard down from time to time."

"It's gonna sound stupid, but I never thought I'd need someone, you know?"

"Needing someone isn't half as scary as being needed. Maybe that's what you're really afraid of. But it makes you rise. And push yourself. It's easy to get lazy in ways we don't even recognize."

Lu exhaled. "It probably doesn't matter anyway. I fucked it up."

"Oh please," Tash said. "You can fix it. You've just gotta decide what you really want."

"I want Paisley."

"Then why are you wasting time with me?"

"Promise me one thing," Lu said. "If it doesn't work out, we never had this conversation."

Tash giggled. "You know it. Good luck."

"Thanks. And have an amazing time tonight. You're probably gonna meet so many of your heroes."

"Totally. You should see the guest list. I still can't believe Monroe invited me. I wish Aidan was here to go with me."

"He'll be back soon, right?" Lu asked.

"Yeah, and I'll be busy 'til then anyway. I have work to do for Monroe, then Tuesday I have to go do the set-up at the gallery. He gets back Wednesday. Then the opening is Thursday night. You'll be there, right?"

"Wouldn't miss it."

"I better go get glamorous. Oh my God, you should see my gown. It looks like liquid gold and has this plunging neckline. It's a showstopper, if I do say so myself. I'm wearing my hair down on one side, with waves. Very old-school Hollywood. And of course, bright red lips."

Lu laughed. "You're gonna crush it. Have fun, babe."

"You too, baby."

***

After exchanging text messages with Paisley, Lu spent an hour pacing around her apartment, waiting for her to arrive. When she heard a gentle knock, she squeezed her eyes shut for a moment and then opened the door.

"Hey, come on in," she said, closing the door behind her. "Thanks for coming here. I would have come to your place if I wasn't working later tonight."

"It's okay," Paisley said, taking a seat on the edge of Lu's bed. "I wanted to apologize to you anyway."

Lu furrowed her brow and sat down next to her. "*You* wanted to apologize?"

"I overreacted. I was going to reach out, but then you didn't try to get in touch with me, and..."

"I'm the one who should apologize," Lu said, taking a deep breath. "You were just calling me out on my shit. And in some ways, you were spot on. But it's not that I don't care or that I don't want to be with you."

Paisley took Lu's hand. "Then what is it?"

"I want to show you something." Lu jumped up and pulled a photograph out of her dresser drawer.

"What's that?" Paisley asked.

Lu plopped back down on the edge of the bed. "It's a picture of my family."

Paisley took the photo and then looked back at Lu.

"They're nothing like your family. I mean, you guys get each other. No one from my family has any clue about who I am. And they don't even try to learn."

"That must have been tough growing up," Paisley said.

"It made me rely on myself. If I wanted something, I had to find a way to make it happen. I could never count on anyone else to do anything for me. Don't get me wrong, they're not bad people. I don't have a horrible sob story." She looked down as if searching for the words. "When we started dating, you asked me why I moved to the West Coast. You asked what I was trying to get away from. See, the thing is, I wasn't really trying to flee *from* something, but rather *to* something."

Paisley smiled.

"And now I don't want to run at all. I just want to be. I've never felt that way before."

Paisley rubbed Lu's hand.

Lu smiled. "I love you and I want to be with you."

"I love you, too," Paisley said.

Lu leaned in, put her hand on Paisley's face, and kissed her. When she pulled back, Paisley said, "So I guess this means you'll be crashing at my place part of the time."

"Actually, what I said about Malibu being too far from work was true." Paisley looked down and bit her lip. Lu continued. "I was thinking, my lease is up soon. I know it's fast, but I was hoping we could get a place together, somewhere in the middle."

Paisley smiled brightly, grabbed Lu, and they fell into the bed.

***

Tash stepped out of the limousine to a frenzy of flashing lightbulbs. Photographers clicked away as she slowly walked the carpet toward Magic Manor. Meryl and Goldie were walking ahead of her, and one of the directors she most admired was following behind her. *This is unbelievable, even if it is just one Cinderella night.*

She walked inside and was immediately handed a glass of champagne. Waiters walked around with trays of caviar blinis, mini salmon *en croute*, and artichoke hearts topped with mushroom duxelles. She was popping a blini into her mouth when a parlor magician started doing an illusion. People gathered around to watch. By the end of the trick, Tash was laughing and chatting with a few other guests, but they all turned to look when Bill and Monroe arrived. Monroe looked stunning in a strapless, black satin gown, her ears and neck dripping with diamonds. Tash caught Monroe's eye and they both tilted their heads in acknowledgement of each other. Monroe held her finger up as if to say, please wait for me. Tash smiled and continued making small talk as Bill and Monroe greeted their guests. Soon, Tash saw Monroe whisper something to Bill. Then she sashayed across the room.

"Tash, you look gorgeous. I'm so glad you could make it."

"I can't thank you enough for the invitation and the gown. This is one of the most exciting nights of my life."

Monroe smiled.

"Oh, and you look beautiful too, Monroe."

"Thank you. I feel wonderful. I had been suffering from terrible insomnia, but I finally started sleeping soundly again." She paused before continuing, "It's the strangest thing and I'm a bit embarrassed to admit it, but it actually started after you told me about Aidan's tour. For some reason, I couldn't get it out of my mind."

Tash crinkled her face. "I guess it stirred something up for you too."

"There was just something about his fast success that took hold of my mind. I don't know if you remember, but we also spoke about why I came to Los Angeles. I hadn't thought about that in years and, well, it's not important why, but that got my head spinning. So yes, in a strange way, your boyfriend's tour was the impetus for some restless nights."

"I'm glad you're feeling better."

Monroe took Tash's hand and looked at her earnestly. "It was your film. I watched your film." She squeezed Tash's hand. "You had never told me what it was about."

Tash smiled. "That was one of my problems with the film festivals and grant proposals. I was terrible at describing it and I think people misunderstood it or wanted it to be something easier to define, something more Hollywood."

Monroe's eyes widened. "When it started with that couple, I thought it was going to be a love story. But that's not really what it is at all."

Tash shook her head. "No, it's not."

Monroe released Tash's hand and then held her hands up as if trying to animate what the film was about. "It's about that thing inside each of us. That thing, that feeling, you know? Possibilities. It's about possibilities."

Tash smiled. "Yes, that's exactly right. I should have had you help me explain it. People didn't get it."

"Well, I did. And Bill did too. I showed it to him and he thought it was brilliant. Hold on, let me get his attention. That's why I invited you; he wants to chat with you."

Tash was dumbfounded as she watched Monroe wave Bill over.

"Well, hello there," he said, extending his hand. "We've seen each other briefly at the house but I don't think we've properly met."

"It's nice to meet you, sir," Tash said, shaking his hand. "Thank you so much for having me."

"Monroe was quite taken with your film. I know you didn't ask her to show it to me; I hope you don't mind that she did. You can't imagine how many people have asked Monroe to show me their headshots, or scripts, or films. She never has before, not once, so I watched your film with deep curiosity. I can see why she was moved. You have a great sensibility. It showed tremendous promise."

Tash blushed and tried to keep her mouth from falling open. "Thank you. I'm extremely honored."

"Let me cut to the chase. A couple of years ago, we acquired several small production companies. One of them specializes in art films, producing pieces for museum theaters, supporting the shorts, and so on. We had the idea to turn it into something, maybe even work with streaming platforms, but the truth is, we haven't done much with it yet. We need to get some talent in there with vision to curate and develop content. Are you available to come in Monday for an interview and to meet the team?"

Tash's jaw dropped. "Uh, I don't even know what to say."

"Say yes."

"Yes, of course. I'll be there."

"Terrific. I'll have my assistant call you to confirm the details. It was wonderful talking with you, but I can see one of my snippiest screenwriters and snarkiest directors huddled together. They're giving me the eye. If I don't go say hello, they'll make my life hell."

Tash laughed. "Of course. Thank you again for the opportunity."

"I'll join you in a minute, darling," Monroe said.

As soon as Bill walked away, Tash's eyes became misty.

"Oh, don't cry dear, you'll ruin your eye makeup."

"Monroe, I don't know how to thank you. I can't believe you did this for me."

"There's no need to thank me. You're talented, truly talented. Tash, you have a passion. I envy that about you. It's something I always longed for."

Tash smiled.

"Just promise you'll meet me for lunch from time to time and you'll tell me if what I'm wearing belongs on the worst-dressed list."

"Of course," Tash said, sniffling.

"I better join Bill before he thinks I defected. Enjoy yourself tonight. There should be quite a lot of magic."

"I will. Monroe, please know how grateful I am. I think you're extraordinary. And I bet you have more passion in you than you realize. It's never too late."

Monroe smiled and sauntered off.

Tash stood, glowing as brightly as her gown, taking in the feeling, the chatter, and the magic.

CHAPTER 19

Tash was standing in the back of the gallery's media room when Patty popped in to check on her.

"How's the system working?" Patty asked.

"It's great," Tash said, turning to face her. "Projecting it on all three walls was a great idea, especially for the opening running scene. You feel like you're moving with them."

"Glad we could make it work. We were prepared for it from a show we did last year, but I always cross my fingers for anything tech."

Tash smiled. "I hear ya."

"I'm dashing out for a lunch meeting. I'll see you Thursday night."

"I'm just gonna run through it a couple more times to make sure there aren't any glitches with the thirty-second delay between showings. Then I'll set up the chairs and head out myself."

"Ellen's up front if you need anything. Make sure to use the white folding chairs. They're stacked in the back room."

"Okay. Thanks, Patty."

As Patty left, the film ended. Tash walked to the center of the dark, empty room, waiting for the film to restart. She was standing still, her mind quiet, when she heard someone step into the doorway and knock on the wall. Thinking Patty forgot something, she turned, just as the film began again. The light hit her face as her images popped up all around her. She gasped. It was Aidan. He was wearing black leather pants, a t-shirt, headphones slung around his shoulders, and the sexiest smile she had ever seen. "Hey there, beauty queen," he said, leaning against the doorframe.

She smiled as the light and images from her film bounced off her face. "Aidan," she said, as if confirming it was really him. "I thought you weren't coming home until tomorrow."

"Yeah, after you called yesterday with your incredible news, I decided to skip the big party. Hitched a ride with one of the crew who had to get back for his kid's birthday."

"How'd you know where to find me?"

"When I got home, I bumped into Darrell. He told me you'd be here."

Tash smiled.

"So, creative development for an artsy production company, a subsidiary of a major studio. I mean, wow. Holy smokes. That's amazing. Congratulations. I'm so proud of you."

"I still can't believe it. I'll be going through submissions and curating content with two other people, who I met and actually really like. I mean, it's not glamorous, but Aidan, can you believe it?"

Aidan smiled, looked her up and down, and then said, "Yeah, I can believe it."

Tash blushed. "I might be able to pitch some of my own work too."

"I'd expect nothing less," he said, walking over. They stood inches apart, staring at each other as the light from the projector hit their faces.

"So, what have you been up to this summer?" Tash asked.

Aidan slipped the headphones off his shoulders and put them on her ears. "This is something new I've been working on." He put his arms around her waist and hit play. Tash listened to his beats as her images swirled around them both.

After a few minutes, she took off the headphones, leaned in, and kissed him.

"God, I missed you," he said.

"Me too. I love you. I'm sorry for how things were before you left. I had to work through some stuff."

"I know. It's all good. So, you said your new job starts November first. Did Monroe ask you for two months or something?"

"No. She's so amazing, she just let me go. I'm already done. I offered to help her find a replacement, but she said she could find someone. I actually think she's going to do it on her own for a bit. She texted me this morning that she's signing up for a class. She can't decide between writing and fashion design. I think she's trying to figure out what's next for her. You know, find her bliss."

"That's cool."

"Yeah. And I'll still see her. She stops by the studio from time to time and made me promise to meet her for lunches."

"So then why aren't you starting the new job right away?"

"I asked for two months. When I start, I want to give it my all and I really want to write my full-length screenplay first, while I have time. I know I should have done it this summer, but I was going through some stuff and…"

"You don't have to explain."

"I know nothing may come of it, but it's just something I need to see through. So, I'm taking two months off to write. With what we're both making now I figured we could swing it. Is that okay?"

"It's perfect, actually."

Tash raised an eyebrow.

"Calvin's two-week UK tour starts the week after next. We bonded, and as a thank you present, he invited us to come along for a vacation, all expenses paid."

Tash grinned.

"When we were in New York, you asked me if I could deejay in LA. Do you remember?"

"I remember."

"Well, can you write in London? I figured we could use the time together. You can write during the day and we can party at night. The clubs are supposed to be the bomb. We could even catch some theater if you need inspiration. So, what do you say, beauty queen? Are you in?"

She watched the images floating around them, and then looked into his eyes. "I'm all in."

SUGGESTED CLASSROOM OR BOOK CLUB USE

1. Compare Prilly from *Low-Fat Love* to Tash in *Film*. What are the similarities or differences you see? What distinguishes their journeys?

2. How does Tash evolve over the course of the three novels?

3. Who is your favorite character from these novels? Why? What, if anything, do you learn from him/her?

4. Compare Jason from *Blue* to Lu from *Film*. What do we learn from each of these characters about bias and assumptions based on status characteristics (e.g. race, sexuality, gender)?

5. As a reader, what was your emotional journey reading each novel? How, if at all, did you reflect on your own life?

6. Which characters resonated the most deeply with you? Which character did you most dislike, and why? Which book was your favorite, and why?

7. Each book is littered with pop culture references. Go back through some of these references. How is pop culture used in each book? What are the stories about pop culture that come through? What is the importance of this aspect of the collection?

8. If for one day you could step into the shoes of any of the characters from these novels, who would you pick? Why? What might you learn from the experience?

9. What is the overall message about relationships that you've taken from this collection?

10. What is the overall message about self-concept or self-esteem that you've taken from this collection?

CREATIVE WRITING ACTIVITIES

1. Pick one of the characters from any of these novels and write his/her story five years later.

2. Pick one of the minor characters from these novels (e.g., Melville, Harold, Darrell) and write his/her story.

3. Write an essay about yourself based on one of the themes in these novels (e.g., self-esteem, romantic relationships, professional struggle, loneliness, depression, grief, pop culture consumption, friendship).

AFTERWORD

These novels were each published as part of the *Social Fictions* series, which I developed after writing *Low-Fat Love*. The *Social Fictions* series comprises full-length literary works – novels, plays, creative nonfiction, and short story and poetry collections – that are informed by research and teaching experiences. Each book includes a brief academic preface. This series or concept did not develop in a vacuum. Following the work of many others, I had been writing about art and social science for years, advocating for artful ways of knowing and artful forms of expression. I merge scholarly and artistic practices in my own work under the rubric of "arts-based research." I believe the line between nonfiction and fiction is blurry. I've written and spoken about these topics extensively. As a result, much has been made over the years about the extent to which a researcher has the ability or right to pen novels. I'd like to briefly share my thoughts.

Every artist brings his/her/their perspective and experiences to bear on their creative process. Our worldviews cannot be separated from our art; who we are is integral to our art-making, across all media. Everything we create comes through our filter. This is true whether you have a fine arts background, a degree in creative writing, or a scientific background. I'm trained as a sociologist and therefore I bring a sociological perspective to every experience, whether it's watching a film, listening to a political debate, or writing a novel. My sociological background is simply a perspective I can't help but apply to any project. It's part of my blueprint or filter. It's a lens and a tool.

We all have different lenses available to us. Many actors have a range of educational and professional experiences in other subject matter, and the same is true across the arts. Next time you find yourself in an art museum, read the curatorial notes about the artists. You'll see that many of the visual artists we hold in high regard have backgrounds in engineering, science, philosophy, and other subjects. Their visual art would not be what it is without these lenses and tools. When we look at an Alexander Calder sculpture, we accept it as a piece of art.

455

We are not more critical of it simply because he has a background in mechanical engineering. In fact, if we are aware of his background, we understand that it allowed him to break ground in the visual arts.

People may be more inclined to critique art created by scholars, just as they may be more apt to critique novels labeled social fiction. Can it be art? Can it be *good* art? I've spent so much time suggesting that the arts can also be an expression of research that I've perhaps neglected to adequately present my novels as literary works. To set the record straight – yes, I am a scholar. I am also a novelist. For me, these practices are intertwined and yet distinct. And as for my novels, they are indeed art.

ACKNOWLEDGEMENTS

Thank you to everyone at Brill | Sense for supporting this book and my growth as an author. Special thanks to John Bennett, Peter de Liefde, Els van Egmond, Dan Carney, Caroline van Erp, Jolanda Karada, Evelien van der Veer, and Robert van Gameren. Thank you to the editorial advisory board members of the *Social Fictions* series for your generosity, and to the early reviewers for your kind endorsements. Heartfelt thanks to Shalen Lowell, the world's best assistant, spiritual bodyguard, and treasured friend. Thank you to Clear Voice Editing for the phenomenal copyediting services. Tori Amos, I couldn't have "made my own pretty hate machine" without you. Thank you for being a creative force and inspiration, professionally and personally. To my social media community and colleagues, as always, thank you boundlessly for your support. My deepest gratitude to my friends and family, especially Tony Adams, Vanessa Alssid, Melissa Anyiwo, Pamela DeSantis, Sandra Faulkner, Ally Field, Robert Charles Gompers, Xan Nowakowski, Laurel Richardson, Mr. Barry Mark Shuman, Jessica Smartt Gullion, and J. E. Sumerau. Celine Boyle, thank you for your comments and edits on these novels. They are stronger because of you. Madeline Leavy-Rosen, you are forever my light. Never settle for low-fat love, because you deserve the real deal. Chase your dreams and have fun along the way. Mark Robins, you're the best spouse in the world. Thank you for the endless support, love, and laughter. I love you always. To all those who haunt these pages, I honor you. Finally, I extend my heartfelt appreciation to all the readers over the years. I'm so grateful to everyone who has taken these characters into their hearts, and every reader who has approached me at a book event or emailed to share his/her/their story. You inspire me beyond words. I'm humbled that you've seen fragments of yourself in these pages. This collection is for every Prilly, every Tash, every you, and every me. We can each be many things in this wonderful life. We are possibilities.

ABOUT THE AUTHOR

Patricia Leavy, Ph.D., is an independent scholar and bestselling author. She was formerly Associate Professor of Sociology, Chair of Sociology & Criminology, and Founding Director of Gender Studies at Stonehill College in Massachusetts. She has published over twenty-five books, earning commercial and critical success in both nonfiction and fiction, and her work has been translated into numerous languages. Her recent titles include *The Oxford Handbook of Methods for Public Scholarship, Handbook of Arts-Based Research, Research Design: Quantitative, Qualitative, Mixed Methods, Arts-Based, and Community-Based Participatory Research Approaches, Method Meets Art: Arts-Based Research Practice Second Edition, Fiction as Research Practice, The Oxford Handbook of Qualitative Research*, and the novels *Spark, Film, Blue, American Circumstance,* and *Low-Fat Love.* She is also series creator and editor for ten book series with Oxford University Press, Guilford Press, and Brill | Sense and is cofounder and co-editor-in-chief of *Art/Research International: A Transdisciplinary Journal.* A vocal advocate of public scholarship, she has blogged for *The Huffington Post, The Creativity Post, Mogul,* and *We Are the Real Deal* and is frequently called on by the US national news media. In addition to receiving numerous accolades for her books, she has received career awards from the New England Sociological Association, the American Creativity Association, the American Educational Research Association, the International Congress of Qualitative Inquiry, and the National Art Education Association. In 2016 Mogul, a global women's empowerment network, named her an "Influencer." In 2018, she was honored by the National Women's Hall of Fame and SUNY-New Paltz established the "Patricia Leavy Award for Art and Social Justice." Please visit www.patricialeavy.com for more information or for links to her social media.

Printed in the United States
By Bookmasters